PB
14x 11/11 v9/12

HTML, XHTML, and CSS for the Absolute Beginner

W17
D0564438

Jerry Lee Ford, Jr.

Course Technology PTR
A part of Cengage Learning

Australia • Brazil • Japan • Korea • Mexico • Singapore • Spain • United Kingdom • United States

3 1336 08623 7980

HTML, XHTML, and CSS for the Absolute Beginner: Jerry Lee Ford, Jr.

Publisher and General Manager, Course Technology PTR: Stacy L. Hiquet

Associate Director of Marketing: Sarah Panella

Manager of Editorial Services: Heather Talbot

Marketing Manager: Mark Hughes

Acquisitions Editor: Mitzi Koontz

Project Editor: Jenny Davidson

Technical Reviewer: Keith Davenport

PTR Editorial Services Coordinator: Jen Blaney

Interior Layout Tech: Value Chain International

Cover Designer: Mike Tanamachi

Indexer: Katherine Stimson

Proofreader: Sara Gullion

© 2010 Course Technology, a part of Cengage Learning.

ALL RIGHTS RESERVED. No part of this work covered by the copyright herein may be reproduced, transmitted, stored, or used in any form or by any means graphic, electronic, or mechanical, including but not limited to photocopying, recording, scanning, digitizing, taping, Web distribution, information networks, or information storage and retrieval systems, except as permitted under Section 107 or 108 of the 1976 United States Copyright Act, without the prior written permission of the publisher.

For product information and technology assistance, contact us at **Cengage Learning Customer & Sales Support, 1-800-354-9706**

For permission to use material from this text or product, submit all requests online at **cengage.com/permissions** Further permissions questions can be emailed to **permissionrequest@cengage.com**

All trademarks are the property of their respective owners.

Library of Congress Control Number: 2009927808

ISBN-13: 978-1-4354-5423-1
ISBN-10: 1-4354-5423-5

Course Technology, a part of Cengage Learning
20 Channel Center Street
Boston, MA 02210
USA

Cengage Learning is a leading provider of customized learning solutions with office locations around the globe, including Singapore, the United Kingdom, Australia, Mexico, Brazil, and Japan. Locate your local office at: **international.cengage.com/region**

Cengage Learning products are represented in Canada by Nelson Education, Ltd.

For your lifelong learning solutions, visit **courseptr.com**

Visit our corporate website at **cengage.com**

Printed in the United States of America
1 2 3 4 5 6 7 11 10 09

To my mother and father for always being there, and to my wonderful children, Alexander, William, and Molly, and my beautiful wife, Mary.

Acknowledgments

This book represents the hard work and effort of a great many people to whom I owe thanks. First, I would like to thank Mitzi Koontz, who was crucial in helping to make this book a reality and who served as the book's acquisitions editor. Special thanks to the book's project editor, Jenny Davidson, for all her hard work and for making sure that all of the different parts of this book came together like they were supposed to. I also owe thanks to this book's technical editor, Keith Davenport, who provided invaluable insight, suggestions, and advice. Last but not least, I want to thank everyone at Course Technology PTR for their contributions and hard work.

About the Author

Jerry Lee Ford, Jr. is an author, educator, and an IT professional with more than 20 years of experience in information technology, including roles as an automation analyst, technical manager, technical support analyst, automation engineer, and security analyst. He is the author of 33 books and co-author of two additional books. His published works include *Ajax Programming for the Absolute Beginner*, *Scratch Programming for Teens*, *Microsoft Visual Basic 2008 Express Programming for the Absolute Beginner*, and *Phrogram Programming for the Absolute Beginner*. Jerry has a master's degree in business administration from Virginia Commonwealth University in Richmond, Virginia, and he has more than five years of experience as an adjunct instructor teaching networking courses in information technology.

Table of Contents

Introduction xvi

Part I **Introducing HTML, XHTML, and CSS** 1

Chapter 1 **Web Page Development 101** 3

Project Preview: The HTML Joke Page 4
Introducing HTML, XHTML, CSS, and Other Web Development Technologies 5
  HTML and XHTML 6
  Cascading Style Sheets 8
  Getting Interactive with JavaScript 9
Introducing the Document Object Model 10
  DOM Basics 10
  Navigating the DOM Tree 10
Understanding How Things Get Done on the World Wide Web 13
Linking Everything Together 14
  Working with Absolute Paths 15
  Relative Paths 16
Working with an (X)HTML Editor 17
Creating a Simple Web Page 17
Back to the HTML Joke Page 19
  Designing the Application 19
  Step 1: Creating a New HTML Document 20
  Step 2: Developing the Document's Markup 20
  Step 3: Loading and Testing the Web Page 22
Summary 23

Chapter 2 **HTML and XHTML Basics** 25

Project Preview: Linked Jokes Application 26
Separating Presentation from Content 27
The Six Flavors of (X)HTML 28
  HTML Standards 28
  XHTML Standards 29
The html Element 31
Dissecting (X)HTML Markup 32

Tag Pairs ... 32
Single Tags ... 33
Learning More about Tags ... 34
Markup Validation ... 35
Configuring Element Attributes ... 38
Standard Element Attributes ... 39
Understanding Element Levels ... 40
Working with Block-Level Elements ... 40
Embedding Inline Elements ... 40
Nesting Elements ... 41
Commenting Your Markup ... 42
Improving Document Organization with White Space ... 42
Finding a Web Host for Your Web Pages ... 44
Back to the Linked Jokes Project ... 45
Designing the Application ... 45
Step 1: Creating New HTML Document ... 45
Step 2: Developing the Document's XHTML ... 45
Step 3: Loading and Testing Your New Web Documents ... 48
Summary ... 48

Part II **Working with (X)HTML ... 51**

Chapter 3 **Creating (X)HTML Document Headings ... 53**

Project Preview: The Math Quiz Application ... 54
Establishing a Document Framework ... 55
Building a Document Template ... 55
Making the Document Template Well Formed ... 56
Adding Elements to the head Section ... 57
The <title> tag ... 58
The <meta> tag ... 59
The <base> tag ... 61
The <style> tag ... 63
The <link> tag ... 66
The <script> tag ... 67
Back to the Math Quiz Page ... 69
Designing the Application ... 69
Step 1: Creating a New HTML Document ... 69
Step 2: Developing the Document's Markup ... 69
Step 3: Performing a Quick Test of the Document ... 72
Step 4: Spicing Things Up with an Internal Style Sheet ... 73
Step 5: Loading and Testing the Math Quiz ... 76
Summary ... 77

Chapter 4 **Adding Content to Your Web Pages.................... 79**

Project Preview: A Knight's Tale.................... 80
Developing the body Section.................... 81
Properly Managing Content.................... 82
Grouping Content.................... 84
  The div Element.................... 85
  The span Element.................... 86
Paragraphs and Headings.................... 86
  The p Element.................... 86
  Heading Elements.................... 88
Working with Smaller Blocks of Text.................... 89
  Displaying Preformatted Test.................... 89
  Displaying Quotes.................... 92
  Working with the blockquote Element.................... 92
  Managing Address Information.................... 93
Working with Inline Elements.................... 94
  Working with the em Element.................... 94
  Working with the strong Element.................... 95
  Working with the small Element.................... 96
  Working with the big Element.................... 96
Organizing Text with Lists.................... 97
  Creating Unordered Lists.................... 97
  Creating Ordered Lists.................... 98
  Creating Definition Lists.................... 99
Line Breaks and Horizontal Rules.................... 100
  The br Element.................... 100
  The hr Element.................... 102
Introducing JavaScript.................... 103
  Integrating JavaScript into Your Web Documents.................... 103
  A JavaScript Example.................... 104
  Learning More About JavaScript.................... 105
Back to the Knights Tale Project.................... 105
  Designing the Application.................... 105
  Step 1: Creating a New XHTML Document.................... 105
  Step 2: Developing the Document's Markup.................... 106
  Step 3: Creating the Document's Script.................... 106
  Step 4: Loading and Testing the Knight's Tale Project.................... 109
Summary.................... 110

Chapter 5 **Delving into Images and Links.................... 111**

Project Preview: The (X)HTML Typing Quiz.................... 112
Let's Get Graphical.................... 114

Image Types 114
Storing Graphic Files Externally 115
Connecting Things Together with Links 121
Creating Links 121
Don't Let Links Send Your Visitors Away 125
Using Links to Set Up Document Downloads 126
Using Links to Facilitate Emailing 127
Other Forms of Content 129
Integrating Video as Content 129
Adding Audio Playback to Your Web Pages 131
Displaying PDF Documents 132
Back to the (X)HTML Typing Quiz 133
Designing the Application 134
Step 1: Creating a New XHTML Document 134
Step 2: Developing the Document's Markup 134
Step 3: Creating the Document's Script 135
Step 4: Loading and Testing the Typing Quiz 140
Summary 140

Chapter 6 **Designing Tables and Forms** **143**

Project Preview: The Number Guessing Game 144
Using Tables to Display Information 145
Basic Table Elements 146
Adding Borders to Your Tables 147
Playing Nice with Non-Graphic Browsers 148
Assigning a Table Heading 150
Defining Heading Row and Column Headings 151
Merging Table Cells 153
Collecting User Input through Forms 154
Defining Controls Using the input Element 156
Adding Buttons Using the button Element 165
Adding a Multiline Text Field Using the textarea Element 165
Adding Drop-Down Lists to Forms 167
Refining Form Structure 173
Adding Descriptive Test to Controls Using the Label Element 173
Working with the fieldset Element 174
A Complete Form Example 176
Advice on Good Form Design 179
Back to the Number Guessing Game 180
Designing the Application 181
Step 1: Creating a New XHTML Document 181
Step 2: Developing the Document's Markup 181
Step 3: Developing the Document's Script 183

Step 4: Loading and Testing the Number Guessing Game ... 188
Summary ... 188

Part III **CASCADING STYLE SHEETS ... 189**

Chapter 7 **AN INTRODUCTION TO CASCADING STYLE SHEETS ... 191**

Project Preview: The Rock, Paper, Scissors Game ... 192
Introducing CSS ... 193
Understanding the Basics of CSS Syntax ... 195
Crafting Rule Selectors ... 196
Universal ... 196
Element ... 196
Class ... 197
Pseudo Class ... 197
ID ... 197
Specifying More Complex Selectors ... 198
Integrating CSS into Your HTML Pages ... 198
Using Inline Styles ... 198
Managing Individual Documents with Embedded Style Sheets ... 199
Leveraging the Power of External Style Sheets ... 203
Understanding How CSS Rules Are Applied ... 206
Specificity ... 206
Cascading ... 208
What to Do When All Else Fails ... 208
Styling Fonts and Color ... 209
Influencing Font Presentation ... 209
Controlling the Presentation of Text ... 213
Specifying Foreground and Background Properties ... 215
Validating CSS Syntax ... 217
Back to the Rock, Paper, Scissors Game ... 217
Designing the Application ... 218
Step 1: Creating a New XHTML Document ... 218
Step 2: Developing the Document's Markup ... 218
Step 3: Adding meta and title Elements ... 219
Step 4: Specifying Document Content ... 219
Step 5: Creating the Document's Script ... 220
Step 6: Creating an External Style Sheet ... 223
Step 7: Loading and Testing the Rock, Paper, Scissors Game ... 224
Summary ... 227

Chapter 8 **Digging Deeper into CSS....................................... 229**

Project Preview: The Fortune Teller Game.. 230
Working with Containers.. 231
  Setting Container Margins.. 231
  Padding Space Between the Container and Its Border.. 232
  Configuring a Container's Border.. 232
Taking Control of Element Placement.. 234
  Static Positioning.. 235
  Absolute Positioning.. 237
  Relative Positioning.. 238
  Fixed Positioning.. 240
  Float Positioning.. 242
Using CSS to Style Your Lists.. 244
  Customizing Markers for Ordered Lists.. 244
  Changing Markers for Unordered Lists.. 247
  Creating Custom List Markers.. 249
Styling Links.. 251
  Modifying the Presentation of Text Links.. 251
  Creating Graphical Links.. 252
Using CSS to Better Integrate Text and Images.. 256
  Wrapping Text Around Graphics.. 256
  Adding a Background Image to Your Web Page.. 258
Styling Your Tables.. 260
  Styling Your Forms.. 267
  Styling Based on Output Device.. 270
Back to the Fortune Teller Game.. 271
  Designing the Application.. 271
  Step 1: Creating a New XHTML Document.. 272
  Step 2: Developing the Document's Markup.. 272
  Step 3: Adding meta and title Elements.. 272
  Step 4: Specifying Document Content.. 272
  Step 5: Creating the Document's Script.. 274
  Step 6: Creating an External Style Sheet.. 276
  Step 7: Loading and Testing the Fortune Teller Game.. 277
Summary.. 280

Part IV **Client-Side Scripting....................................... 283**

Chapter 9 **Client-Side Scripting....................................... 285**

Project Preview: The Word Decoder Challenge.. 285
Introducing JavaScript.. 287

Working with JavaScript ... 288
    What about Browsers That Do Not Support JavaScript? ... 289
    Creating a Simple JavaScript ... 290
    Running Your JavaScripts ... 290
Different Ways of Integrating JavaScript into Your Documents ... 291
    Embedding JavaScripts in the head Section ... 291
    Embedding JavaScripts in the body Section ... 293
    Storing Your JavaScripts Externally ... 294
    Embedding JavaScript Statements inside HTML Tags ... 294
Documenting Your Scripts ... 294
Dealing with Different Types of Values ... 295
Storing and Retrieving Data ... 295
    Defining JavaScript Variables ... 296
Working with Collections of Data ... 297
    Accessing Array Elements ... 298
    Processing Arrays with Loops ... 299
    Manipulating and Comparing Data ... 300
    Performing Mathematic Calculations ... 300
    Assigning Values to Variables ... 301
    Comparing Values ... 303
Making Decisions ... 304
    Working with the if Statement ... 304
    Generating Multiline if Statements ... 305
    Handling Alternative Conditions ... 306
    Nesting if Statements ... 307
    Evaluating Conditions with the switch Statement ... 308
Using Loops to Work Efficiently ... 310
    Creating a Loop Using the for Statement ... 310
    Creating a Loop Using the while Statement ... 312
    Creating a Loop Using the do. . .while Statement ... 313
    Breaking out of Loops ... 314
Organizing Your JavaScripts into Functions ... 315
    Defining Functions ... 315
    Executing Functions ... 316
    Creating Interactive Web Pages Using Event-Driven Scripts ... 318
    Different Types of Javascript Events ... 318
    Managing Window Events ... 319
    Handling Mouse Events ... 320
Back to the Word Decoder Challenge Project ... 322
    Designing the Application ... 322
    Step 1: Creating a New XHTML Document ... 322
    Step 2: Developing the Document's Markup ... 322
    Step 3: Adding meta and title Elements ... 323
    Step 4: Specifying Document Content ... 323

- Step 5: Creating the Document's Script 324
- Step 6: Creating an External Style Sheet 328
- Step 7: Loading and Testing the Word Decoder Challenge Game 330
- Summary 330

Chapter 10 **Building Websites 331**

- Project Preview: www.tech-publishing.com 331
- Designing a Website from the Ground Up 335
  - Document Project Objectives 335
  - Organization Content 336
  - Outlining a Common Page Structure 337
  - Creating a Rough Mockup of the Web Page Template 337
  - Creating a Common Document Template 337
  - Developing a Common CSS Style Sheet for the Website 337
  - Build-out the Documents That Make Up the Website 338
- Back to the www.tech-publishing.com Website 338
  - Designing the Website 338
  - Step 1: Outlining Objectives for the Website 338
  - Step 2: Sketching Out the Site's Structure 339
  - Step 3: Outlining Template Content 339
  - Step 4: Sketching Out a Web Page Design 340
  - Step 5: Creating Template Markup 341
  - Step 6: Developing the Site's External CSS File 344
  - Step 7: Assembling Document Files 350
  - Step 8: Testing the New Website 362
- Summary 363

Part V **Appendixes 365**

Appendix A **What's on the Companion Website? 367**

- Downloading the Book's Source Code 368

Appendix B **What Next? 369**

- HTML Resources 369
  - Wikipedia's HTML and XHTML Pages 370
  - WC3's HTML 4.01 Specification Page 370
  - WC3's XHTML Specifications 371
- Resources for Cascading Style Sheets 371
  - Wikipedia's Cascading Style Sheets Page 372

WC3's Cascading Style Sheets Page 372
XML Resources 373
Wikipedia's XML Page 373
W3C's Extensible Markup Language (XML) Page 374
JavaScript Resources 375
Wikipedia's JavaScript Page 375
JavaScript Tutorial 376
Essential Development Tools 377
Web Page Editors 377
Graphics Editors 379
FTP Clients 382
Link Checkers 383
The Author's Website 384

Glossary 387

Index 393

INTRODUCTION

Welcome to *HTML, XHTML, and CSS Programming for the Absolute Beginner*! Web development today involves a combination of different technologies that together facilitate the development of websites and web pages. But what are these technologies and how do you work with them? These are the questions that this book is going to answer for you.

For many people the Internet is a mystery. They set up an Internet account with a local Internet service provider and then open their browser and before they know it, they are learning, shopping, and playing games online. Accessing the Internet in this manner is simple and intuitive. It usually does not take long before you start discovering and visiting websites created by family and friends. You may start hearing new terms like HTML, XHTML, and CSS. These three terms represent markup and presentation languages that are used as the basis for creating all of the websites you see on the Internet.

This book will provide an overview of the markup languages that form the foundation of web page development on the Internet (HTML and XHTML). It will also show you how to control and manage the presentation of content on your web pages using Cascading Style Sheets (CSS). By the time you make it to the end of the book, you will understand the fundamentals of HTML, XHTML, and CSS and will have used them to develop many different types of web pages.

To help make learning how to work with these technologies as fun and interesting as possible, this book will utilize a hands-on instructional approach that emphasizes learning by doing. This will be accomplished through the development of a series of projects that will show you how to create web pages that tell jokes, perform silly tasks, and create computer games.

So, whether you are a student who has just signed up for an introductory web development class, a computer hobbyist interested in rolling up his sleeves and having some fun, or just someone with an idea for creating a new website, this book will provide everything you need to get up and running quickly. By the time you are done, you'll have plenty of hands-on experience and will be prepared to start developing your own website.

Why HTML, XHTML, and CSS?

Since its rise from relative obscurity to worldwide recognition in the mid-1990s, the Internet has been a force to be reckoned with. It has quickly grown from a medium that served up text to one that incorporates text, graphics, audio, and video and has become a learning and research tool. It has also become an essential engine for business and education and has come to rival radio, television, and newspapers as a source of news and entertainment. In short, the Internet has become an indispensable component of modern life.

At its core, the Internet is all about displaying and sharing documents. While other technologies are sometimes involved, most web pages are created using HTML and XHTML and their appearance is usually controlled by CSS. There is no getting around it, if you want to join the world's global community by creating your own website, then you must learn how to work with HTML, XHTML, and CSS. This book will help to overcome this barrier.

Who Should Read This Book?

HTML, XHTML, and CSS Programming for the Absolute Beginner is designed to teach first-time programmers, computer enthusiasts, and anyone else interested in creating web pages how to become a web developer. Once you have learned the basics, you will be surprised how easy it is to get started. If you can use a computer to surf the Internet or play games, then you can become a web developer and carve out your own little niche in cyberspace.

While basic knowledge of how to work with a computer and surf the Internet is assumed, no prior web development or programming experience is required for you to be able to complete this book. Although prior programming experience would obviously be helpful, as would a basic understanding of HTML, XHTML, JavaScript, the DOM and CSS, it is not required.

A goal of this book is to teach you everything you need to get your own website up and running while at the same time making your learning experience as fun and enjoyable as possible. This will be accomplished using a games-based instructional approach, through the creation of web-based computer jokes, wacky projects, and games. If this approach to learning web development sounds appealing then keep reading. You will be creating web pages and developing websites in no time at all.

What You Need to Begin

To create web pages you need to work with things like HTML, XHTML, CSS, and JavaScript. However, you do not need to purchase any of these software languages. They are all free and already available to you on your computer. You do not have to download or install anything to use them. However, you will need a few software tools to get started. In order to create web pages, you need a text editor with which you can create and save your web pages.

Web pages are saved as plain text files. If you are a Windows user, you can use Notepad. If you are a Mac OS X user, you can configure TextEdit to save your web pages as plain text files. If you are a UNIX or Linux user, you can use vi or any text-editing utility supported by your operating system. Of course, there are plenty of sophisticated high-end web page editors that you can buy that include many extra bells and whistles. If you are interested in learning more about these types of editors, check out Appendix B.

In addition to a good editor, you will need access to at least one or two different web browsers, like Windows Internet Explorer, in order to load and test your web pages to make sure they look and operate like you want them to. In order to build a real website, you will need access to the Internet. You will also need access to a web server on which to upload your web pages. For most people this means setting up an account with a web service provider that will host your website. Chapter 1 provides advice on how to find a good website provider.

You will also need the ability to transfer or upload the files that make up your web pages to your website. Many providers offer you a GUI interface that allows you to do so. However, you may want to instead download and install a free or inexpensive FTP client application to help you transfer your files. Check out Appendix B for a list of good FTP clients.

Testing with Different Web Browsers

In order to create interactive web pages that are both entertaining and useful, you need to learn a little something about programming. In this book, this means learning the fundamentals of JavaScript scripting. Because of small differences in the way that modern web browsers are designed, JavaScript sometimes works slightly differently on various browsers, resulting in small alterations in the way that web pages appear and operate.

In order to ensure that your web pages look and work the way you want them to, you must test them using a number of different web browsers. At a minimum, you will want to test your web pages using Microsoft's Internet Explorer (http://www.microsoft.com/windows/Internet-explorer/) and Apple's Safari (www.apple.com/safari/). Internet Explorer only runs on Microsoft Windows while Safari runs on both Windows and Mac OS X. In addition to these two browsers, you will also want to download and install the very popular Firefox browser (www.firefox.com). This browser runs on both Windows and Mac OS X. In addition to these three web browsers, you may also want to consider testing with one or two of the following web browsers as well.

- **Opera.** A popular third-party Windows browser (www.opera.com).
- **Deepnet Explorer.** A Windows browser with a built-in RSS newsreader (www.deepnetexplorer.com).
- **Konqueror.** A popular Linux browser (http://www.konqueror.org).

- **Camino.** A popular Mac OS X browser (http://caminobrowser.org).
- **Google Chrome.** A new Windows browser developed by Google (www.google.com/chrome).

All of the figures and examples that you will see in this book will be demonstrated using Internet Explorer 8, Safari 3, or Firefox 3.

Things That You Need to Know

In order to fully utilize the information provided by this book, you need to have a basic understanding of computers and the Internet. You also need a website that you can work with or at the very least, you should be interested in creating one. Other than this, the book will provide everything else you need to get started. By the time you are done, you'll know how to create and edit web pages and entire websites. In doing so, you will learn about many different web development technologies, including HTML, XHTML, CSS, XML, and JavaScript scripting.

How This Book Is Organized

Although I wrote this book based on the assumption that it would be read sequentially, it does cover a wide variety of topics, and depending on your technical background and experience, you may want to jump around, picking and choosing the topics that you want to learn more about. *HTML, XHTML, and CSS Programming for the Absolute Beginner* is organized into five parts. Part I of this book consists of two chapters that provide an introduction to web-page development and cover HTML and XHTML basics. You will learn how things work on the world wide web, how URLs are formulated, and how to create web pages.

Part II consists of four chapters that explain how to create HTML and XHTML document headings and show you how to organize web page content using things like paragraphs, headings, lists, and so on. You will learn how to work with images and add links to your web pages. You will also learn how to design and display information in tables and forms.

Part III shows you how to control the presentation of your web pages by teaching you the ins and outs of working with Cascading Style Sheets or CSS. You will learn how to create internal and external style sheets, how to add backgrounds, how to manage different types of media, how to specify colors and fonts, and how to style tables and forms.

Part IV provides an overview of client-side scripting using JavaScript, offering you the programming skills needed to build interactive web pages. You will learn how to create embedded and external JavaScripts and how to use them to respond to events. You will also learn how to programmatically interact with and control the web browser's document object model (DOM), which is crucial to web scripting. Using JavaScript, you will learn how to access and dynamically modify different parts of web pages by making changes to the DOM.

Part V consists of two appendices and a glossary. The first appendix provides an overview of all the web development projects presented in this book and explains how to download the book's source code from its companion website. The second appendix is designed to assist you in furthering your web development knowledge and education by providing a list of online resources. You will also learn about different applications and software services to assist you in the development of your web pages.

Conventions Used in This Book

To make this book easier to read and understand, a number of special conventions have been applied that are designed to highlight critical information and to emphasize specific information. These conventions are as follows.

- *Italics*. Whenever an important programming term is used for the first time, I will highlight the word in italics to give it additional emphasis. This will let you know that the term is one that you will want to make sure you remember and understand.

I will provide tips on how to do things differently and will point out different techniques that you can use to become a more effective and productive web developer.

From time to time, I will point out situations where you are most likely to run into problems and will also provide advice on how to deal with those situations or, better yet, prevent them from ever occurring in the first place.

I will provide different types of tricks and shortcuts, designed to help you work more efficiently and become a better web developer.

Challenges

Every chapter in this book ends by guiding you through the development of a new web project. Immediately following each project, I will provide a series of suggestions or challenges that you can implement to improve the chapter project and further expand your web development skills.

Part I

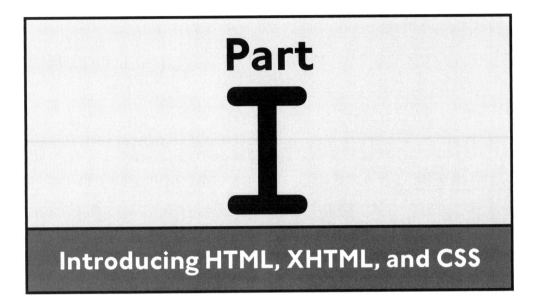

Introducing HTML, XHTML, and CSS

Web Page Development 101

If you can surf the Internet, operate a DVD player, or create a Microsoft Word document, you too can create your own web pages. This chapter introduces the HTML and XHTML markup languages, which web developers use to develop web pages, and CSS, which is used to provide styling information that affects the appearance and presentation of web pages. You will also be introduced to the DOM (document object model), which organizes web page contents into a hierarchy allowing it to be easily referenced, and to JavaScript, which is a scripting language used to create dynamic web pages that interact with visitors. You will also learn how links are used to connect things together and will end by learning how to create your very first web page.

Specifically, you will learn:

- About the differences between HTML and XHTML markup languages
- About the role of CSS in influencing web page presentation
- About JavaScript and its role in creating interactive websites
- How links are used to tie together the pages of your website and to connect them to outside world

Project Preview: The HTML Joke Page

In this chapter and in each chapter that follows, you will learn how to create a new web project. Learning web development though hands-on exercises and instruction makes learning a lot of fun. This chapter's project is the HTML Joke Page. The web page displays a joke and its punch line when displayed, as shown in Figure 1.1.

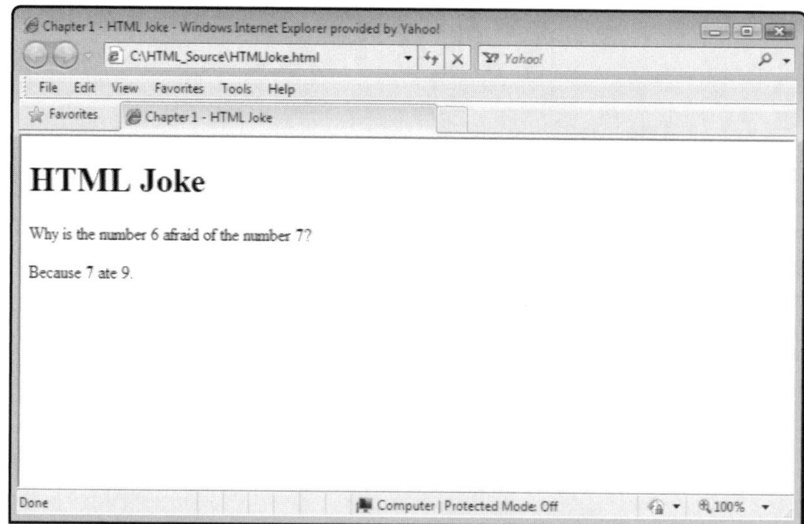

Figure 1.1

Displaying the HTML Joke Page using Internet Explorer 8.

As you can see, there is not a lot to this web page, just some text that displays the joke and its punch line. Still, by learning how to create this simple web page, you will learn the basic steps involved in creating all kinds of web pages.

Properly designed web pages should display in a consistent fashion regardless of which web browser they display in. Figures 1.2 and 1.3 show how this same web page looks when displayed using different web browsers.

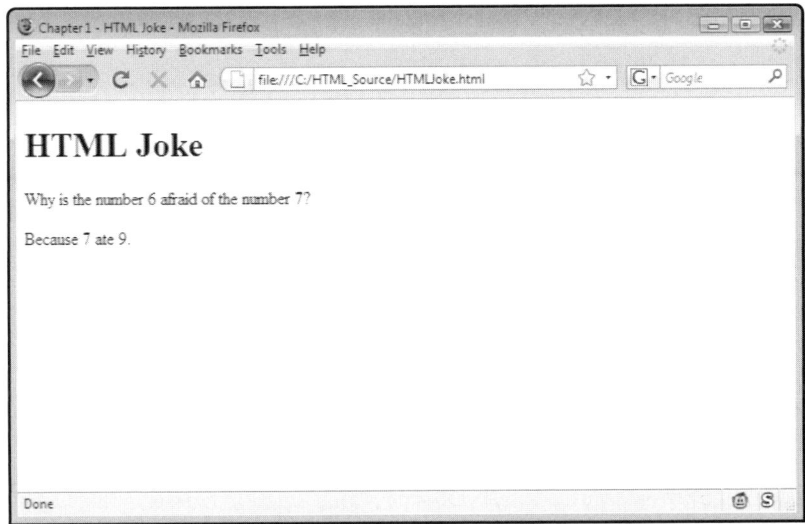

FIGURE 1.2

Displaying the HTML Joke Page using Mozilla Firefox 3.

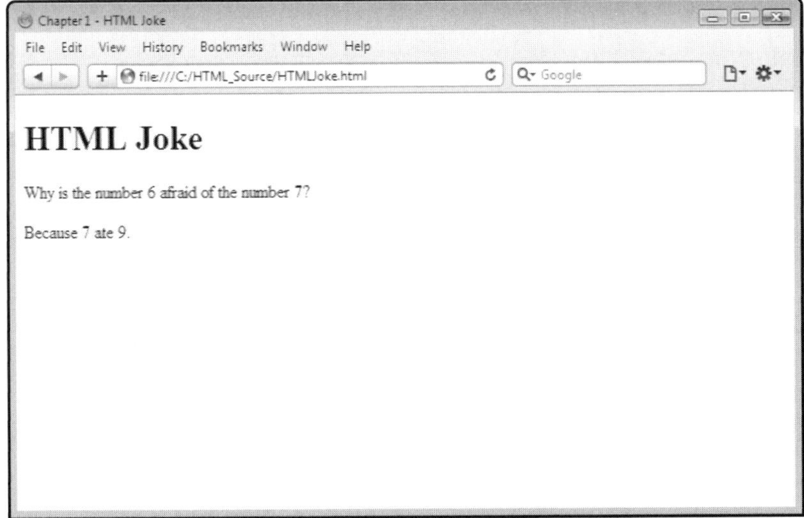

FIGURE 1.3

Displaying the HTML Joke Page using Apple Safari 3.

Introducing HTML, XHTML, CSS, and Other Web Development Technologies

The development of web pages and websites involves a number of different programming languages that together allow web developers to create unique, interesting, and interactive web pages. These languages include:

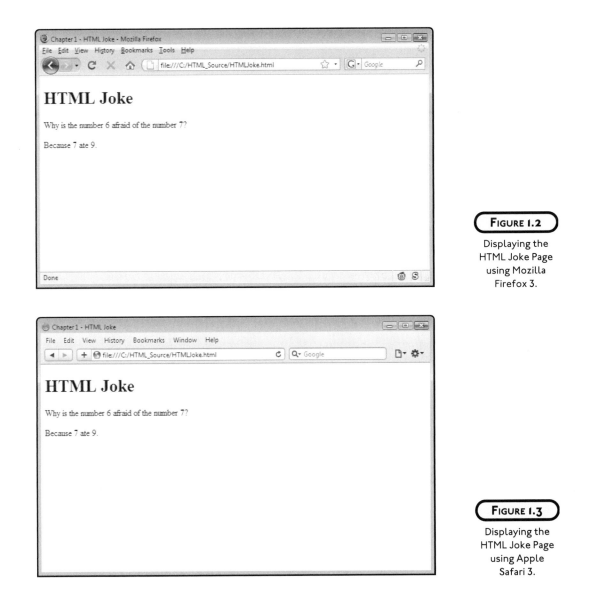

- HTML
- XHTML
- CSS
- JavaScript

Each of these languages is introduced and discussed in this chapter and then reviewed in detail in later chapters. These languages have been around for years and are supported by recognized industry standards. The complementary nature of these languages produces a robust web development environment.

Many people use the terms web document and web page interchangeably. In this book, a distinction is made between the two terms. The term web document is used to refer to text files containing markup code and the term web page is used to refer to the result that is displayed and made visible to web surfers when a web document is loaded and rendered by a web browser or similar device.

HTML and XHTML

HTML and XHTML are markup languages. *Markup languages* are languages that "mark up" plain text so it is formatted and displayed in a web browser in interesting and useful ways. Web pages are *rendered* (displayed) by browsers when they load a copy of your web documents (plain text files containing markup). Users load web documents by entering the web document's URL into the browser. As this book will demonstrate, most web pages are made up of nothing more than plain text files consisting of HTML or XHTML (and perhaps a little CSS).

It All Started with HTML

HTML or *Hypertext Markup Language* is a markup language that was created based on SGML or Standard Generalized Markup Language. First appearing in the early 1990s, HTML has long served as the standard markup language for the Internet. *XHTML*, otherwise known as the *Extensible Hypertext Markup Language*, is a markup language that is very similar to HTML, except that it is based on XML rather than SGML. *XML* (*Extensible Markup Language*) represents a more restrictive subset of SGML, resulting in tighter syntax that yields more consistent results when markup is rendered by browsers.

HTML was created for the purpose of describing the structure of text-based web documents. HTML suffers from a number of irregularities. XHTML was created to addresses these irregularities. XHTML has a predictable syntax. Markup, be it HTML or XHTML, is the glue that binds all of the content in your web documents together.

Over the years, HTML has been enhanced a number of times. HTML 1.0 was published in 1993. HTML 2.0 made its debut in 1995. HTML 3.0 appeared in 1996 and HTML 4.0 was published in 1997. The most current version of HTML, HTML 4.01, arrived on the scene in 1999. Even as new features have been added to HTML, old features have also been deprecated. Deprecated features are marked for eventual removal from the language. As such, their usage is highly discouraged.

Along Came XHTML

XHTML 1.0 arrived on the scene in 2000 and was originally intended to be the replacement for HTML. XHTML is an update of HTML 4.01 that follows the more restrictive rules of XML. XML is an extensible language that allows you to define your own elements. However, XHTML version 1.0 does not support the definition of custom tags. Instead, you must stick with the elements defined as part of the XHTML 1.0 specification.

The changes that were made to make the leap from HTML to XHTML were primarily small ones. The primary purpose of the first version of XHTML was to adapt HTML to make it compliant with XML. As a result, the two markup languages remain very similar and the way things are done in one language is often identical to the way things are done in the other. XHTML documents are required to be well formed. To conform to XML, all XHTML elements must be written in lowercase and all elements must also be closed. HTML is a lot more lenient in both of these circumstances, allowing upper- or lower-case spelling and open elements. Unlike HTML, XHTML forces you to enclose all attribute values inside quotation marks (single or double). Although HTML sometimes imposed this requirement, it often allows you to do away with it.

The movement from HTML to XML results in a simplified and less complicated markup language. It also means that the markup language has become compatible with all kinds of XML tools, simplifying the presentation of content on resource-constrained devices like cellular phones and other types of handheld devices.

Where We Are Now

HTML 4.01 was intended to be the final version of HTML. Despite XHTML's many improvements and wide adoption, many web developers continue to use HTML. Recognizing HTML's continued importance and the need for further improvements, W3C has resumed work on the development of a new version of HTML, HTML 5.0. This will provide web developers who support large amounts of HTML additional time to make the transition to XHTML. At the same time the W3C is also working on the next version of XHTML, XHTML 5. New web developers, however, should plan on working exclusively with XHTML. This will save the trouble of having to convert down the road.

Because HTML and XHTML are so closely related, what works in one language often works identically in the other language. As a result, web developers have taken to referring to both languages generically as (X)HTML. This text adopts this approach, using the term *(X)HTML* to refer to both languages, except where specific differences between the two languages need to be pointed out.

HTML and XHTML are sets of open standards maintained by the *World Wide Web Consortium* (*W3C*). The W3C is a non-profit organization dedicated to the development of open standards, ensuring that things on the Internet work smoothly by providing everyone with a consistent and agreed upon set of rules.

Cascading Style Sheets

In the early days of web page development, web page developers were limited to the default presentation capabilities built into HTML. However, HTML's presentation capabilities were very limited, forcing web developers to get creative. The result was often poor development techniques in which HTML elements were used in ways that were never intended. To address some of its presentation shortcomings, some of HTML's elements were enhanced to provide them with additional presentation capabilities. For example, numerous elements were given new attributes that could be used to control their spacing, color, text size, etc.

Unfortunately, the inclusion of both structure and presentation into the same markup only served to weaken both aspects. Of particular difficulty was the fact that embedding presentation directly into markup made it difficult to modify the appearance and presentation of a web page or website because altering the way things looked typically meant making changes to elements throughout web documents. The end result was markup that was more difficult to understand and update.

An answer to this challenge soon came along in the form of *Cascading Style Sheet* or *CSS*. CSS is a style sheet language that web developers use to specify the presentation of web page content. CSS is its own language with its own rules and syntax. CSS provides you with the ability to separate markup from presentation through the creation of style sheets that specify how web documents should be rendered when displayed.

CSS provides web developers with a means of applying a consistent look and feel to web pages. CSS lets you specify things like font type, color, and size as well as background styles, borders, and alignment. CSS alleviates the need for web developers to have to repeatedly configure the presentation of elements within web documents. Instead, CSS lets you define style rules once and then applies those rules to every matching page element.

CSS made its debut back in 1997. However, it got off to a relatively slow start. It took years for it to work its way into mainstream web development. Today, CSS is a widely adopted standard sponsored and maintained by the W3C. By teaching you how to control the presentation of your web pages using CSS, this book will help you to avoid making many of the mistakes that web developers have traditionally made when building new web pages and sites.

You will get an early introduction to CSS in Chapter 3 followed by a more in-depth presentation of CSS in Chapters 7 and 8. By the time you are done, you will know how to develop web documents whose content and presentation are kept separate, resulting in web documents that are more streamlined and easy to maintain and update. As a result, you'll be able to make major or minor changes that affect the look and feel of entire websites through the modification of CSS, without having to change your content and markup.

Getting Interactive with JavaScript

In order to create web pages that are truly dynamic and capable of doing more than simply displaying static content, you need to learn how to work with a client-side programming language. Many such languages are available. Of these, JavaScript is by far the most commonly used. JavaScript programs are small text-based scripts that are downloaded as part of web documents and then executed within web browsers.

A *client-side programming language* is one that executes within a browser on the user's computer as opposed to a server-side language, which executes on web servers located on the internet.

JavaScripts give you, as a web developer, the ability to create truly interactive content. You can write JavaScripts that respond to user activity such as mouse movements and key presses, or to validate user input, such as ensuring that a phone number is formatted correctly. JavaScript is an interpreted programming language. This means that scripts written in JavaScript are not precompiled (made executable) at development time. Instead, scripts are converted to an executable format only when downloaded into the web browser for execution. Because it is an interpreted language, JavaScripts tend to execute a little slower than other compiled programming languages. However, thanks to the speed of modern computers and Internet connections, this impact is hardly noticeable.

JavaScript is also an object-based programming language. As such, it views everything within an (X)HTML document and the browser as *objects*. One key feature of JavaScript that is essential to the development of interactive web pages is the ability to trigger the execution of scripts based on the occurrence of different types of events. An *event* is an action that occurs when the user interacts with your web pages. As explained in Chapter 9, events occur for all sorts of reasons, such as when visitors first access a web page or when they leave it. Events also occur when visitors click on form buttons, key input into text fields, and so on.

Introducing the Document Object Model

Web documents are made up of many different types of elements. As you will learn, web browsers organize these elements using something called the *document object model* or *DOM*. The DOM provides the ability for scripts and CSS to access and update the content and style of web documents.

DOM Basics

The DOM is provided by the browser. The DOM provides a means through which JavaScripts can access and interact with web document content. By programmatically manipulating DOM objects, web developers can dynamically update web pages. Every time a browser loads a web document, it renders an HTML page. At the same time, the browser creates a DOM tree map in memory specifying all of the elements in the web document.

Back at the end of the 1990s, web browsers provided inconsistent support for the DOM, often putting their own unique spin on things. As a result, web browsers did not always display content the same way. In 1998, W3C published the first DOM standard. In April 2004, DOM 3 was published. DOM 3 is still the current standard. All modern web browsers support DOM 3. As a result, different web browsers now render much more consistent results when displaying web pages.

Within the DOM, objects are organized in a hierarchy. At the top of this hierarchy is the `document` object. The `document` object ties together all of the elements in the document into a tree-like structure. Every element defined in a web document is represented by its own object in the DOM. The result is a collection of related objects with parent, child, and sibling relationships. Using a scripting language like JavaScript, you can use these relationships as a means of navigating the DOM tree. Further, you can use methods and properties provided by these objects to interact with and control them, allowing you to do things like make elements appear and disappear. You can also use CSS and the DOM to modify web documents by changing things like their color, size, and so on.

Navigating the DOM Tree

As already noted, the `document` object sits at the top of the DOM tree as depicted in Figure 1.4. The `document` object provides programmatic access to all of the objects that make up a web document.

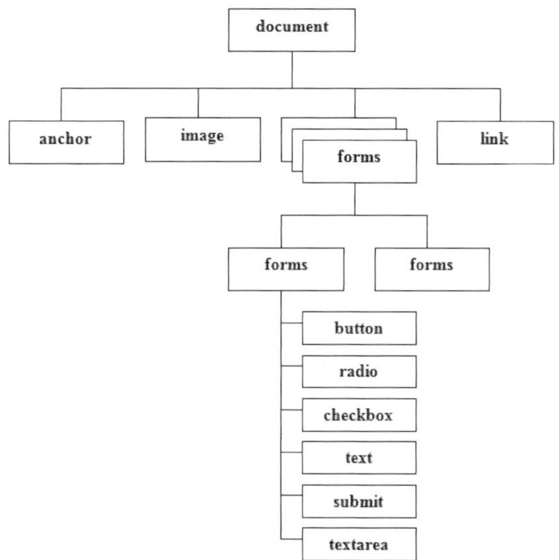

FIGURE 1.4

The document object provides easy access to all of the elements located on a web document.

The document object resides at the top of the tree. Underneath it are all of the other objects that make up the web document. As an example of how web documents are mapped out by the DOM, take a look at the following web document.

```
<!DOCTYPE html PUBLIC "-//W3C//DTD XHTML 1.0 Strict//EN"
  "http://www.w3.org/TR/xhtml1/DTD/xhtml1-strict.dtd">

<html xmlns="http://www.w3.org/1999/xhtml" lang="en" xml:lang="en">

  <head>
    <title>DOM Example</title>
  </head>

  <body>
    <h1>The Three Bears</h1>
    <p>Once upon a time there were three bears.</p>
  </body>

</html>
```

This small XHTML page contains a title element, a level 1 heading (h1), and a paragraph (p) element. Figure 1.5 shows the web page that is displayed when this web document is loaded and rendered by Internet Explorer.

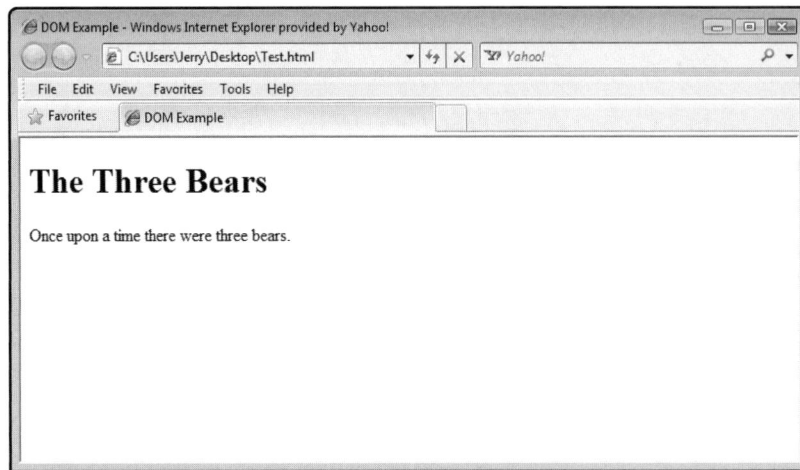

FIGURE 1.5

An example of the web document once it has been rendered by Internet Explorer.

The browser's internal view of the web document's content is quite different from what the web surfers see. Figure 1.6 provides a graphical representation of the DOM tree that the browser will create in memory when it loads the web document.

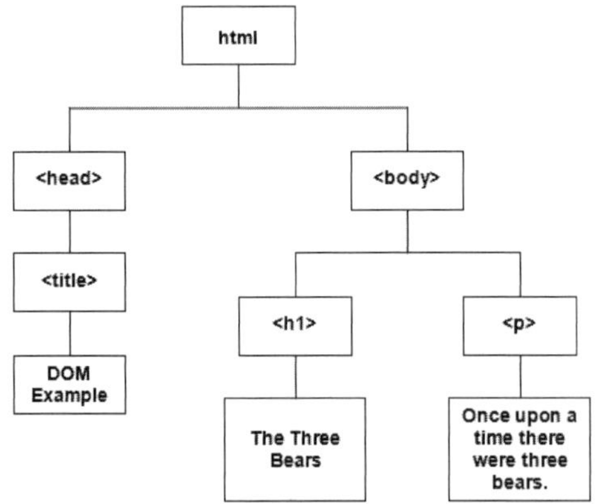

FIGURE 1.6

A graphic representation of the DOM tree that the browser will produce in memory as it renders the web document.

As you will learn later in this book, you can assign an optional `id` attribute to the elements that make up your web documents. You can then use each element's assigned `id` to programmatically interact with the element or to alter its presentation by applying one or more CSS rules to it. To learn more about the DOM, visit www.w3c.org/DOM.

Understanding How Things Get Done on the World Wide Web

People use many different types of devices to connect to the Internet. Most people surf the Internet using their computer and a web browser like Microsoft Internet Explorer. A *web browser* is a software application that processes HTML and XHTML documents and renders web pages based on the contents of those documents. The following list identifies a number of today's most commonly used web browsers.

- **Internet Explorer.** Windows browser (www.microsoft.com/windows/Internet-explorer/).
- **Safari.** Mac OS X browser (www.apple.com/safari/).
- **Firefox.** Windows, Mac OS X, and Linux browser (www.firefox.com).
- **Opera.** Windows, Mac OS X, and Linux browser (www.opera.com).
- **Deepnet Explorer.** Windows browser (www.deepnetexplorer.com).
- **Konqueror.** Linux browser (www.konqueror.org).
- **Camino.** Mac OX S browser (caminobrowser.org).
- **Google Chrome.** Windows browser (www.google.com/chrome).

Despite all of the standardization that has occurred in recent years with HTML, XHTML, CSS, and JavaScript, there are still small differences in the way that browsers render content. As a result, it is important that you test your web pages using at least two or three of the browsers listed above.

There are, however, many other ways that people connect to the Internet, including things like Internet-enabled cell phones, specialized text-to-speech devices that assist visually challenged people who surf the Internet. Regardless of which software program or device people are using, they all have one thing in common: they are designed to process (X)HTML documents and to render web pages based on the content provided in those documents.

Some of the people that visit your website may not use any of the above browsers. These users might have visual problems and surf the Internet using special text-to-voice applications or they may use browsers like Lynx. Shown in Figure 1.7, Lynx only supports text-based browsing. Text-only browsing allows for really fast browsing.

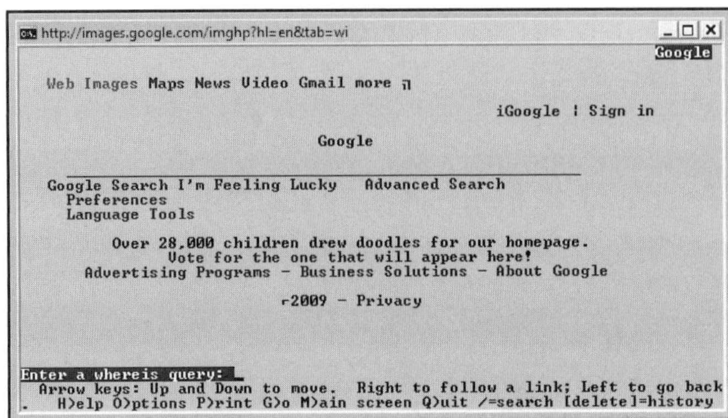

FIGURE 1.7

Using the Lynx browser to visit `www.google.com`.

Most websites depend heavily on the use of graphics to help deliver their message. This can create a range of challenges for web developers. Fortunately, as you will learn in Chapter 5, there are ways of providing content specifically designed to service the needs of these types of users.

LINKING EVERYTHING TOGETHER

In order to access anything on the Internet, you must know its *URL* or *Uniform Resource Locator*. For example, to access Microsoft's website you would enter a URL of www.microsoft.com in your browser's URL field and press Enter. Every website has one. In fact, every page of every website has a URL as well. URLs are defined using the syntax shown in Figure 1.8.

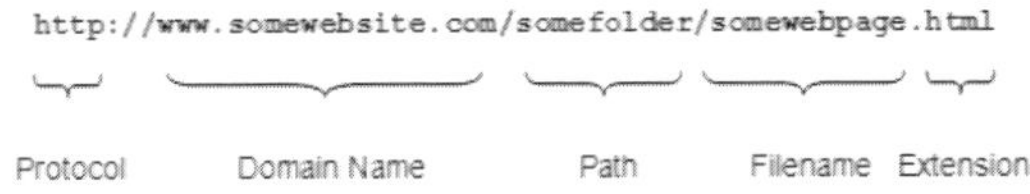

FIGURE 1.8

A URL is made up of multiple components that together identify the location of a resource on the web.

As you can see in Figure 1.8, every URL consists of the following components.

- **Protocol.** A set of rules that governs communications and the exchange of data between computers over a network. You will specify *http* (*HyperText Transfer Protocol*), which is a protocol that governs the transmission of hypertext-encoded data between computers on a network.
- **Domain Name.** Identifies the website where the specified web page or resources resides.

- **Path.** A hierarchical list of folders in which a web page of file resides.
- **Filename.** The name of the file to be retrieved and loaded.
- **Extension.** The file's file extension, typically .htm or .html.

URLs begin by specifying the http protocol, which is separated from the remaining text in the URL by the :// characters. Domain Name specifies the name of the website where the web page or file resides. Just like your computer, web servers can store files in a hierarchical collection of folders. Path specifies the folder in which the document is stored. The / character is used to separate the domain name from the path. The / character is also used to delineate every folder specified in the path. The path is followed by another / and then the name of the file to be retrieved, followed by a dot and the file's file extension, which in the case of web pages is either .htm or .html. Specifying the correct extension is important, since a website may have files that share the same name but different file extensions.

You may use either .htm or .html as the file extension of your web pages. The three-character .htm file extension dates back to the days of MS-DOS when all files had to have three character file extensions. You may use either file extension you want. Throughout this book the more familiar .html extension will be used.

URLs are essential to the operation of the web. They provide an easy, intuitive way of specifying where things reside. URLs are also used in the construction of links, providing the foundation for navigation between web pages. Path information in URLs can be specified using either absolute or relative values, both of which are discussed in the sections that follow.

Working with Absolute Paths

An *absolute URL* is one that specifies a text string that contains a fully qualified path that identifies the exact location of a resource on the Internet. An absolute URL specifies the protocol, domain name, complete path showing all folders as well as a filename and extension. Absolute URLs are used when creating links to external web pages that exist outside of your website. For example, the following string is an example of a typical absolute URL.

```
http://www.apple.com/education/it-professionals/index.html
```

Here, an absolute path of /education/it-professionals/ shows the exact location within which the index.html web page resides at the www.apple.com domain.

Most web servers are configured to automatically load a default web page when a URL specifies a folder instead of a filename. More often than not, the default web page is named `index.html`. So, if you wanted, you could rewrite the previous URL as shown below and the web server will serve up the same web page.

http://www.apple.com/education/it-professionals/

Relative Paths

A *relative URL* is one that specifies the location of a file relative to the location of the current web page. A relative URL allows you to point to a file location by specifying only its path and file information. Relative URLs allow you to shorten paths. For example, if you need to create a link to a file that resides in the same folder as the web page, all you have to do is specify the filename and extension of the other file as demonstrated here:

```
help.html
```

Another advantage of working with relative URLs is that they can make the movement of websites from one server to another a lot easier. All you would have to do is copy all of the files that make up your website from one web server to another and as long as you used relative URLs to connect your web pages, everything should still work. No changes required.

If on the other hand, you need to refer to a file that resides in a parent folder, then use a relative URL, type ../ followed by the name of the file.

```
../help.html
```

If the file being referenced is, say, three folders up in the folder hierarchy, you do as demonstrated here:

```
../../../help.html
```

If it's easier, you can specify the location of a file starting from the location of the website's *root* or top-most folder. Just enter a / followed by the path to the folder where the file resides, as demonstrated here:

```
/projects/helpfiles/help.html
```

When a string indicating a path begins with the / character, that opening / character always represents the root folder.

Working with an (X)HTML Editor

The development of web documents differs from the development of other documents like word publishing and spreadsheets in one key way: to create and view the results of a web document in its final rendered form, you must work with two different applications. First, you must have a text or code editor with which you can create the text file that makes up your (X)HTML document. Once you have created and edited your web document, you must then use a web browser to view the resulting web page.

If after reviewing your work you decide to make additional changes, all you have to do is re-edit the text of the document's file and save it. Once complete, you can click on the web browser's refresh button to update the display of the resulting web page. In no time at all, you will quickly master the process and find the transition between editor and browser to be second nature.

There are plenty of high-end web editors available. Some of these editors include features like color-coding, automatic indentation, as well as access to prewritten code snippets. Some editors even come with built-in browsers of their own, saving you the hassle of having to work with two separate applications. I recommend that you stick with your computer's default text editor for now. This keeps things simple and allows you to focus on the fundamentals of web page development. Once you have mastered this, you can always upgrade to a higher-end editor and take advantage of all its bells and whistles.

Creating a Simple Web Page

This chapter has used the term *document* frequently to refer to plain text files containing (X) HTML statements. Documents, when rendered by web browsers, are used as the basis for creating web pages, made up of the content outlined in documents. All XHTML Strict 1.0 documents share a common format that must be strictly adhered to. This format consists of the `DOCTYPE` element, which is followed by the `html` element and its contents.

```
<!DOCTYPE html PUBLIC "-//W3C//DTD XHTML 1.0 Strict//EN"
  "http://www.w3.org/TR/xhtml1/DTD/xhtml1-strict.dtd">
<html xmlns="http://www.w3.org/1999/xhtml" lang="en" xml:lang="en">

  <head>

  </head>

  <body>
```

```
  </body>

</html>
```

Note the extra use of blank spaces and lines in the previous example. Their usage has no effect on the resulting document other than to improve its readability for the developer. When rendered by a web browser, this extra white space is ignored. Also note the use of indentation for some of the document's elements, which is used strictly for the purpose of visually formatting and organizing the hierarchical relationship of elements to one another.

Lastly, note that the DOCTYPE element, located at the beginning of the document, though written on two lines, is actually a single statement. It was spread out over two lines to improve its presentation within this book. To show that the second part of the statement is related to the first part, the second part was indented two spaces.

The html element serves as the document's *root element* and acts as a container in which all other elements are stored. Specifically, the html element contains the head and body elements. The head element contains other elements that are used to provide information about the document and its contents. The body element contains all of the document's contents, which when rendered by the web browser is presented as web page content. Every XHTML document that you create will follow this same format, varying only if you decide to work with a different version of XHTML.

Aside from the DOCTYPE element, every element in an (X)HTML document must be placed inside the opening <html> and closing </html> tags that make up the html element. Otherwise, the document is regarded as invalid resulting in unpredictable results.

If, however, you decide to work with HTML documents, both the DOCTYPE and opening html element will vary slightly, as demonstrated here:

```
<!DOCTYPE HTML PUBLIC "-//W3C//DTD HTML 4.01//EN"
  "http://www.w3.org/TR/html4/strict.dtd">

<html>

  <head>

  </head>
```

```
  <body>

  </body>

</html>
```

In this example, a document adhering to HTML 4.01 version strict has been laid out.

Back to the HTML Joke Page

It is now time to turn your attention to the development of this chapter's project, the HTML Joke page. When loaded into the web browser, this document, named HTMLJoke.html, will present visitors with a web page that displays the text for a humorous joke along with the text for that joke's punch line.

Since this book has yet to introduce you to the intricacies of (X)HTML development, don't worry if you do not fully understand what each individual statement is doing. For now, keep your attention on the overall process being followed. Things will become clear as you make your way through this book. By the time you have finished this book, web pages like the HTML Joke page will seem quite elementary to you.

Designing the Application

To help keep things simple, the development of this application will be performed in three steps, as outlined here:

1. Create a new HTML document.
2. Develop the document's markup.
3. Load and test the HTML page.

Although this web project is relatively simple, its development will walk you through the basics steps involved in creating and testing most web pages. As long as you take your time and follow along carefully with all of the instructions that are provided, you should not have any trouble creating and then testing your own copy of this web document.

In order to be able to share your web pages with the world, you will have to find a web host. Advice on how to find a web host is provided in Chapter 2. For now, you will learn how to test the execution of your web pages, locally on your own computer.

Step 1: Creating a New HTML Document

The first step in the creation of this project is the creation of an empty text file. Begin by opening your preferred code or text editor; Microsoft Notepad will work just fine on Windows and TextEdit will do on Mac OS X. Of course, you can use any editor that can save its output as a text file. Create and save a new, empty text file. Name the file HTMLJokes.html and save it.

To keep things simple and make your web pages easy to access and maintain, consider creating a dedicated folder to store them in. For example, when developing the web documents for this book, a folder named HTML_Source was created on the computer's local C: drive. You'll see that reflected in the URL field of a number of the figures shown in this and other chapters.

Step 2: Developing the Document's Markup

The next step in creating the HTML Joke project is to develop the web document's markup. Begin by adding the following elements to the HTMLJokes.html document.

```
<!DOCTYPE HTML PUBLIC "-//W3C//DTD HTML 4.01//EN"
  "http://www.w3.org/TR/html4/strict.dtd">

<html>

  <head>

  </head>

  <body>

  </body>

</html>
```

These statements are identical to those for the HTML template that you were introduced to earlier in this chapter. These elements including the `DOCTYPE` element, which specifies the version of HTML being used, and the elements needed to outline the document's `html`, `head`, and `body` sections. At this point you have supplied everything needed to create a valid, well-formed HTML page. If you were to save and load this document into your browser you would see a blank web page. Of course, to create a web page of value, you must add content to it. In the case of the HTML Joke project, this includes the addition of both `head` and `body` elements.

Modifying the head Section

To complete the document's head section, modify it by embedding the meta and title elements as shown here:

```
<head>
  <meta http-equiv="Content-type" content="text/html; charset=UTF-8">
  <title>Chapter 1 - HTML Joke</title>
</head>
```

The meta element shown here is used to specify the content type and character set used by the document. The title element is used to specify a text string that will be displayed in the web browser's titlebar. You will learn more about how to work with both of these elements in Chapter 3.

Specifying Document Content

The web page's content is provided by the document's body section. It consists of a level 1 heading and two paragraphs that display a joke and the joke's accompanying headline. To update the document's body section with the elements required to tell the joke, modify the document's body section as shown here:

```
<body>
  <h1>HTML Joke</h1>
  <p>Why is the number 6 afraid of the number 7?</p>
  <p>Because 7 ate 9.</p>
</body>
```

Without getting into the specifics now, the h1 element displays a heading identifying the joke. Then two p elements are used to display the requisite text content.

The Finished HTML Document

Once you have modified the document's body section, your copy of the web document is complete. The following example shows what the document looks like once it has been completely assembled.

```
<!DOCTYPE HTML PUBLIC "-//W3C//DTD HTML 4.01//EN"
  "http://www.w3.org/TR/html4/strict.dtd">

<html>

  <head>
    <meta http-equiv="Content-type" content="text/html; charset=UTF-8">
```

```
    <title>Chapter 1 - HTML Joke</title>
  </head>

  <body>
    <h1>HTML Joke</h1>
    <p>Why is the number 6 afraid of the number 7?</p>
    <p>Because 7 ate 9.</p>
  </body>

</html>
```

Although this book's primary focus is on the use of XHTML, its first project was done using HTML to demonstrate the similarities of the two markup languages. To convert this HTML document to an XHTML document, all you have to do is to modify the document's `DOCTYPE` and `html` elements as shown here in bold:

```
<!DOCTYPE html PUBLIC "-//W3C//DTD XHTML 1.0 Strict//EN"
  "http://www.w3.org/TR/xhtml1/DTD/xhtml1-strict.dtd">

<html xmlns="http://www.w3.org/1999/xhtml" lang="en" xml:lang="en">

<head>
    <meta http-equiv="Content-type" content="text/xhtml; charset=UTF-8" />
    <title>Chapter 1 - XHTML Joke</title>
  </head>

  <body>
    <h1>XHTML Joke</h1>
    <p>Why is the number 6 afraid of the number 7?</p>
    <p>Because 7 ate 9.</p>
  </body>

</html>
```

Step 3: Loading and Testing the Web Page

As you are about to see, you can easily load and display your web document from your own computer using your web browser, without having to upload it to the Internet. This makes testing your document quick and easy. To do so, open your preferred web browser and then execute the following procedure.

1. Click on the browser's File menu and select the Open File command. This displays a standard file open dialog.
2. Using the dialog window, navigate to the folder where you stored the web page and select it.
3. Click on the Open button. The browser will then load and display the document, as demonstrated in Figure 1.9.

FIGURE 1.9

An example of how the HTML Joke page looks when loaded using the Opera Web browser.

You can also load and test the HTMLJokes.html file by opening the folder in which you stored it and then double-clicking on it.

Well, that's it. As you can see, the steps required to create a basic web page are very straightforward. More complex web projects, involving multiple web pages and internal and external CSS and JavaScript files, require additional files and their development is a little more complicated, as you will see in later chapters.

SUMMARY

This chapter provided an introduction to HTML and XHTML, the markup languages used to develop web documents, and to Cascading Style Sheets or CSS, a web development language used to affect the appearance and presentation of web pages. You were also introduced to the document object model or DOM. Using the DOM, web developers are able to programmatically interact with and further control the presentation of web pages. You also learned how links are used to tie things together on and between web documents. On top of all this, you learned how to create your first HMTL and XHTML documents.

Challenges

1. **As currently written, the HTML Joke document displays a web page with a single joke shown on it as well as the joke's punch line. To make the page more interesting, consider adding additional jokes to the web document.**
2. **Try modifying the document title by changing the contents of its** `title` **element, as shown here, to a test string of your own choosing.**
   ```
   <title>Chapter 1 - HTML Joke</title>
   ```
3. **Replicate these changes in the XHTML version of this web page.**

HTML and XHTML Basics

A key part of understanding how to develop web pages is to know the syntax rules and requirements of how to work with (X)HTML tags and their attributes. In this chapter, you will review the different HTML and XHTML standards available to web developers and will learn how to specify which version you plan to use in your web documents. You will learn the different ways in which elements are formulated and will review basic tag construction. You will also learn how to configure tag attributes and to work with standard tag attributes. This chapter will also explain how to improve the organization and presentation of statements in your web pages and will provide advice on what to look for when selecting a web host for your website.

Specifically, you will learn:

- About the six versions of (X)HTML and how to specify which version you are working with using the `html` element
- How to work with single tags and tag pairs
- How to validate your (X)HTML documents
- How to modify element attributes
- How to comment your (X)HTML markup and to make effective use of white space

Project Preview: Linked Jokes Application

In this chapter's web development project, you will learn how to create a new XHTML application named linkedjokes.html. This web application will consist of three web documents. The first document displays a pair of jokes, as shown in Figure 2.1.

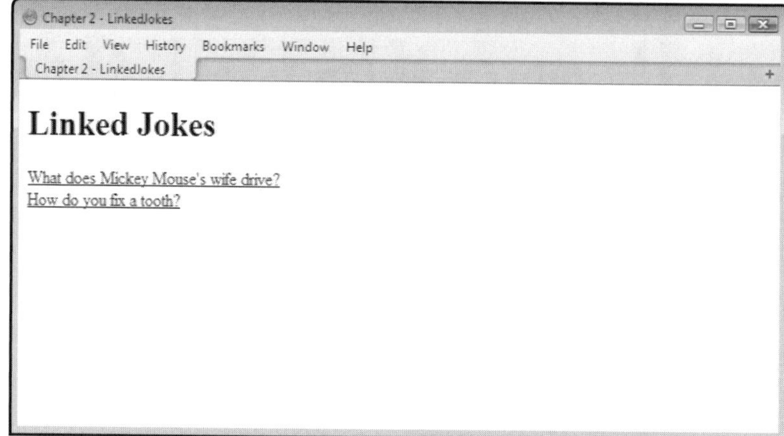

Figure 2.1

Using the Apple Safari browser to load the linkedjokes.html page.

Answers to each joke are provided in two separate web documents, one per joke. To view the answer for a given joke, the user must click on that joke's link. Figure 2.2 shows the web page that is loaded when the user clicks on the link for the first joke.

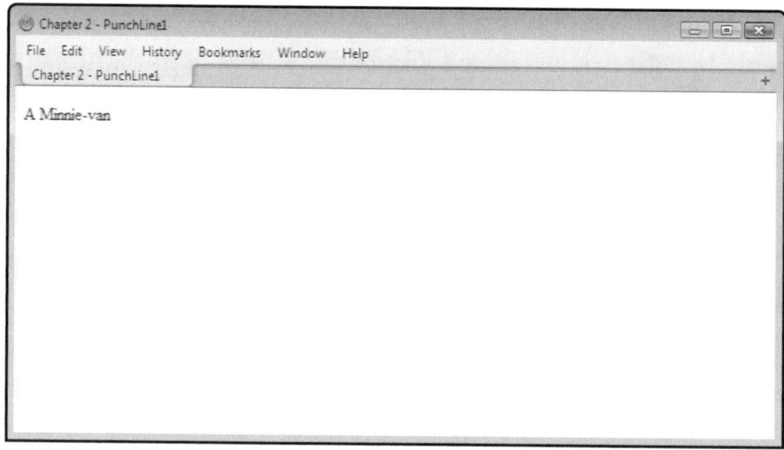

Figure 2.2

This page is automatically loaded when the user clicks on the first link on the page.

Likewise, to view the answer for the second joke, the user must click on that joke's link. Figure 2.3 shows the punch line that is displayed when the link for the second joke has been clicked.

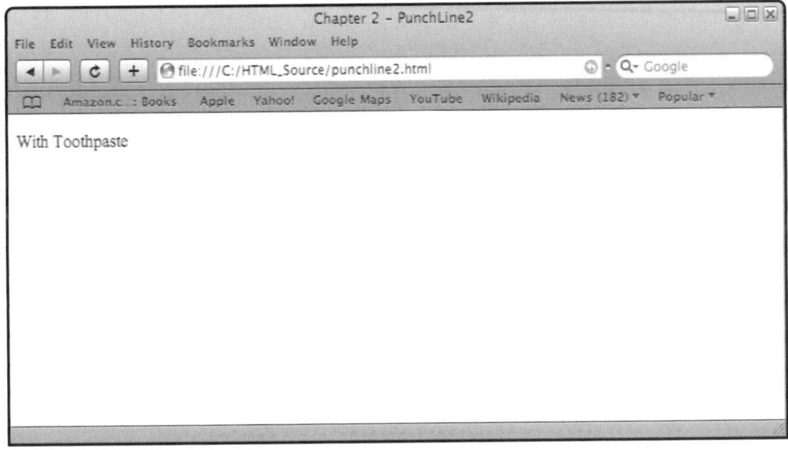

FIGURE 2.3

This page is automatically loaded when the user clicks on the second link on the page.

SEPARATING PRESENTATION FROM CONTENT

The basic purpose of (X)HTML is to provide structure to web documents. It provides a collection of elements that allow web developers to organize web documents in meaningful ways, identifying things like headings, paragraphs, and so on.

In the old days, before the widespread availability of CSS, web developers had limited control over the presentation of text within their web pages. To cope with this problem, a number of attributes were added to HTML that gave developers a bit of control over the appearance of a web document's content. However, this intermixing of content and presentation led to markup code that was not always easy to understand and support because of all of the extra presentation attributes that had to be added to document elements in order to try to manage their appearance.

Finally, along came Cascading Style Sheets or CSS in the late 1990s. CSS is its own language separate and distinct from (X)HTML. CSS allows web developers to define presentation rules in a stylesheet, which can then be applied to (X)HTML elements. Style sheets can be defined separately from markup inside web documents or externally in CSS files, separating content from presentation even further. Once created, external style sheets can be applied to any number of (X)HTML documents, allowing for the centralized administration of presentation for any number of web documents using a single style sheet.

Thanks to the widespread use of CSS, web developers can now separate content from presentation by using (X)HTML to outline a web document's design and organization and CSS to specify the appearance of that content. The result is web documents that are significantly easier to understand and update. The focus of this chapter is on the development of properly structured or *well-formed* (X)HTML. Concerns over presentation will be saved for later chapters.

The Six Flavors of (X)HTML

In total there are currently six different versions of HTML and XHTML, referred to collectively throughout this book as (X)HTML. There are three current versions of HTML named Transitional, Frameset, and Strict and three roughly parallel versions of XHTML also named Transitional, Frameset, and Strict. You specify which version of HTML or XHTML you are working with in a special element located at the beginning of every (X)HTML page known as the *Document Type Declaration* or *DOCTYPE* element. The `DOCTYPE` element tells web browsers what version of (X)HTML is being used so that the browser knows what set of rules to follow when rendering and displaying the document's content.

Technically, the `DOCTYPE` declaration is not an HTML element. Its sole purpose is to indicate a document's type. It must be placed at the top of all (X)HTML documents and must be defined exactly as outlined in the sections that follow, with no variation in syntax or capitalization. Other than white space, no other statements may precede the DOCTYPE declaration.

Technically speaking, to be compliant with XML standards, all XML documents should include an XML declaration statement before the `DOCTYPE` declaration. The XML declaration statement is used to identify the document as an XML document and to specify the document character encoding method. An example of an XML declaration statement is shown here:

```
<?xml version="1.0" encoding="UTF-8"?>
```

Unfortunately, not all web browsers, most notably Internet Explorer, are able to properly interpret the XML declaration statement. As a result, these browsers may render web pages inconsistent with your expectations. Because of limited browser support, it is best to omit the XML declaration statement.

HTML Standards

As already stated, there are three different current versions of HTML, each of which defines a similar but slightly different standard that specifies the rules that must be followed in order to generate well-formed documents.

HTML 4.01 Transitional

HTML 4.01 Transitional supports all HTML elements, including a number of presentation elements. Its purpose is to help web developers make the transition from earlier versions of HTML to HTML 4.01. To work with this version of HTML, you must add the following DOCTYPE element to be beginning of your HTML pages, typed exactly as shown here:

```
<!DOCTYPE HTML PUBLIC "-//W3C//DTD HTML 4.01 Transitional//EN"
  "http://www.w3.org/TR/html4/loose.dtd">
```

HTML 4.01 Frameset

HTML 4.01 Frameset is identical to HTML 4.01 Transition but includes added support for dealing with frames. Frames are an older web development methodology in which web pages were organized into different sections or frames, into which separate HTML pages are loaded. To work with this version of HTML, you must add the following DOCTYPE element to the beginning of your HTML pages, exactly as shown here:

```
<!DOCTYPE HTML PUBLIC "-//W3C//DTD HTML 4.01 Frameset//EN"
  "http://www.w3.org/TR/html4/frameset.dtd">
```

HTML 4.01 Strict

HTML 4.01 Strict excludes support for older presentation-based HTML elements, deferring to CSS to provide for web page presentation. Well-formed HTML pages that use this version will display more consistent results when rendered by different web browsers. To work with this version of HTML, you must add the following DOCTYPE element to the beginning of your HTML pages, typed exactly as shown here:

```
<!DOCTYPE HTML PUBLIC "-//W3C//DTD HTML 4.01//EN"
  "http://www.w3.org/TR/html4/strict.dtd">
```

XHTML Standards

As is the case with HTML, there are also three different current versions of XHTML. All three are similar but vary slightly in regards to the rules that must be followed in order to generate well-formed documents.

XHTML 1.0 Transitional

XHTML 1.0 Transitional, as its name implies, is a version of XHTML designed to support web developers who are in the process of converting from HTML to XHTML. As such, it retains support for a number of deprecated features, which, if present do not prevent a document from being well formed. To work with this version of XHTML, you must add the following DOCTYPE element to the beginning of your HTML pages, exactly as shown here:

```
<!DOCTYPE html PUBLIC "-//W3C//DTD XHTML 1.0 Transitional//EN"
  "http://www.w3.org/TR/xhtml1/DTD/xhtml1-transitional.dtd">
```

XHTML 1.0 Frameset

XHTML 1.0 Frameset is designed to support web pages that still rely on the use of framesets. A frameset is a mechanism for laying out web pages into separate frames or panes, each of which displays its own web page. Frames are a deprecated feature in both Strict and Transitional XHTML. To work with this version of XHTML, you must add the following DOCTYPE element to the beginning of your HTML pages, exactly as shown here:

```
<!DOCTYPE html PUBLIC "-//W3C//DTD XHTML 1.0 Frameset//EN"
  "http://www.w3.org/TR/xhtml1/DTD/xhtml1-frameset.dtd">
```

XHTML 1.0 Strict

XHTML 1.0 Strict, as its name implies, is the most stringent of the three versions of XHTML. As such, presentation and other deprecated features are not allowed and syntax rules must be rigidly adhered to in order for an XHTML document to be regarded as being well formed. To work with this version of XHTML, you must add the following DOCTYPE element to the beginning of your HTML pages, exactly as shown here:

```
<!DOCTYPE html PUBLIC "-//W3C//DTD XHTML 1.0 Strict//EN"
  "http://www.w3.org/TR/xhtml1/DTD/xhtml1-strict.dtd">
```

Unless otherwise specifically noted, all of the examples that are presented in this book will be done using XHTML 1.0 Strict.

Back in the early days of CSS, web browsers did not provide uniform levels of support for the language. Browsers of the day often interpreted CSS in accordance with their own rules in place of the official standard. To overcome this challenge, browser developers introduced DOCTYPE switching. With DOCTYPE switching, browsers assume that any document with a properly defined DOCTYPE is well formed and exactly follows the standard applications to its definition and will render the page in compliance mode.

If, however, the DOCTYPE is not properly defined or present, the browser will render the document in quirks mode. *Quirks mode* is more lenient than compliance mode and may result in less than desirable presentation of the document. In contrast, documents rendered in compliance mode are rendered in a far more predictable manner.

The HTML Element

The html element marks the beginning of a document's markup and is referred to as the document's root element. In (X)HTML documents the html element is defined by an opening <html> tag and a corresponding closing </html> tag. In HTML documents the html element is used without any attributes, as demonstrated here:

```
<!DOCTYPE HTML PUBLIC "-//W3C//DTD HTML 4.01//EN"
  "http://www.w3.org/TR/html4/strict.dtd">
 <html>
  <head>
  </head>

  <body>
  </body>
 </html>
```

In XHTML documents, you must include a required xmlns attribute in the head element and assign it a value of http://www.w3.org/1999/xhtml. This attribute specifies the location where the XHTML namespace resides. This namespace defines all of the elements and attributes supported by XHTML.

In addition, you should specify the optional lang and xml:lang attributes. These attributes specify the language in which the web document has been written. The following example demonstrates how the html element will appear in all of the XHTML examples that you will see in this book.

```
<!DOCTYPE HTML PUBLIC "-//W3C//DTD HTML 4.01//EN"
  "http://www.w3.org/TR/html4/strict.dtd">
 <html xmlns="http://www.w3.org/1999/xhtml" lang="en" xml:lang="en">
  <head>
  </head>

  <body>
  </body>
 </html>
```

XHTML is based on XML. XML is an extensible markup language. It allows for the creation of custom elements. However, XHTML 1.0 only supports a predefined collection of elements as specified in its namespace. XHTML 1.0 does not support the definition of custom elements. XHTML 1.1 and XHTML 2 will allow web developers to introduce custom elements through the development of a customized namespace. However, neither of these versions of XHTML has been published as an official standard yet.

Dissecting (X)HTML Markup

(X)HTML consists of numerous elements that you must learn how to use as a web developer. (X)HTML elements are made up of tags. Tags are used to mark the beginning and end of document content. Tag names are descriptive. They instruct web browsers as to the type of content they contain, so that the browsers will know how to render the document's content.

(X)HTML tags are enclosed within < and > brackets. The opening bracket (<) identifies the beginning of the tag. It is followed by the tag name. Tag names end with a closing bracket (>). (X)HTML consists of many different tags, each of which serves a different and distinct purpose. For example, the `<p>` tag specifies the beginning of a paragraph and the `<h1>` tag specifies the beginning of a heading.

Tag Pairs

Most (X)HTML tags work in pairs, including a start and an end tag. Tag pairs have the following syntax.

```
<tag>content</tag>
```

Here, ***content*** represents the content that is embedded within the two tags. The start tag identifies the beginning of an element and the end tag identifies where the element ends. For example, the following elements are all made up of tag pairs.

```
<h1>Little Red Riding Hood</h1>
<p>There once was a little girl named Little Red Riding Hood.</p>
```

Here, the first pair of tags defines a level one heading. It begins with the `<h1>` start tag and ends with the `</h1>` tag. The second pair defines a paragraph. It begins with the `<p>` tag and ends with the `</p>` tag. As you can see, all end tags include a / character, which sets them apart from start tags. These two tags and everything in between them is an element. Elements form the building blocks with which (X)HTML documents are created.

As already stated, (X)HTML supports two primary types of tags: tag pairs and single tags. A pair tag is a set of two tags that identify the beginning and the ending of an element. Figure 2.4 provides a high-level breakdown on the components of an (X)HTML element tag pair.

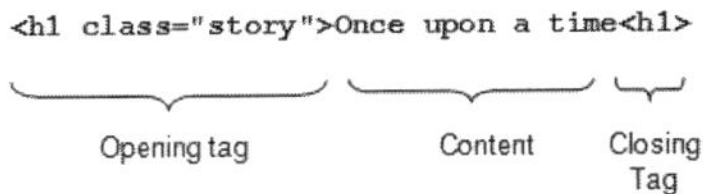

Figure 2.4

Elements are composed of an opening tag, content, and a closing tag.

As depicted in Figure 2.5, elements also consist of attributes.

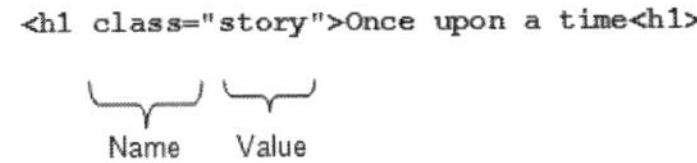

Figure 2.5

An attribute is made up of a name and an assigned value.

Single Tags

Not all elements require closing tags. Elements that do not have an end tag are referred to as single or empty tags. Single tags do not contain any contents. While HTML will let you get away without supplying an end tag in many situations, XTHML mandates that all elements must be closed. To comply with this rule, all single tags are self-closed, which is accomplished by placing a / before the closing >, as demonstrated here:

```
<tag/>
```

Unfortunately, since XHTML is based on XML and older browsers do not support XHTML, problems arise when these browsers attempt to process XHTML pages within single tags. To prevent these browsers from running into trouble when they try to render your web pages, you need to include a blank space in front of the closing / character, as demonstrated here:

```
<tag />
```

This little trick allows older browsers to ignore the closing slash, since it's not supported. Newer browsers, on the other hand, are smart enough to ignore the extra space and correctly interpret the tag. Three examples of how you should formulate single tags are provided here:

```
<br />
<hr />
<img src= "logo.gif" />
```

The first tag is used to insert a line break. The second tag inserts a horizontal rule (a line) across a web page, and the third example uses an image element (<img />) to insert an external image file into the web page at a specified location. Don't worry right now what each of these tags do. You learn about them in greater detail later in this book.

This book teaches you how to work with both (X)HTML and CSS. One easy way to determine which type of content you are looking at is to look and see if code has been embedded within the < and > characters (e.g., (X)HTML) or within { and } characters (e.g., CSS).

Learning More about Tags

Throughout this book you will be introduced to different types of tags, all of which support a host of different attributes. While you will be introduced to many of the elements that support these tags, there is not enough room in this book to define and present every possible attribute belonging to every available (X)HTML tag. Instead, you'll be introduced to the most commonly used tags and the most commonly used attributes.

If you find that you need to know more about any of the tags or tag attributes covered in this book, you can visit http://www.w3schools.com/tags/default.asp, as shown in Figure 2.6.

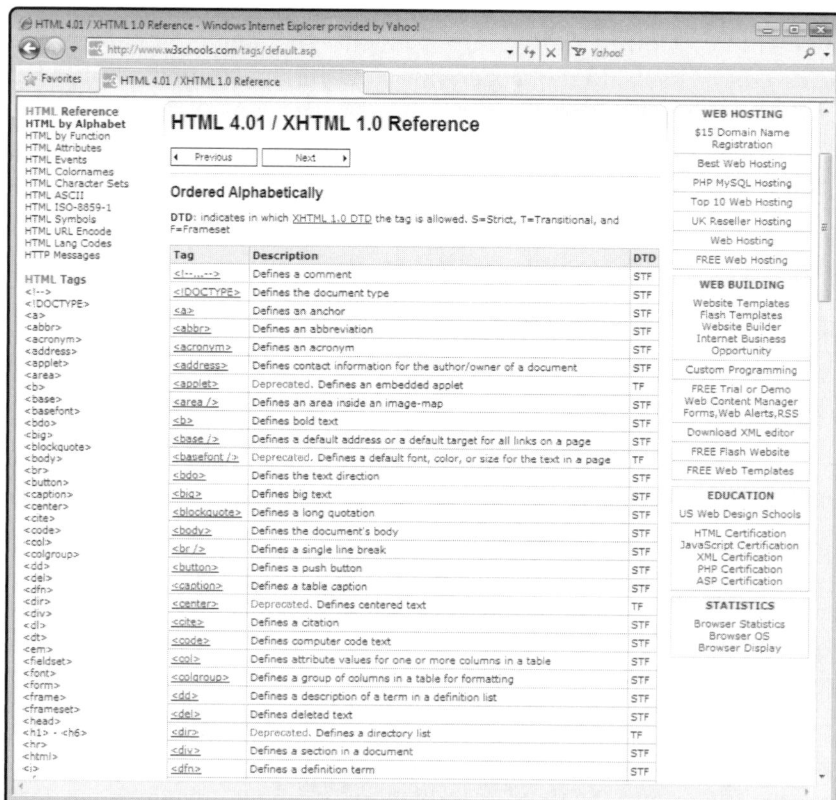

Tag	Description	DTD
<!--...-->	Defines a comment	STF
<!DOCTYPE>	Defines the document type	STF
<a>	Defines an anchor	STF
<abbr>	Defines an abbreviation	STF
<acronym>	Defines an acronym	STF
<address>	Defines contact information for the author/owner of a document	STF
<applet>	Deprecated. Defines an embedded applet	TF
<area />	Defines an area inside an image-map	STF
<b>	Defines bold text	STF
<base />	Defines a default address or a default target for all links on a page	STF
<basefont />	Deprecated. Defines a default font, color, or size for the text in a page	TF
<bdo>	Defines the text direction	STF
<big>	Defines big text	STF
<blockquote>	Defines a long quotation	STF
<body>	Defines the document's body	STF
 	Defines a single line break	STF
<button>	Defines a push button	STF
<caption>	Defines a table caption	STF
<center>	Deprecated. Defines centered text	TF
<cite>	Defines a citation	STF
<code>	Defines computer code text	STF
<col>	Defines attribute values for one or more columns in a table	STF
<colgroup>	Defines a group of columns in a table for formatting	STF
<dd>	Defines a description of a term in a definition list	STF
<del>	Defines deleted text	STF
<dir>	Deprecated. Defines a directory list	TF
<div>	Defines a section in a document	STF
<dfn>	Defines a definition term	STF

Figure 2.6

Detailed information about every HTML and XTHML tag is available online.

As shown in Figure 2.6, the HTML 4.01 / XHTML 1.0 Reference at www.w3schools.com provides information about every available tag. To review a document for a given tag, all you have to do is click on its tag name and you will be presented with everything there is to know about the tag, as demonstrated in Figure 2.7.

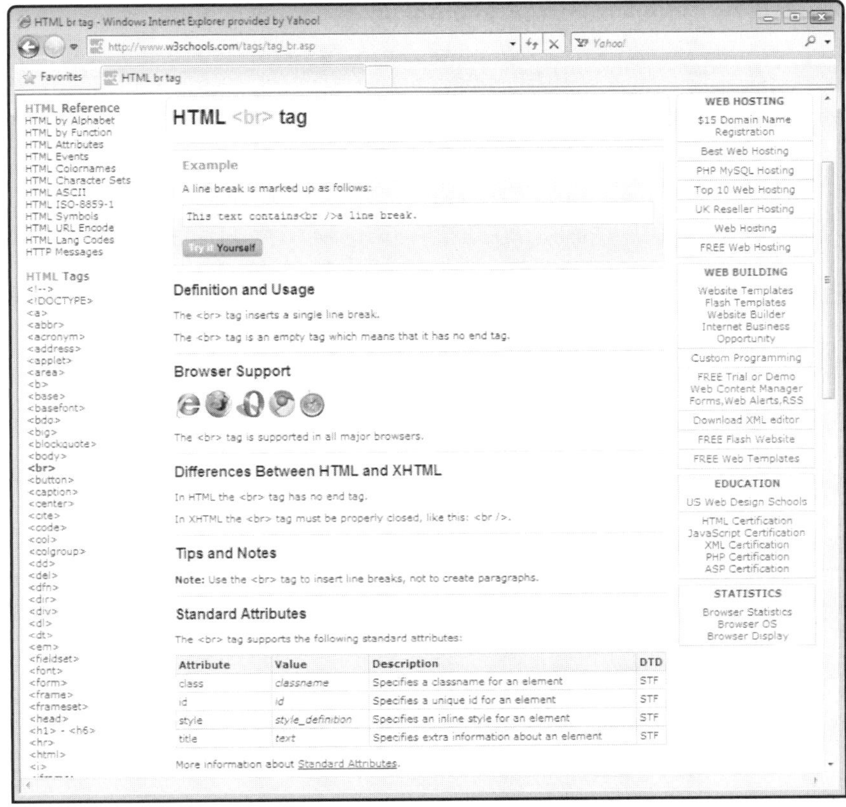

FIGURE 2.7

An example of the information that is returned when you look up the <br> tag.

As shown in Figure 2.7, the information provided about each tag includes an example of its usage, a list of browsers that support it, an explanation of differences in the way the tag is supported between HTML and XHTML, and a detailed listing of all the tag's attributes.

Markup Validation

In order to render (X)HTML documents in a consistent and predictable manner, you must ensure that they are well formed, meaning that your document should strictly adhere to whatever HTML or XHTML standard you have decided to work with. In this book, that's XHTML Strict. Failure to create well-formed documents will result in unpredictable results.

Beyond taking care when developing your (X)HTML documents, you can ensure that your documents are well formed by taking advantage of a free markup validation service provided by W3C, located at `validator.w3.org` as shown in Figure 2.8.

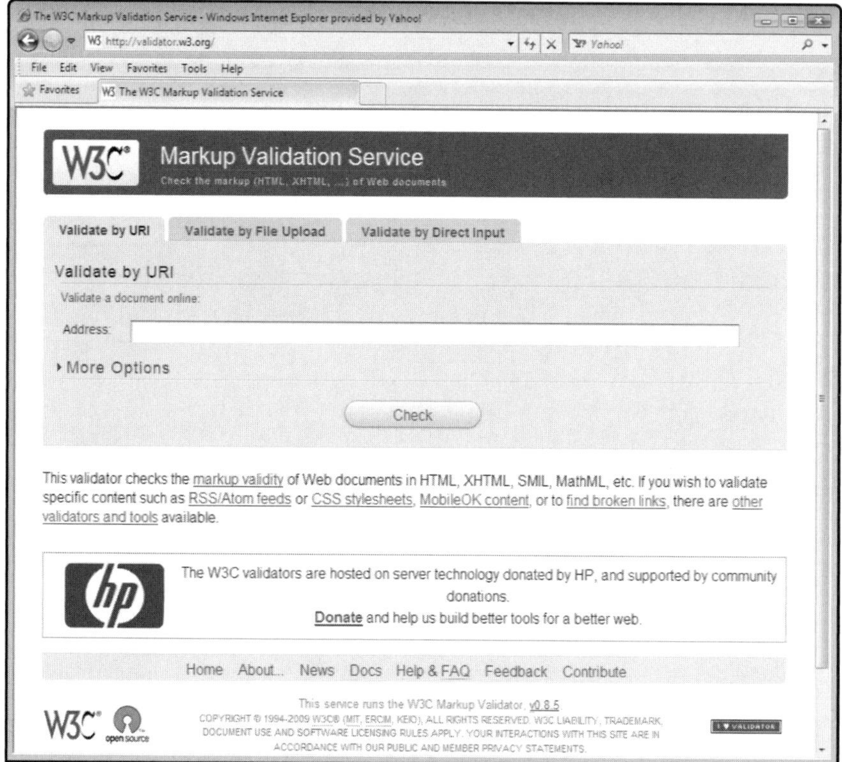

FIGURE 2.8

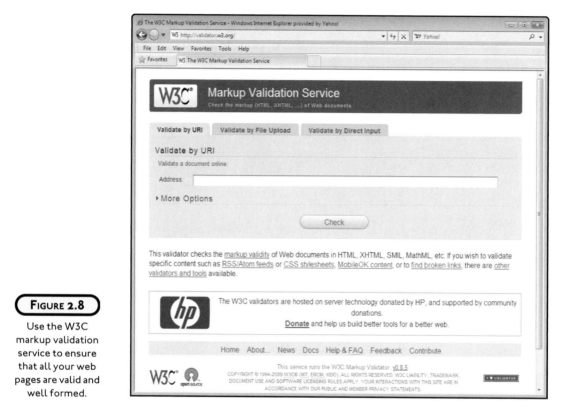

Use the W3C markup validation service to ensure that all your web pages are valid and well formed.

Using this free service, you can ensure that all of your web documents are valid and therefore should render in most web browsers in a consistent and predictable manner. You can use this service in any of three ways. First, if you have uploaded your document to the Internet, you can enter its URL. Second, if your web page still resides on your computer, you can upload it as a file. Finally, you can copy and paste the contents of your page into a form provided by the service. Regardless of which option you select, the service will analyze your markup and display its results, allowing you to ensure that your (X)HTML documents are well formed and to fix them if they are not.

Most web browsers are able to deal with documents that are not well formed. However, the results generated from (X)HTML documents that are not well formed may cause less than desirable results that differ from browser to browser.

Figure 2.9 shows an example of the results you will see when an HTML 4.01 document is well formed.

FIGURE 2.9

Error and Warning messages would have been displayed if the document was not well formed.

Similarly, Figure 2.10 shows the results that are displayed when an XHTML 1.0 Strict document is well formed.

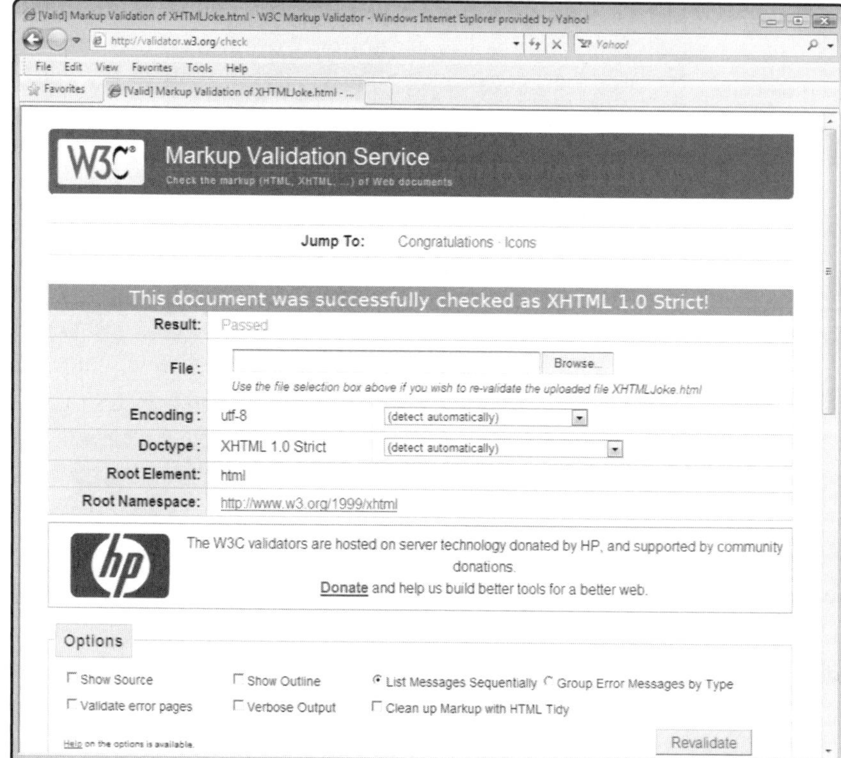

Figure 2.10

Well-formed markup should display consistently in different web browsers.

Configuring Element Attributes

Most (X)HTML elements support a range of attributes, which you can modify to configure the appearance and behavior, or the element based on its use in current circumstances. Like all XHTML syntax, attributes must be spelled in all lowercase. HTML allows for both upper- and lowercase. For example, the anchor element `<a>` uses the `href` attribute to specify the URL to which the link points, as demonstrated here:

```
<a href="http://www.microsoft.com">Microsoft's website</a>
```

Attributes are always specified after the element name and are only allowed in opening elements or in single elements before the self-closing tag. Most elements support a number of different attributes, allowing you to specify as many as you want in any order that makes sense to you, provided you separate each with a blank space. Note that according to XML syntax rules, you must specify attribute values within matching double-quotation marks using the syntax outlined here:

```
<tag attribute="value" attribute="value" . . . attribute="value">
```

(X)HTML elements support many different types of attributes. Many attributes are limited to specific values while others can take any text value you assign them. To determine which types of attributes are supported by each type of (X)HTML element, visit http://www.w3schools.com/tags/default.asp.

Element attributes are made up of an attribute name followed by the equals sign and then an assigned value, as demonstrated here:

```
<p id="Intro">A long time ago in a far away land…</p>
```

Here, a paragraph element has been assigned an `id` of `Intro`. `Id` is a universal attribute that can be assigned to any (X)HTML element. The `id` attribute will allow the paragraph to be referenced from elsewhere within the document, perhaps by a CSS style rule that set the font type, style, or size of the text that makes up the paragraph. Note that the quotation marks around the `id`, though optional in HTML, are required in XHTML strict.

Standard Element Attributes

As you learn different (X)HTML elements throughout this book, you will be introduced to many of the attributes that the elements support. However, there are a number of universal attributes that are common to just about every element. Use of these elements is entirely optional but often helpful. These elements are outlined below and demonstrated throughout the rest of the book.

`title`

`title` is an optional attribute that is used to assign a title to an element. Most browsers display the contents specified by the title in a tooltip when the mouse pointer is moved over the rendered element.

`id`

`id` is an optional attribute that specifies a unique name or identifier for an element, allowing the element to be referenced elsewhere, typically by CSS or JavaScript. When assigning a name to an `id`, the following rules apply:

- Each `ID` must be unique throughout the document
- Class names are made up of letters and numbers
- Class names are also limited to the following special characters: underscore (_) and hyphen (-)

`class`

`class` is an optional attribute used to define an element as being part of a class, allowing it along with all elements of that class to be referenced as a group. Any number of elements can be assigned to the same class. In addition, an element can be assigned to two or more classes. Classes are often used in conjunction allowing all elements within the same class to be assigned the same presentation rules. Classes are also used in conjunction with scripting. When working with classes, the following rules apply:

- When an element is assigned to more than one class, class assignments must be separated by spaces
- You may use any letter or number
- The first character must be a letter
- Except for the underscore (_) and hyphen (-) no special character can be used

`style`

The optional `style` attribute allows you to embed inline styling inside elements. Inline styles are seldom used by web developers, who generally defer to external style sheets and their inherent benefits. External style sheets are covered in Chapters 7 and 8.

Understanding Element Levels

There are two ways of working with (X)HTML elements, block level and inline. Block-level elements are used to display content on its own line, separate from other contents. Inline elements are designed to enclose small amounts of text embedded within block-level elements.

Working with Block-Level Elements

Block-level elements are elements that display their content on their own line, apart from other element content. An example of such an element is the `p` (paragraph) element, which is used to organize text into its own separate block, as demonstrated here:

```
<p>Perhaps today is a good day to die!</p>
```

Other examples of block-level elements include the `div` element and each of the heading elements (`h1`, `h2`, `h3`, `h4`, `h5`, and `h6`).

Embedding Inline Elements

Inline elements enclose smaller amounts of text for the purpose of highlighting them in some fashion. Block-level elements can stand on their own within an (X)HTML document. They may also be embedded within other block statements. Inline elements cannot stand on their own. To use them, they must be embedded within a block-level element as demonstrated here:

```
<p>The first letter of people's names <strong>should</strong> always be
capitalized.</p>
```

In this example, the inline strong element, which places strong emphasis on a word or words, has been embedded within a p element. An inline element can, however, contain another inline element provided the outer inline element resides within a block-level element, as demonstrated here:

```
<p>The first letter of people's names <em><strong>should</strong></em> always
be capitalized.</p>
```

Here, the em element has been added around the strong element to further add emphasis to a word within a p element.

Nesting Elements

Most (X)HTML elements allow you to embed them within other elements. You must properly nest embedded elements to provide valid and well-formed (X)HTML documents. Otherwise, errors will occur, as demonstrated in the following example.

```
<p>The first letter of people's names <em><strong>should</em></strong> always
be capitalized.</p>
```

Here, the em and strong elements are not properly embedded.

When embedded elements are within one another, it is essential that you remember to complete the inner element before you close the outer tags, as demonstrated here:

```
<div><p>Hello World!</p></div>
```

Failure to follow this simple rule will result in errors. An example of improperly nested elements is provided here:

```
<div><p>Hello World!</div></p>
```

Some (X)HTML elements are specifically designed to be used in a nested manner. Examples of these types of elements include the <ol>, which defines an ordered list, and <li> element, which defines an item within a list. The following example demonstrates these two types.

```
<ol>
  <li>Apples</li>
  <li>Oranges</li>
  <li>Pears</li>
  <li>Grapes</li>
</ol>
```

Commenting Your Markup

(X)HTML consists of a collection of English-like tags, which is the basis for defining elements. Despite this, (X)HTML documents can be quite complex. One way to make your document easier to understand and support is to embed comments inside your documents that explain what is going on and why you have laid out your documents in the manner you have.

(X)HTML comments are created by embedding text within an opening `<!--` tag and a closing `-->` tag. For example,

```
<!-- The following paragraph introduces the story's main character. -->
<p>Once upon a time there was a wizard named Gandor.</p>
```

If you need to, you can spread comments over multiple lines, as demonstrated here:

```
<!-- The following paragraph introduces
the story's main character. -->
<p>Once upon a time there was a wizard named Gandor.</p>
```

One common use of comments is to temporarily comment out one or more elements when developing and testing documents. For example, when troubleshooting a problem with a document you might temporarily comment out one or more elements that you suspect to be the source of the problem in order to see how the rest of the document is rendered when those elements are not processed.

Web browsers will not display the contents stored in a document's embedded comments. You should use them liberally throughout your documents to document every major part of the document.

Improving Document Organization with White Space

One nice feature of (X)HTML is that you are permitted to use white space at will for improved formatting of your documents without affecting the document in any meaningful way (other than increasing its size). You add white space to your documents by inserting extra spaces and line breaks into your documents.

When web browsers load (X)HTML documents, they automatically ignore all of the extra white space by collapsing all extra space down to a single space. For example, in the following example, extra white space has been added before and after different elements in order to make the resulting statements easier to view and maintain.

```
<div>

  <p>

      Once there was a hero named <em>Mighty Molly</em>!

  </p>

</div>
```

When rendered by the browser, the output generated by this example is identical to that generated by the following example. However, as you can see, it is clearly easier to view and understand what is going on in the first example thanks to the extra white space.

```
<div><p>Once there was a hero named <em>Mighty Molly</em>!</p></div>
```

Likewise, this third example will be rendered in an identical manner.

```
<div>

      <p>

   Once    there    was    a    hero    named
      <em>Mighty Molly</em>!

      </p>

  </div>
```

As this example shows, the overuse of white space in this third example has become anti-productive. Obviously too much of a good thing is not always good. When rendered by the browser, this example's output, shown next, is the same as the other examples.

```
Once there was a hero named Mighty Molly
```

If you need to preserve white space, you can enclose your content within the pre element, covered in Chapter 4.

Finding a Web Host for Your Web Pages

In Chapter 1, you learned how to create a web page and test it by using the browser to open a copy of the web page stored on your own computer. However, in order to be able to share your website with the rest of the world, you need to upload your web documents to a web server. A web server is simply a specially configured server that is connected to the Internet and whose purpose is to accept requests from web browsers and return specified web pages and other types of content.

If you do not already have a web host, there are a number of different ways of finding a good web host for your web pages. You could begin your search by checking with your Internet service provider. Sometimes Internet service providers offer their customers a little web server space as part of their service. Another option for finding a host for your web pages is one of any number of free website hosts like Google (http://googlewebhosting.net/). The price that you pay for free services like this is the display of advertisements on your web pages, typically in the form of banners. A third option that you can pursue is to find a web host provider. You have to pay a little for this service but it is often the best choice. For as little at $7.95 per month, a good web host provider will provide you with space to store your best pages, multiple e-mail accounts, support for advanced features like PHP, MySQL, Ruby on Rails, Perl, Python, website statistics, and many other options. An example of one such web host is site5 (www.site5.com).

Once selected, your web host will provide the URL of your website, which might be something like www.*hostname*.com/*sitename*. Here, *hostname* is the name of your web host and *sitename* is the name of your website.

Once you have found a web host you are comfortable with, your provider will give you instructions on how to access your website and how to upload and manage your web pages. Most web hosts allow you to upload web pages one of two ways. First, you are usually given a graphical user interface through which you can upload and manage your web documents. Second, you can usually use *FTP*, which stands for *File Transfer Protocol*. Using an FTP client and the FTP address provided by your web host, you can upload and download files from your website. You'll also be able to create a folder structure within which to store your files.

There are a number of very good FTP clients available for download on the Internet. Examples include FileZilla (filezilla-project.org/).

Once you have uploaded your web pages, you can then access and view them using your web browser.

Back to the Linked Jokes Project

Now it is time to return your attention to the Linked Jokes project. In this project, you will create three separate XHTML documents. The first document will display two jokes, each of which is also a link that when clicked instructs the browser which of the other two XHTML documents it should load. As you can see, rather than display the jokes and punch lines all on the same web page, this chapter's project uses links to control navigation from a primary page to two other pages.

Designing the Application

As was the case with preceding chapter projects, you will develop the Linked Jokes project in a series of steps as outlined here:

1. Create the project's HTML documents.
2. Develop the document's markup.
3. Load and test the HTML page.

What makes this project different from the HTML Jokes project that you created in Chapter 1 is the movement of joke punch lines to external web pages, which are loaded and displayed in the web browsers when their corresponding links are clicked.

Step 1: Creating New HTML Document

The first step in the creation of this project's web document is the creation of the empty text files. Begin by opening your preferred code or text editor and creating and saving the following three files, using the names outlined here:

- **LinkedJokes.html.** The main landing page whose URL visitors will use to view this web application.
- **PunchLine1.html.** A web page that is loaded when visitors click on the link for the first joke on the LinkedJokes.html document.
- **PunchLine2.html.** A web page that is loaded when visitors click on the link for the second joke on the LinkedJokes.html document.

Step 2: Developing the Document's XHTML

The next step in creating the Linked Jokes project is the development of the markup for all three of the project's web documents. Begin by adding the following elements to the LinkedJokes.html document.

```
<!DOCTYPE HTML PUBLIC "-//W3C//DTD HTML 4.01//EN"
  "http://www.w3.org/TR/html4/strict.dtd">

<html xmlns="http://www.w3.org/1999/xhtml" lang="en" xml:lang="en">

  <head>

  </head>

  <body>

  </body>

</html>
```

These statements include the DOCTYPE element and the base set of elements required to build an XHTML page. The next step in the development of the Linked Jokes project is to finish the LinkedJokes.html document and to create the project's other two documents.

Completing the LinkedJokes.html Document

To complete the LinkedJokes.html document, you need to modify it by embedding the meta and title elements as shown next. The meta element specifies the content type and character set used by the document and the title element specifies a text string that will be displayed in the web browser's titlebar.

```
<head>
  <meta http-equiv="Content-type" content="text/xhtml; charset=UTF-8" />
  <title>Chapter 2 - LinkedJokes</title>
</head>
```

You also need to update the document's body section by modifying it, as shown here:

```
<body>
  <h1>Linked Jokes</h1>
  <a href="punchline1.html">What does Mickey Mouse's wife drive?</a><br />
  <a href="punchline2.html">How do you fix a tooth?</a>
</body>
```

This markup consists of a level 1 heading and two links that display the document's jokes. When clicked, these links instruct the browser to load and display the documents specified by each link's href attribute.

Creating the PunchLine1.html Document

Next, open the PunchLine1.html documents, add the following statements to it, and then save the file.

```
<!DOCTYPE html PUBLIC "-//W3C//DTD XHTML 1.0 Strict//EN"
  "http://www.w3.org/TR/xhtml1/DTD/xhtml1-strict.dtd">

<html xmlns="http://www.w3.org/1999/xhtml" lang="en" xml:lang="en">

  <head>
    <meta http-equiv="Content-type" content="text/xhtml; charset=UTF-8" />
    <title>Chapter 2 - PunchLine1</title>
  </head>

  <body>
    <p>A Minnie-van</p>
 </body>

</html>
```

As you can see, this web document is very similar to the LinkedJokes.html pages, except that instead of two links, it displays a paragraph showing the punch line for one of the game's jokes.

Creating the PunchLine2.html Document

Lastly, open the PunchLine2.html documents, add the following statements to it, and then save the file.

```
<!DOCTYPE html PUBLIC "-//W3C//DTD XHTML 1.0 Strict//EN"
  "http://www.w3.org/TR/xhtml1/DTD/xhtml1-strict.dtd">

<html xmlns="http://www.w3.org/1999/xhtml" lang="en" xml:lang="en">

  <head>
    <meta http-equiv="Content-type" content="text/xhtml; charset=UTF-8" />
    <title>Chapter 2 - PunchLine2</title>
  </head>

  <body>
    <p>With Toothpaste</p>
```

```
 </body>

</html>
```

As you can see, the only difference between this and the PunchLine1.html document is the content stored in the `title` element and the content located in the `body` section's paragraph element.

Step 3: Loading and Testing Your New Web Documents

At this point, all three documents that make up the Linked Jokes project have been completed and you are ready to load and view the results of your work. To do so, open your favorite web browser and then execute the following procedure.

1. Click on the browser's File menu and select the Open File command. This displays a standard file open dialog.
2. Using the dialog window, navigate to the folder where you stored the web page and select it.
3. Click on the Open button. The browser will then load and display the specified document as was demonstrated back in Figure 2.1.

If anything looks out of place on your version of this project, go back and recheck your work. If, after clicking one of the links located on the main page you see an error indicating that the specified web page cannot be found, double-check the URL that you entered into the browser and make sure that the case used within the links matches the case you used when you saved both the PunchLine1.html and PunchLine2.html files.

Summary

This chapter provided an overview of (X)HTML syntax rules and outlined the requirements of how to work with tags and tag elements. You learned about all six (X)HTML standards, how they compare to one another, and how to specify the one you want to work with in your web document. You learned about the different ways in which elements are formulated and how to construct tags. You were introduced to (X)HTML standard tags and learned how to improve document organization and presentation using white space and comments. You also received guidance on what to look for in a web host.

Challenges

1. As currently written, the Link Jokes web application only displays two jokes. Consider modifying it to suit your own personal style by replacing or adding to its collection of jokes.
2. Consider adding more text to the document using the p (paragraph) element that explicitly instructs the user to click on a joke in order to see its punch line.
3. After making changes to your web documents, consider visiting www.validator.w3.org and ensuring that they are still well formed.

Part II

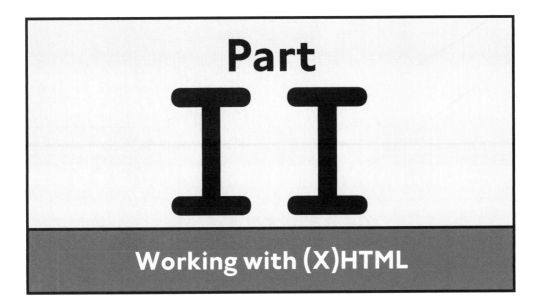

Working with (X)HTML

Creating (X)HTML Document Headings

All (X)HTML pages are made up of two primary sections: the head and body. This chapter focuses on the head section, which is responsible for specifying information about the documents and its content. With the exception of the <title> tag, which displays a text string in browser title bars, none of the contents of all of the head section are displayed. Instead, the tags stored in the head section are used to do things like provide information for search engines, define CSS style sheets used within documents, and define scripts embedded within the document.

Specifically, you will learn how to use:

- The <title> tag to display a text string in the browser's title bar
- The <meta> tag to provide keyword data used by search engines
- The <base> tag to reduce the size of links
- The <style> tag to create internal style sheets
- The <link> tag to link external style sheets to documents
- The <script> tag to add scripts to your documents

Project Preview: The Math Quiz Application

In this chapter, you will learn how to create a new web project call the Math Quiz application. To take the quiz, the user must have a pencil and a sheet of paper on which to write and record his answer. The Math Quiz presents the user with instructions for completing the quiz, as shown in Figure 3.1.

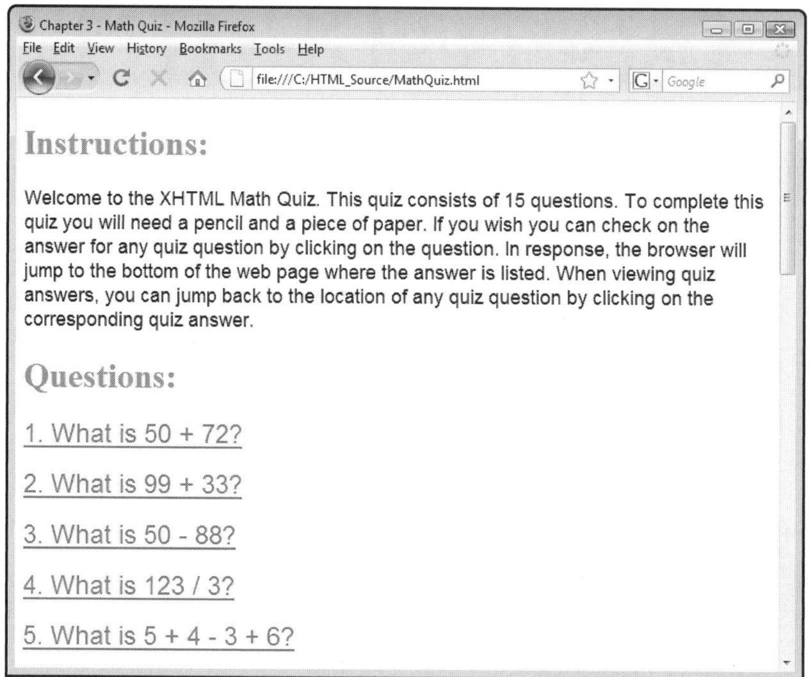
Chapter 3 - Math Quiz - Mozilla Firefox
File Edit View History Bookmarks Tools Help
file:///C:/HTML_Source/MathQuiz.html
Google
Instructions:
Welcome to the XHTML Math Quiz. This quiz consists of 15 questions. To complete this quiz you will need a pencil and a piece of paper. If you wish you can check on the answer for any quiz question by clicking on the question. In response, the browser will jump to the bottom of the web page where the answer is listed. When viewing quiz answers, you can jump back to the location of any quiz question by clicking on the corresponding quiz answer.
Questions:
1. What is 50 + 72?
2. What is 99 + 33?
3. What is 50 - 88?
4. What is 123 / 3?
5. What is 5 + 4 - 3 + 6?

Figure 3.1

The quiz consists of 15 arithmetic questions.

As shown in Figure 3.2, the quiz consists of 15 separate math questions. Answers to all 15 questions are provided at the bottom of the web page.

Every question on the page is actually a link that when clicked jumps down and displays its corresponding answer. Likewise, every answer is also a link that when clicked returns you to its corresponding question. As this web page demonstrates, links can be used to control navigation within web pages and not just between them.

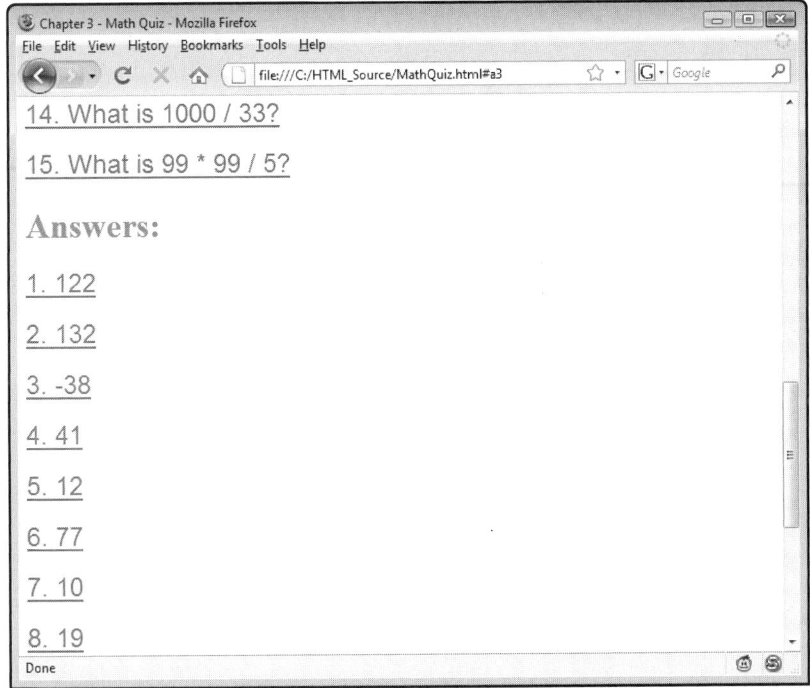

FIGURE 3.2

Answers to each question are provided at the bottom of the web page.

Establishing a Document Framework

Every (X)HTML document is made up of three parts, outlined here:

- `DOCTYPE` **declaration.** Tells the browsers what version of HTML or (X)HTML is being used.
- **Document head section.** Provides information about the document, including its title, style information, and scripts.
- **Document body.** Outlines the content that is rendered in the browser and made visible to visitors.

In Chapter 2 you learned how to specify a web document `DOCTYPE`. The focus of this chapter is on the development of a web document's head section. Chapters 4 to 6 will cover the development of a web document's `body` section.

Building a Document Template

While every (X)HTML page is unique, they all have these three parts in common. Going forward in this book, all examples will be presented using (X)HTML Strict. As such, it is a good idea to create a template that you can use as the basis for creating all other documents. As a first step in creating this template, create a document like the one shown here:

```
<!DOCTYPE html PUBLIC "-//W3C//DTD XHTML 1.0 Strict//EN"
  "http://www.w3.org/TR/xhtml1/DTD/xhtml1-strict.dtd">

<html xmlns="http://www.w3.org/1999/xhtml" lang="en" xml:lang="en">

  <head>

  </head>

  <body>

  </body>
</html>
```

The DOCTYPE element is essential because it is responsible for telling the browser what version of (X)HTML should be applied when rendering the contents of the document. The specifics of the DOCTYPE statement were reviewed in Chapter 1. The rest of the document is contained within the html element, which itself is made up of the body and head elements.

To be well formed, the html element's opening <html> tag must at a minimum include an xmlns attribute, which is used to specify the XML namespace used by the (X)HTML document (http://www.ww3.org/1999/xhtml). Optionally, you may also include the lang and xml:lang: attributes. Both the lang and xml:lang attributes are used to specify the language in which the document has been written.

Making the Document Template Well Formed

If you take the document template that was just explained and validate it at http://validator.w3.org, you see that an error and two warnings are raised. The error and one of the warnings note that no character encoding is found. This can be corrected by adding a <meta> tag to the document's head section. The other warning occurs because a <title> tag has not been included in the head section. The following example addresses all of these problems and results in a well-formed (X)HTML page with no errors or warnings.

```
<!DOCTYPE html PUBLIC "-//W3C//DTD XHTML 1.0 Strict//EN"
  "http://www.w3.org/TR/xhtml1/DTD/xhtml1-strict.dtd">

<html xmlns="http://www.w3.org/1999/xhtml" lang="en" xml:lang="en">
```

```
  <head>
    <meta http-equiv="Content-type" content="text/xhtml; charset=UTF-8" />
    <title></title>
  </head>

  <body>

  </body>

</html>
```

Technically, the inclusion of the <meta> is not required. However, it is recommended that you use it anyway. This will help ensure that all browsers properly render your documents and will eliminate the warning messages displayed if you validate your web documents at validator.w3.org.

Adding Elements to the head Section

With the exception of the `<title>` tag, none of the tags that you place within the head section of your (X)HTML pages result in the display of any content that is visible to the user. However, the content that you add to the head section of your (X)HTML pages plays an important role in the presentation of documents and the interactivity of resulting web pages. For example, the head section is where you define a document's style rules, title, and the meta content that web search engines use when indexing your web pages.

The head section supports a number of different tags. The list of tags that you can use in the head section is outlined next. Their use is demonstrated in detail through the rest of this chapter.

- `<title>`—This tag displays a text string in the browser's title bar
- `<meta>`—This tag is used to provide keyword data used by Internet search engines
- `<base>`—This tag is used to shorten the size of links
- `<style>`—This tag is used to embed an internal style sheet into a document
- `<link>`—This tag is used to set up a link to an external style sheet document
- `<script>`—This tag is used to add scripts to your documents

Even though the contents of the head section do not get displayed by the web browser, visitors to your web pages can still see your web page's content by viewing its source. To do so, all users have to do is load your web page and then click on View > Source (Internet Explorer) or View > View Source (Apple Safari) or View > Page Source (Mozilla Firefox).

The <title> tag

The `<title>` tag is used to display a text string in the browser's title bar. You should always include a title on every document. The title clearly identifies the web page to visitors. Search engines display the title when they generate a list of web pages as the result of user queries. As a result, the title may be the first thing web surfers see when your site appears in a search engine's output.

Web browsers also use a document title when generating bookmarks for web pages and for the generation of bookmark names. When you formulate the text for your document, make sure that you keep it concise and yet descriptive of what the document is all about. The following document provides an example of how to use the `<title>`tag.

```
<!DOCTYPE html PUBLIC "-//W3C//DTD XHTML 1.0 Strict//EN"
  "http://www.w3.org/TR/xhtml1/DTD/xhtml1-strict.dtd">

<html xmlns="http://www.w3.org/1999/xhtml" lang="en" xml:lang="en">

  <head>
    <title>XYZ's Graphic Design and Publishing</title>
  </head>

  <body>

  </body>

</html>
```

Note that all you have to do to supply a title for your document is to type the desired text between the `<title>` and `</title>` tags. Figure 3.3 demonstrates how the title appears when the document is loaded into Internet Explorer, Mozilla Firefox, and Apple Safari.

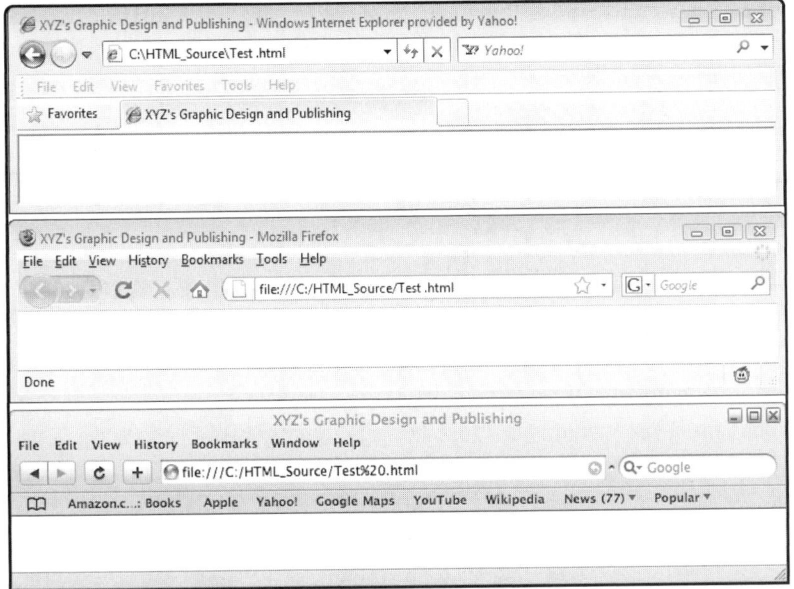

FIGURE 3.3

A demonstration of the use of the `title` element.

The <meta> tag

The most common means by which web surfers find new websites is through search engines. Search engines regularly search the Internet indexing new websites. You have the ability to influence the content that search engines collect through the use of metadata, documented in the head section of documents using `<meta>` tags. Metadata is a term used to describe data about data.

The use of metadata is an important component in the marketing of web pages. But it is only a small part of a well-constructed marketing campaign. To learn more about how to attract people to your website, check out *Increase Your Web Traffic in a Weekend* (ISBN# 1598634828) by Jerry Lee Ford, Jr.

Using meta tags, you can define suggested keywords and descriptions for search engines. For example, the following document contains three meta elements. The first element uses the `<meta>` tag's `name` element to specify a list of keywords for search engines to index. The words themselves are specified in a comma-separated list using the tag's `content` attribute. The second meta element specifies a descriptive statement for search engines to use their search result listing when displaying information about the web page. The third meta element, which you have seen before, uses the `http-equiv` attribute to connect or associate the value assigned to the `Content` attribute with the HTTP response header. The meta element also uses the `charset` attribute to specify the character-encoding scheme used by the document.

In addition to keywords and description, the <meta> tag's name attribute also supports author and summary as possible values.

```
<!DOCTYPE html PUBLIC "-//W3C//DTD XHTML 1.0 Strict//EN"
  "http://www.w3.org/TR/xhtml1/DTD/xhtml1-strict.dtd">

<html xmlns="http://www.w3.org/1999/xhtml" lang="en" xml:lang="en">

  <head>
    <meta name="keywords" content="Games, Jokes, Riddles, Stories" />
    <meta name="description" content="Play free on-line games" />
    <meta http-equiv="Content-type" content="text/xhtml; charset=UTF-8" />
    <title>Chapter 1 - XHTML Joke</title>
  </head>

  <body>

  </body>

</html>
```

You can also use the meta tag's http-equiv attribute to instruct web browsers to perform certain actions. For example, the following element would be used to instruct the browser to automatically refresh the contents of the document every 30 seconds.

```
<meta http-equiv="refresh" content="30" />
```

Older web browsers may not support the use of the <meta> tag's http- equiv attribute. In which case, redirection will fail. As a result, it is a good idea to also display a link with a test message on your web page instructing visitors who are not automatically redirected to click on the link.

Similarly, you can use a meta element to automatically redirect visitors to another web page, as demonstrated here:

```
<!DOCTYPE html PUBLIC "-//W3C//DTD XHTML 1.0 Strict//EN"
  "http://www.w3.org/TR/xhtml1/DTD/xhtml1-strict.dtd">

<html xmlns="http://www.w3.org/1999/xhtml" lang="en" xml:lang="en">
```

```
<head>
 <meta http-equiv="refresh" content="5; url= http://www.courseptr.com" />
 <meta http-equiv="Content-type" content="text/xhtml; charset=UTF-8" />
 <title>Redirection Example</title>
</head>

<body>
  <h1>The resource you are looking for has moved.</h1>
  <h2>Your browser will automatically be redirected in 5 seconds to:</h2>
  <p>
    <a href="http://www.courseptr.com">http://www.courseptr.com</a>
  </p>
</body>

</html>
```

Here, visitors are redirected from the current web page to a page located at http://www.courseptr.com after a 5-second delay. In the event that the visitor's browser does not support meta tag redirection, a link has been provided for visitors to click on. Figure 3.4 shows an example of what visitors will see when this document is initially loaded into their browser.

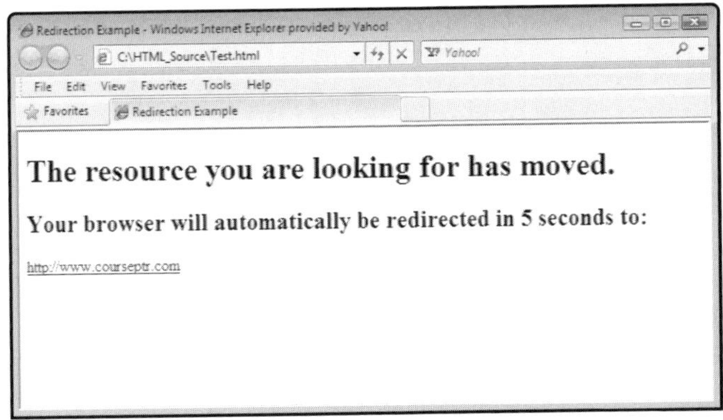

FIGURE 3.4

A simple redirection example.

The <base> tag

If you find that you are creating a web page that has a lot of links to files residing at the same location, you can shorten the URL reference to those files using the base element to specify the URL for all common links. The `<base>` tag has just one required attribute, `href`, which specifies the base URL for all of the links. By using the `<base>` tags to specify a base URL, you shorten the length of any URL that has the same base URL. This not only helps keep things simple but makes your documents easier to maintain. For example, if the location of all files using the base URL changes, all you would have to do is modify the contents of the <base> tag to point to the new location and everything will work.

To see an example of how to set up a base URL, take a look at the following example.

```
<!DOCTYPE html PUBLIC "-//W3C//DTD XHTML 1.0 Strict//EN"
  "http://www.w3.org/TR/xhtml1/DTD/xhtml1-strict.dtd">

<html xmlns="http://www.w3.org/1999/xhtml" lang="en" xml:lang="en">

  <head>
    <meta http-equiv="Content-type" content="text/xhtml; charset=UTF-8" />
    <base href="http://www.courseptr.com/" />
    <title>Demo - Working with the Base element</title>
  </head>

  <body>
    <h1>Book Categories</h1>
    <p><a href="ptr_catalog.cfm?group=Programming">Programming Topics</a>
      </p>
    <p><a href="ptr_catalog.cfm?group=Operating Systems">Operating
      Systems</a></p>
    <p><a href="ptr_catalog.cfm?group=Certification">Certification</a></p>
    <p><a href="ptr_catalog.cfm?group=Macintosh">Macintosh</a></p>
  </body>

</html>
```

When loaded, the browser will pre-append the base URL to each of the URLs in the four link elements. Figure 3.5 shows the resulting web page after it has been rendered by the browser.

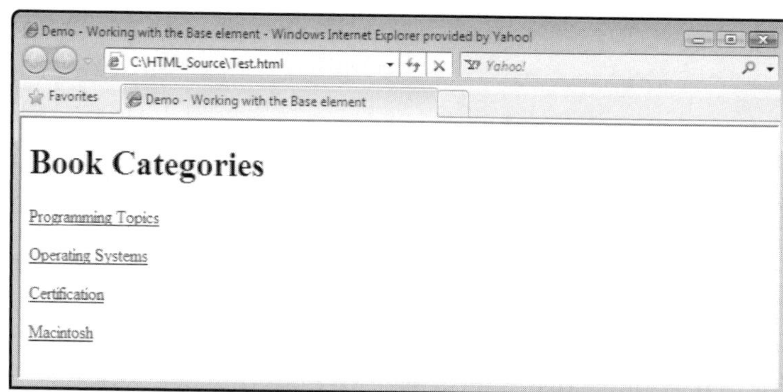

FIGURE 3.5

Using the base element to shorten the length of your links.

The <style> tag

There are several ways in which you can influence the way browsers present the appearance of your documents. These options include inline tags, internal style sheets, and external style sheets. Internal style sheets are embedded within web documents using the `<style>` tag. This tag has one required attribute named `type`, which must be assigned a value of `text/css`. The following web document demonstrates the use of the `<style>` tag.

```
<!DOCTYPE html PUBLIC "-//W3C//DTD XHTML 1.0 Strict//EN"
  "http://www.w3.org/TR/xhtml1/DTD/xhtml1-strict.dtd">

<html xmlns="http://www.w3.org/1999/xhtml" lang="en" xml:lang="en">

  <head>
    <meta http-equiv="Content-type" content="text/xhtml; charset=UTF-8" />
    <style type="text/css">
      h1 {color: red;}
      a {font: 24px arial, courier;
         color: green;}
    </style>
    <title>Chapter 2 - LinkedJokes</title>
  </head>

  <body>
    <h1>Linked Jokes</h1>
    <a href="punchline1.html">What does Mickey Mouse's wife drive?</a><br />
    <a href="punchline2.html">How do you fix a tooth?</a>
  </body>

</html>
```

As you can see, the `style` element consists of both a start and an end tag. The starting style tag is written as `<style type="text/css">`. This internal style sheet consists of various rules that govern the presentation of the web document level 1 heading and link elements. Here, all level 1 headings are displayed in red and all links are displayed using a 24-pixel font. If the computer that has loaded the web document supports the arial font, that font is used. If the arial font is not present then the courier font is used. If that font is also not present, the computer default font is used. Figure 3.6 shows how this web document looks when loaded using Internet Explorer.

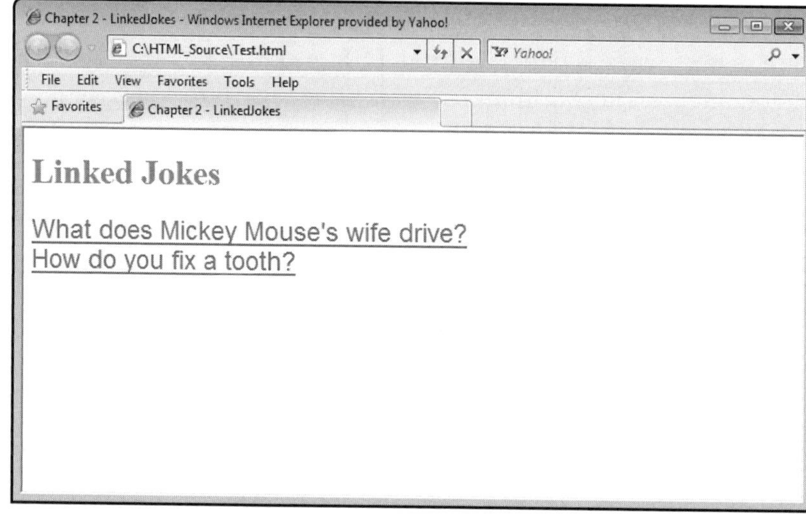

FIGURE 3.6

An example of a web page whose font type and color have been styled using an internal style sheet.

The previous web document contains two links. The first link points to a web page named punchline1.html and the second link points to a web page named punchline2.html. The contents of the punchline1.html file are shown next. Note that this file also contains its own internal style sheet. This style sheet contains a single rule that sets the font size, type, and color for all paragraph (p) elements.

```
<!DOCTYPE html PUBLIC "-//W3C//DTD XHTML 1.0 Strict//EN"
  "http://www.w3.org/TR/xhtml1/DTD/xhtml1-strict.dtd">

<html xmlns="http://www.w3.org/1999/xhtml" lang="en" xml:lang="en">

  <head>
    <meta http-equiv="Content-type" content="text/xhtml; charset=UTF-8" />
    <style type="text/css">
      p {font: 24px arial, courier;
         color: green;}
    </style>
    <title>Chapter 2 - PunchLine1</title>
  </head>

  <body>
    <p>A Minnie-van</p>
 </body>

</html>
```

Figure 3.7 shows how the contents of this page appear when loaded by the web browser.

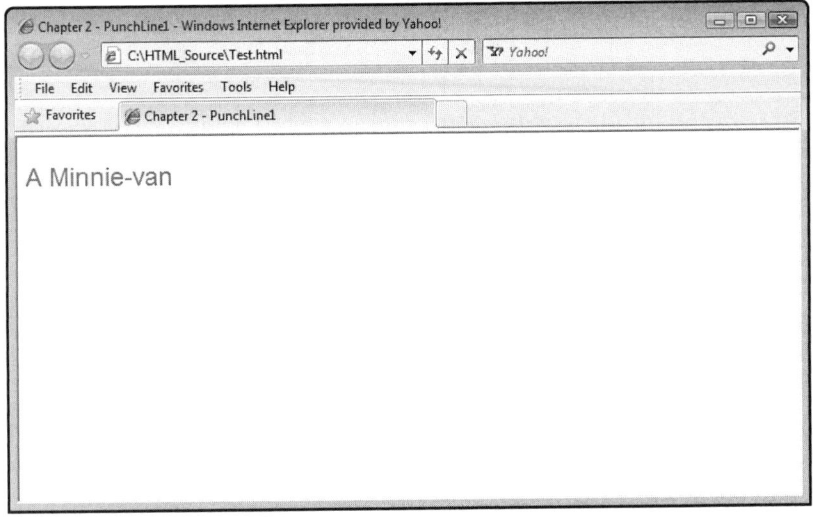

FIGURE 3.7

The text for the web page's paragraph (p) elements is displayed as green text.

The contents of the punchline2.html file are shown next. Note that this file also contains its own internal style sheet. This style sheet contains a single rule that sets the font size, type, and color for all paragraph (p) elements.

```
<!DOCTYPE html PUBLIC "-//W3C//DTD XHTML 1.0 Strict//EN"
  "http://www.w3.org/TR/xhtml1/DTD/xhtml1-strict.dtd">

<html xmlns="http://www.w3.org/1999/xhtml" lang="en" xml:lang="en">

  <head>
    <meta http-equiv="Content-type" content="text/xhtml; charset=UTF-8" />
    <style type="text/css">
      p {font: 24px arial, courier;
         color: green;}
    </style>
    <title>Chapter 2 - PunchLine2</title>
  </head>

  <body>
    <p>With Toothpaste</p>
 </body>

</html>
```

Internal style sheets help to separate document structure from presentation. However, web developers seldom use internal style sheets, preferring instead to use external style sheets. You will learn all about internal and external style sheets in Chapters 7 and 8.

The <link> tag

The `link` element is used to define a relationship with another document. One common use of the `link` element is to establish a link to an external style sheet document. External style sheets, like their internal style sheet counterparts, provide web developers with the ability to style web page presentations. The following web document demonstrates how to use the `link` element to connect an external style sheet.

```
<!DOCTYPE html PUBLIC "-//W3C//DTD XHTML 1.0 Strict//EN"
  "http://www.w3.org/TR/xhtml1/DTD/xhtml1-strict.dtd">

<html xmlns="http://www.w3.org/1999/xhtml" lang="en" xml:lang="en">

  <head>
    <meta http-equiv="Content-type" content="text/xhtml; charset=UTF-8" />
    <link rel="stylesheet" type="text/css" href="test.css" />
    <title>Chapter 2 - LinkedJokes</title>
  </head>

  <body>
    <h1>Linked Jokes</h1>
    <a href="punchline1.html">What does Mickey Mouse's wife drive?</a><br />
    <a href="punchline2.html">How do you fix a tooth?</a>
  </body>

</html>
```

As you can see, the `link` element consists of a single, self-closed tag. Note that in this example, the `link` element makes use of the following attributes.

- **`rel`**. Defines the relationship with the external document, which in the case of external style sheets is `stylesheet`.
- **`type`**. Specifies the MIME type of the linked document, which in the case of an external style sheet is `text/css`.
- **`href`**. Specifies the URL for the style sheet.

The name of the external style called in this example is test.css. This file is stored in the same folder as the web document. Like (X)HTML documents, CSS external style sheets are made up of plain text. The contents of this external style sheet are shown next.

```
h1 {color: red;}
a {font: 24px arial, courier; color: green;}
```

This external style sheet contains two rules. The first rules instruct the browser to display all headings in red and all links in green, using a 24-pixel font and either arial or courier font. As you can see, external style sheets do not include opening and closing `<style>` tags. Figure 3.8 shows an example of the contents of the external file sheet file.

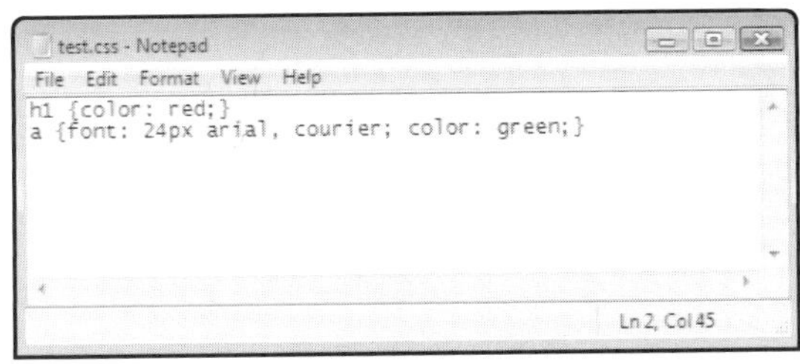
test.css - Notepad
File Edit Format View Help
h1 {color: red;}
a {font: 24px arial, courier; color: green;}
Ln 2, Col 45

FIGURE 3.8

An example of a simple external style sheet.

The <script> tag

In order to create web pages that provide your visitors with an interactive experience, you need to learn how to work with one of any number of web-based computer-programming languages. One of the most popular and most widely used is JavaScript. *JavaScript* is a scripting language that executes within web browsers and which can be used to execute scripts embedded within web pages.

Although you can add scripts to the `head` or `body` sections of your documents, it is recommended that you always add them to the `head` section. This will ensure that they are loaded into memory before the browser renders the content in the `body` section, making the scripts available for use whenever they are needed. In order to add a script to your documents, you must use the `<script>` tag. The `<script>` tag supports a number of attributes, including:

- `language`. Identifies the script as JavaScript.
- `type`. Specifies the MIME type of the script.
- `scr`. Specifies a URL that provides a link to a file that contains a JavaScript.

The following web document demonstrates how to use the `script` element to embed a script within a web document.

```
<!DOCTYPE html PUBLIC "-//W3C//DTD XHTML 1.0 Strict//EN"
  "http://www.w3.org/TR/xhtml1/DTD/xhtml1-strict.dtd">

<html xmlns="http://www.w3.org/1999/xhtml">

  <head>
    <meta http-equiv="Content-type" content="text/xhtml; charset=UTF-8" />
    <title>Chapter 1 - XHTML Joke</title>
    <script language="javascript" type="text/javascript">
    <!-- Start hiding JavaScript statements
      window.alert("Hello World!");
    //End hiding JavaScript statements -->
    </script>
  </head>

<body>

</body>

</html>
```

As you can see, since the JavaScript is embedded within the web document itself, only the `language` and `type` attributes were used. Figure 3.9 shows the output that is displayed when this script is loaded by the Apple Safari web browser.

FIGURE 3.9

Using JavaScript to display a message in a popup dialog window.

The following statements demonstrate how to call upon an external JavaScript from within a web document.

```
<script src="Test.js" language="javascript" type="text/javascript">
</script>
```

As you can see, the `src` attribute has been used to specify the location of the external JavaScript in place of embedded JavaScript statements.

Chapter 9 provides a good overview of JavaScript and its use in the dynamic generation of interactive content.

Back to the Math Quiz Page

Okay, it's time to turn your attention back to the development of the Math Quiz project. Once loaded into a web browser, this document will present your visitors with instructions for taking a 15-question math quiz along with the quiz itself. Answers to each question are provided at the bottom of the web page. Your visitors can jump back and forth between questions and answers by clicking on individual questions and answers. Specifically, every question is individually linked to its corresponding answer at the bottom of the page and every answer is linked back to its corresponding question.

As you can see, this chapter's project uses links to control navigation within a web page as opposed to using them to establish links to other external web pages, as was demonstrated in Chapter 2's project.

Designing the Application

As is the case with all of the web projects in this book, you will develop the Math Quiz project in a series of steps, as outlined here:

1. Create a new HTML document.
2. Develop the document's markup.
3. Test the HTML page.
4. Spice things up with a little CSS.
5. Perform a final test.

As you work on this web document, pay particular attention to how links are formed and note the appearance of the resulting web page content before and after the document's internal style sheet is applied.

Step 1: Creating a New HTML Document

The first step in creating this project's web document is to create an empty text file. Using your preferred code or text editor, create and save a new, empty text file. Name the file MathQuiz.html and save it in the same location as all of your other web documents.

Step 2: Developing the Document's Markup

The next step in creating the Math Quiz project is to write the web document's markup. Let's begin by adding the following standard set of elements to the MathQuiz.html document.

```
<!DOCTYPE html PUBLIC "-//W3C//DTD XHTML 1.0 Strict//EN"
  "http://www.w3.org/TR/xhtml1/DTD/xhtml1-strict.dtd">

<html xmlns="http://www.w3.org/1999/xhtml" lang="en" xml:lang="en">

  <head>

  </head>

  <body>

  </body>

</html>
```

At this point you have supplied everything needed to create a valid, well-formed HTML page. All that remains is for you to add the markup required to complete the document's `head` and `body` section.

Updating the head Section

To complete the document's `head` section, modify it by embedding the `meta` and `title` elements, as shown here:

```
<head>

  <meta http-equiv="Content-type" content="text/xhtml; charset=UTF-8" />
  <title>Chapter 3 - Math Quiz</title>

</head>
```

The `meta` element specifies the document's content type and character set, and the `title` element specifies a text string to be displayed in the web browser's titlebar.

Specifying Document Content

The web document content is provided by the document's `body` section, which is made up of a number or heading (`h1`), paragraph (`p`), and link (`a`) elements. Begin the development of the `body` section's markup by adding the following statements to it.

```
<h1>Instructions:</h1>

<p>Welcome to the XHTML Math Quiz. This quiz consists of 15 questions.
   To complete this quiz you will need a pencil and a piece of paper.
   If you wish you can check on the answer for any quiz question by
   clicking on the question. In response, the browser will jump to the
   bottom of the web page where the answer is listed. When viewing quiz
   answers, you can jump back to the location of any quiz question
   by clicking on the corresponding quiz answer.</p>
```

As you can see, the h1 element encloses a heading that identifies the location of the quiz's instructions, which are embedded within a p element that follows the h1 element. Next, add the following statement to the end of the body section. These statements consist of another h1 element that identifies the beginning of the quiz's list of questions followed by a series of 15 p elements. Embedded within each paragraph is a link (a) element. Each link is identified by a unique id assignment. Each link href attribute points to a named element located at the end of the page. The text for each link is then displayed.

One of the objectives of this book is to provide you with a new web project at the end of each chapter. Unfortunately, the tradeoff of this approach means that in the early chapters you must use a number of (X)HTML elements before they have been formally instructed and explained. All of the elements that you see in this project are explained in detail in Chapter 4. For now, just follow along with the explanations that are provided and type in everything exactly as you see it. If necessary, you can return and review this project again after completing Chapter 4.

```
<h1>Questions:</h1>

<p><a id="q1" href="#a1">1. What is 50 + 72?</a></p>
<p><a id="q2" href="#a2">2. What is 99 + 33?</a></p>
<p><a id="q3" href="#a3">3. What is 50 - 88?</a></p>
<p><a id="q4" href="#a4">4. What is 123 / 3?</a></p>
<p><a id="q5" href="#a5">5. What is 5 + 4 - 3 + 6?</a></p>
<p><a id="q6" href="#a6">6. What is 7 * 11?</a></p>
<p><a id="q7" href="#a7">7. What is 4 * 5 / 2</a></p>
<p><a id="q8" href="#a8">8. What is 10 * 2 + 6 - 7?</a></p>
<p><a id="q9" href="#a9">9. What is 50 + 72?</a></p>
<p><a id="q10" href="#a10">10. What is 50 / 5 * 6?</a></p>
```

```
<p><a id="q11" href="#a11">11. What is 3 * 3 * 3 * 3 / 9?</a></p>
<p><a id="q12" href="#a12">12. What is 5 / 2 + 4.5 + 3?</a></p>
<p><a id="q13" href="#a13">13. What is 22 - 5 - 3 - 1?</a></p>
<p><a id="q14" href="#a14">14. What is 1000 / 33?</a></p>
<p><a id="q15" href="#a15">15. What is 99 * 99 / 5?</a></p>
```

Now that we have written all of the markup required to outline the web document's questions, it is time to add the markup responsible for displaying answers to all of the quiz's questions. As was the case in the markup used to display the quiz questions, the markup for the answers also consists of a (link) elements embedded within p (paragraph) elements. The markup is provided below and should be added to the end of the document's body section.

```
<h1>Answers:</h1>

<p><a id="a1" href="#q1">1. 122</a></p>
<p><a id="a2" href="#q2">2. 132</a></p>
<p><a id="a3" href="#q3">3. -38</a></p>
<p><a id="a4" href="#q4">4. 41</a></p>
<p><a id="a5" href="#q5">5. 12</a></p>
<p><a id="a6" href="#q6">6. 77</a></p>
<p><a id="a7" href="#q7">7. 10</a></p>
<p><a id="a8" href="#q8">8. 19</a></p>
<p><a id="a9" href="#q9">9. 122</a></p>
<p><a id="a10" href="#q10">10. 60</a></p>
<p><a id="a11" href="#q11">11. 9</a></p>
<p><a id="a12" href="#q12">12. 10</a></p>
<p><a id="a13" href="#q13">13. 15</a></p>
<p><a id="a14" href="#q14">14. 30.30</a></p>
<p><a id="a15" href="#q15">15. 1960.2</a></p>
```

Step 3: Performing a Quick Test of the Document

At this point, your copy of the Math Quiz application should be ready for testing. To do so, open your preferred web browser and then execute the following procedure.

1. Click on the browser's File menu and select the Open File command. This displays a standard file open dialog.
2. Using the dialog window, navigate to the folder where you stored the web page and select it.
3. Click on the Open button. The browser will then load and display the specified document.

Once loaded and rendered in your browser, the Math Quiz should look like the example shown in Figure 3.10.

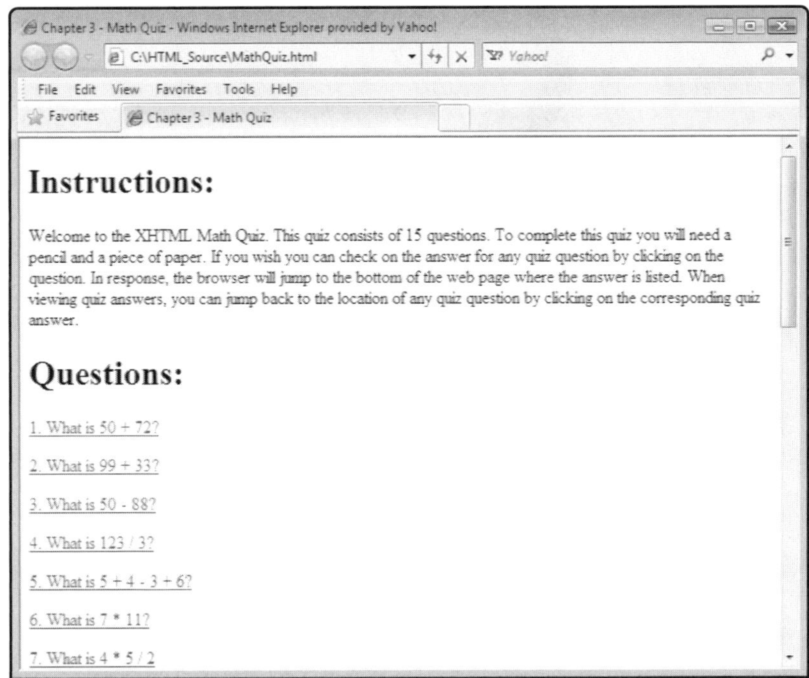

FIGURE 3.10

The quiz consists of arithmetic questions.

As you can see, by default, the text displayed on the resulting web page is displayed in black, except for the question and answer links, which are displayed in blue. The page's content is displayed using the browser's default font type and size.

Step 4: Spicing Things Up with an Internal Style Sheet

Rather than accept this default presentation, let's spice things up a bit by adding a CSS internal style sheet to the web document. Specifically, you will modify the presentation of the document by modifying its default colors, font sizes, and font types.

Embedding an Internal Style Sheet

As you learned earlier in this chapter, to add an internal style sheet to a web document, you must add the `style` element to the document's `head` section. To do so, embed the following CSS markup to the document's `head` section.

```
<style type="text/css">
  h1 {color: red;}
  a {font: 24px arial, courier;
     color: green;}
  p {color: black;
     font: 18px arial, courier;}
</style>
```

(X)HTML uses elements made up of tags to organize content. (X)HTML tags are created by placing them within < and > characters. CSS, on the other hand, uses rules when specifying presentation. CSS rules are embedded within { and } characters. The first rule listed above instructs the browser to display all `h1` (heading) elements using the color red. The next CSS rule instructs the browser to display the document's links using a font that is 24 pixels high using arial font. If the arial font is not supported on the user's computer, courier is used. Lastly, link text is displayed in green color.

The third and final CSS rule instructs the browser to display all `p` (paragraph) text in black, using a font size of 18 pixels and the arial font (courier is not supported).

A detailed review of CSS and its syntax is provided in Chapters 7 and 8.

The Finished HTML Document

Your copy of the Math Quiz's web document should now be complete. To make sure that you have assembled it correctly, compare your document against the following completed example.

```
<!DOCTYPE html PUBLIC "-//W3C//DTD XHTML 1.0 Strict//EN"
  "http://www.w3.org/TR/xhtml1/DTD/xhtml1-strict.dtd">

<html xmlns="http://www.w3.org/1999/xhtml" lang="en" xml:lang="en">

  <head>

    <meta http-equiv="Content-type" content="text/xhtml; charset=UTF-8" />

    <style type="text/css">
      h1 {color: red;}
      a {font: 24px arial, courier;
```

```
      color: green;}
    p {color: black;
      font: 18px arial, courier;}
  </style>

  <title>Chapter 3 - Math Quiz</title>

</head>

<body>

  <h1>Instructions:</h1>

  <p>Welcome to the XHTML Math Quiz. This quiz consists of 15 questions.
    To complete this quiz you will need a pencil and a piece of paper.
    If you wish you can check on the answer for any quiz question by
    clicking on the question. In response, the browser will jump to the
    bottom of the web page where the answer is listed. When viewing quiz
    answers, you can jump back to the location of any quiz question
    by clicking on the corresponding quiz answer.</p>

  <h1>Questions:</h1>

  <p><a id="q1" href="#a1">1. What is 50 + 72?</a></p>
  <p><a id="q2" href="#a2">2. What is 99 + 33?</a></p>
  <p><a id="q3" href="#a3">3. What is 50 - 88?</a></p>
  <p><a id="q4" href="#a4">4. What is 123 / 3?</a></p>
  <p><a id="q5" href="#a5">5. What is 5 + 4 - 3 + 6?</a></p>
  <p><a id="q6" href="#a6">6. What is 7 * 11?</a></p>
  <p><a id="q7" href="#a7">7. What is 4 * 5 / 2</a></p>
  <p><a id="q8" href="#a8">8. What is 10 * 2 + 6 - 7?</a></p>
  <p><a id="q9" href="#a9">9. What is 50 + 72?</a></p>
  <p><a id="q10" href="#a10">10. What is 50 / 5 * 6?</a></p>
  <p><a id="q11" href="#a11">11. What is 3 * 3 * 3 * 3 / 9?</a></p>
  <p><a id="q12" href="#a12">12. What is 5 / 2 + 4.5 + 3?</a></p>
  <p><a id="q13" href="#a13">13. What is 22 - 5 - 3 - 1?</a></p>
  <p><a id="q14" href="#a14">14. What is 1000 / 33?</a></p>
  <p><a id="q15" href="#a15">15. What is 99 * 99 / 5?</a></p>
```

```
    <h1>Answers:</h1>

    <p><a id="a1" href="#q1">1. 122</a></p>
    <p><a id="a2" href="#q2">2. 132</a></p>
    <p><a id="a3" href="#q3">3. -38</a></p>
    <p><a id="a4" href="#q4">4. 41</a></p>
    <p><a id="a5" href="#q5">5. 12</a></p>
    <p><a id="a6" href="#q6">6. 77</a></p>
    <p><a id="a7" href="#q7">7. 10</a></p>
    <p><a id="a8" href="#q8">8. 19</a></p>
    <p><a id="a9" href="#q9">9. 122</a></p>
    <p><a id="a10" href="#q10">10. 60</a></p>
    <p><a id="a11" href="#q11">11. 9</a></p>
    <p><a id="a12" href="#q12">12. 10</a></p>
    <p><a id="a13" href="#q13">13. 15</a></p>
    <p><a id="a14" href="#q14">14. 30.30</a></p>
    <p><a id="a15" href="#q15">15. 1960.2</a></p>

  </body>

</html>
```

Step 5: Loading and Testing the Math Quiz

Okay, it is time to retest your copy of the Math Quiz document to ensure that it looks and works as previously described. If your web browser is still open from the last time you tested the web page, just click on its relation\refresh button. Otherwise, open your browser again and reload your document. Figure 3.11 shows the resulting web page that is rendered when the document is loaded.

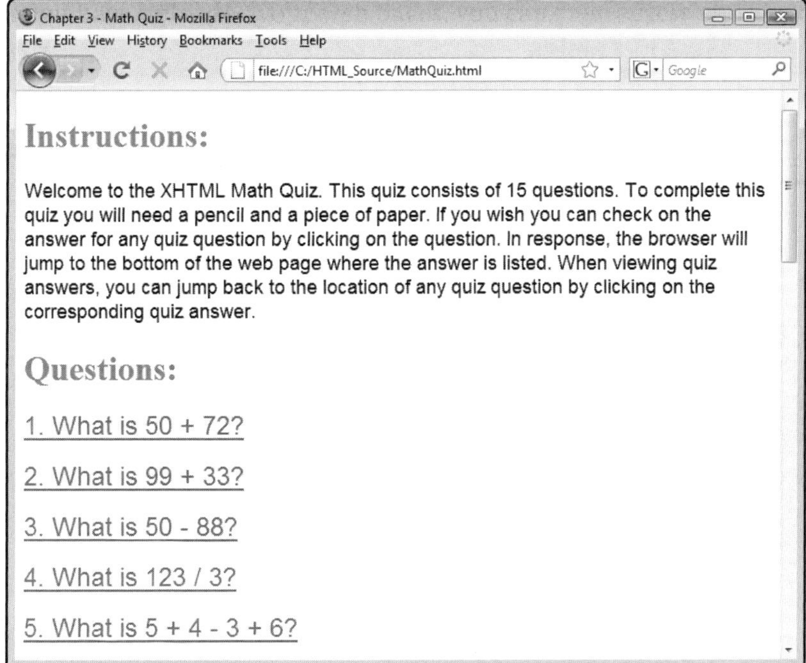

Chapter 3 - Math Quiz - Mozilla Firefox
File Edit View History Bookmarks Tools Help
file:///C:/HTML_Source/MathQuiz.html
Google
Instructions:
Welcome to the XHTML Math Quiz. This quiz consists of 15 questions. To complete this quiz you will need a pencil and a piece of paper. If you wish you can check on the answer for any quiz question by clicking on the question. In response, the browser will jump to the bottom of the web page where the answer is listed. When viewing quiz answers, you can jump back to the location of any quiz question by clicking on the corresponding quiz answer.
Questions:
1. What is 50 + 72?
2. What is 99 + 33?
3. What is 50 - 88?
4. What is 123 / 3?
5. What is 5 + 4 - 3 + 6?

FIGURE 3.11

The quiz consists of 15 arithmetic questions.

SUMMARY

This chapter focused on the development of your (X)HTML page's `head` section. This included learning how to use the `<title>` tag to display a text string in the browser's title bar and the `<meta>` tag to provide keyword and descriptive data for search engines. You also learned how to use the `<base>` tags to reduce tag size and the `<style>` and `<link>` tags to work with internal and external style sheets. Lastly, you learned how to work with the `<script>` tag to add scripts to your documents. On top of all this, you learned how to create the Math Quiz web application.

Challenges

1. Consider expanding on the Math Quiz by adding additional questions and answers to it.
2. Improve web page navigation by adding an extra link at the top and bottom of the document, which when clicked jumps the user from the top to the bottom of the web page and vice versa.
3. Consider expanding the text that provides the user with instructions, explaining the number of questions that must be answered in order to pass the quiz.
4. Try to modify the web page's presentation by experimenting with the rules located in its internal style sheet, assigning different font colors, font types, and sizes.

Adding Content to Your Web Pages

All (X)HTML documents are made up of two primary sections, the head and body section. This chapter focuses on the body section, which displays all of the content that the people who visit your web pages will see. In other words, it's where all the real exciting action is. You will learn how to work with a wide number of (X)HTML elements, including elements that display headings, text, lists, line breaks, as well as elements that allow you to emphasize text, highlight phrases, and quote text. Understanding how to work with these elements is essential because they provide web browsers with the instruction they require in order to know how to render web page content in a format that is understandable to people.

Specifically, you will learn:

- How to group contents using the div and span elements
- How to format text using headings and paragraphs
- Different ways of highlighting and emphasizing text
- How to organize data using different types of lists
- How to create line breaks and horizontal rules
- How to integrate JavaScript into your web documents

Project Preview: A Knight's Tale

In this chapter's web project you will learn how to create a new web application that creates a story based on user input. This project will provide an early preview of JavaScript and its ability to interact with the user through popup dialog windows. Figure 4.1 shows the popup dialog that is displayed when the web page containing the JavaScript is loaded into the browser.

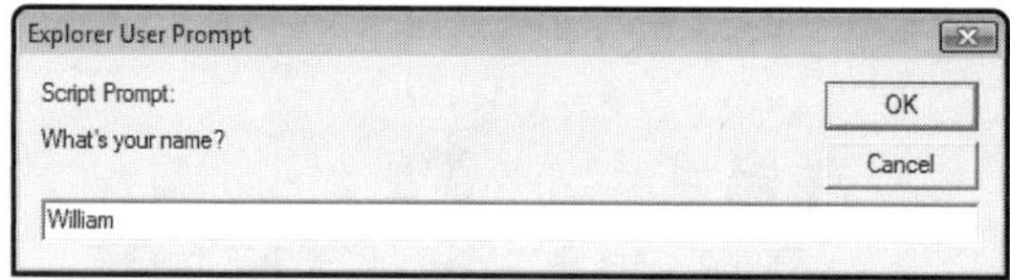

Figure 4.1

The script prompts the user to enter his name.

Once the user answers the script's first question, a second question is presented, as demonstrated in Figure 4.2.

Figure 4.2

The script prompts the user for additional information.

The user enters information into the popup dialog by typing it into the popup dialog's text field and clicking on its OK button. Once the script has collected all of the information it needs to tell its story, the execution of the script concludes by displaying a popup dialog window like the one shown in Figure 4.3.

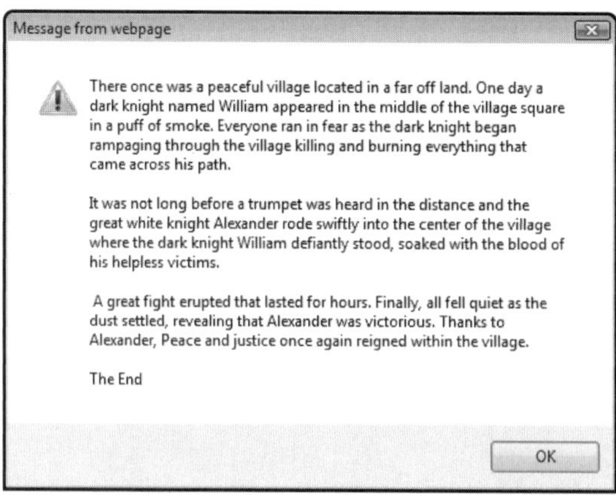

Message from webpage
There once was a peaceful village located in a far off land. One day a dark knight named William appeared in the middle of the village square in a puff of smoke. Everyone ran in fear as the dark knight began rampaging through the village killing and burning everything that came across his path.
It was not long before a trumpet was heard in the distance and the great white knight Alexander rode swiftly into the center of the village where the dark knight William defiantly stood, soaked with the blood of his helpless victims.
A great fight erupted that lasted for hours. Finally, all fell quiet as the dust settled, revealing that Alexander was victorious. Thanks to Alexander, Peace and justice once again reigned within the village.
The End
OK

Figure 4.3

Information collected from the user is integrated into the story that is told.

Developing the body Section

Now that you know how to formulate the DOCTYPE element, the head element, and how to work with all of the elements that can be applied to the head section of your (X)HTML documents, it's time to focus on the fun part of web development: the content that is displayed in the browser window. With the exception of the head section's title element, the only content that is displayed when your web documents are loaded and rendered by the browser is the content that you embed within your web document's body section.

Content is a term that loosely refers to everything that people see and hear when they load web pages into their web browser. Content includes any text, graphics, audio, and video visible to your visitors.

All content displayed by the web browser must be placed within your web document's body section. The body section is made up of a starting <body> tag and a closing </body> tag, as highlighted here:

```
<!DOCTYPE HTML PUBLIC "-//W3C//DTD HTML 4.01//EN"
  "http://www.w3.org/TR/html4/strict.dtd">

<html xmlns="http://www.w3.org/1999/xhtml" lang="en" xml:lang="en">

  <head>

  </head>

  <body>

  </body>

</html>
```

Although older versions of HTML supported a number of different attributes for the <body> tag, these attributes have been deprecated in XHTML Strict 1.0.

The body element is a block element. It can only contain other block-level elements. It cannot contain text or an inline element. To be used, text and inline elements must first be embedded within other block-level elements. Any content placed outside of the opening <body> tag and the closing `</body>` tag will make the document invalid and thus poorly formed. Any such text will display inconsistently in different browsers or might not even be displayed at all.

Properly Managing Content

(X)HTML supplies a host of different elements, each of which is designed to work with a specific type of content. There are elements for working with things like headings and paragraphs. There are also elements that are designed to emphasize or highlight text in various meaningful ways. There are even elements for creating and presenting text in different types of lists. In many cases, you can use different elements to produce similar results. However, these elements are best used when properly matched up to the semantic requirements of your documents. Part of your challenge as a web developer is to thoughtfully and carefully select the proper element with which to display text within your web documents.

As Table 4.1 shows, (X)HTML supports a wide range of tags, each of which is designed for a specific purpose. There are far too many different types of tags to attempt to cover them all within this book. The rest of this chapter is dedicated to reviewing and demonstrating the use of a number of the most commonly used (X)THML elements, explaining proper application and usage of these elements. If you want to learn more about any tag not covered in this book, you can do so by visiting www.w3schools.com/tags/.

Table 4.1 (X)HTML Tags Available in the body Section

(X)HTML Tag	Description	DTD Support	Deprecated
<!--	Identifies the beginning of a comment	STF	
-->	Identifies the end of a comment	STF	
<a>	Creates an anchor	STF	
<abbr>	Identifies an abbreviation	STF	
<acronym>	Defines an acronym	STF	
<address>	Defines document contact information	STF	
<applet>	Creates an embedded applet	TF	Yes
<area />	Marks an area within an image map	STF	
<b>	Highlights text in bold	STF	
<bdo>	Specifies the direction of text	STF	
<big>	Specifies text size as big	STF	
<blockquote>	Defines a lengthy quote	STF	
 	Inserts a line break	STF	
<button>	Creates a push button	STF	

<caption>	Supplies a table caption	STF	
<center>	Centers text	TF	Yes
<cite>	Defines a citation	STF	
<code>	Identifies computer code	STF	
<col>	Sets attribute values for table columns	STF	
<colgroup>	Creates a table column group	STF	
<dd>	Provides a term description in a definition list	STF	
<del>	Identifies deleted text	STF	
<dir>	Specifies a directory listing	TF	Yes
<div>	Groups related content within a document	STF	
<dfn>	Specifies a definition term	STF	
<dl>	Specifies a definition list	STF	
<dt>	Defines a term within a definition list	STF	
<em>	Emphasizes text	STF	
<fieldset>	Sets a form	STF	
<font>	Specifies font, color, and size attributes for text	TF	Yes
<form>	Creates a form	STF	
<frame />	Creates a frame	F	
<frameset>	Outlines a frameset	F	
<h1>	Defines level 1 heading	STF	
<h2>	Defines level 2 heading	STF	
<h3>	Defines level 3 heading	STF	
<h4>	Defines level 4 heading	STF	
<h5>	Defines level 5 heading	STF	
<h6>	Defines level 6 heading	STF	
<hr />	Generates a horizontal line	STF	
<i>	Displays text in italic	STF	
<iframe>	Creates an inline frame	TF	
<img />	Adds an image to a document	STF	
<input />	Creates an input control	STF	
<ins>	Identifies text as being inserted text	STF	
<isindex>	Adds a searchable index to a document	TF	Yes
<kbd>	Displays text as keyboard text	STF	
<label>	Creates a label for an input element	STF	
<legend>	Adds a caption to a fieldset element	STF	
<li>	Creates a list item	STF	
<map>	Creates an image-map	STF	
<menu>	Creates a menu list	TF	Yes
<noframes>	Provides alternate content for browsers that do not support frames	TF	

<noscript>	Specifies alternate content for browsers with JavaScript support	STF	
<object>	Creates an embedded object	STF	
<ol>	Creates an ordered list	STF	
<optgroup>	Creates a collection of related options for a select list	STF	
<option>	Specifies a select list option	STF	
<p>	Creates a paragraph	STF	
<param>	Specifies an object parameter	STF	
<pre>	Displays preformatted text	STF	
<q>	Displays text as a short quotation	STF	
<s>	Strikes through text	TF	Yes
<samp>	Renders text as sample computer code	STF	
<script>	Encloses client-side scripts	STF	
<select>	Creates a drop-down list	STF	
<small>	Renders text in a small format	STF	
<span>	Identifies a small incline section of text	STF	
<strike>	Strikes through text	TF	Yes
<strong>	Renders text in a strong format	STF	
<sub>	Subscripts text	STF	
<sup>	Superscripts text	STF	
<table>	Creates a table	STF	
<tbody>	Identifies table body content	STF	
<td>	Establishes a cell within a table	STF	
<textarea>	Creates a multi-line text form input control	STF	
<tfoot>	Identifies table footer content	STF	
<th>	Creates a table heading	STF	
<thead>	Groups the table heading content	STF	
<tr>	Creates a table row	STF	
<tt>	Lays out text in teletype format	STF	
<u>	Underlines text	TF	Yes
<ul>	Creates an unordered list	STF	
<var>	Defines a variable part within a text string	STF	

The DTD Support column indentifies which versions of XHTML 1.0 support each tag (legend: SIStrict, TITransitional, FIFrameset).

Grouping Content

All but two (X)HTML elements that you will learn about in this chapter have some sort of semantic meaning. For example, the block-level `p` element is used to create paragraphs and the inline `em` element is used to add emphasis to a select portion of text. The `div` and `span` elements, on the other hand, have no semantic value of their own. Their primary purpose is to group contents into discreet units so that it can be further manipulated by CSS or JavaScript.

The div Element

The div element is one of just two generic elements in (X)HTML. The div element is a block-level element whose only purpose is to group related elements together. By grouping two or more elements together, web developers can more easily manipulate them via CSS or JavaScript.

Despite its semantic limitation, the div element is one of the most used (X)HTML elements. In fact, it is often used so frequently that web developers have assigned a name to the practice of excessive div usage: *divitis*.

The div element is made up of an opening <div> tag and a closing </div> tag. This block-level element can contain text or any other block or inline element. When rendered, the div element begins on its own line. Otherwise, its use has no impact on content presentation.

The following example demonstrates the use of the div element. As you can see it has been used to group together a heading and two paragraphs.

```
<div>
  <h1>A Short Fairy Tale</h1>
  <p>Once upon a time there was a brave king named William the Great.
    King William ruled over a mountainous land on the far side of
    the world. This reign was known as the golden age of learning
    and enlightenment.</p>
  <p>One dark night an evil monster began to prey upon his people
    and their lands. The king called upon his bravest knights to go
    out and face the dread beast. One by one all of the knights
    were defeated. Finally, with no one left to turn to, King
    William rode out to face the monster. After a long and bloody
    struggle, King William killed the monster and once again
    brought hope and freedom to the people.</p>
  <p>The End</p>
<div>
```

By grouping various elements inside the div element, you simplify the application because you can apply style rules just once to the div element instead of having to create separate rules for each of its enclosed elements.

The span Element

The span element, like the div element, has no semantic value of its own. This element is similar to the div element except that instead of being block-level, span is an inline element. As such, its purpose is to offset a portion of text located within a block-level element as demonstrated here:

```
<p>Once upon a time there was a brave king named William the Great.
   King William ruled over a mountainous land on the far side of
   the world. This reign was known as the <span>golden age of learning
   and enlightenment</span>.</p>
```

Here, the span element has enclosed a portion of the content within a p element. When written in this manner, you can affect the presentation of the text enclosed by the span element using CSS.

Paragraphs and Headings

(X)HTML provides a number of different types of elements that allow you to display text. Two of the most basic and commonly used types of content are paragraphs and headings. Heading elements are used to add titles to web pages. Paragraphs are used to group sentences together into units. In some cases, these may be the only two elements required to build many text-only web pages.

The p Element

One of the most commonly used (X)HTML elements used in the development of web documents is the paragraph (p) element. A paragraph is a collection of one or more sentences that elaborate on a particular thought or that discusses a specific topic. Paragraphs are created using the p element. This element is a block-level element that begins with the <p> tag and ends with the </p> tag. Paragraphs can only contain text and inline elements. Every paragraph begins on its own line and is followed by a blank line after it ends.

Web browsers are often very forgiving applications--so much so that they often allow web developers to get away with sloppy markup. One common error made by web developers is the omission of the required closing </p> tag. Be careful not to make this mistake. The result may be the inconsistent presentation of your content across different browsers.

By default, paragraph text is left-aligned. HTML provides an `align` attribute that can be used to apply any of the following values to paragraphs: `right`, `left`, `center`, `justify`. However, the `align` attribute has been deprecated in XHTML 1.0 and therefore its use should be avoided. CSS's text-align property can be used to manage paragraph alignment.

As an example of how to work with the paragraph element, take a look at the following example, which shows an XHTML document made up of three paragraphs.

```
<!DOCTYPE html PUBLIC "-//W3C//DTD XHTML 1.0 Strict//EN"
  "http://www.w3.org/TR/xhtml1/DTD/xhtml1-strict.dtd">

<html xmlns="http://www.w3.org/1999/xhtml" lang="en" xml:lang="en">

  <head>
    <meta http-equiv="Content-type" content="text/xhtml; charset=UTF-8" />
    <title>Chapter 4 - Paragraph Demo</title>
  </head>

  <body>
    <p>Once upon a time there was a brave king named William the Great.
       King William ruled over a mountainous land on the far side of
       the world. This reign was known as the golden age of learning
       and enlightenment.</p>
    <p>One dark night an evil monster began to prey upon his people
       and their lands. The king called upon his bravest knights to go
       out and face the dread beast. One by one all of the knights
       were defeated. Finally, with no one left to turn to, King
       William rode out to face the monster. After a long and bloody
       struggle, King William killed the monster and once again
       brought hope and freedom to the people.</p>
    <p>The End</p>
  </body>

</html>
```

Figure 4.4 shows how this example looks when rendered by Internet Explorer.

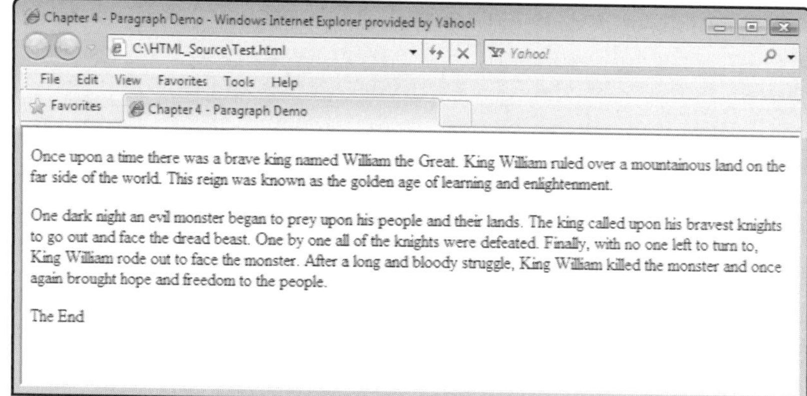

FIGURE 4.4

An example of a web page whose content is displayed in three paragraphs.

Web developers sometimes embed extra paragraph elements in their web documents in order to add additional white space. This practice should be avoided. Instead, the proper way of inserting additional white space in your web documents is through the application of CSS.

Heading Elements

(X)HTML supports six different levels of headings named `h1`, `h2`, `h3`, `h4`, `h5`, and `h6`. Heading elements are intended to be used as titles of headings for sections of text within documents. The `h1` element represents the highest or more important type of heading. The `h6` element represents the lowest or least important type of heading. Used together, the range of headings supported by (X)HTML allows you to establish a hierarchy showing the relative importance of information within your web documents.

The following example demonstrates how to work with each of the six headings and provides an indication of what each head looks like with respect to each other.

```
<h1>Level 1 Heading</h1>
<h2>Level 2 Heading</h2>
<h3>Level 3 Heading</h3>
<h4>Level 4 Heading</h4>
<h5>Level 5 Heading</h5>
<h6>Level 6 Heading</h6>
```

Figure 4.5 shows how this example looks when rendered by the Apple Safari web browser. As you can see, web browsers display headings at varying sizes using a bold font.

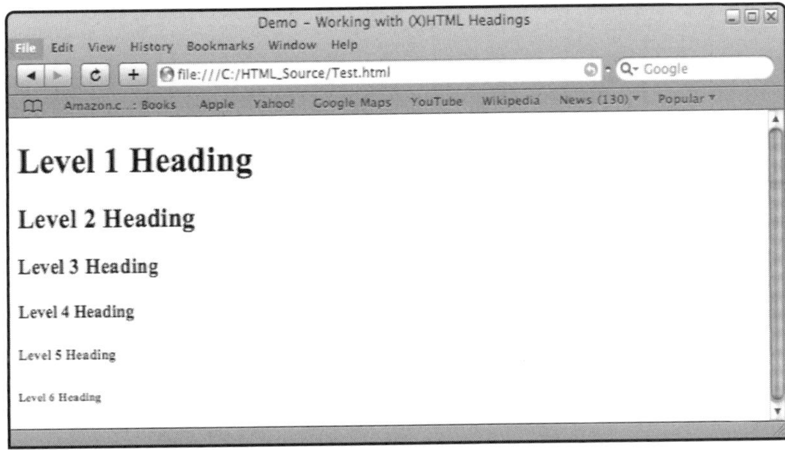

FIGURE 4.5
(X)HTML headings present text in a range of different-sized text.

Although not required, you should try to use only one `h1` heading element per page, since there should only be one high-level heading per page. You can use as many other types of headings as you need. However, you should use them in sequence, starting with `h1` and working your way down to `h6`, unless you have a compelling need to use headings out of sequence.

Like most (X)HTML elements, you can use CSS, covered in Chapters 7 and 8, to modify the appearance of heading elements.

Working with Smaller Blocks of Text

Headings provide an effective means of adding titles and different levels of headings to your web pages, and paragraphs are perfect for organizing text into sections. Using these elements you can effectively manage and organize large collections of text. However, there are times when you will need to work with block-level text that is not a heading and not well suited for display as paragraphs. The next five sections review a number of alternative block-level elements.

Displaying Preformatted Test

By default, web browsers remove any extra white space or blank lines found between text when rendering and displaying text, as demonstrated here:

```
<body>
  <p>
    1
    2
```

```
    3
    4
    5
  </p>
</body>
```

Figure 4.6 shows how the browser displays the output generated by the previous example.

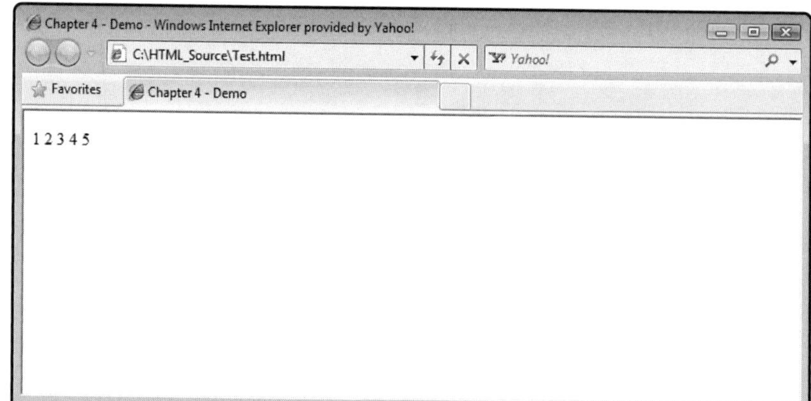

FIGURE 4.6

By default, web browsers remove extra white space.

To modify the browser's default behavior, you can exercise a degree of control over how text is displayed using the `br` element to insert line breaks within your documents, as demonstrated here:

```
<body>
<body>
  <p>
    1<br />
    2<br />
    3<br />
    4<br />
    5
  </p>
</body>
```

Figure 4.7 shows how the browser displayed the output generated by the previous example.

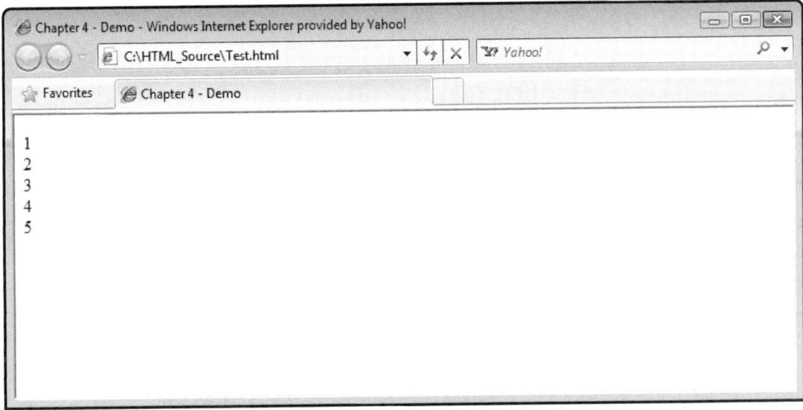

FIGURE 4.7

The br element can be used to insert line breaks within text strings.

If you want to preserve the text formatting in your web documents, you can use the pre element. This element instructs browsers to display text exactly as out laid out within your web documents, as demonstrated here:

```
<body>
  <pre>
      1
      2
      3
      4
      5
  </pre>
</body>
```

Figure 4.8 shows how the browser displayed the output generated by the previous example.

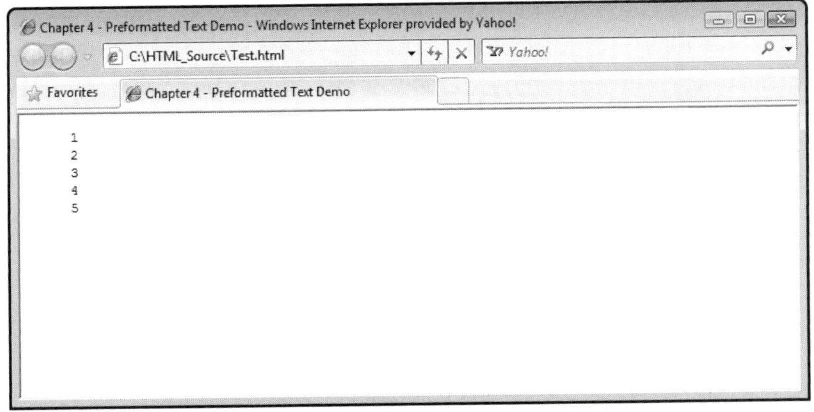

FIGURE 4.8

You can use the pre element to preserve text layout.

Displaying Quotes

Another element that you may want to use is the q element, which displays embedded text as a quotation. Generally speaking, you should use this element to quote text that is no longer than two lines. For anything longer, you should use the blockquote element instead. The following example demonstrates the use of this element.

```
<body>
  <q>Better to remain silent and be thought a fool than to speak
     out and remove all doubt.</q>
</body>
```

As shown in Figure 4.9, web browsers automatically enclose quoted text within quotation marks.

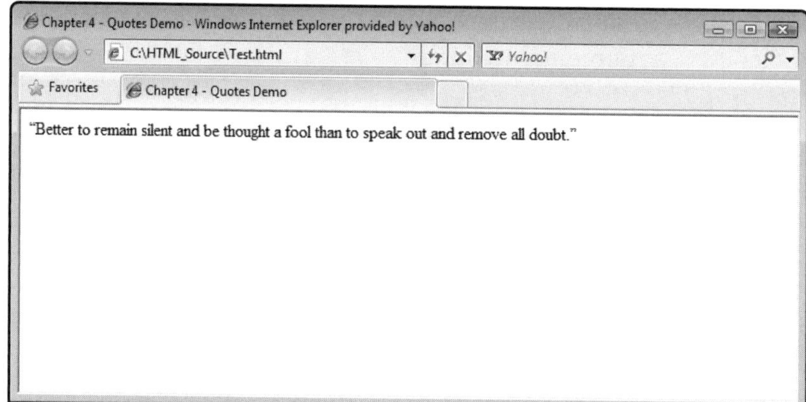

FIGURE 4.9

Use the q element to display short quotations.

Working with the blockquote Element

Like the q element, the blockquote is used to display quotations. Specifically, the q element is designed to display short quotations (1-2 lines) and the blockquote is designed to format longer quotations. By default, browsers automatically display white space before and after the blockquote. The following example demonstrates the use of this element.

```
<body>
  <blockquote>
    Fourscore and seven years ago our fathers brought forth upon this
    continent a new nation, conceived in liberty, and dedicated to the
    proposition that all men are created equal... We here highly resolve
    that these dead shall not have died in vain, that this nation, under
    God, shall have a new birth of freedom; and that government of the
```

```
    people, by the people, and for the people, shall not perish from
    the earth.
  </blockquote>
</body>
```

As shown in Figure 4.10, web browsers automatically indent text contained within a `blockquote` element.

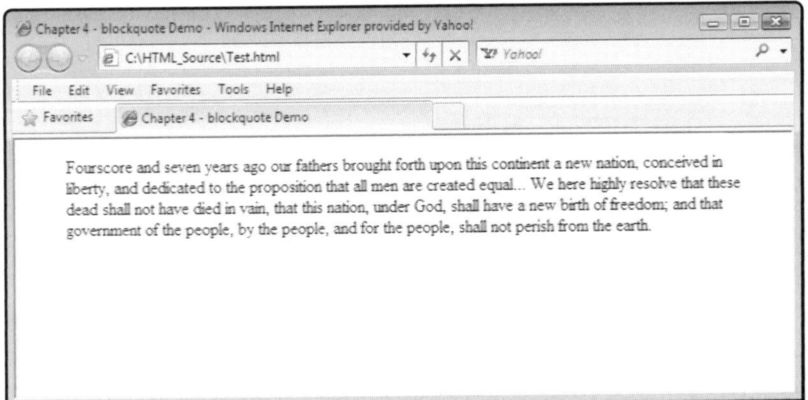

FIGURE 4.10

Use the `blockquote` element to display longer quotations.

Managing Address Information

Another block-level element that you can use is the `address` element. As its name implies, this element structures address information. Web developers often use it when adding contact information to web pages. The following example demonstrates the use of this element. Note the use of the `br` element to help manage the format of the example.

```
<body>
  <address>
    Mr. Big<br />
    Big Shots Incorporated<br />
    1103 Sunset Avenue<br />
    Richmond, Virginia 23233
  </address>
</body>
```

As shown in Figure 4.11, web browsers automatically render text embedded within the address element in *italic* and add a line break before and after the element.

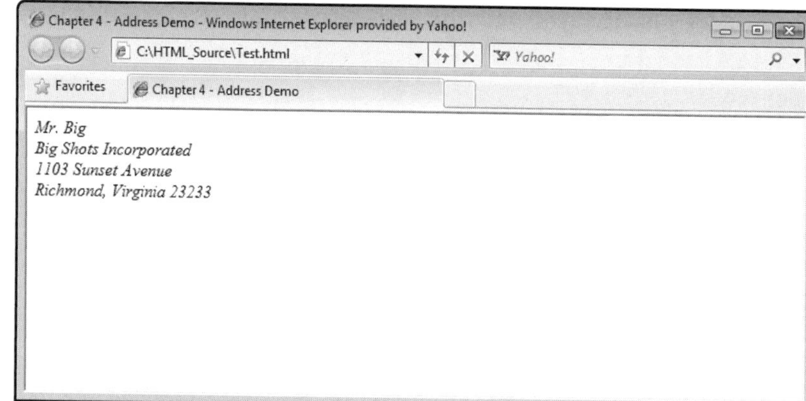

FIGURE 4.11

The address elements are used to format address information.

WORKING WITH INLINE ELEMENTS

To give you further control over how to define the structure of text within your web documents, (X)HTML provides a number of inline elements that let you emphasize text, make it more strongly emphasized, and change its influence by indicating its importance relative to its size. The next four sections review a number of commonly used inline elements that can be used to help structure text.

The inline elements covered in the next four sections not only influence text structure but also have an impact on its appearance. As such, it is easy to fall into the trap of using these elements strictly for presentation purposes. However, you are better served using CSS for control presentation. Take care when working with these inline elements to apply them only when it makes good structural sense to do so.

Working with the em Element

Using the em element you can provide additional meaning to inline text by displaying it in italics. Although this element has qualities that affect text presentation, it has not been deprecated. The following example demonstrates the use of this element.

```
<body>
  <p>With three seconds to go William hit a <em>three pointer</em> to
    win the game.</p>
</body>
```

Figure 4.12 shows how Internet Explorer rendered text embedded within an em element.

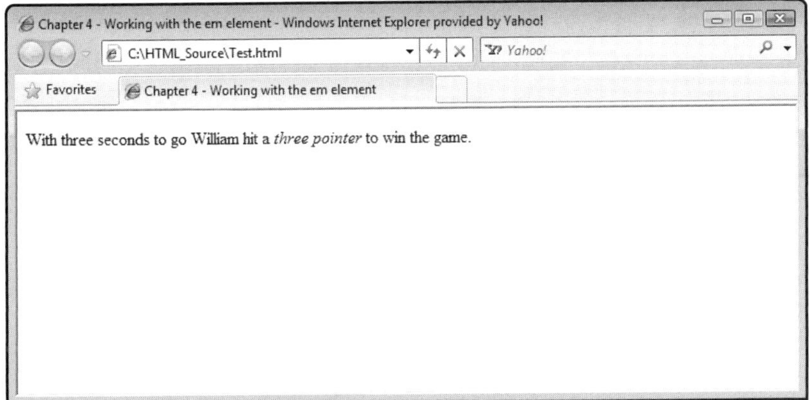

FIGURE 4.12

Use the em element to place additional emphasis on inline text.

Working with the strong Element

Using the strong element, you can provide additional meaning to inline text by displaying it in a **stronger** format. Although this element has qualities that affect text presentation, it has not been deprecated. The following example demonstrates the use of this element.

```
<body>
  <p>With three seconds to go William hit a <strong>three pointer
    </strong> to win the game.</p>
</body>
```

Figure 4.13 shows how Internet Explorer rendered text embedded within a strong element.

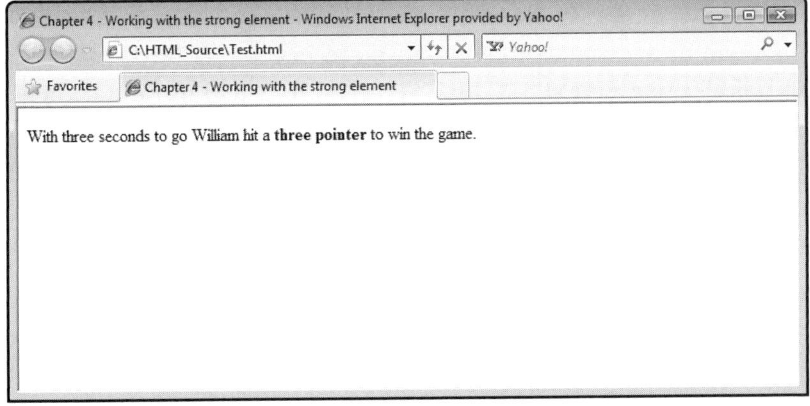

FIGURE 4.13

Use the strong element to display inline text in a strong manner.

Working with the small Element

Using the `small` element you can provide additional meaning to inline text by displaying it in a reduced font size. Although this element has qualities that affect text presentation, it has not been deprecated. The following example demonstrates the use of this element.

```
<body>
  <p>With three seconds to go William hit a <small>three pointer
     </small> to win the game.</p>
</body>
```

Figure 4.14 shows how Internet Explorer rendered text embedded within a `small` element.

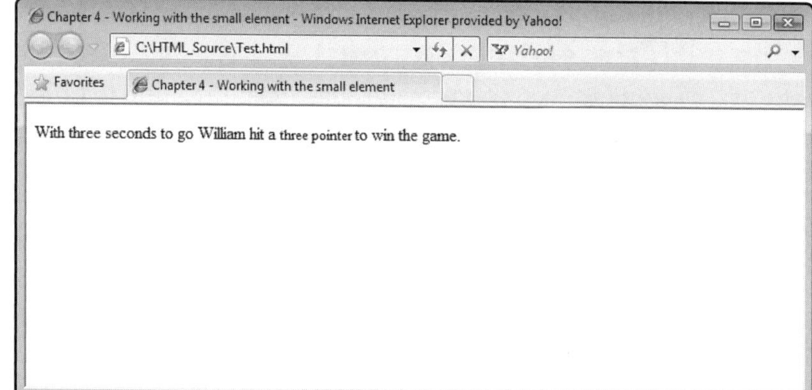

FIGURE 4.14

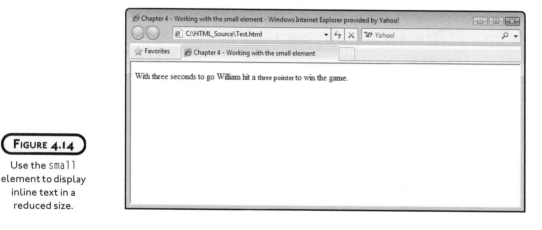

Use the `small` element to display inline text in a reduced size.

Working with the big Element

Using the `big` element you can provide additional meaning to inline text by displaying it in an enlarged font size. Although this element has qualities that affect text presentation, it has not been deprecated. The following example demonstrates the use of this element.

```
<body>
  <p>With three seconds to go William hit a <big>three pointer</big>
     to win the game.</p>
</body>
```

Figure 4.15 shows how Internet Explorer rendered text embedded within a `big` element.

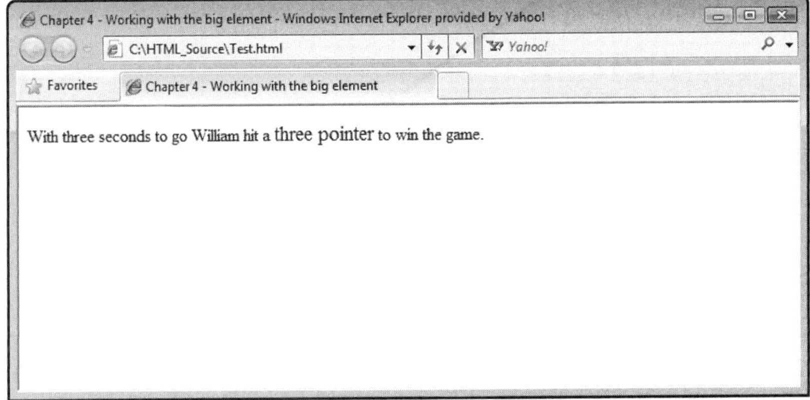

Figure 4.15

Use the `big` element to display inline text in an enlarged size.

Organizing Text with Lists

Another way of organizing content is to display it in a list. Lists help structure text by organizing it into intuitive and meaningful collections. (X)HTML supports three types of lists: unordered, ordered, and defined lists.

Creating Unordered Lists

An unordered list is a collection of related items. The order in which items appear in the list is not important. In order to create an unordered list, you need to work with two elements, `ul` and `il`. The `ul` element is used to define an unordered list. The `il` element is used to embed an item with the list. The following example demonstrates how these two elements work in tandem to generate lists.

```
<body>
  <h1>To Do List</h1>
  <ul>
    <li>Put up shelves in the garage</li>
    <li>Cut down trees in the back yard</li>
    <li>Clean out the family car</li>
    <li>Reorganize the attack</li>
    <li>Hold a yard sale</li>
  </ul>
</body>
```

Figure 4.16 shows how Internet Explorer rendered the list from the previous example.

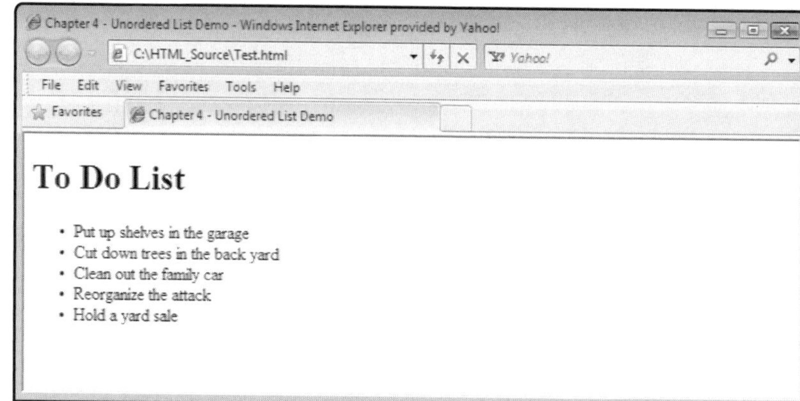

FIGURE 4.16

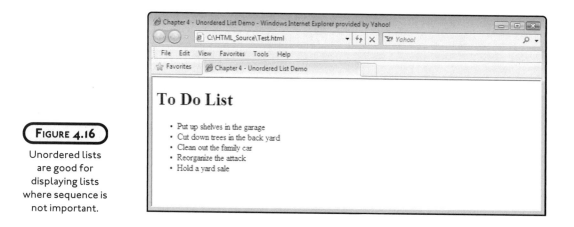

Unordered lists are good for displaying lists where sequence is not important.

Creating Ordered Lists

An ordered list is a collection of related items. The order in which items appear in the list is important. In order to create an ordered list, you need to work with two elements, `ol` and `il`. The `ol` element is used to define an ordered list and the `il` element is used to embed an item within the list. By default, the browsers will render numbered lists. However, using CSS, you can render lists using letters of the alphabet or using roman numerals. The following example demonstrates how these two elements work in tandem to order lists.

```
<body>
  <ol>
    <li>Oil and sharpen the chain saw. </li>
    <li>Explain to kids that they are too old for a tree house. </li>
    <li>Make sure kids are not in tree house! </li>
    <li>Cut down trees in the back yard. </li>
  </ol>
</body>
```

Figure 4.17 shows how Internet Explorer renders the ordered list outlined in the previous example.

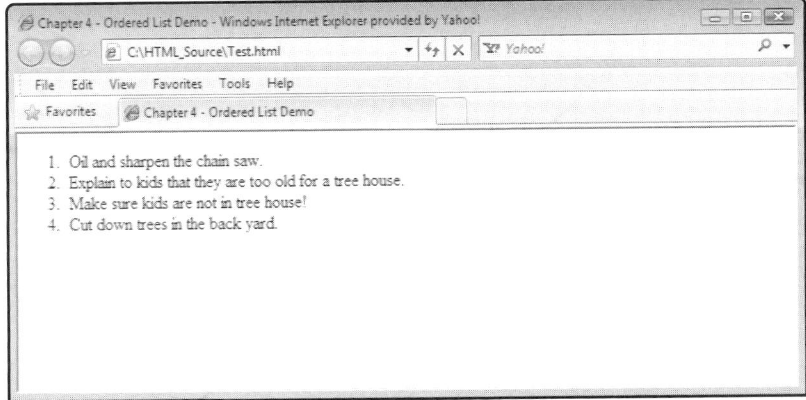
Chapter 4 - Ordered List Demo - Windows Internet Explorer provided by Yahoo!
C:\HTML_Source\Test.html
File Edit View Favorites Tools Help
Favorites
Chapter 4 - Ordered List Demo
1. Oil and sharpen the chain saw.
2. Explain to kids that they are too old for a tree house.
3. Make sure kids are not in tree house!
4. Cut down trees in the back yard.

FIGURE 4.17

Ordered lists are good for displaying lists where the order of items in the list is important.

Creating Definition Lists

A definition list is a collection of terms and their definitions. In order to create a definition list, you need to work with three elements, `dl`, `dt`, and `dd`. The `dl` element is used to define a definition list. The `dt` element is used to define a term in the list, and the `dd` element is used to add a definition for that term. The `dd` element may also include things like paragraphs, links, and images. The following example demonstrates how these three elements work in tandem to order definition lists.

```
<body>
  <h1>Terms:</h1>
  <dl>
    <dt>HTML</dt>
    <dd>
      An acronym for HyperText Markup Language, a popular markup
      language used to develop web pages on the world wide web.
    </dd>
    <dt>XHTML</dt>
    <dd>
      An acronym for Extensible Hypertext Markup Language, a popular
      markup language that combines the qualities of HTML and XML.
    </dd>
    <dt>CSS</dt>
    <dd>
      An acronym for Cascading Style Sheets, a popular style sheet
      language used to influence the presentation of contents in
```

```
      documents created using markup languages.
    </dd>
  </dl>
</body>
```

Figure 4.18 shows how Internet Explorer renders the definition list outlined in the previous example.

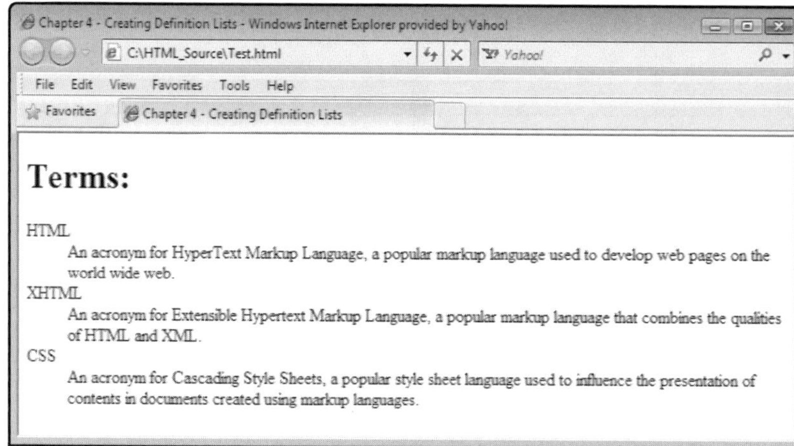

FIGURE 4.18

Definition lists are perfect for defining lists of terms and definitions.

LINE BREAKS AND HORIZONTAL RULES

(X)HTML provides two handy elements that you can use to organize content within web pages. These elements let you execute line breaks and add horizontal rules (lines) to your web pages. Though handy, these elements should be used stringently and with care and not abused for the purpose of presentation where CSS can be used.

The br Element

By default, web browsers automatically wrap text when it reaches the edge of the browser window, breaking lines between words. Using the `br` element, you can introduce line breaks yourself, when needed. The `br` element is an empty element made up of a single tag using the syntax outlined here:

```
<br />
```

The following example demonstrates how to use the `br` element to control the format of paragraph text.

```
<!DOCTYPE html PUBLIC "-//W3C//DTD XHTML 1.0 Strict//EN"
  "http://www.w3.org/TR/xhtml1/DTD/xhtml1-strict.dtd">

<html xmlns="http://www.w3.org/1999/xhtml" lang="en" xml:lang="en">

  <head>
    <meta http-equiv="Content-type" content="text/xhtml; charset=UTF-8" />
    <title>Chapter 4 - Line Break Demo</title>
  </head>

  <body>
    <h1>Jor-El's Message to Kal-El in Superman II</h1>
    <p>You will travel far, my little Kal-El, but we will never leave you,
       even in the face of our deaths.<br />
       You will make my strength your own.<br />
       You will see my life through your eyes, as your life will be seen
       through mine.<br />
       The son becomes the father. And the father, the son.</p>
  </body>

</html>
```

When executed, this example produces the output shown in Figure 4.19.

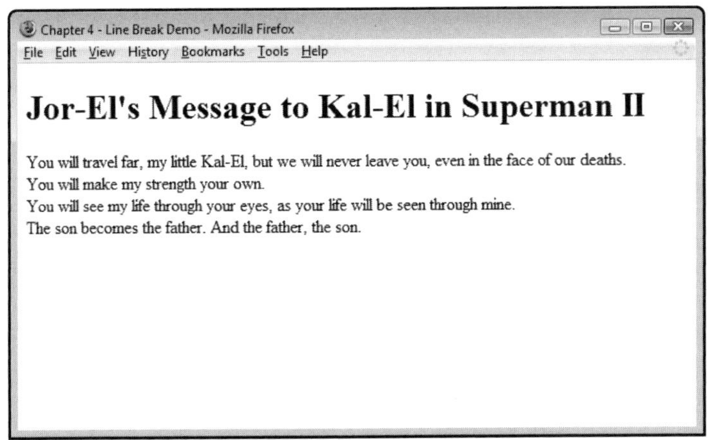

FIGURE 4.19

Using line breaks to mark the end of lines.

Web developers have often inappropriately used the br element as a means of inserting repeated numbers of blank lines in web pages. Don't make this same mistake. Instead, use CSS to manage margin size and add padding as necessary to add any blank space you need. Instead, you should limit your use of the br element to controlling line breaks within text.

The hr Element

The hr (horizontal rule) element is used to add a horizontal line to web pages. Its purpose is to divide web pages into different sections, separating one section of contents from another. The hr element is an empty element and has the following syntax.

```
<hr />
```

The hr element is a block-level element. It appears on its own line. You can use CSS to configure how browsers treat horizontal rules, specifying top and bottom margins, width, etc. The following example demonstrates how the hr element can be used in (X)HTML documents.

```
<!DOCTYPE html PUBLIC "-//W3C//DTD XHTML 1.0 Strict//EN"
  "http://www.w3.org/TR/xhtml1/DTD/xhtml1-strict.dtd">

<html xmlns="http://www.w3.org/1999/xhtml" lang="en" xml:lang="en">

  <head>
    <meta http-equiv="Content-type" content="text/xhtml; charset=UTF-8" />
    <title>Chapter 4 - Horizontal Rule Demo</title>
  </head>

  <body>
    <h1>Report Card</h1>
    <p>For Alexander Lee Ford</p>
    <h2>Science</h2>
    <p>1st Term: A+</p>
    <p>2nd Term: A+</p>
    <hr />
    <h2>Math</h2>
    <p>1st Term: A</p>
    <p>2nd Term: A+</p>
    <hr />
    <h2>English</h2>
    <p>1st Term: B+</p>
```

```
    <p>2nd Term: A</p>
  </body>

</html>
```

When executed, this example produces the output shown in Figure 4.20.

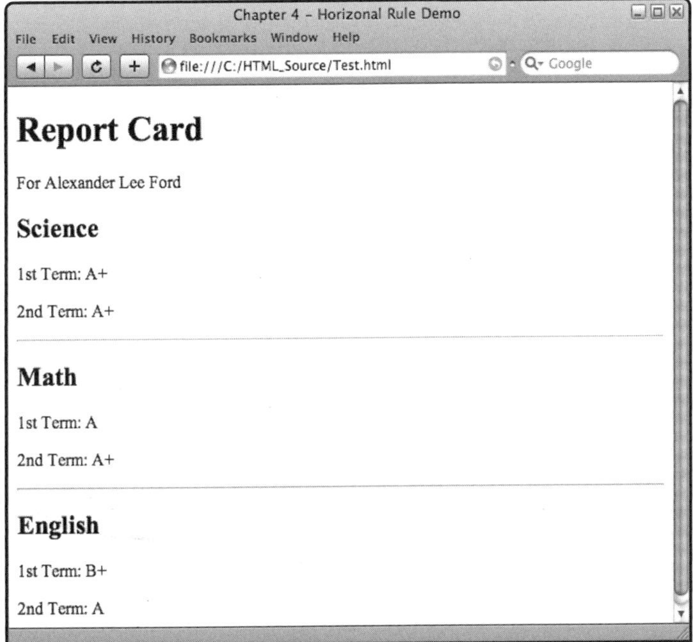

Figure 4.20

Using horizontal rules to organize a web page's content.

Introducing JavaScript

The primary focus of this book is on HTML, XHTML, and CSS. However, web development requires that you learn how to work with a number of different languages and technologies. In order to continue to provide more interesting and fun web projects in each succeeding chapter, it is necessary to delve a little into JavaScript early on. Otherwise, all the book's web projects would have to be based on simple, static contents. While useful, it is not very exciting and significantly limits the types of web projects and games that you can tackle.

Integrating JavaScript into Your Web Documents

JavaScript is an interpreted programming language, which means that JavaScripts are not converted to an executable form until the HTML page they reside in is processed. In Chapter 3, you learned how to work with the `script` element and to use it to embed scripts within your web documents. You also learned how to use the script element to reference external JavaScript files.

The drawback to interpreted scripts is that they execute slower than programs written in compiled programming languages, which are converted into executable code at development time.

A JavaScript Example

JavaScript is regarded as a flexible programming language. JavaScript imposes a minimal set of syntax rules that govern the formulation of statements. JavaScript statements begin and end on the same line. However, if necessary, you can continue a statement onto another line using concatenation (explained in Chapter 9). If you want, you can even place two or more statements on the same line if you separate them with semicolons (;). Semicolons identify the end of statements.

The following example demonstrates how easy it is to integrate a JavaScript into a web document.

```
<!DOCTYPE html PUBLIC "-//W3C//DTD XHTML 1.0 Strict//EN"
  "http://www.w3.org/TR/xhtml1/DTD/xhtml1-strict.dtd">

<html xmlns="http://www.w3.org/1999/xhtml" lang="en" xml:lang="en">

  <head>
    <meta http-equiv="Content-type" content="text/xhtml; charset=UTF-8" />
    <title>Chapter 9 - Creating a JavaScript function</title>
    <script type = "text/javascript">
        window.alert("JavaScript programming is fun and powerful.");
    </script>
  </head>

  <body>
  </body>

</html>
```

As you can see, the JavaScript has been embedded within the web document's head section. The script begins with an opening <script> tag. The tag's type attribute is set to "text/javascript". This instructs the browser as to what languages it needs to process. The JavaScript ends with the closing </script> tag. In between is a single JavaScript statement that tells the browser to display a text message in a popup dialog window.

JavaScript can be very small as in the case of this example. They can also consist of hundreds or thousands of lines of code statements, creating complex web applications capable of interacting with the user. Javascript supports a full range of programming statements that provide the ability to define and store data, implement conditional logic, and to set up loops that are capable of processing unlimited amounts of data. A good understanding of JavaScript is essential to any web developer.

Learning More About JavaScript

The first eight chapters of this book focus exclusively on HTML, XHTML, and CSS. However, all of the chapter game projects going forward are going to involve the use of JavaScript. As a result, you may find it useful to skip on to Chapter 9, where JavaScript is covered in detail, and read up on JavaScript before continuing on with the rest of the book. If you don't think you are ready to tackle JavaScript just yet, then for now you should keep your focus on basic concepts that are covered in each chapter and when you are presented with a little JavaScript, simply accept high-level explanations that are provided and key it in as instructed.

Back to the Knights Tale Project

Alright, now it is time to return your attention to this chapter's project, a Knights Tale. This web project consists of a single web document containing an embedded JavaScript, which when executed interacts with the user using different types of popup dialog windows.

The first two popup dialog windows displayed by this web application will display two buttons, OK and Cancel. In order for the application to work correctly, the user must key in the required information to the popup window's text file and click on the OK button. If the user fails to enter anything or clicks on the Cancel buttons instead of the OK buttons, things will not work correctly.

Designing the Application

The development of this web application will be performed in four steps, as outlined here:

1. Create a new XHTML document.
2. Develop the document's markup.
3. Develop the document's JavaScript.
4. Load and test the XHTML page.

Step 1: Creating a New XHTML Document

As has been the case with all of the web projects that you have worked on up to this point in the book, the first step is the creation of an empty text file. Do so using your preferred code or text editor and then save and name the file KnightsTale.html.

Step 2: Developing the Document's Markup

The second step in the development of the Knights Tale project is to assemble the web document's markup. Begin by adding the following elements to the KnightsTale.html file.

```
<!DOCTYPE html PUBLIC "-//W3C//DTD XHTML 1.0 Strict//EN"
  "http://www.w3.org/TR/xhtml1/DTD/xhtml1-strict.dtd">

<html xmlns="http://www.w3.org/1999/xhtml" lang="en" xml:lang="en">

  <head>

  </head>

  <body>

  </body>

</html>
```

Next, let's ensure that the head section is well formed by adding the following elements to it.

```
<meta http-equiv="Content-type" content="text/xhtml; charset=UTF-8" />
<title>A Knight's Tale</title>
```

Unlike all of the other projects that you have worked on in this book, the web page that is rendered with this project does not display anything. It is completely blank. Therefore, as shown next, there is no markup for you to add to the body section.

Step 3: Creating the Document's Script

The Knights Tale application makes use of a JavaScript embedded within its head section. As you learned in Chapter 3, in order to embed a JavaScript within an (X)THML document, you must use the script element. So, the first step in the creation of the script is to add the following statement to bottom of the web document's head section.

```
<script type = "text/javascript">

</script>
```

Unfortunately, while the vast majority of web surfers use web browsers that support JavaScript, there are some that do not. Since these browsers do not understand JavaScript and do not know what to do with it, they may end up displaying the script's code statement on the resulting web page, which is clearly not what you are going to want to happen. To prevent this behavior, it is common practice to begin all JavaScript code with the (X)HTML comments shown here:

```
<script type = "text/javascript">
<!-- Start hiding JavaScript statements

// End hiding JavaScript statements -->
</script>
```

This enables browsers that know how to work with JavaScripts to do so but at the same time it allows browsers that do not support JavaScript to ignore everything between the opening and closing comments. So, if you have not already done so, modify your JavaScript as shown above.

Now it's time to add the code statements that make up the JavaScript. To do so, type everything you see below in between the opening and closing comment statements that you just added to the document.

```
var hero;
var villain;
var tale;

hero = prompt("What's your name?", "");
villain = prompt("What's your best friend's name?", "");

tale = "There once was a peaceful village located in a far off " +
       "land. One day a dark knight named " + villain +
       " appeared in the middle of the village square in a " +
       "puff of smoke. Everyone ran in fear as the dark knight " +
       "began rampaging through the village killing and " +
       "burning everything that came across his path. \n\n" +
       "It was not long before a trumpet was heard in the " +
       "distance and the great white knight " + hero +
       " rode swiftly into the center of the village where the " +
       "dark knight " + villain + " defiantly stood, soaked with " +
       "the blood of his helpless victims. \n\n A great " +
       "fight erupted that lasted for hours. Finally, all " +
       "fell quiet as the dust settled, revealing that " +
       hero + " was victorious. Thanks to " + hero + ", peace " +
```

```
        "and justice once again reigned within the village. \n\n" +
        "The End";

alert(tale);
```

This script defines three variables, which are locations in memory where data is stored, and then displays two popup dialog windows that prompt the user to type in his name and the name of a friend. This information is stored in variables. Next, a large text string is created and assigned to a variable named `tale`. Because the text of the story is so large, it is broken up into a series of smaller strings, which are then concatenated together. If you look closely, you see that the instances of the `hero` and `villain` variables have been embedded within the story. As a result, their contents will be displayed in place of their names when the story is finally displayed. The last statement shown above executed a built-in JavaScript function named `alert()`, passing the `tale` variable as an argument. When executed, this function will display the application's final popup dialog window and display the value assigned to `tale` (e.g., the text that makes up the story).

The Finished HTML Document

At this point, your copy of the KnightsTale.html document should be complete. To make sure that you have assembled it correctly, take a look at the following example, which shows what the finished document should look like.

```
<!DOCTYPE html PUBLIC "-//W3C//DTD XHTML 1.0 Strict//EN"
  "http://www.w3.org/TR/xhtml1/DTD/xhtml1-strict.dtd">

<html xmlns="http://www.w3.org/1999/xhtml" lang="en" xml:lang="en">

  <head>

    <meta http-equiv="Content-type" content="text/xhtml; charset=UTF-8" />
    <title>A Knight's Tale</title>

    <script type = "text/javascript">
    <!-- Start hiding JavaScript statements

      var hero;
      var villain;
      var tale;

      hero = prompt("What's your name?", "");
```

```
      villain = prompt("What's your best friend's name?", "");

      tale = "There once was a peaceful village located in a far off " +
             "land. One day a dark knight named " + villain +
             " appeared in the middle of the village square in a " +
             "puff of smoke. Everyone ran in fear as the dark knight " +
             "began rampaging through the village killing and " +
             "burning everything that came across his path. \n\n" +
             "It was not long before a trumpet was heard in the " +
             "distance and the great white knight " + hero +
             " rode swiftly into the center of the village where the " +
             "dark knight " + villain + " defiantly stood, soaked with " +
             "the blood of his helpless victims. \n\n A great " +
             "fight erupted that lasted for hours. Finally, all " +
             "fell quiet as the dust settled, revealing that " +
             hero + " was victorious. Thanks to " + hero + ", peace " +
             "and justice once again reigned within the village. \n\n" +
             "The End";

      alert(tale);

    // End hiding JavaScript statements -->
    </script>

  </head>

  <body>

  </body>

</html>
```

Step 4: Loading and Testing the Knight's Tale Project

Okay, it is time to open your favorite web browser, load your new web page, and see how things have turned out. To do so, open your preferred web browser and then execute the following procedure.

1. Click on the browser's File menu and select the Open File command. This displays a standard file open dialog.

2. Using the dialog window, navigate to the folder where you stored the web page and select it.
3. Click on the Open button. The browser will load and display the specified document.

If everything works as you expect it to, try loading the web document using one or two other browsers and make sure that its content is displayed in a consistent manner.

Summary

The primary focus of this chapter was on the development and presentation of content stored within the `body` section of your web documents. As part of this presentation, this chapter provided an overview of many of the elements that are essential to the organization and structuring of text on web pages. This included learning about elements that display headings, text, lists, line breaks, emphasize text, highlight phrases, and quote text. You also learned how to execute controlled line breaks and to add horizontal rules to your web pages. To top things off, you learned how to create the Knights Tale application.

Challenges

1. **As currently written, once the user has finished reading the web application's story, he is left with a blank web page to look at. Consider modifying the XHTML document by adding markup to the `body` section that instructs the user to click on the browser's refresh button to reload the application and run it again.**
2. **As currently written, the KnightsTale.html file contains an embedded JavaScript file. To streamline this file's contents, create a new copy of the application and externalize its JavaScript. To do so, create a new file named KnightsTale.js and move the code statements that make up the application's JavaScript into it (less the opening `<script>` and closing `</script>` tags and their associated comment statements). Next, modify the KnightsTale.html file by adding `src = "KnightsTale.js"` as an attribute to the opening `<script>` tag. Note: if you need help with this challenge, you can download a working example of it from this book's companion web page located at www.courseptr.com/downloads/.**

Delving into Images and Links

Although text is the dominant form of content on most websites, there are plenty of other types of media in use, most notably graphics. In this chapter, you will learn about the different types of graphics that are used on the web. You will learn how to display graphics on your web pages and to provide alternative text descriptions of graphics to support browsers that have problems working with graphics. You will also learn how to use graphics when setting up links and to use links as navigation controls that connect your pages together and to other web pages. In addition to all this you will learn how to work with audio and video and to display other types of media content.

Specifically, you will learn how to:

- Use links to manage site navigation
- Use links to set up document downloads
- Use graphics when constructing links
- Embed and control the playback of audio and video
- Display PDF files within web pages

Project Preview: The (X)HTML Typing Quiz

In this chapter's web project, you will learn how to create an online quiz that evaluates the user's typing skills. Specifically, you will develop an online application that presents the users with five sentences and challenges them to retype those sentences exactly as they are shown. Any mistake in spelling, punctuation, or case will result in an error. To pass the quiz, users must retype at least three sentences correctly.

When loaded, the application begins by displaying the popup dialog windows shown in Figure 5.1.

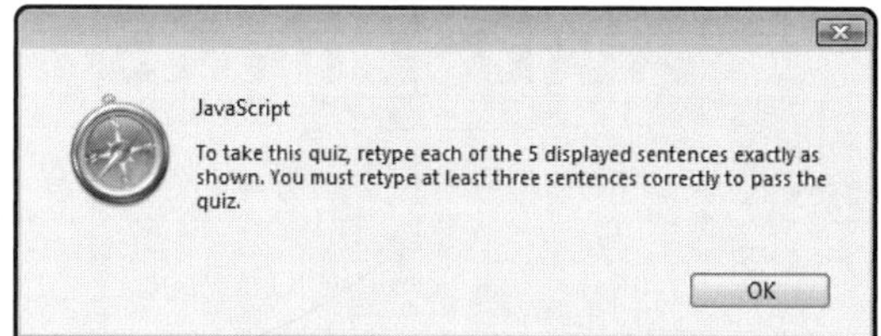

Figure 5.1

An example of the application's opening popup Window as seen using Apple Safari.

The user is presented with a brief explanation of the rules for taking the typing quiz and must click on OK to continue. In response, the first of five challenge sentences is displayed, as demonstrated in Figure 5.2.

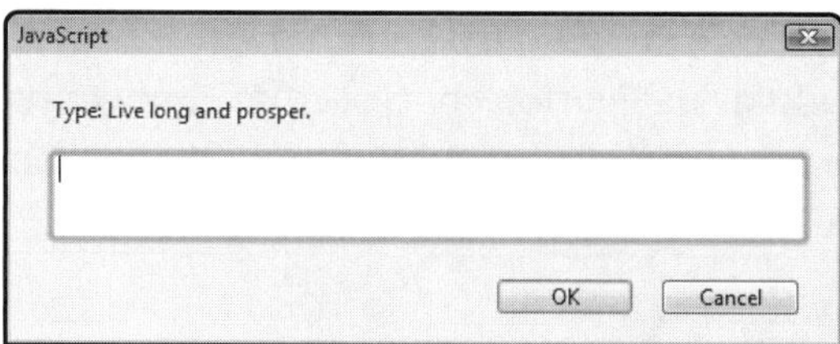

Figure 5.2

Sentences must be retyped in the popup dialog window's text field.

To submit an answer, the user must retype the sentence exactly as it is displayed in the window's text field and then click on the OK button. Mistyping the sentence or clicking on the window's Cancel button will result in an incorrect answer.

As demonstrated in Figure 5.3, the web application provides the user with immediate feedback after each answer is submitted.

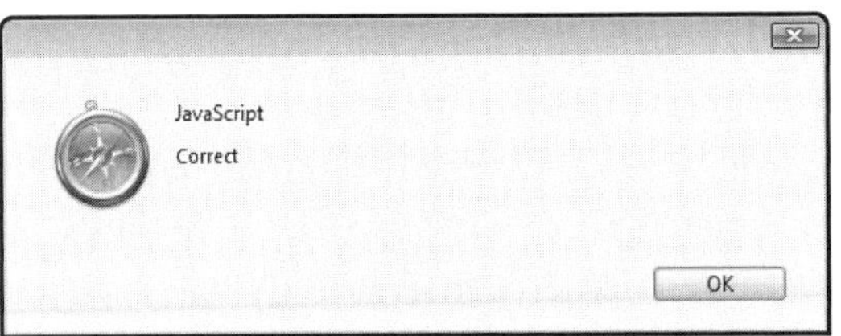

FIGURE 5.3

The user can keep track of progress by keeping count of the number of correctly retyped sentences.

At the end of the quiz, the application totals up the user's score and displays a message indicating whether the user passed or failed the quiz, as demonstrated in Figure 5.4.

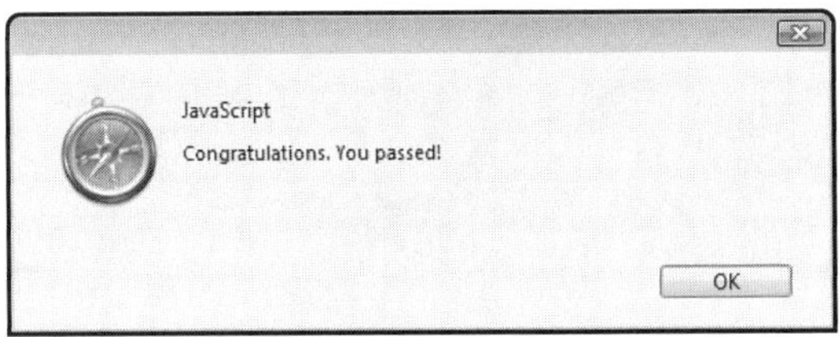

FIGURE 5.4

The user has passed the typing quiz.

As soon as the user acknowledges her results by clicking on the OK button, the screen shown in Figure 5.5 is displayed, instructing the user how to restart the test.

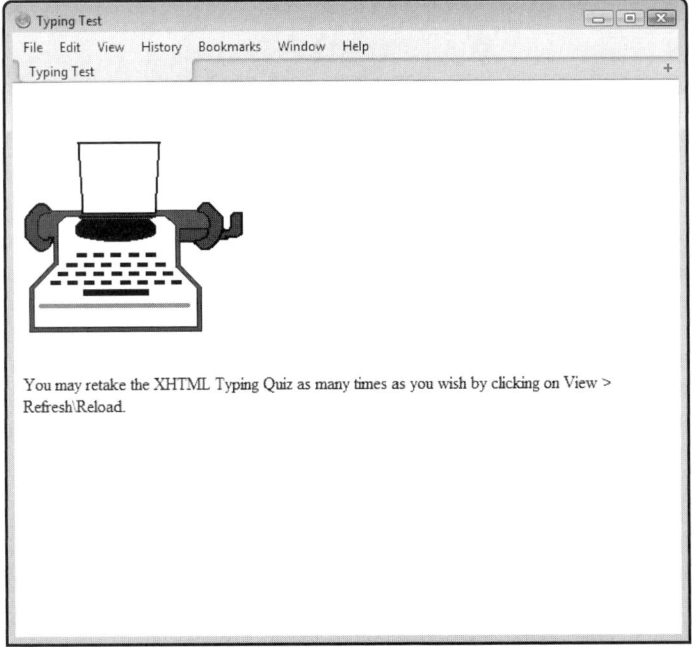

FIGURE 5.5

The user is permitted to retake the test as many times as is desired.

Let's Get Graphical

Up to this point in the book, focus has been almost exclusively on the use of text. However, sometimes ideas, messages, and concepts are better articulated through graphics like photographs, charts, graphs, drawings, maps, and so on. Many web developers use graphics to help establish a website's overall layout and presentation, using them to establish a consistent theme across their web pages. As demonstrated in Figure 5.6, many online websites carefully integrate their company's logo and branding into their website.

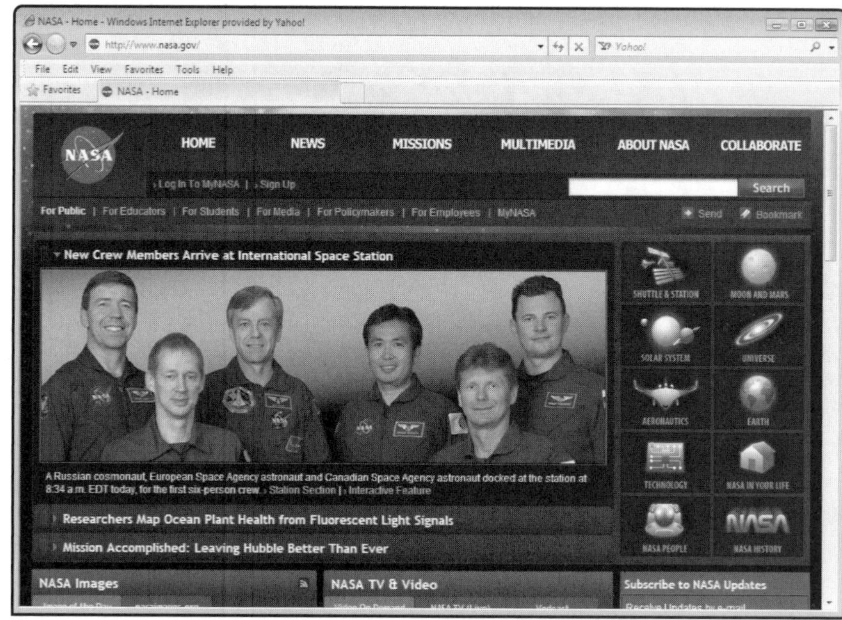

Figure 5.6

An example of how graphics can be used to create a visually powerful and theme-oriented web page.

To be effective, graphics must be properly used; otherwise, they can backfire on you, resulting in web pages that look overloaded, convoluted, and unattractive. XHTML lets you work with graphics using either of two elements, the `img` or `object` element. Of these two options, the `img` element is by far the most commonly used. The `img` element is an inline element that can be used to work with all types of image files.

Image Types

There are many different types of graphics. Unfortunately, not all graphics are equally supported by all operating systems. As a result, it is best to stick with the universally supported graphics formats listed here:

- **GIF (Graphics Interchange Format).** Best used for images with less than 256 colors but that require great detail.
- **JPEG (Joint Photographic Experts Group).** Best used for photos and other graphics files that contain a larger range of colors.
- **PNG (Portable Network Graphics).** Best used for photos and other graphics files that contain a larger range of colors.

Any good graphics editor will support all three of these graphic formats and will allow you to convert files from one format to another. All three of these graphic formats are designed to compress the size of their files, making them well suited for the Internet where bandwidth is always a concern. JPEG files reduce the size of graphic files by reducing the number of pixels used to represent the image. The result is a loss of image quality. JPEGs do, however, retain a great deal of color information making them appropriate for storing photographs and other high-color images.

Unlike JPEG files, GIF files are limited to 256 colors but are capable of rendering great detail. Rather than sacrifice pixels, GIF files reduce the number of colors. Because they retain all pixels, GIF files are good for storing detailed line art, maps, graphs, charts, and other low-color graphics. GIF files provide two features that make them unique when compared to JPEGs. First, GIF files can have transparent backgrounds, meaning that if you overlay an image on top of another image, the bottom image will become a background for the GIF file. You can also create animated GIF files. These types of GIF files are actually made up of two or more frames that are rotated, giving the impression that the GIF file is in motion.

PNG files are a relatively new graphic file format. Like GIF files, PNG files retain all pixel data. PNG files support transparency. However, unlike GIF files, PNG files are not limited to 256 colors. In fact, PNG files can support 24-bit color, allowing them to rival JPEG files, though PNG files tend to be a little larger than their JPEG counterparts.

As you can see, all three of these graphic file types have their advantages and disadvantages and you will probably end up using different combinations of all three. The important thing is that you avoid using other graphic file types.

Storing Graphic Files Externally

Unlike text, images displayed on web pages are external content. They are not embedded in the web document. Instead, they reside in external files that are then referenced from within the web document. Web browsers render images in two steps. First, the web document's markup must be downloaded and then any external image files are downloaded.

Working with the img Element

The img element is an inline element, and as such must be embedded within a block-level element to be used. In order to generate well-formed pages, you must include the src and alt attributes. The src attribute is used to specify the URL location of the graphic file. The alt attribute provides an alternative text string that is displayed in the event the browser is unable to display the graphic file. The alt attribute allows you to specify up to 1,024 characters and should be used to provide descriptions that provide visitors with an effective understanding of the image and what it depicts. The following example demonstrates the use of the img element to display a graphic file named fishing.jpg, which is located in the same folder as the web document. An alternative description has also been provided.

```
<img src = "fishing.jpg" alt = "Picture of a little boy fishing" />
```

Specifying Graphic File Dimensions

Because web browsers download and render images in a two-step process, documents with many images may take a while to fully download and render, especially for users with slow Internet connections. As a result, users may begin reading page content while the images on the document are still being downloaded. The web browser will reserve space for each image file defined on a web document. However, since images vary in terms of width and height, there is no guarantee that the browser will allocate the correct amount of space required to display the image unless you provide it with information on the dimensions of each graphic. You can do this by adding the width and height attributes to the img element, as demonstrated in the following example.

```
<!DOCTYPE html PUBLIC "-//W3C//DTD XHTML 1.0 Strict//EN"
  "http://www.w3.org/TR/xhtml1/DTD/xhtml1-strict.dtd">

<html xmlns="http://www.w3.org/1999/xhtml" lang="en" xml:lang="en">

  <head>
    <meta http-equiv="Content-type" content="text/xhtml; charset=UTF-8" />
    <title>Chapter 5 - Missing Graphics Demo</title>
  </head>

  <body>
    <div>
      <img src = "fishing.jpg" width = "356" height = "267"
        alt = "Picture of a little boy fishing" />
      <img src = "teapot.jpg" width = "356" height = "267"
        alt = "Picture of a teapot" />
      <img src = "cats.jpg" width = "356" height = "267"
```

```
      alt = "Picture of two cats" />
    </div>
  </body>

</html>
```

As you can see, the `width` and `height` attributes have been included as part of all three of the web document's `image` elements. As a result, web browsers that support the display of graphics will reserve the proper amount of space for each graphic file. Figure 5.7 shows the web page that is created when this example is loaded and rendered using Apple Safari.

By default, all images appear in their actual size when rendered and displayed. If you specify reduced `width` and `height` attribute settings, it should look okay when rendered. However, to conserve bandwidth you should resize the graphics using your favorite graphic application to the size you want them to be.

If, on the other hand, you specify `width` and `height` attribute values that are larger than the graphic being download, the resulting image may appear choppy. Again, you will be better served editing your graphics and assigning the right width and height before you use them on your web pages. Check out Appendix B for information on several good graphic applications.

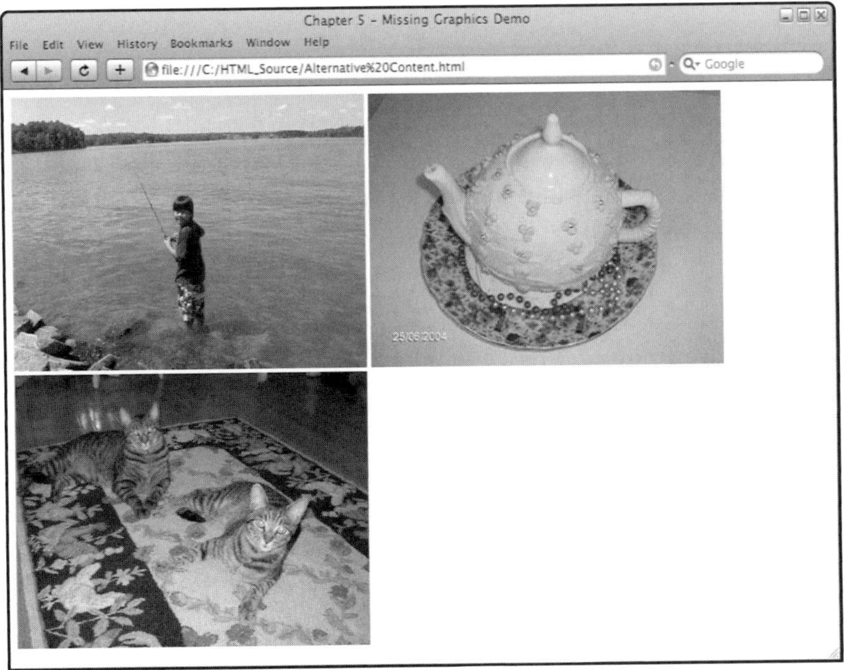

FIGURE 5.7

An example of how the web page looks when rendered by Apple Safari.

Figure 5.8 shows an example of what users will see in the event the web browser is unable to display the specific images.

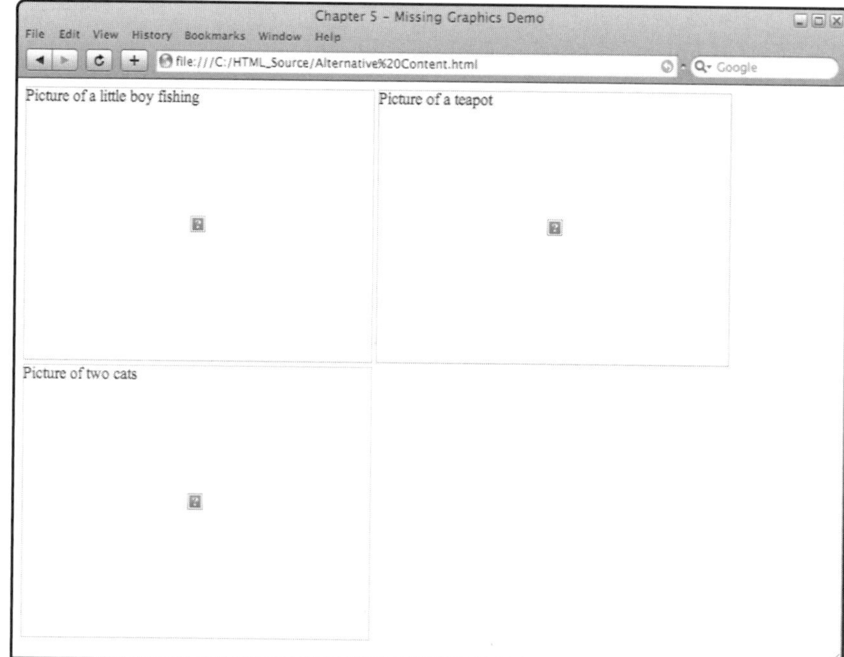

FIGURE 5.8

A demonstration of how alternative content is displayed in the event the graphics cannot be displayed.

There can be any number of reasons why a browser is unable to display graphic files. The browser may be a text-only browser. The graphic files may have been renamed, moved, or deleted. Regardless, as Figure 5.8 demonstrates, by including the required `alt` attribute you can still provide visitors with an idea of what they are missing.

To create well-formed web documents, you must include the `alt` attribute as part of every `img` element. However, since not all images are meant to serve as content, there may be images that don't convey any information at all and whose only purpose is to be aesthetically pleasing. For these types of graphics, you should assign an empty string (e.g., `alt = ""`) when specifying an `img` element `alt` attribute.

Controlling How Text and Graphics Are Displayed

By default, web browsers will display images alongside text. To demonstrate this, take a look at the following example.

```
<!DOCTYPE html PUBLIC "-//W3C//DTD XHTML 1.0 Strict//EN"
  "http://www.w3.org/TR/xhtml1/DTD/xhtml1-strict.dtd">

<html xmlns="http://www.w3.org/1999/xhtml" lang="en" xml:lang="en">

  <head>
    <meta http-equiv="Content-type" content="text/xhtml; charset=UTF-8" />
    <title>Chapter 5 - Graphic and Text Layout</title>
  </head>

  <body>
    <p>
      Fun in the sun.
      <img src = "fishing.jpg" width = "356" height = "267"
        alt = "Picture of a little boy fishing" />
      We spent the day fishing and relaxing in the sun.
    </p>
  </body>

</html>
```

Here, text and an `img` element have all been placed within a `p` element. Figure 5.9 shows how the web browser will render this missed content on the resulting web page.

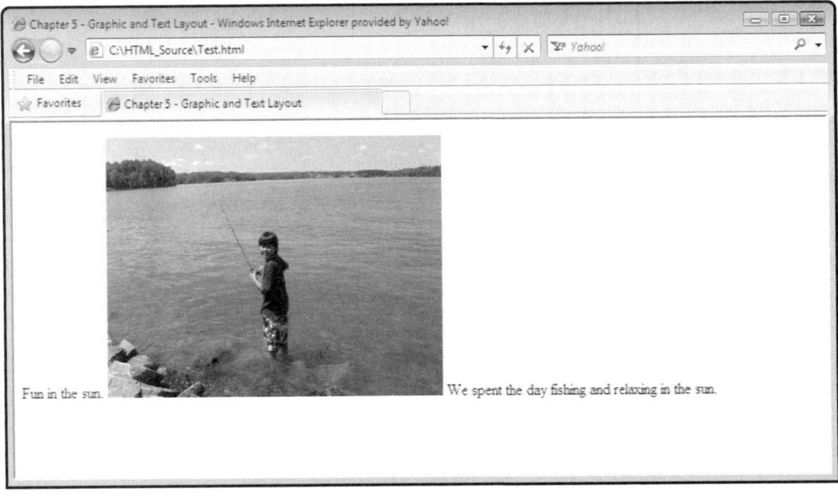

FIGURE 5.9

Web browsers automatically align graphics and text.

If you want to separate the display of text and graphics, you can do so by enclosing them in their own respective block-level elements, as demonstrated in the following example.

```
<!DOCTYPE html PUBLIC "-//W3C//DTD XHTML 1.0 Strict//EN"
  "http://www.w3.org/TR/xhtml1/DTD/xhtml1-strict.dtd">

<html xmlns="http://www.w3.org/1999/xhtml" lang="en" xml:lang="en">

  <head>
    <meta http-equiv="Content-type" content="text/xhtml; charset=UTF-8" />
    <title>Chapter 5 - Graphic and Text Layout</title>
  </head>

  <body>
    <p>Fun in the sun.</p>
    <p><img src = "fishing.jpg" width = "356" height = "267"
      alt = "Picture of a little boy fishing" /></p>
    <p> We spent the day fishing and relaxing in the sun.</p>
  </body>

</html>
```

Figure 5.10 shows how the block-level format changes have affected the way the content of the resulting web page looks when it is rendered by the browser.

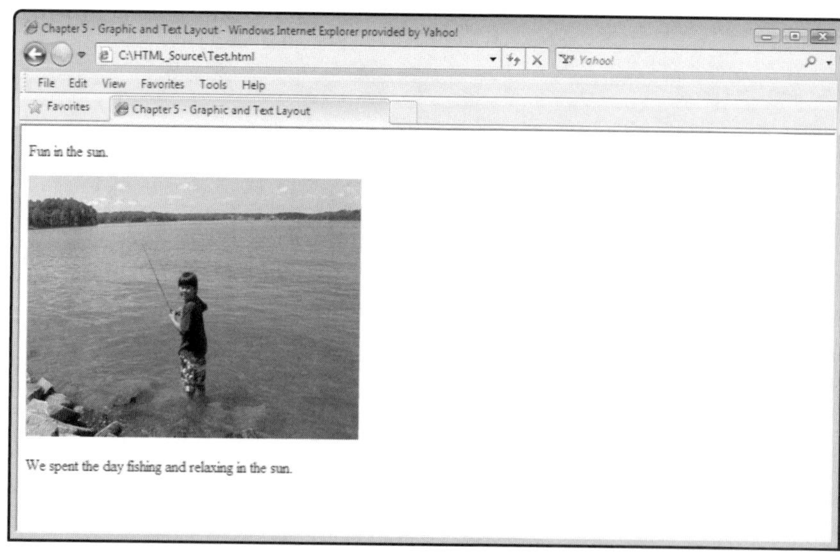

FIGURE 5.10

Using block-level elements to separate graphics and text.

Using CSS, you can exercise precise control over how text and graphics are displayed on your web pages. CSS is covered in Chapters 7 and 8.

Connecting Things Together with Links

Links, also known as hyperlinks, are used to connect things together on the Internet. They are in fact the glue that binds everything together to create the world wide web as we know it. Web browsers generally display links as underlined text. If you move the mouse pointer over a link it usually changes into a different shape, often a hand with a pointing finger. Click on the link and the web browser will navigate to the link's specified URL. Links can be set up for any of the following scenarios.

- To establish a link to another page.
- To establish a link to a location within the same page.
- To other types of documents in order to facilitate file downloads.
- To email addresses partially automating email generation.

Creating Links

Links are built using the anchor (`a`) element, which anchors a target URL to a location on a web page. The anchor element is an inline element, so to use it you must embed it within a block-level element, as demonstrated here:

```
<p><a href = "http://www.apple.com">Click Me</a></p>
```

Here, the anchor element's `href` attribute is used to specify the URL of the target file. The text (`Click Me`) embedded within the opening `<a>` tag and closing `</a>` tags is displayed in the browser. The link is activated when the user clicks on this text.

Setting Up Text Links

The most common use of links is to link to another external web document. To set up a link to an external document, you must know the document's full URL, as demonstrated in the following example:

```
<p><a href = "http://www.microsoft.com">Visit Microsoft</a></p>
```

Here, a link has been set up to the Microsoft website. When clicked, the web browser will leave the web page containing the link and load Microsoft's main web page. Web developers also use links as the basis for facilitating navigation between web documents on their own websites, as demonstrated in the following example.

```
<!DOCTYPE html PUBLIC "-//W3C//DTD XHTML 1.0 Strict//EN"
  "http://www.w3.org/TR/xhtml1/DTD/xhtml1-strict.dtd">

<html xmlns="http://www.w3.org/1999/xhtml" lang="en" xml:lang="en">

  <head>
    <meta http-equiv="Content-type" content="text/xhtml; charset=UTF-8" />
    <title>Chapter 5 - Navigation Links Demo</title>
  </head>

  <body>
    <p>
      <a href = "home.html">Home</a> |
      <a href = "products.html">Products</a> |
      <a href = "support.html">Support</a> |
      <a href = "downloads.html">Downloads</a> |
      <a href = "help.html">Help</a>
    </p>
  </body>

</html>
```

Here, five links have been defined that together form a text-based navigation bar that is often placed at the top and bottom of web pages to provide visitors with a means of navigating between web pages. Because these links are to local web pages that reside within the same folder as the current web page, relative URLs have been used. Figure 5.11 shows an example of the collection of links that are displayed when this web document is loaded into the browser.

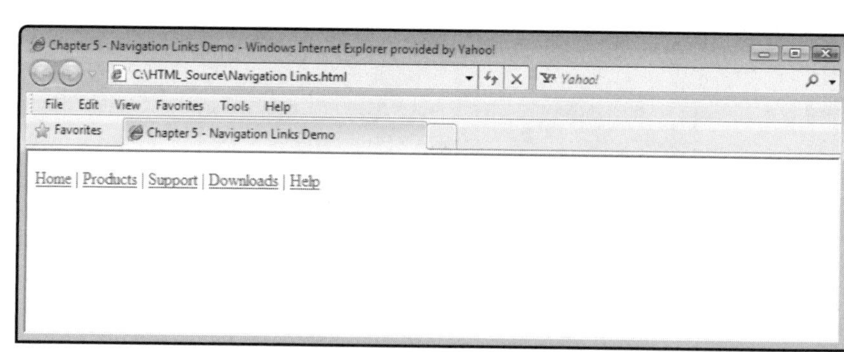

FIGURE 5.11

Using links to create text-based navigation controls.

One of the problems with links is that things on the Internet tend to change a lot. Any links that you set up to external pages can be broken at any time if their author deletes, renames, or moves them. Likewise, if you rearrange things within your own website, you run the risk of forgetting to update your site's internal links. Broken links result in errors like the one shown in Figure 5.12, which is the last thing you want the people that visit your website to see when they click on your links.

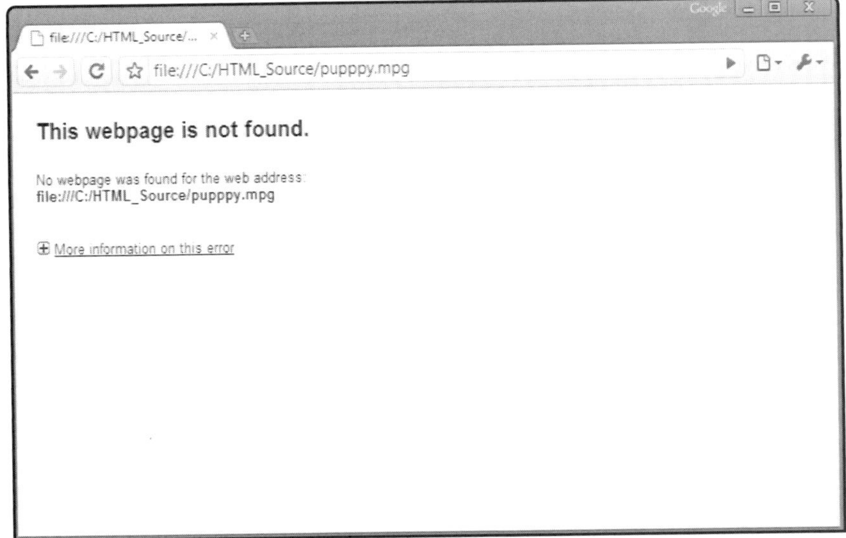

FIGURE 5.12

An example of a broken link as viewed using Google Chrome.

Fortunately, there are a number of very good free and low-cost links checker web services and applications available that you can use to keep an eye on the status of all your website's links. Read Appendix B to learn more about them.

Setting Up Graphics Links

So far all of the links we've discussed have been text-based, but as the following example shows, you can substitute graphics in place of text. This allows you to create things like graphics menus and custom button controls.

```
<!DOCTYPE html PUBLIC "-//W3C//DTD XHTML 1.0 Strict//EN"
  "http://www.w3.org/TR/xhtml1/DTD/xhtml1-strict.dtd">

<html xmlns="http://www.w3.org/1999/xhtml" lang="en" xml:lang="en">
```

```
<head>

  <meta http-equiv="Content-type" content="text/xhtml; charset=UTF-8" />
  <title>Chapter 5 - Downloading the Puppy Video Demo</title>
</head>

<body>

  <div>
    <a href = "help.html" target = "_blank"><img src = "help.gif"
      alt = "Click to access help" /></a>
  </div>

</body>

</html>
```

Here, a graphic image (a black button labeled Help) is displayed as shown in Figure 5.13. When the user moves the mouse pointer over the button, the shape of the pointer changes. When clicked, a new web document is opened in its own browser window. Note that by default, links load target web pages into the current browser window. However, by adding the target attribute, which is discussed in the next section, to the link, you override this behavior by instructing the browser to open a new browser window.

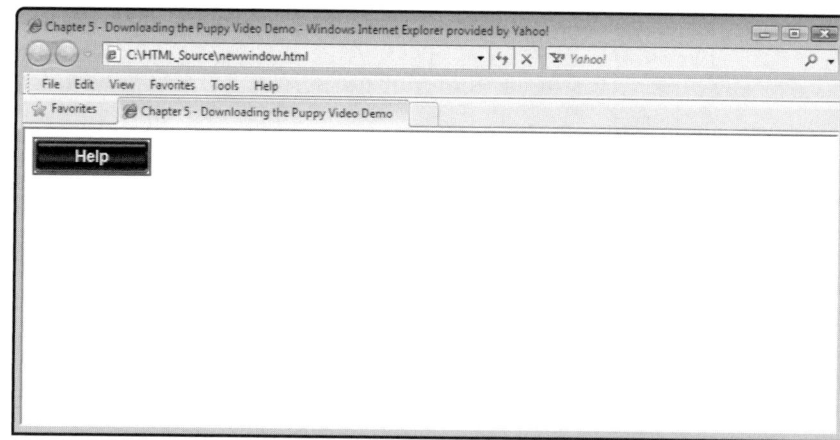

FIGURE 5.13

Configuring a graphic image to serve a link.

Don't Let Links Send Your Visitors Away

By default, a clicked link sends your visitors away from your website to the web page specified in the link. However, successful websites don't get that way by sending visitors away, but by keeping them around as much as possible. One way of providing your visitors with helpful links without sending them away is to create links that when clicked open a new window for the target page. This way, your visitors don't have to leave your website to explore one of your links.

The trick to creating links that open a new window is to include the anchor element's `target` attribute when defining a link and to assign a value of `_blank` to the attribute. An example of how to set up this type of link is shown here:

```
<!DOCTYPE html PUBLIC "-//W3C//DTD XHTML 1.0 Strict//EN"
  "http://www.w3.org/TR/xhtml1/DTD/xhtml1-strict.dtd">

<html xmlns="http://www.w3.org/1999/xhtml" lang="en" xml:lang="en">

  <head>
    <meta http-equiv="Content-type" content="text/xhtml; charset=UTF-8" />
    <title>Chapter 5 - Opening a Link in a New Window</title>
  </head>

  <body>
    <p>
      <p><a href = http://www.apple.com target = "_blank">Click Me</a></p>
    </p>
  </body>

</html>
```

Figure 5.14 shows the result that occurs when you run this example and click on the page's link.

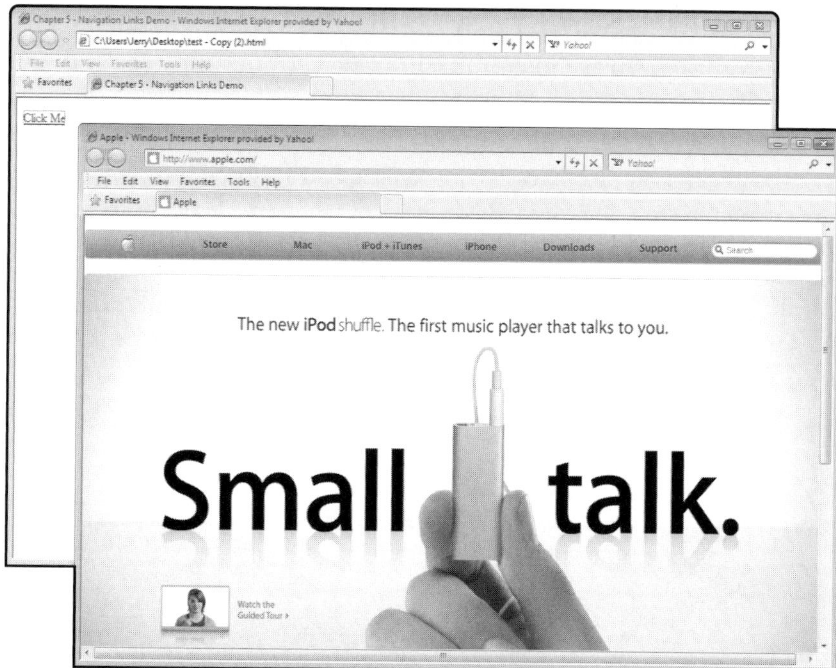

FIGURE 5.14

Keep your visitors by opening links in their own window.

Using Links to Set Up Document Downloads

You can set up links to point to any type of file. This includes files like Microsoft Office documents, PDF files, and Zip archive documents. Since web browsers are not built to work with these types of files, a couple of things may happen. First, if the browser has a plug-in that can handle the document, which is typically the case for PDF files, it may open and display the file. Once displayed, visitors can view or save the PDF. For other types of files, the browser may display a window that allows your visitors to download and save the files.

The following example demonstrates how to set up a web page that displays links to three different files.

```
<!DOCTYPE html PUBLIC "-//W3C//DTD XHTML 1.0 Strict//EN"
  "http://www.w3.org/TR/xhtml1/DTD/xhtml1-strict.dtd">

<html xmlns="http://www.w3.org/1999/xhtml" lang="en" xml:lang="en">

  <head>
    <meta http-equiv="Content-type" content="text/xhtml; charset=UTF-8" />
    <title>Chapter 5 - Downloading Files Demo</title>
  </head>
```

```
<body>
  <h1>Download Options</h1>
  <div>
    <a href = "WhitePaper.doc">
       Download free white paper document (Word)</a><br />
    <a href = "WhitePaper.pdf">
       Download free white paper document (PDF)</a><br />
    <a href = "WhitePaper.zip">
       Download free white paper document (Zip)</a>
  </div>
</body>

</html>
```

Figure 5.15 shows how the resulting web page looks when loaded. Using this example as a model, you can create a "Downloads" page on your website where you might post all kinds of free files.

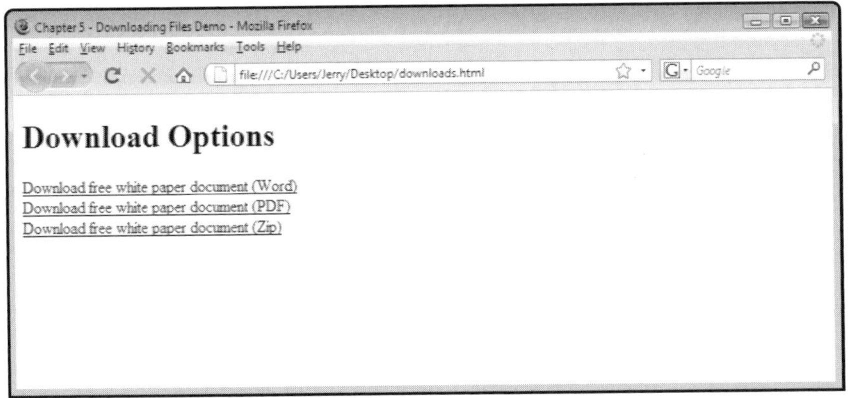

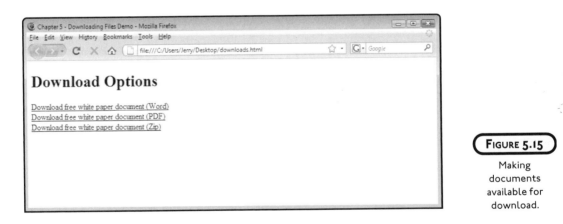

FIGURE 5.15
Making documents available for download.

Using Links to Facilitate Emailing

Have you ever visited a website that displayed a link labeled Contact Us that when clicked automatically opened your email application and created a new email addressed to the website? Perhaps the title of the email was also included? If you want, you can use a link to replicate this same technique on your own web pages, as demonstrated here:

```
<!DOCTYPE html PUBLIC "-//W3C//DTD XHTML 1.0 Strict//EN"
  "http://www.w3.org/TR/xhtml1/DTD/xhtml1-strict.dtd">
```

```
<html xmlns="http://www.w3.org/1999/xhtml" lang="en" xml:lang="en">

  <head>
    <meta http-equiv="Content-type" content="text/xhtml; charset=UTF-8" />
    <title>Chapter 5 - Email Demo</title>
  </head>

  <body>
    <p>
      <a href="mailto:jerry@tech-publishing.com">Contact Us</a>
    </p>
  </body>

</html>
```

When clicked, this page's link will automatically start the user's default email application and copy the email address specified by the `href` attribute, less the required `mailto:` keyword into the application's To field. As a result, all the user has to do is supply a subject and message text and then click on Send to submit the email. Figure 5.16 shows an example.

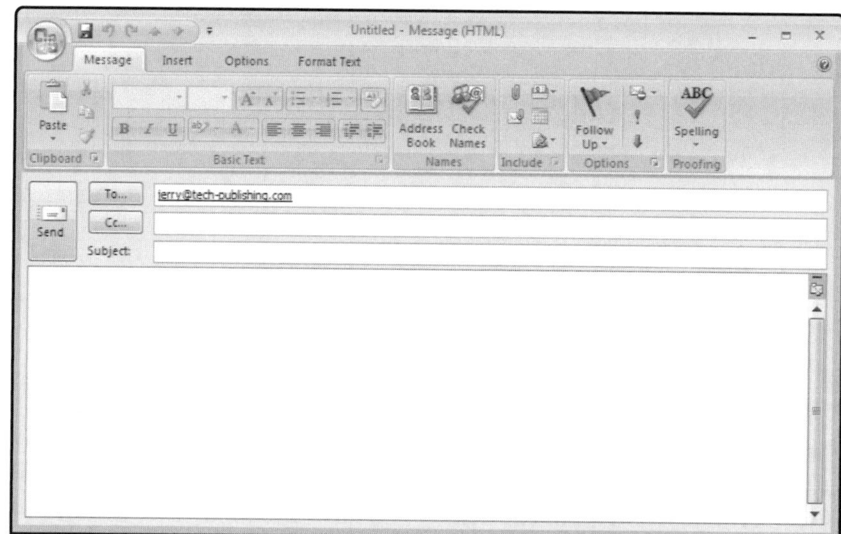

FIGURE 5.16

Use a link to make it easy for your visitors to send you an email.

Unfortunately, spammers have found that a good way of collecting email addresses is to collect them from web pages that use links to generate emails. So, unless you want to risk making it easier for spammers to get a hold of your email address, you might want to think hard before using this technique and instead use a form to collect visitor input. Forms are discussed in Chapter 6.

Other Forms of Content

As you have no doubt witnessed, websites are capable of displaying all kinds of content other than text and graphics. This includes content like audio and video. In order to work with this type of content you need to become familiar with the `object` element. In addition to audio and video, this element lets you include objects like java applets, ActiveX, Flash, and PDF in your web pages.

The key to working with video and audio in XHTML 1.0 Strict is to master use of the `object` element. The `object` element is an inline element. The `object` element supports a number of attributes that are used to define the media you are working with. These attributes include:

- **data.** Specifies the object's URL.
- **type.** Specifies the object's MIME type.
- **width.** Sets the object's width in pixels or as a percentage of its parent element.
- **height.** Sets the object's height in pixels or as a percentage of its parent element.

Integrating Video as Content

In order to use the `object` elements to embed and play audio and video files within your web documents, you must use the `object` element in conjunction with the `param` element. The `param` element must be nested within `object` elements in order to provide additional information needed to control interaction with the media, as demonstrated in the following example.

```
<!DOCTYPE html PUBLIC "-//W3C//DTD XHTML 1.0 Strict//EN"
  "http://www.w3.org/TR/xhtml1/DTD/xhtml1-strict.dtd">

<html xmlns="http://www.w3.org/1999/xhtml" lang="en" xml:lang="en">

  <head>
    <meta http-equiv="Content-type" content="text/xhtml; charset=UTF-8" />
    <title>Chapter 5 - Playing a MPG Video</title>
  </head>
```

```
  <body>
    <div>
      <object data = "puppy.mpg" type = "video/mpeg" width = "600"
        height = "480">
        <param name = "src" value = "puppy.mpg" />
        <param name = "autoplay" value = "true" />
      </object>
    </div>
  </body>

</html>
```

Here a video named puppy.mpg has been added to a web page using the `object` element. Two `param` elements were added that specify the name and location of the mpg file and instruct the browser to automatically start the playback of the video when the web page has finished loading. Figure 5.17 shows an example of the video as it is being played using the Internet Explorer browser.

FIGURE 5.17

An example of how to play a video on your web page.

Adding Audio Playback to Your Web Pages

The playback of audio is not much different than the playback of video. The following example demonstrates how to display a control that manages audio playback.

```
<!DOCTYPE html PUBLIC "-//W3C//DTD XHTML 1.0 Strict//EN"
  "http://www.w3.org/TR/xhtml1/DTD/xhtml1-strict.dtd">

<html xmlns="http://www.w3.org/1999/xhtml" lang="en" xml:lang="en">

  <head>
    <meta http-equiv="Content-type" content="text/xhtml; charset=UTF-8" />
    <title>Chapter 5 - Playing an audio file</title>
  </head>

  <body>
    <div>
      <object type="audio/x-wav" data="test.wav" width="250" height="30">
        <param name="src" value="test.wav" />
        <param name="autoplay" value="true" />
        <param name="autoStart" value="1" />
      </object>
    </div>
  </body>
</html>
```

As you can see, a wave file named test.wav will be played. The `object` element's `type` attribute has been set to `audio/x-wav` and the `data` attribute has been set to `test.wav`. The dimensions of the playback control have also been specified. Next, three `param` elements are used to specify the location of the wave file and instruct the browser to initiate playback of the wave file.

Figure 5.18 shows how the resulting web page looks when this document is loaded using the opera web browser.

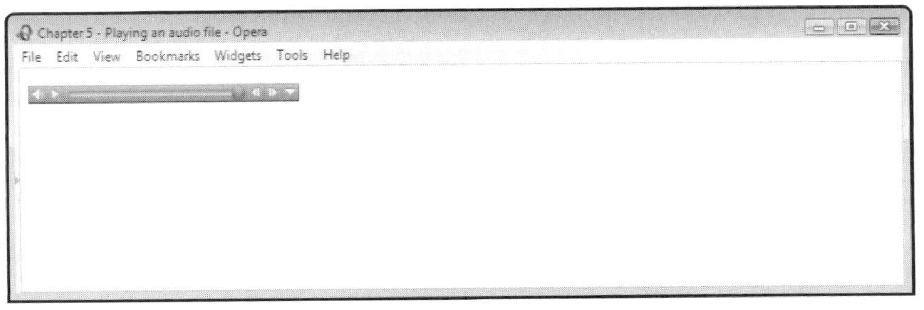

FIGURE 5.18

An example of how to play an audio file on your web page.

If you prefer, you can remove the display of the playback control from the web page by setting the `object` element's `width` and `height` attributes to `0`, as demonstrated in the following example.

```
<!DOCTYPE html PUBLIC "-//W3C//DTD XHTML 1.0 Strict//EN"
  "http://www.w3.org/TR/xhtml1/DTD/xhtml1-strict.dtd">

<html xmlns="http://www.w3.org/1999/xhtml" lang="en" xml:lang="en">

  <head>
    <meta http-equiv="Content-type" content="text/xhtml; charset=UTF-8" />
    <title>Chapter 5 - Playing an audio file</title>
  </head>

  <body>
    <div>
      <object type="audio/x-wav" data="test.wav" width="0" height="0">
        <param name="src" value="test.wav" />
        <param name="autoplay" value="true" />
        <param name="autoStart" value="1" />
      </object>
    </div>
  </body>

</html>
```

Displaying PDF Documents

In addition to video and audio content, you can add other types of content to your web documents using the `object` element. For example, the following web document shows how to use the `object` element to embed the display of a PDF document as content within a web page.

```
<!DOCTYPE html PUBLIC "-//W3C//DTD XHTML 1.0 Strict//EN"
  "http://www.w3.org/TR/xhtml1/DTD/xhtml1-strict.dtd">

<html xmlns="http://www.w3.org/1999/xhtml" lang="en" xml:lang="en">

  <head>
    <meta http-equiv="Content-type" content="text/xhtml; charset=UTF-8" />
    <title>Chapter 5 - Displaying a PDF Document</title>
```

```
  </head>

  <body>
    <div>
      <object data="test.pdf" type="application/pdf" width="600"
        height="480">
      </object>
    </div>
  </body>

</html>
```

Figure 5.19 shows an example of the output that is produced when this example is rendered using Google's Chrome browser.

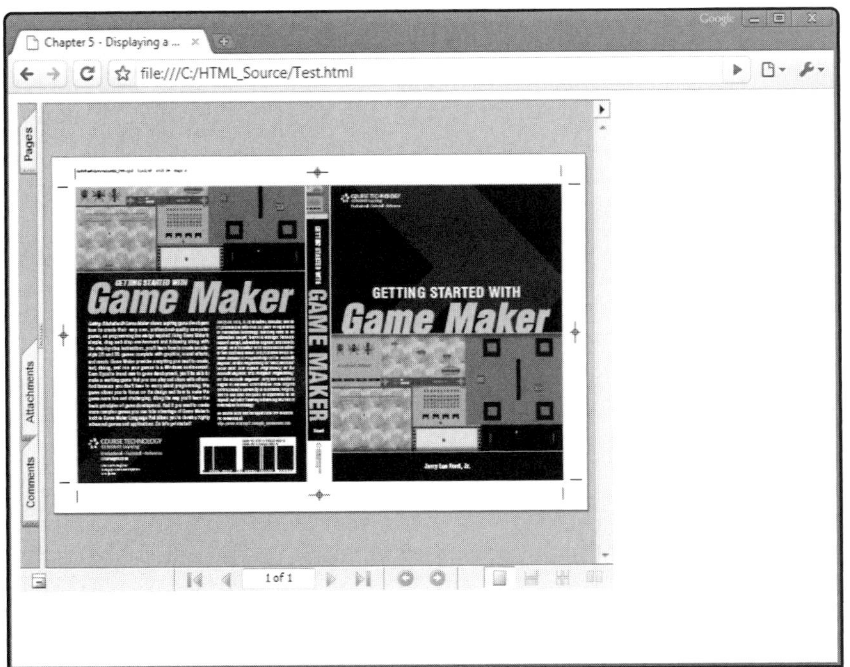

FIGURE 5.19

Displaying a DPF file as part of the content in a web page.

BACK TO THE (X)HTML TYPING QUIZ

Alright, now it is time to return your attention to this chapter's project, the (X)HTML Typing Quiz. This web application presents the user with five sentences and challenges him to retype them exactly as shown. The user can take as much time as needed to retype each sentence but must retype it exactly as shown. Any change in spelling, case, or punctuation will result in an error. To pass the quiz the user must retype at least three sentences correctly.

Designing the Application

The development of this web application will be performed in four steps, as outlined here:

1. Create a new XHTML document.
2. Develop the document's markup.
3. Develop the document's JavaScript.
4. Load and test the XHTML page.

Step 1: Creating a New XHTML Document

This application consists of an XHTML document and a graphics file named typewriter.jpg. The first step in the creation of this project is the creation of the application's web document. Do so using your preferred code or text editor and then save and name the file typingquiz.html. Next, open your web browser and go to http://www.courseptr.com/downloads and download the source code for this project, including the project's graphic file. Place a copy of the typewriter.jpg file in the same folder as the project's XHTML file.

Step 2: Developing the Document's Markup

The second step in the development of the Typing Quiz application is to begin putting together the web document's markup. Begin by adding the following elements to the typingquiz.html file.

```
<!DOCTYPE html PUBLIC "-//W3C//DTD XHTML 1.0 Strict//EN"
  "http://www.w3.org/TR/xhtml1/DTD/xhtml1-strict.dtd">

<html xmlns="http://www.w3.org/1999/xhtml" lang="en" xml:lang="en">

  <head>

  </head>

  <body>

  </body>

</html>
```

With the web document's core elements in place, let's ensure that the document is well formed by adding the following elements to its head section.

```
<meta http-equiv="Content-type" content="text/xhtml; charset=UTF-8" />
<title>Typing Quiz</title>
```

To wrap up your work on the document's markup, add the following statements to the body section.

```
<div><img src = "typewriter.gif" width = "222" height = "236"
  alt = "Picture of an old style manual typewriter" /></div>

<p>You may retake the (X)HTML Typing Quiz as many times as
    you wish by clicking on View > Refresh\Reload.</p>
```

As you can see, the img element is used to embed an image file named typewriter.jpg in the web document. The image file's width and height are set and an alternative text string is provided. Note that since the img element is an inline element, it must be enclosed within a block-level element, in this case the div element. Lastly, a paragraph has been added that provides instructions for taking the quiz.

Step 3: Creating the Document's Script

In order to manage the administration of the quiz and its interaction with the user, the web document includes a JavaScript. This script will manage the display of the web application's popup dialog windows and the analysis of each of the user's typed answers. To begin work on this script, add the following statements to the web document's head section.

```
<script type = "text/javascript">
<!-- Start hiding JavaScript statements

// End hiding JavaScript statements -->
</script>
```

The next step in the development of the script file is to declare its variables and to assign their initial values. To do this, add the following statements to the script file.

```
var noCorrect = 0;

var s1 = "Live long and prosper.";
var s2 = "In the end there can be only one.";
var s3 = "Indeed, perhaps today is a good day to die.";
var s4 = "If I had to choose, I would say that it is good to be ";
```

```
    s4 = s4 + "loved but better to be feared.";
var s5 = "Ask not what your country can do for you but what you ";
    s5 = s5 + "can do for your country.";

var intro = "To take this quiz, retype each of the 5 displayed " +
            "sentences exactly as shown. You must retype at " +
            "least three sentences correctly to pass the quiz."
```

The rest of the script's statements, shown next, should be added to the end of the script file.

```
alert(intro);

challenge = prompt("Type: " + s1, "");
if (challenge == s1) {
  alert("Correct");
  noCorrect = noCorrect + 1
} else {
  alert("Incorrect");
}

challenge = prompt("Type: " + s2, "");
if (challenge == s2) {
  alert("Correct");
  noCorrect = noCorrect + 1
} else {
  alert("Incorrect");
}

challenge = prompt("Type: " + s3, "");
if (challenge == s3) {
  alert("Correct");
  noCorrect = noCorrect + 1
} else {
  alert("Incorrect");
}

challenge = prompt("Type: " + s4, "");
if (challenge == s4) {
  alert("Correct");
```

```
  noCorrect = noCorrect + 1
} else {
  alert("Incorrect");
}

challenge = prompt("Type: " + s5, "");
if (challenge == s5) {
  alert("Correct");
  noCorrect = noCorrect + 1
} else {
  alert("Incorrect");
}

if (noCorrect > 2) {
  alert("Congratulations. You passed!");
} else {
  alert("Sorry but you failed.");
}
```

Without getting too much into the details of the script's programming logic, what these statements do is display a series of seven popup dialog windows that show the application's instructions, each of its five challenge sentences, and the user's final result.

To learn more about JavaScript, make sure that you review Chapter 9.

The Finished HTML Document

Okay, assuming you have been following along carefully with all of the steps that have been outlined, your copy of the Typing Quiz should be ready for testing. To make sure that you have assembled everything correctly, take a look at the following example, which shows what the finished document should look like.

```
<!DOCTYPE html PUBLIC "-//W3C//DTD XHTML 1.0 Strict//EN"
  "http://www.w3.org/TR/xhtml1/DTD/xhtml1-strict.dtd">

<html xmlns="http://www.w3.org/1999/xhtml" lang="en" xml:lang="en">

  <head>
```

```
<meta http-equiv="Content-type" content="text/xhtml; charset=UTF-8" />
<title>Typing Test</title>

<script type = "text/javascript">
<!-- Start hiding JavaScript statements

  var noCorrect = 0;

  var s1 = "Live long and prosper.";
  var s2 = "In the end there can be only one.";
  var s3 = "Indeed, perhaps today is a good day to die.";
  var s4 = "If I had to choose, I would say that it is good to be ";
      s4 = s4 + "loved but better to be feared.";
  var s5 = "Ask not what your country can do for you but what you ";
      s5 = s5 + "can do for your country.";

  var intro = "To take this quiz, retype each of the 5 displayed " +
              "sentences exactly as shown. You must retype at " +
              "least three sentences correctly to pass the quiz."

  alert(intro);

  challenge = prompt("Type: " + s1, "");
  if (challenge == s1) {
     alert("Correct");
     noCorrect = noCorrect + 1
  } else {
     alert("Incorrect");
  }

  challenge = prompt("Type: " + s2, "");
  if (challenge == s2) {
     alert("Correct");
     noCorrect = noCorrect + 1
  } else {
     alert("Incorrect");
  }
```

```
    challenge = prompt("Type: " + s3, "");
    if (challenge == s3) {
       alert("Correct");
       noCorrect = noCorrect + 1
    } else {
       alert("Incorrect");
    }

    challenge = prompt("Type: " + s4, "");
    if (challenge == s4) {
       alert("Correct");
       noCorrect = noCorrect + 1
    } else {
       alert("Incorrect");
    }

    challenge = prompt("Type: " + s5, "");
    if (challenge == s5) {
       alert("Correct");
       noCorrect = noCorrect + 1
    } else {
       alert("Incorrect");
    }

    if (noCorrect > 2) {
      alert("Congratulations. You passed!");
    } else {
      alert("Sorry but you failed.");
    }

  // End hiding JavaScript statements -->
  </script>

</head>

<body>

  <div><img src = "typewriter.gif" width = "222" height = "236"
```

```
    alt = "Picture of an old style manual typewriter" /></div>

  <p>You may retake the (X)HTML Typing Quiz as many times as
     you wish by clicking on View > Refresh\Reload.</p>


</body>

</html>
```

Step 4: Loading and Testing the Typing Quiz

To test your new web application, start up you favorite web browser and use it to load the typingquiz.html file by executing the following steps.

1. Click on the browser's File menu and select the Open File command. This displays a standard file open dialog.
2. Navigate to the folder where you stored the web page and select it.
3. Click on the Open button.

If all goes as it should, continue testing your application using one or two other web browsers. You might want to validate that it is well formed by visiting thhp://validator.w3.org.

SUMMARY

This chapter provided a good overview of how to integrate graphics into your web pages. You learned about JPEG, GIF, and PNG files and their advantages and disadvantages. You learned about the importance of providing alternative content for graphics, and you learned how to create graphic links, set up site navigation, and to set up document downloads. On top of all this, this chapter showed you how to work with the `object` element and how to use it to seamlessly integrate audio and video into your web documents. You even learned how to embed the display of PDF files as part of web page content. In addition, you learned how to create the Typing Quiz web application.

Challenges

1. As currently written, the Typing Quiz displays a somewhat bland looking graphic of a typewriter when the web page is rendered in the browser. Consider taking steps to spruce things up a bit by replacing this image with one that is a bit more interesting.
2. Consider adding a link to the bottom of the page that points back to your main website; perhaps mention that more interesting things await there.
3. If you feel up to the challenge, try to add to the text to make it more difficult.

Designing Tables and Forms

Displaying text is essential to web page development. So far, you have learned how to display text in headings, paragraphs, and lists and to emphasize text structure using an assortment of other elements. Another way of organizing text is using tables. Tables can help you streamline the display of any data that can be organized in rows and columns. Another important aspect of web development is the collection of input from the people who visit your web pages, which is essential to the creation of interactive websites. If you have already used search engines or purchased anything online, you already have plenty of experience working with forms. This chapter will expand your web development skills by teaching you how to display information in tables and collect it using forms.

Specifically, you will learn how to:

- Organize and display data using forms
- Create forms with borders, row, and column headers, and merged cells
- Collect user input using forms
- Work with different types of text fields, buttons, and drop-down lists
- Improve form organization using labels and fieldsets

Project Preview: The Number Guessing Game

This chapter's web project is the Number Guessing Game. This game challenges the player to try to guess a randomly generated number in the range of 1 to 10 in as few guesses as possible. The player makes guesses by clicking on one of ten radio controls that make up the application's form, as demonstrated in Figure 6.1.

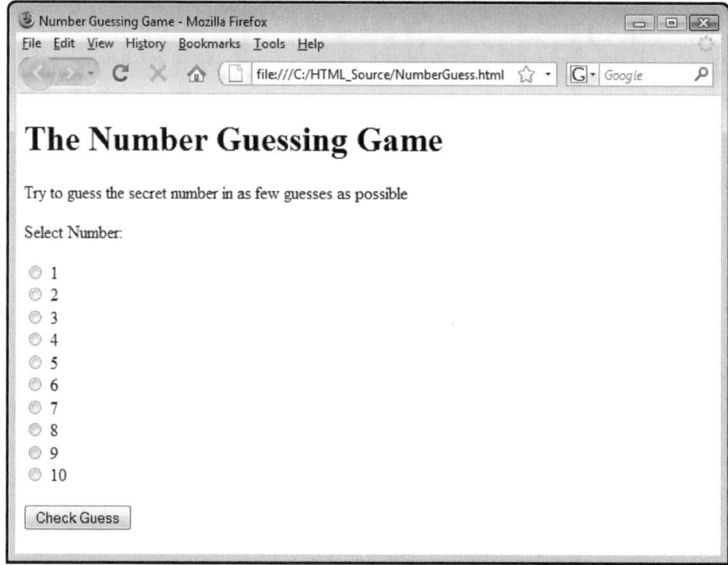

Figure 6.1

The game is made up of a form that consists of 10 radio controls and a button control.

Once the player has selected the radio control representing his guess, the button control labeled `Check Guess` must be clicked. The game will then compare the player's input against the game's secret number in order to determine whether the player has won the game or needs to keep on playing. Figure 6.2 shows an example of the message that the game displays in the event the player's guess was higher than the secret number.

Game play continues until the player finally guesses the secret number. Once the correct number has been selected, the message shown in Figure 6.3 is displayed, informing the player that he has won the game.

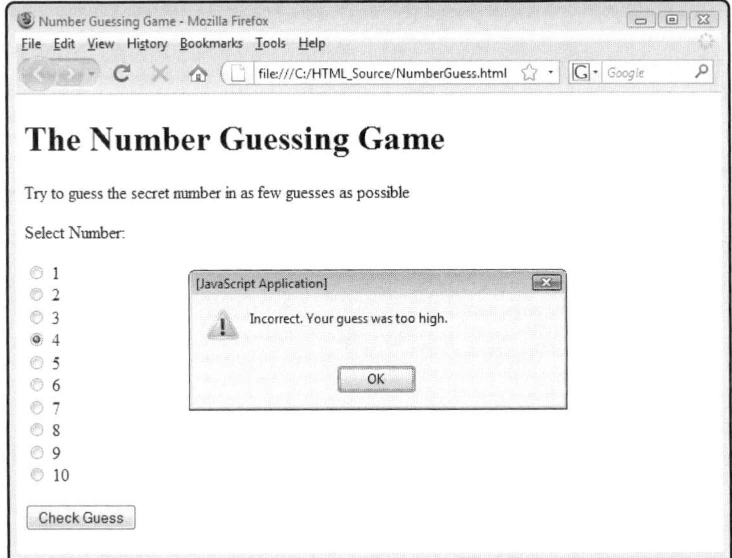

FIGURE 6.2

The player can use the messages provided by the game to help guide his next move.

FIGURE 6.3

The message congratulates the player and explains how to restart the game.

USING TABLES TO DISPLAY INFORMATION

Tables provide a convenient way of displaying collections of related data that lend themselves to a tabular format. To create tables, you need to learn how to work with three elements: table, tr, and td. The table element is made up of the <table> tag, which marks the beginning of a table, and the `</table>` tag, which marks the end of a table. Inside the `table` element, rows are established using the `<tr>` and `</tr>` tags and individual cells within those rows are created using the `<td>` and `</td>` tags (the letters "td" stand for table data, which can be text, lists, forms, images, etc.).

Basic Table Elements

The following example demonstrates how to use the `table`, `tr`, and `td` elements to construct a simple table made up of four rows with three cells per row. As you can see, `<tr>` and `</tr>` tags are used to define each row in the table and `<td>` and `</td>` tags are used to enclose the content of every cell in each row.

```
<table>
  <tr>
    <td>Lakers</td>
    <td>Los Angeles</td>
    <td>West</td>
  </tr>
  <tr>
    <td>Celtics</td>
    <td>Boston</td>
    <td>East</td>
  </tr>
  <tr>
    <td>Magic</td>
    <td>Orlando</td>
    <td>East</td>
  </tr>
  <tr>
    <td>Cavaliers</td>
    <td>Cleveland</td>
    <td>East</td>
  </tr>
</table>
```

As Figure 6.4 demonstrates, the browser automatically sizes the table and its rows and cells based on the contents contained in the table. However, as you will learn in Chapter 8, you can use CSS to control table formatting.

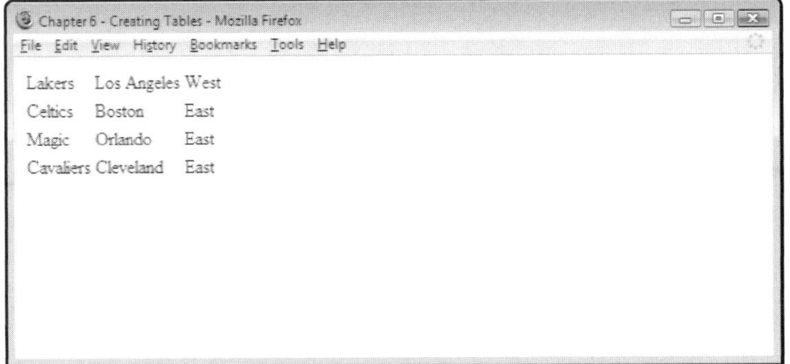

FIGURE 6.4

An example of a table made up of three rows and four columns.

Adding Borders to Your Tables

In order to make tables easier for people to view and understand, it is often helpful to add a border to them, showing the outer edges of the table while also distinguishing rows and cells. To accomplish this feat, all you have to do is to add the `border` attribute to the `form` element, as demonstrated here:

```
<table border = "1">
  <tr>
    <td>Lakers</td>
    <td>Celtics</td>
    <td>Magic</td>
    <td>Cavaliers</td>
  </tr>
  <tr>
    <td>Los Angeles</td>
    <td>Boston</td>
    <td>Orlando</td>
    <td>Cleveland</td>
  </tr>
  <tr>
    <td>West</td>
    <td>East</td>
    <td>East</td>
    <td>East</td>
  </tr>
</table>
```

As you can see, the `table` element's `border` attribute has been assigned a value of 1. This instructs the browser to draw a 1-pixel thick border around the table and its rows and cells. When rendered, this example displays the table shown in Figure 6.5.

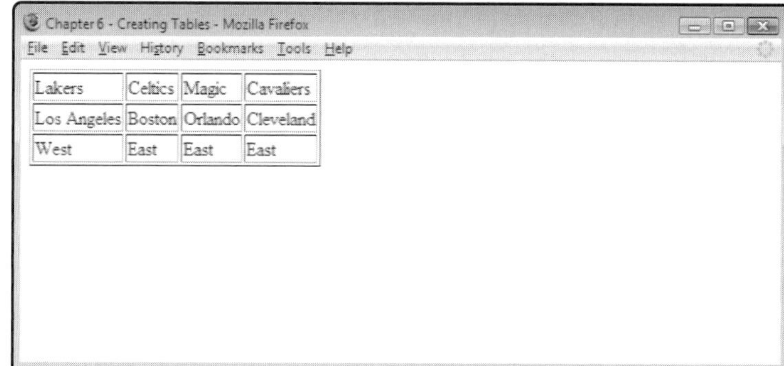

FIGURE 6.5

An example of a table with a border set to a thickness of 1.

Figure 6.6 shows an example of how the table would look if you changed the value assigned to the `border` attribute from 1 to 10.

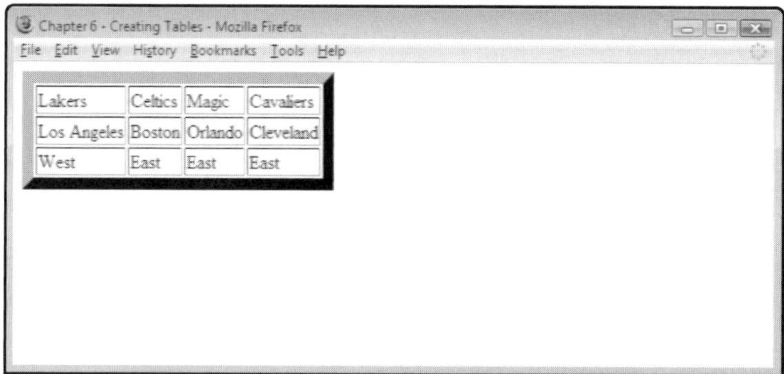

FIGURE 6.6

An example of a table with a border set to a thickness of 10 pixels.

Note that in both examples, the browser automatically left aligns the table's data.

Playing Nice with Non-Graphic Browsers

Unfortunately, non-visual browsers can have trouble rendering tables. To help ensure that these browsers display table data in a useful fashion, use the `summary` and `scope` elements when defining (X)HTML tables. The `summary` element provides a text string that can be used by browsers that reply on text-to-voice speech synthesizers. This element is ignored by visual browsers. The `scope` element helps non-visual browsers determine how to lay out a table by providing header information that helps identify columns (`col`) and rows (`row`).

The following example demonstrates how to use both the `table` element's `summary` attribute and the `td` element's `scope` attribute.

```
<table border = "1" summary = "Popular NBA Basketball Teams">
  <tr>
    <td scope = "col">Team</td>
    <td scope = "col">City</td>
    <td scope = "col">Conference</td>
  </tr>
  <tr>
    <td scope = "row">Lakers</td>
    <td>Los Angeles</td>
    <td>West</td>
  </tr>
  <tr>
    <td scope = "row">Celtics</td>
    <td>Boston</td>
    <td>East</td>
  </tr>
  <tr>
    <td scope = "row">Magic</td>
    <td>Orlando</td>
    <td>East</td>
  </tr>
  <tr>
    <td scope = "row">Cavaliers</td>
    <td>Cleveland</td>
    <td>East</td>
  </tr>
</table>
```

Figure 6.7 demonstrates how this example looks when viewed using the Lynx text-only browser.

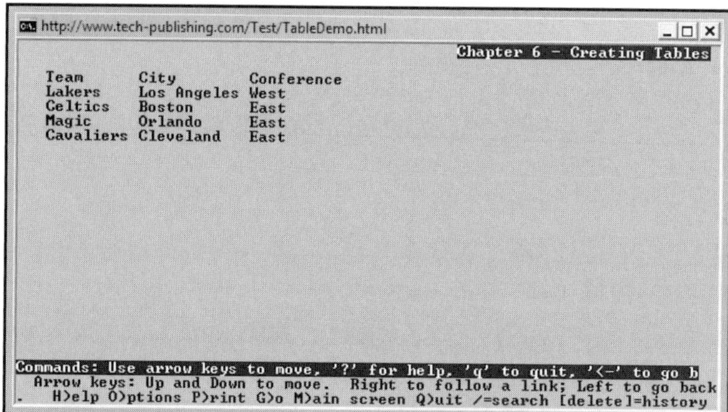

FIGURE 6.7

An example of a table displayed using the Lynx browser.

Assigning a Table Heading

You may find it helpful to display a heading for your tables, providing a high-level description of its contents. The way to do this is to use the `caption` element, as demonstrated in the following example.

```
<table border = "1" summary = "Popular NBA Basketball Teams">
  <caption>Popular NBA Teams</caption>
  <tr>
    <td scope = "col">Team</td>
    <td scope = "col">City</td>
    <td scope = "col">Conference</td>
  </tr>
  <tr>
    <td>Lakers</td>
    <td>Los Angeles</td>
    <td>West</td>
  </tr>
  <tr>
    <td>Celtics</td>
    <td>Boston</td>
    <td>East</td>
  </tr>
  <tr>
    <td>Magic</td>
    <td>Orlando</td>
    <td>East</td>
  </tr>
```

```
  <tr>
    <td>Cavaliers</td>
    <td>Cleveland</td>
    <td>East</td>
  </tr>
</table>
```

To add a caption to a table, you must embed the caption's text between `<caption>` and `</caption>` tags. You are limited to one `caption` element per table and that element should be placed after the table's opening tag. Figure 6.8 provides an example of how this table will look when loaded by the browser.

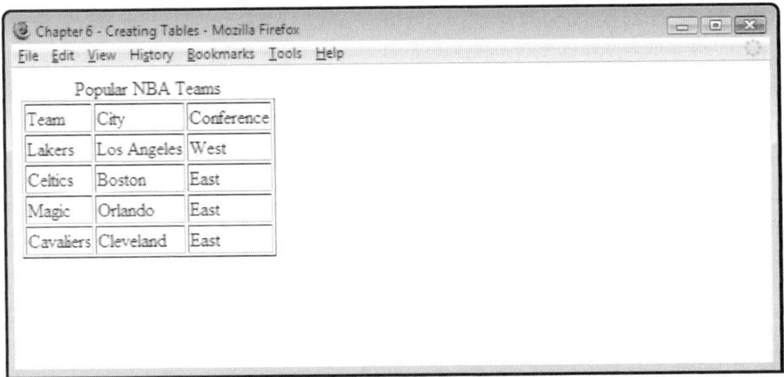

FIGURE 6.8
An example of a table with a table heading.

Note that the heading displayed by the `caption` element is always displayed above the table and not within the table itself.

Defining Heading Row and Column Headings

It is often useful to add a heading to a table at the top of each column (`col`) or to the left of each row (`row`). To do so, you use the `th` element, as demonstrated in the following example.

```
<table border = "1" summary = "Popular NBA Basketball Teams">
  <caption>Popular NBA Teams</caption>
  <tr>
    <th scope = "col">Team</th>
    <th scope = "col">City</th>
    <th scope = "col">Conference</th>
  </tr>
  <tr>
    <td>Lakers</td>
```

```
    <td>Los Angeles</td>
    <td>West</td>
  </tr>
  <tr>
    <td>Celtics</td>
    <td>Boston</td>
    <td>East</td>
  </tr>
  <tr>
    <td>Magic</td>
    <td>Orlando</td>
    <td>East</td>
  </tr>
  <tr>
    <td>Cavaliers</td>
    <td>Cleveland</td>
    <td>East</td>
  </tr>
</table>
```

Figure 6.9 shows how this table will look once loaded by a browser.

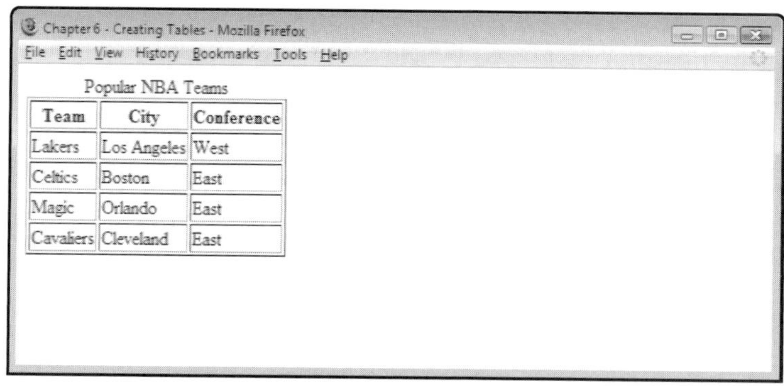

FIGURE 6.9

An example of a table with a column heading.

Row and column headings are typically displayed in bold to make them stand out and are usually centered within their cells.

Merging Table Cells

One neat structural trick that you often see in (X)HTML tables is the use of merged cells, in which two or more cells are merged together to create a single large cell. Merged cells can be used to display multi-column or multi-row headings. To merge cells horizontally across a table, you need to add the `colspan` attribute to the appropriate `th` or `td` element. Similarly, to merge cells vertically in a table, you need to add the `rowspan` attribute to the appropriate `th` or `td` element. The following example demonstrates how to use the `colspan` attribute to set up a table header that spans the entire top row of a table.

```
<table border = "1" summary = "Popular NBA Basketball Teams">
  <caption>Popular NBA Teams</caption>
  <tr>
    <th colspan = "3">2008 - 2009 Season</th>
  </tr>
  <tr>
    <th scope = "col">Team</th>
    <th scope = "col">City</th>
    <th scope = "col">Conference</th>
  </tr>
  <tr>
    <td>Lakers</td>
    <td>Los Angeles</td>
    <td>West</td>
  </tr>
  <tr>
    <td>Celtics</td>
    <td>Boston</td>
    <td>East</td>
  </tr>
  <tr>
    <td>Magic</td>
    <td>Orlando</td>
    <td>East</td>
  </tr>
  <tr>
    <td>Cavaliers</td>
    <td>Cleveland</td>
    <td>East</td>
```

```
  </tr>
</table>
```

Note that in this example, `colspan` has been assigned a value of 3, instructing the browser to span the header across all three cells in the table. Figure 6.10 shows how the table looks when the (X)HTML page that contains it is loaded into the browser.

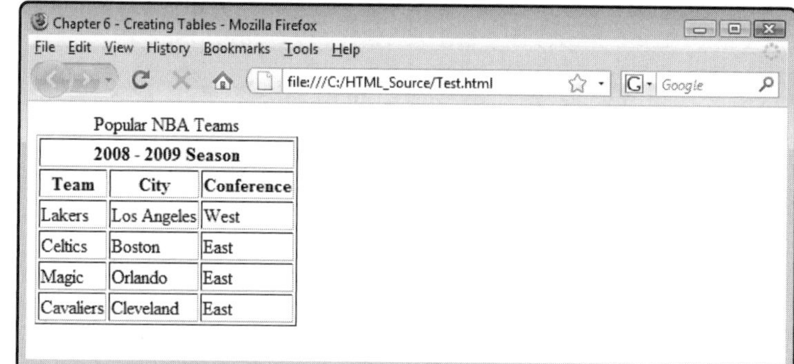

Popular NBA Teams

2008 - 2009 Season		
Team	**City**	**Conference**
Lakers	Los Angeles	West
Celtics	Boston	East
Magic	Orlando	East
Cavaliers	Cleveland	East

FIGURE 6.10

An example of how to merge table cells.

COLLECTING USER INPUT THROUGH FORMS

Communication on the Internet is a two way street, facilitated by things like email and instant messaging. One way that many websites interact with their visitors is through forms. A *form* is a location on a web page where visitors can provide input. Forms are made up of controls like text fields, check boxes, radio buttons, drop-down lists, and push buttons. The data collected by a control is that control's value. To work with a control, your visitors must select it, placing *focus* on the control. To submit form data, most forms require that visitors click on a Submit button, at which time the form's data is packed up and sent to a form handler.

Forms are defined using the `form` element, which is made up of an opening `<form>` tag and a closing `</form>` tag. Once filled in, forms are processed by a form handler. A *form handler* is a program or script that usually executes on a web server, although a form's handler can instead be a JavaScript located on the same document as the form. Its purpose is to validate and process the contents of forms. This may mean storing the user's input in a server database or file or using it to generate a highly customized web page.

When submitted, form data is sent to a form handler as name/value pairs. Therefore, one of the requirements of every form is that all form elements be named.

Forms have one required attribute. This attribute is `action`. It is used to specify the URL of the form handler. Another optional `form` element attribute that is usually used is the `method` attribute. This attribute specifies how to send data to a web server for processing by the form handler. The `method` attribute supports the following values.

- **get.** Sends form contents to the form handler by adding it to the URL string.
- **post.** Sends form contents to the form handler using the Hypertext Transfer Protocol.

In addition to sending form data using the form element attribute's `get` and `post` options, you can also send form data via email. When you use this option, the form data is sent as a text file made up of name/value pairs. Though not practical for large amounts of data, this option can be used effectively in situations where small amounts of data are transmitted. To use this option, you must formulate the `form` element as demonstrated next. Note the use of the required `mailto:` keyword, which is separated from the desired email address by a colon.

```
<form action = "mailto:xxx@website.com" action = " post">
```

Including a statement like this one in your web documents opens them up to spammers who search the internet looking for email accounts to add to their email lists, so use this option sparingly.

If the `method` attribute is omitted, a default of `get` is assumed. The following example shows an XHTML document that can be used as a template for creating forms that send form data to a form handler. In this example, the form data is sent to a form handler script named processdata.cgi, which resides on the same server as the web document.

```
<!DOCTYPE html PUBLIC "-//W3C//DTD XHTML 1.0 Strict//EN"
  "http://www.w3.org/TR/xhtml1/DTD/xhtml1-strict.dtd">

<html xmlns="http://www.w3.org/1999/xhtml" lang="en" xml:lang="en">

  <head>
    <meta http-equiv="Content-type" content="text/xhtml; charset=UTF-8" />
    <title>Chapter 6 - Building Forms</title>
  </head>

  <body>

    <form action = "/cgi-bin/processdata.cgi" method = "post">
```

```
    </form>

  </body>

</html>
```

As you can see, the form element is block level. In addition, it can only contain other block-level elements. If inline elements are to be used, they must be placed within block-level elements inside the form.

The form element provides a structure within which specialized form elements are stored. In addition to specialized form elements, forms can also contain regular (X)HTML elements, like paragraphs and headings, or any other (X)HTML element that adds to the forms structure.

Defining Controls Using the input Element

One of the most versatile and commonly used form elements is the input element. It can be used to generate a wide variety of different types of form controls. The input element is an inline element, so to use it you must enclose it within a block element as you will see demonstrated repeatedly in the many form examples that follow. The range of controls that you can generate using the input element is listed here:

- Text fields
- Password fields
- File controls
- Checkbox controls
- Radio buttons
- Button controls
- Image control
- Hidden control
- Submit button
- Reset button

To tell the browser what type of control you want when working with the input element, you must specify the control's type using the input element's type attribute. The browser will then generate the corresponding type of control when the form is rendered.

Creating Text Controls

If you add an `input` element to a form and set its `type` attribute's value to `text` (`input type = "text"`), a single-line text field control is added to your form. By default, most browsers will display the text field as a rectangular text control with a text background and an inset border. Most browsers will automatically set the text field's length to approximately 25 characters wide.

Text fields are perfect for collecting small amounts of text input from your visitors. If you need to collect more than a few words, you should use the `textarea` control, discussed later in this chapter. The following example demonstrates how to create a table containing a text control.

```
<p>
  <label for = "name">Enter your name:</label>
  <input type = "text" id = "name" name = "name" size = "20"
    maxlength = "20" value = "Enter your name here" />
</p>
```

As you can see, the `input` element that is defined in this example specifies a number of optional attributes that further configure the resulting text control. The attributes are explained here:

- **size.** Sets the width, in terms of number of characters, of the text field.
- **maxlength.** Defines the total number of characters of input (including blank spaces) that the text field can accept.
- **value.** Specifies a text string to be displayed inside the text field as its default input.

Figure 6.11 shows how the previous example looks when loaded into the web browser.

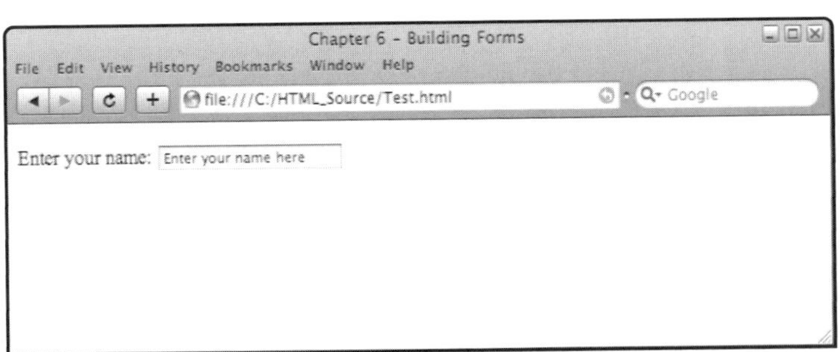

Figure 6.11

Using a text control to collect text input from your visitors.

Creating Password Controls

A password control is a text field with a twist—any text typed into it is masked using asterisks or bullet characters to prevent it from being seen by spying eyes. To add a password control to a form, all you have to do is add an `input` element to a form and set its `type` attribute's value to `password` (`input type = "password"`). A password control is a single-line text field. By default, most browsers will display the text field as a rectangular text control with a text background and an inset border.

The following example demonstrates how to add a password control to a form.

```
<p>
  <label for = "password">Enter your password:</label>
  <input type = "password" id = "password" name = "password"
    size = "10" maxlength = "10" />
</p>
```

As you can see, in this example the `input` element specifies a number of optional attributes. These include the `size` and `maxlength` attributes, which work exactly the same here as they do for the `text` control. If you want, you can use the `value` attribute to add a default value for the control, though its usage with this control is certainly questionable.

Figure 6.12 shows how the previous example looks when loaded into the web browser.

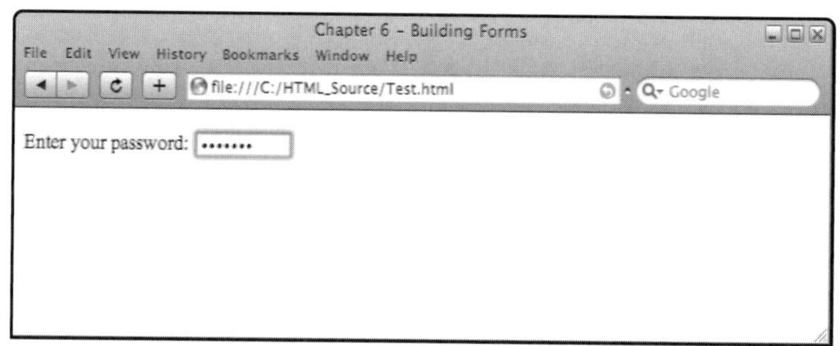

Using a password control to prevent snooping eyes from seeing text input.

Creating File Controls

By setting the `input` element's `type` attribute to file (`input type= "File"`), you can add a control to your form that allows your visitors to select and upload files from their computer as part of the form's data. This control usually displays as a text field with a corresponding button that when clicked displays a standard file dialog. Visitors can specify the file to upload by selecting it via this dialog or by simply keying in the location of the file directly to the control's text field. You can control the width of the control's text field by setting the `input` element's `size` attribute to a desired length (in characters).

The following example demonstrates how to add a file control to a form.

```
<p>
  <label for = "file">Upload your file:</label>
  <input type = "file" id = "file" name = "file"
    size = "50" accept = "text/css, text/html, text/plain" />
</p>
```

Note the addition of the `accept` attribute, which is used to specify MIME types, restricting the types of files displayed in the standard dialog window to only those specified. Figure 6.13 shows how this example looks when loaded by the Internet Explorer browser.

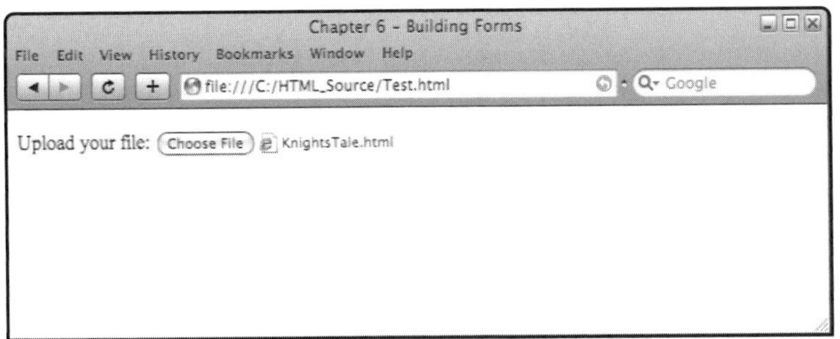

FIGURE 6.13

Using a file control to allow visitors to upload files as form input as seen using Internet Explorer.

Figure 6.13 shows the file control as it will appear on most web browsers. One exception is Apple Safari, which, as demonstrated in Figure 6.14, does not display a text field as part of the control. Instead, Safari displays only the file's name (without its path) and a small icon, identifying the selected file's type.

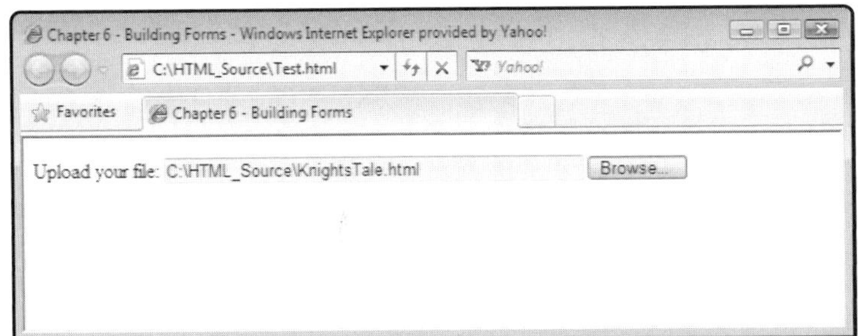

FIGURE 6.14

Using a file control to allows visitors to upload files as form input as seen using Apple Safari.

Creating Checkbox and Radio Controls

Another way of collecting visitor input is through the use of checkbox and radio controls. A checkbox control is a control that displays a small square, which visitors can click on to select or unselect the control. A selected checkbox control displays a checkmark or similar character inside the control. An unselected checkbox simply appears as an empty box.

Checkbox controls are useful in situations when you want your visitors to select between two choices. You can display a series of checkbox controls to present visitors with individual choices, in which case each checkbox control works independently of the other checkbox controls. Checkbox controls are created by setting the `input` element's `type` attribute to `checkbox` (`type= "checkbox"`).

Checkbox controls are normally displayed within a `label` element, which provides descriptive text that lets visitors know what the checkbox control's choices represent. Usually, you will want to use the `input` element's `value` element to assign a value to your checkbox controls. This value is returned as part of the form's data to the form's handler if the checkbox control has been checked. If you want, you can pre-check a checkbox control by assigning the `input` element's checked attribute a value of `checked` (`checked = "checked"`).

Radio controls are similar to checkbox controls in that they allow visitors to choose options. They differ from checkbox controls in that radio controls can be configured to work in groups (just assign every radio control the same name). When used in groups, radio controls work very much like buttons on stereo radios in that you may have many buttons to choose but only one can be selected (pressed) at a time.

Like checkbox controls you can and should always use the `input` element's `value` attribute to assign a value to a radio control; otherwise, the form handler won't be able to tell which radio button was pressed. You may also use the `checked` attribute to pre-select a given radio control. The following example demonstrates how to work with both the checkbox and radio controls.

```
<p>Pick your size:</p>
<p>
  <input type = "checkbox" id = "checkbox1" name = "checkbox1"
    value = "Small" checked = "checked" />
  <label for = "checkbox1">Small</label><br />
  <input type = "checkbox" id = "checkbox2" name = "checkbox2"
    value = "Medium" />
  <label for = "checkbox2">Medium</label><br />
  <input type = "checkbox" id = "checkbox3" name = "checkbox3"
    value = "Large"/>
  <label for = "checkbox3">Large</label><br />
  <input type = "checkbox" id = "checkbox4" name = "checkbox4"
    value = "Extra Large" />
  <label for = "checkbox4">Extra Large</label>
</p>

<p>Choose a color:</p>
```

```
<p>
  <input type = "radio" id = "radio1" name = "radio"
    value = "Red" />
  <label for = "radio1">Red</label><br />
  <input type = "radio" id = "radio2" name = "radio"
    value = "Blue" checked = "checked" />
  <label for = "radio2">Blue</label><br />
  <input type = "radio" id = "radio3" name = "radio"
    value = "Green" />
  <label for = "radio3">Green</label><br />
</p>
```

Figure 6.15 shows how this example will look when rendered by the browser.

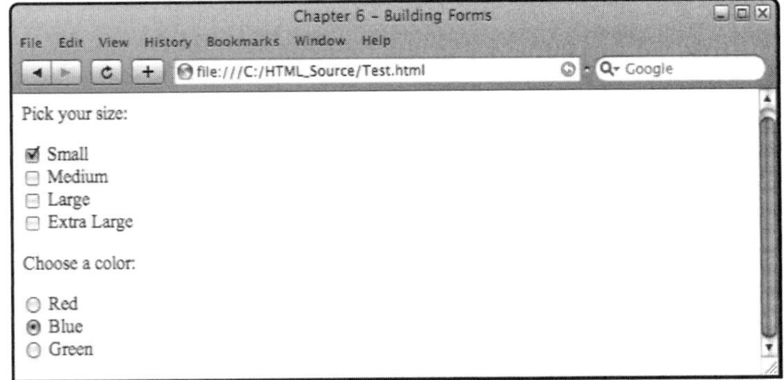

FIGURE 6.15

Letting visitors make selections using checkbox and radio button controls.

Creating Button Controls

By assigning an input element `type` attribute a value of `button` (`input type = "button"`) you can add a button control to a form. Button controls do not perform any predetermined functions. Instead, they are generic controls that are usually used to trigger the execution of JavaScript. Button controls can display text, set by assigning a text string to the `input` element's `value` attribute. The following example demonstrates how to add button controls to a form.

```
<p>
  <input type = "button" id = "button1" name = "button1"
    value = "Open" />
  <input type = "button" id = "button2" name = "button2"
    value = "Save" />
  <input type = "button" id = "button3" name = "button3"
```

```
    value = "Print" />
  <input type = "button" id = "button4" name = "button4"
    value = "Help" />
</p>
```

Figure 6.16 shows how the resulting form looks when rendered by a browser.

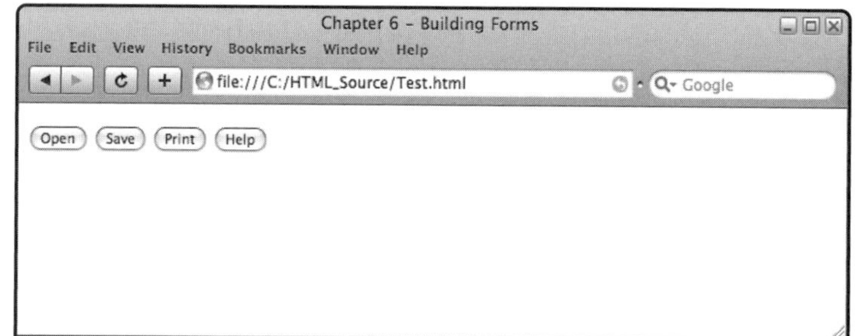

FIGURE 6.16

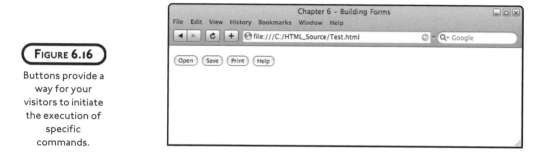

Buttons provide a way for your visitors to initiate the execution of specific commands.

Creating Image Controls

In addition to working with generic button controls, you also have the option of using graphics as a substitute for buttons. To set this up all you have to do is assign a `type` of `image` to an `input` element (`input type = "image"`). You can then use the input element's `src` attribute to specify the URL of the graphic to be displayed and the `alt` attribute to specify an alternative test string for non-graphic browsers.

In most cases, you will want to use graphics that are designed to look like buttons when working with this type of control. There are plenty of free websites that you can visit that will help you create graphic buttons for your web pages. (Check out www.buttongenerator.com as an example of one such site.)

The following example demonstrates how to add a series of three graphic button controls to a form.

If you want to re-create this example, you can download copies of the three graphics that are used from this book's companion web page (www.courseptr.com/downloads).

```
<p>
  <input type = "image" id = "image1" name = "image1"
    src = "start.gif" alt = "Click here to start" />
  <input type = "image" id = "image2" name = "image2"
```

```
    src = "quit.gif" alt = "Click here to quit" />
  <input type = "image" id = "image3" name = "image3"
    src = "help.gif" alt = "Click here for help" />
</p>
```

Figure 6.17 shows how the resulting form looks when this example is loaded into a web browser.

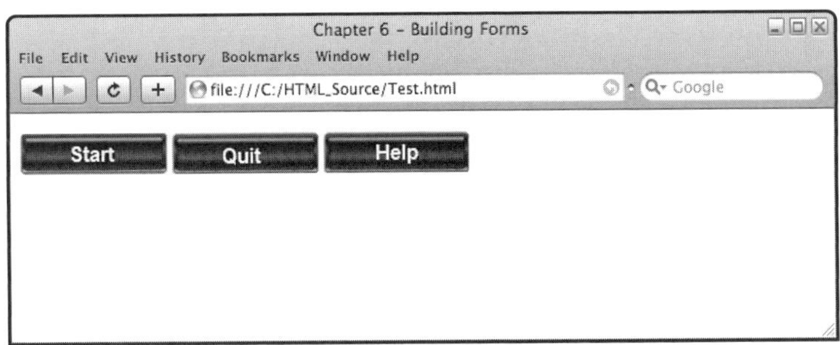

FIGURE 6.17

You can use any graphic you want when creating an image control.

Creating a Hidden Control

One type of form control that you never see is the hidden control. As its name implies, this control is kept hidden from the users. Though not often used, web developers sometimes use the control to store a small piece of information, like a calculated value, in the form. The data stored in a hidden control is passed along with the rest of the form's data when submitted to the form handler.

The following example demonstrates how to add a hidden control to a form. The contents of a hidden control can easily be manipulated by JavaScripts after the page loads.

```
<p>
  <input type = "hidden" id = "hidden" name = "hidden"
    value = "12/31/2012" />
</p>
```

Creating Submit and Reset Button Controls

In addition to creating generic button controls, as demonstrated earlier, you can add two specialized button controls to your forms. If you assign a `type` of `submit` (`input type = "submit"`) to an `input` element, you add a Submit button that when clicked, submits form data to the form handler. The form handler is set by adding the `action` attribute to the `form` element. You can assign the text to be displayed on the Submit button by assigning a text string to the `type` attribute's `value` attribute. If the `value` attribute is omitted, a default text string that says Submit Query or perhaps just Submit is displayed.

If you assign a type of reset (input type = "reset") to an input element, you add a reset button to your form that when clicked, resets and clears the contents of a form back to its initial values. You can assign the text string displayed on the Reset button using the input control's value attribute. If omitted, a default string of Reset is usually displayed. Few developers use the Reset button anymore because experience has shown that it is easily accidentally clicked, frustrating visitors when the data that they have provided unrepentantly disappears.

The following example demonstrates how to add a Submit and Reset button to a form.

```
<!DOCTYPE html PUBLIC "-//W3C//DTD XHTML 1.0 Strict//EN"
  "http://www.w3.org/TR/xhtml1/DTD/xhtml1-strict.dtd">

<html xmlns="http://www.w3.org/1999/xhtml" lang="en" xml:lang="en">

 <head>
   <meta http-equiv="Content-type" content="text/xhtml; charset=UTF-8" />
   <title>Chapter 6 - Building Forms</title>
 </head>

 <body>
   <form action = "/cgi-bin/processdata.cgi" method = "post">
     <p>
      <label for = "order_no">Enter your 12 character order number:</label>
      <input type = "text" id = "order_no" name = "order_no" size = "12"
        maxlength = "12" />
     </p>
     <p>
      <input type = "submit" id = "submit_button" name = "submit_button"
        value = "Retrieve Order Information" />
      <input type = "reset" id = "reset_button" name = "reset_button"
        value = "Reset Form" />
     </p>
   </form>
 </body>

</html>
```

Figure 6.18 shows how the form created in this example looks when rendered by the browser. Note that the default text displayed on the Submit and Reset controls has been modified in this example.

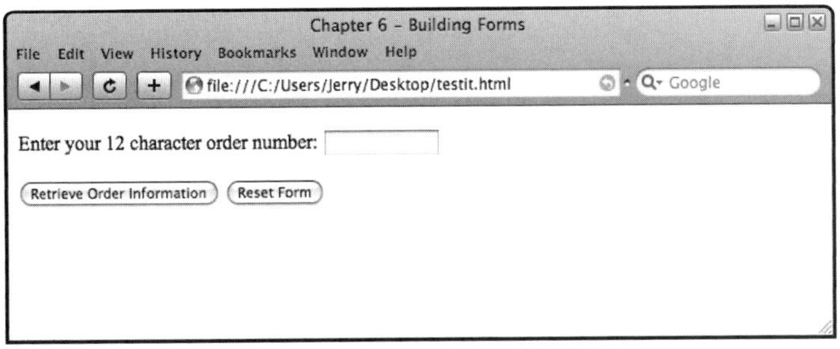

FIGURE 6.18
Controlling form submission and form reset.

Adding Buttons Using the button Element

As you have seen, you can use the `input` element to create all kinds of controls. (X)HTML also supports a number of other form controls, each of which is created using its own specific element. The `button` element is one such control. To work with the `button` element, you must specify a value of `button`, `submit`, or `reset` for its required type attribute. The `button` element works just like the controls created using the `input` element's `button`, `submit`, and `reset` types.

The following example demonstrates how to use the `button` element to add a button to a form.

```
<p>
  <button type = "button" id = "home_page" name = "home_page">
    Click here to return home
  </button>
</p>
```

Figure 6.19 shows how the resulting form looks when this example is loaded into a web browser.

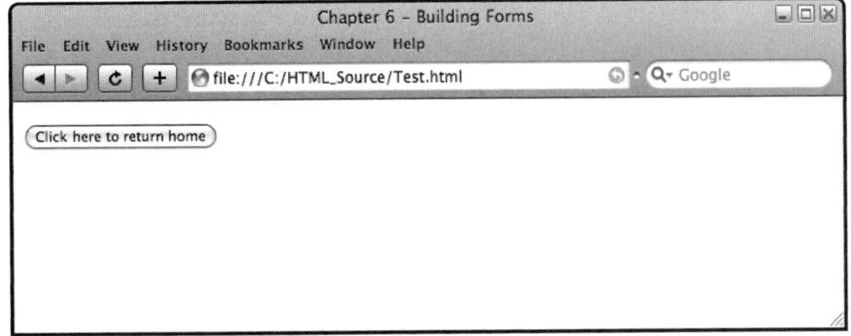

FIGURE 6.19
Defining a custom button control.

Adding a Multiline Text Field Using the textarea Element

Earlier you learned how to add a single-line text field to a form by assigning a type of `text` to the `input` element's `type` attribute. This control is perfect for collecting small amounts of text.

However, if you need to collect anything longer than a single line, you will want to use the textarea element to create a multiline text field instead. The size of the resulting control is established by assigning a numeric value to the element's rows and cols attributes. If the amount of text that visitors enter exceeds the size of the control, the browser will automatically display scroll bars.

The textarea control is a block-level element, with a starting and ending tag. The following example demonstrates how to add a textarea control to a form, making it 10 rows tall and 60 characters wide.

```
<p>
  <label for = "contact_us">Enter your message below:<br /></label>
  <textarea id = "contact_us" name = "contact_us" rows = "10" cols="60">
  </textarea>
</p>
```

In this example, the textarea control is displayed as a large multiline text field, as demonstrated in Figure 6.20.

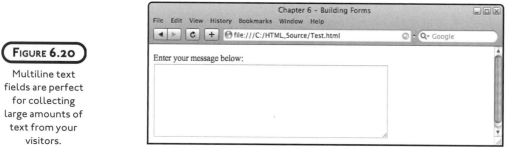

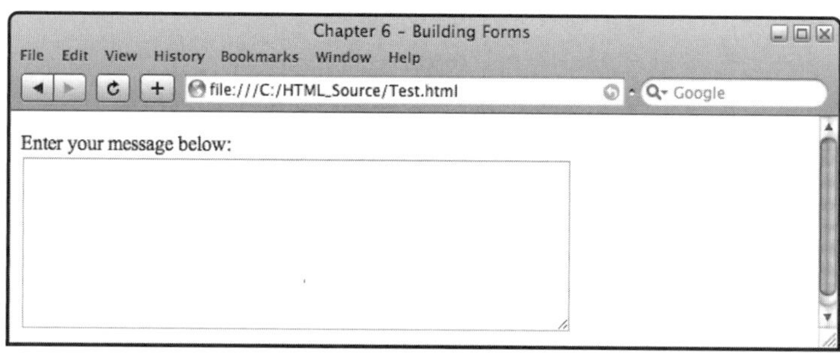

FIGURE 6.20

Multiline text fields are perfect for collecting large amounts of text from your visitors.

Even though it is a block-level control, the textarea element cannot contain other elements. It can remain empty or it can contain text. If you want, you can pre-populate a textarea control with text, as demonstrated here:

```
<p>
  <label for = "contact_us">Enter your message below:<br /></label>
  <textarea id = "contact_us" name = "contact_us" rows = "10" cols="60">
  To send us a message, overtype this text with your own text.
  </textarea>
</p>
```

Adding Drop-Down Lists to Forms

Another type of form control that you have no doubt come across many times on the internet is the drop-down control. You can add drop-down list controls of your own to your forms using the `select` and `option` elements. You can even group and label list contents using the `optgroup` element. Two forms of this control are supported. The first is a single-line drop-down list that expands when clicked to show a list of options from which the user can select. The second form of this control is a multiline control that displays a specified number of rows using the `select` element's optional `size` attribute.

Creating Drop-Down Lists Using the select Element

The first step in creating a drop-down list is to use the `select` element to establish the control, as shown here:

```
<p>
  <label for = "select_team">Select your team:</label>
  <select id = "select_team" name = "select_team">
  </select>
</p>
```

As shown in this example, by default the browser will render a single-line drop down list.

Adding Items to Drop-Down Lists Using the option Element

To create useful drop-down lists, you must populate the `select` element with items, which is done using instances of the `option` element. The `option` element is made up of an opening `<option>` and a closing `</option>` tag. The `option` element can only contain text. This text is displayed as an option in the drop-down list when displayed. Each option appears on a line by itself. The following example shows a form that consists of a single-line drop-down list that contains a listing of every team in the NBA.

```
<p>
  <select id = "select_team" name = "select_team">
    <option value = "" selected = "selected">- Pick a team -</option>
    <option>Celtics</option>
    <option>Nets</option>
    <option>Knicks</option>
    <option>76ers</option>
    <option>Raptors</option>
    <option>Mavericks</option>
    <option>Rockets</option>
    <option>Grizzlies</option>
```

```
    <option>Hornets</option>
    <option>Spurs</option>
    <option>Bulls</option>
    <option>Cavaliers</option>
    <option>Pistons</option>
    <option>Pacers</option>
    <option>Bucks</option>
    <option>Nuggets</option>
    <option>Timberwolves</option>
    <option>Trail Blazers</option>
    <option>City Thunder</option>
    <option>Jazz</option>
    <option>Hawks</option>
    <option>Bobcats</option>
    <option>Heat</option>
    <option>Magic</option>
    <option>Wizards</option>
    <option>Warriors</option>
    <option>Clippers</option>
    <option>Lakers</option>
    <option>Suns</option>
    <option>Kings</option>
  </select>
</p>
```

Figure 6.21 shows how the drop-down list looks when displayed by the browser.

As you can see in Figure 6.21, the drop-down list displays a small arrow button that when clicked, displays all of the options that have been added. To select an entry from the list, all the user has to do is click it. The selected option will be returned as the control's assigned value when passed to the form's handler. The list will then collapse and display the selected entry in a single field. As shown in Figure 6.21, the browser will automatically display a scroll bar in the event the list of options is too long to be displayed at one time. If you include the optional `width` attribute as part of the `select` element, you can pre-configure the width of the drop-down list.

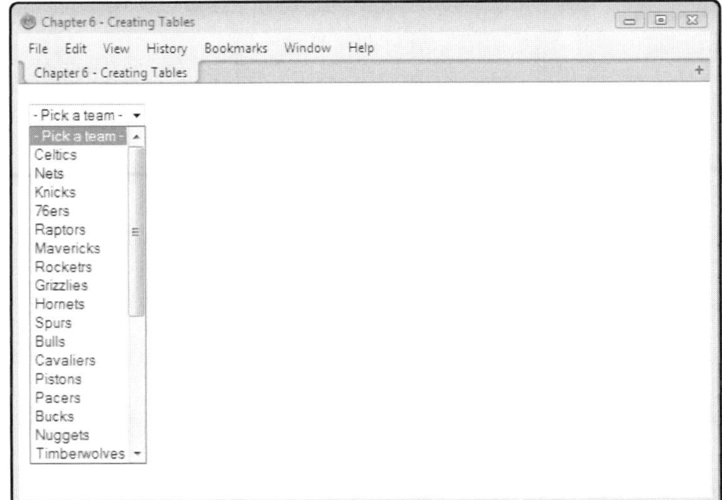

FIGURE 6.21

Drop-down lists let you present your visitors with a pre-determined list of options from which to choose.

By default, the list entry selected by the user is passed as part of the form's data to the form handler. If you want to preselect an option, just add the optional `selected` attribute to the desired option (`selected = "selected"`). Typically, the first option defined in a `select` element is made the default value as was the case in the previous example.

If you want, you can substitute the value that is returned when an option is selected by specifying an optional value attribute to each option element, as demonstrated here:

```
<option value = "Boston Celtics"> Boston</option>
<option value = "New Jersey Nets"> Nets</option>
<option value = "New York Knicks"> Knicks</option>
<option value = "Philadelphia 76ers"> 76ers</option>
```

When one of these four options is selected, the assigned value is returned in place of the text that the user saw.

Adding Categories to Drop-Down Lists Using the optgroup Element

Sometimes it helps to organize `option` elements into labeled groups. This is done by embedding `optgroup` elements within the `select` element. The `optgroup` element has a required `label` attribute that is displayed within the drop-down lists. Most browsers display the `optgroup` element label in bold or italics font. By placing instances of this element at different locations within this list, you can organize its `option` elements into groups, as demonstrated in the following example.

```
<p>
  <select id = "select_team" name = "select_team">
    <option value = "" selected = "selected">- Pick a team -</option>
    <optgroup label = "Atlantic">
    <option>Celtics</option>
    <option>Nets</option>
    <option>Knicks</option>
    <option>76ers</option>
    <option>Raptors</option>
    <optgroup label = "Southwest">
    <option>Mavericks</option>
    <option>Rockets</option>
    <option>Grizzlies</option>
    <option>Hornets</option>
    <option>Spurs</option>
    <optgroup label = "Central">
    <option>Bulls</option>
    <option>Cavaliers</option>
    <option>Pistons</option>
    <option>Pacers</option>
    <option>Bucks</option>
    <optgroup label = "Northwest">
    <option>Nuggets</option>
    <option>Timberwolves</option>
    <option>Trail Blazers</option>
    <option>City Thunder</option>
    <option>Jazz</option>
    <optgroup label = "Southeast">
    <option>Hawks</option>
    <option>Bobcats</option>
    <option>Heat</option>
    <option>Magic</option>
    <option>Wizards</option>
    <optgroup label = "Pacific">
    <option>Warriors</option>
    <option>Clippers</option>
    <option>Lakers</option>
    <option>Suns</option>
```

```
    <option>Kings</option>
  </select>
</p>
```

Figure 6.22 shows the resulting drop-down list that is created when this example is loaded by the browser. As you can see, each `optgroup` element is displayed as a heading in the resulting drop-down list. Note that the `optgroup` elements are strictly informational; they cannot be selected. Only `option` elements can be selected.

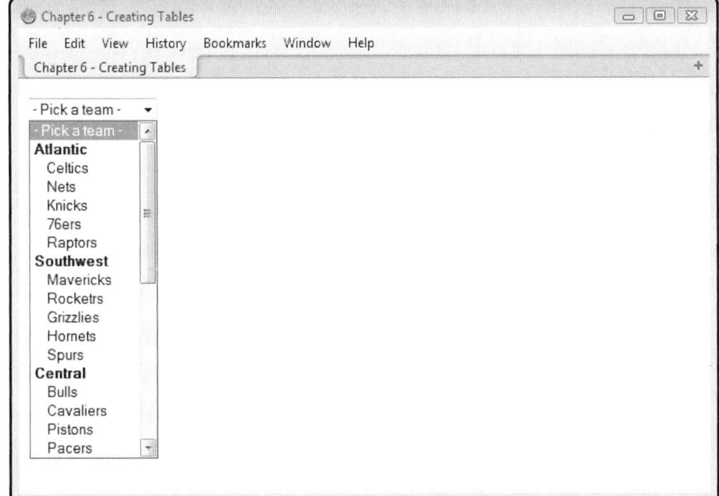

FIGURE 6.22

You can group drop-down list options to improve the organization of the list.

Creating a Multiline Drop-Down List

As previously stated, you can use the `select` element to create a multiline control. To do so, you must set the optional `multiple` attribute to `multiple` (`multiple = "multiple"`) as demonstrated in the following example. Multiline controls allow users to select one or more options by holding down the Shift, Control, or Command key while selecting different list options.

```
<p>
  <select id = "select_team" name = "select_team" size = "20"
    multiple = "Multiple">
    <optgroup label = "Atlantic">
    <option>Celtics</option>
    <option>Nets</option>
    <option>Knicks</option>
    <option>76ers</option>
    <option>Raptors</option>
```

```
    <optgroup label = "Southwest">
    <option>Mavericks</option>
    <option>Rockets</option>
    <option>Grizzlies</option>
    <option>Hornets</option>
    <option>Spurs</option>
    <optgroup label = "Central">
    <option>Bulls</option>
    <option>Cavaliers</option>
    <option>Pistons</option>
    <option>Pacers</option>
    <option>Bucks</option>
    <optgroup label = "Northwest">
    <option>Nuggets</option>
    <option>Timberwolves</option>
    <option>Trail Blazers</option>
    <option>City Thunder</option>
    <option>Jazz</option>
    <optgroup label = "Southeast">
    <option>Hawks</option>
    <option>Bobcats</option>
    <option>Heat</option>
    <option>Magic</option>
    <option>Wizards</option>
    <optgroup label = "Pacific">
    <option>Warriors</option>
    <option>Clippers</option>
    <option>Lakers</option>
    <option>Suns</option>
    <option>Kings</option>
  </select>
</p>
```

Here, a multiline drop-down list has been defined. Note that the `size` attribute has also been specified, setting the size of the control to 20 lines. Omitting the `size` attribute puts you at the mercy of the browser, resulting in inconsistent list presentation. Figure 6.23 shows the form that is displayed when this example is displayed.

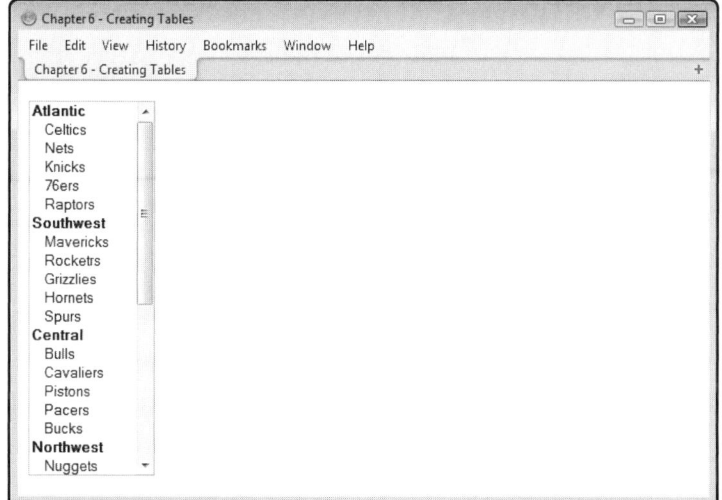

FIGURE 6.23

Multiline drop-down lists don't collapse down to a single line and support multiple selections.

REFINING FORM STRUCTURE

Like the rest of your (X)HTML pages, you need to ensure that your forms have a structure that is intuitive and structurally useful. You can use normal (X)HTML elements like headings and paragraphs to provide structure to your forms. In addition, (X)HTML provides several form-specific elements that provide additional structure.

Adding Descriptive Text to Controls Using the Label Element

As you have already seen numerous times in this chapter, you can use the `label` element to add descriptive text to forms. The `label` element is an inline element. As demonstrated in the following example, the `label` element is used to display text on forms.

```
<p>
  <label for = "username">Enter your name:</label>
  <input type = "text" id = "username" name = "username" size = "20"
    maxlength = "20" value = "Enter your name here" />
</p>
```

Here, a `label` element is used to supply a descriptive label for an element named `username`. The `label` element's optional `for` attribute is used to associate the `label` control with a specific element, based on that element's name.

Working with the fieldset Element

Another structure form control is the `fieldset` element, which is a block-level element that is used to group related collections of form elements into groups. By grouping controls together into logical collections, you can improve the readability of your forms. Grouping related form elements together in this manner makes them easier for your visitors to work with because it makes them more intuitive.

By default, `fieldset` elements display a thin border around all of the form controls that are embedded within them. To better understand the advantage of using the `fieldset` element to help add structure to your forms, take a look at this example.

```
<p>Pick your size:</p>
<fieldset>
  <input type = "checkbox" id = "checkbox1" name = "checkbox1"
    value = "Small" checked = "checked" />
  <label for = "checkbox1">Small</label><br />
  <input type = "checkbox" id = "checkbox2" name = "checkbox2"
    value = "Medium" />
  <label for = "checkbox2">Medium</label><br />
  <input type = "checkbox" id = "checkbox3" name = "checkbox3"
    value = "Large"/>
  <label for = "checkbox3">Large</label><br />
  <input type = "checkbox" id = "checkbox4" name = "checkbox4"
    value = "Extra Large" />
  <label for = "checkbox4">Extra Large</label>
</fieldset>

<p>Choose a color:</p>
<fieldset>
  <input type = "radio" id = "radio1" name = "radio"
    value = "Red" />
  <label for = "radio1">Red</label><br />
  <input type = "radio" id = "radio2" name = "radio"
    value = "Blue" checked = "checked" />
  <label for = "radio2">Blue</label><br />
  <input type = "radio" id = "radio3" name = "radio"
    value = "Green" />
  <label for = "radio3">Green</label><br />
</fieldset>
```

Here, a form has been visually organized into two logical sections using two `fieldset` elements. The first `fieldset` element was used to group a collection of four checkbox controls and the second `fieldset` element was used to group a set of three radio controls.

Figure 6.24 shows how the resulting form looks when the web page containing it is rendered by the browser.

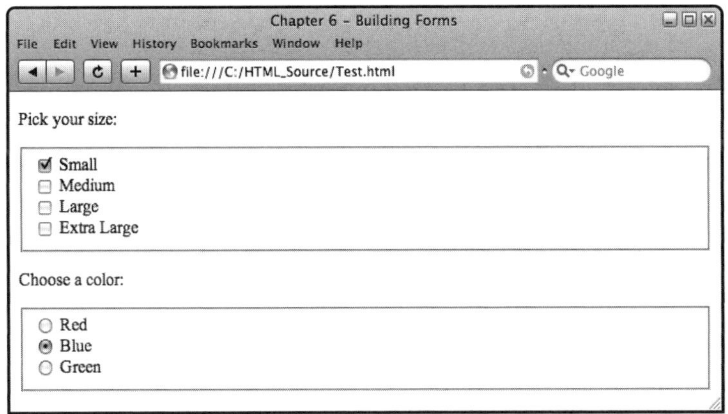

FIGURE 6.24

Using `fieldset` elements to group collections of controls.

You can make your `fieldset` elements even more useful if you include a `legend` element when working with them. A `legend` element allows you to specify a text string that is displayed as a special type of heading at the top of the `fieldset` element. Most browsers place the text specified by the `legend` element in the upper-left corner of the fieldset, embedding it within the `fieldset` element's border. When used, the `legend` element must be embedded within a `fieldset` element, usually as its first statement.

As an example of the impact that the `legend` element has on a `fieldset`, look at the following example.

```
<fieldset>
  <legend>Pick your size:</legend>
  <input type = "checkbox" id = "checkbox1" name = "checkbox1"
    value = "Small" checked = "checked" />
  <label for = "checkbox1">Small</label><br />
  <input type = "checkbox" id = "checkbox2" name = "checkbox2"
    value = "Medium" />
  <label for = "checkbox2">Medium</label><br />
  <input type = "checkbox" id = "checkbox3" name = "checkbox3"
    value = "Large"/>
```

```
  <label for = "checkbox3">Large</label><br />
  <input type = "checkbox" id = "checkbox4" name = "checkbox4"
    value = "Extra Large" />
  <label for = "checkbox4">Extra Large</label>
</fieldset>

<fieldset>
  <legend>Choose a color:</legend>
  <input type = "radio" id = "radio1" name = "radio"
    value = "Red" />
  <label for = "radio1">Red</label><br />
  <input type = "radio" id = "radio2" name = "radio"
    value = "Blue" checked = "checked" />
  <label for = "radio2">Blue</label><br />
  <input type = "radio" id = "radio3" name = "radio"
    value = "Green" />
  <label for = "radio3">Green</label><br />
</fieldset>
```

By adding a `legend` element to a `fieldset` element, you can strengthen the structure of the `fieldset` element's contents. Figure 6.25 shows how the form created by the previous examples will look when rendered by the browser.

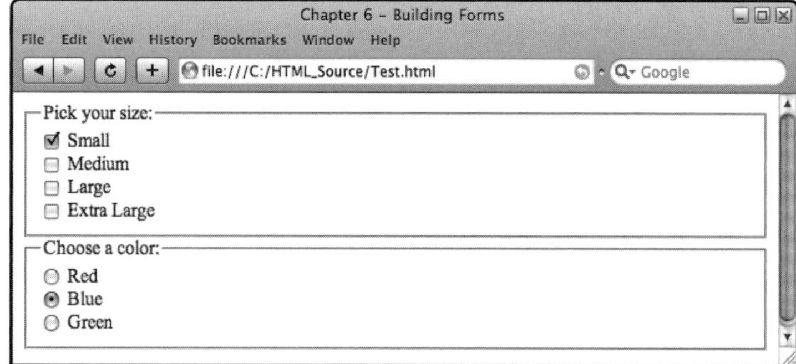

FIGURE 6.25

Using the `legend` element to add a caption to a `fieldset`.

A Complete Form Example

To help tie together everything that you have learned in this chapter about working with forms, let's look at a more complete example of a form that is made up of a number of different elements.

```
<!DOCTYPE html PUBLIC "-//W3C//DTD XHTML 1.0 Strict//EN"
  "http://www.w3.org/TR/xhtml1/DTD/xhtml1-strict.dtd">

<html xmlns="http://www.w3.org/1999/xhtml" lang="en" xml:lang="en">

  <head>
    <meta http-equiv="Content-type" content="text/xhtml; charset=UTF-8" />
    <title>Chapter 6 - Building Forms</title>
  </head>

  <body>

    <h1>Joe's Custom T-Shirts</h1>

    <form action = "/cgi-bin/processdata.cgi" method = "post">

      <p>
        <label for = "name">Last name: (8 character max.)</label>
        <input type = "text" id = "name" name = "name" size = "8"
          maxlength = "8" />
      </p>

      <p>
        <label for = "number">Jersey number: (2 character max.)</label>
        <input type = "text" id = "number" name = "number" size = "2"
          maxlength = "2" />
      </p>

      <fieldset>
        <legend>Pick your size:</legend>
        <input type = "checkbox" id = "checkbox1" name = "checkbox1"
          value = "Small" checked = "checked" />
        <label for = "checkbox1">Small</label><br />
        <input type = "checkbox" id = "checkbox2" name = "checkbox2"
          value = "Medium" />
        <label for = "checkbox2">Medium</label><br />
        <input type = "checkbox" id = "checkbox3" name = "checkbox3"
          value = "Large"/>
```

```
      <label for = "checkbox3">Large</label><br />
      <input type = "checkbox" id = "checkbox4" name = "checkbox4"
        value = "Extra Large" />
      <label for = "checkbox4">Extra Large</label>
    </fieldset>

    <fieldset>
      <legend>Choose a color:</legend>
      <input type = "radio" id = "radio1" name = "radio"
        value = "Red" />
      <label for = "radio1">Red</label><br />
      <input type = "radio" id = "radio2" name = "radio"
        value = "Blue" checked = "checked" />
      <label for = "radio2">Blue</label><br />
      <input type = "radio" id = "radio3" name = "radio"
        value = "Green" />
      <label for = "radio3">Green</label><br />
    </fieldset>

    <p>
      <input type = "submit" id = "submit_button" name = "submit_button"
        value = "Submit Order Information" />
      <input type = "reset" id = "reset_button" name = "reset_button"
        value = "Reset Form" />
    </p>
  </form>

 </body>

</html>
```

In this example, a form is defined that will submit the data it collects to a program running on the web server using the `form` method's `post` method. The first four `form` elements on the page are a pair of labels and text controls. The first text control is named `name` and configured to be eight characters long and to accept eight characters of input. The second text control is named `number` and is set to a size and length of two characters. Note that both pairs of controls are embedded within their own paragraphs, keeping them separate and meeting XHTML Strict 1.0's requirement that all form elements be placed within block-level elements.

Next, a set of five checkbox controls is displayed. Note that a `fieldset` control has been used to visually group the checkbox controls together. A `legend` element has been added to assign it a descriptive header. A `label` element has been included for each checkbox control, providing a descriptive text string that identifies each checkbox's value. Also, note that the first of the four checkbox controls has been pre-selected.

A second `fieldset` is then used to group four radio controls. Again, a `legend` element has been specified. Note that the second radio button has been selected. The last two controls on the form are a Submit and a Reset button. Figure 6.26 shows how this table looks when rendered by the browser.

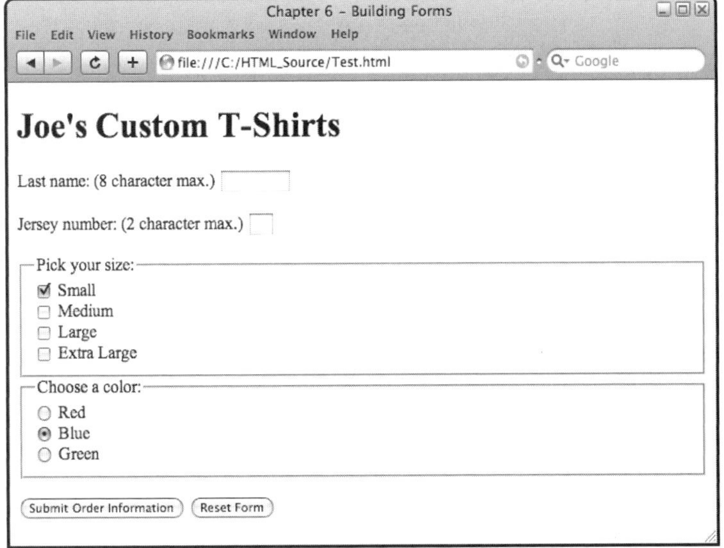

FIGURE 6.26

An example of a complete form made up of multiple form controls.

ADVICE ON GOOD FORM DESIGN

As you have seen, there is a lot to form design. You have to know how to work with a number of different types of elements and element attributes. In addition to creating forms that are functionally correct, you also need to consider the structural and organizational aspects of your forms. Specifically, you need to make sure that the forms you create are well organized, easy to fill out, and as intuitive as you can make them.

To design forms that are really useful and easy for your visitors to understand, their layout should provide a clear and intuitive path that is easy for your visitors to scan and understand without a lot of work. It is often a good idea to provide your visitors with instructions on how to fill out your forms, letting them know what information they will need to have on hand to fill out your form and what you will do with the information they provide to you. If you do not want to crowd the web page with instructional text, you might instead display a link at the top of your form to a help page that explains how to complete the form.

As you develop your forms, make sure you always provide labels for every control. Also, include visual markers where appropriate. Be explicit regarding information that you want to collect and the format you need it in. For example, if you are using a text field to collect a person's birth date and you want that information entered using a format of mm/dd/yy, then make sure the control's label tells the user what format to use when keying in their birth date.

Always keep an eye on the overall layout of your forms. Present form controls in a logical matter. Group related controls together and when appropriate take advantage of fieldsets as a means of grouping related elements together. This can help make your forms easier for your visitors to scan. It also helps to point out any relationships between related controls.

If your forms have required fields, mark them as such so that your visitors know precisely what information they need to provide. One way of doing this is to place an asterisk beside these fields. Alternatively, you might make the labels for these fields bold or display them in a different color.

Always keep in mind that filling out large and complex forms is not a lot of fun. This can discourage your visitors. As a general rule, do your best to keep things short and simple. Whenever possible, streamline your forms by eliminating the collection of unnecessary optional data. Also, when possible, provide default values for your controls. If your visitors need to change these values, they can; otherwise, they can simply accept these values and move along.

If you have added text controls to your form and limited the amount of text they can contain using the `maxlength` attribute, make sure that you let your visitors know about the limitation. If your website makes use of multiple forms, be consistent in their design and presentation.

Once you have learned how to work with JavaScript, covered in Chapter 9, make sure that you include scripts in your web page that validate form content and user feedback when errors are found. Also, consider providing examples of valid input when informing a visitor that invalid input has been collected in one of the form's controls.

Back to the Number Guessing Game

All right, now it is time to return your attention to this chapter's project, the Number Guessing Game. The object of this game is to guess a randomly generated secret number in as few guesses as possible. To submit guesses, the player must click on one of ten radio buttons, representing guesses of 1 to 10. Once the player makes a selection, he must click on a button labeled Check Guess in order to signal the end of the current turn. The game will then process the player's input using a JavaScript and determine whether the player's guess was correct, too low, or too high.

Designing the Application

The development of this game will be performed in a number of steps, as outlined here:

1. Create a new XHTML document.
2. Outline the document's markup.
3. Develop the document's JavaScript.
4. Load and test the HTML page.

Step 1: Creating a New XHTML Document

As has been the case with all of the web projects that you have worked on up to this point in the book, the first step in the creation of this game project is to create a new text file. Do so using your preferred code or text editor, naming the file NumberGuess.html and storing it in the same folder as all of your other (X)HTML projects.

Step 2: Developing the Document's Markup

The next step in the creation of the Number Guessing Game is to assemble the web document's markup. Create these statements by adding the following elements to the NumberGuess.html file.

```
<!DOCTYPE html PUBLIC "-//W3C//DTD XHTML 1.0 Strict//EN"
  "http://www.w3.org/TR/xhtml1/DTD/xhtml1-strict.dtd">

<html xmlns="http://www.w3.org/1999/xhtml" lang="en" xml:lang="en">

  <head>

    <meta http-equiv="Content-type" content="text/xhtml; charset=UTF-8" />
    <title>Number Guessing Game</title>
  </head>

  <body>

  </body>

</html>
```

As you can see, all of the statements needed to create a well-formed XHTML page have been provided, including the web page's `meta` and `title` elements. Once you have completed this task, it's time to add the statements representing the document's content, which consists of a heading, followed by a paragraph, and then a form. To do so, embed the following statements into the document's `body` section.

```
<h1>The Number Guessing Game</h1>
<p>Try to guess the secret number in as few guesses as possible</p>

<form action = "NumberGuess.html">

  <p>Select Number:</p>
    <input type = "radio" id = "radio1" name = "radio" value = "1" />
    <label for = "radio1">1</label><br />

    <input type = "radio" id = "radio2" name = "radio" value = "2" />
    <label for = "radio2">2</label><br />

    <input type = "radio" id = "radio3" name = "radio" value = "3"/>
    <label for = "radio3">3<label><br />

    <input type = "radio" id = "radio4" name = "radio" value = "4" />
    <label for = "radio4">4</label><br />

    <input type = "radio" id = "radio5" name = "radio" value = "5" />
    <label for = "radio5">5</label><br />

    <input type = "radio" id = "radio6" name = "radio" value = "6" />
    <label for = "radio6">6</label><br />

    <input type = "radio" id = "radio7" name = "radio" value = "7" />
    <label for = "radio7">7</label><br />

    <input type = "radio" id = "radio8" name = "radio" value = "8" />
    <label for = "radio8">8</label><br />

    <input type = "radio" id = "radio9" name = "radio" value = "9" />
    <label for = "radio9">9</label><br />
```

```
      <input type = "radio" id = "radio10" name = "radio" value = "10" />
      <label for = "radio10">10</label>
    </p>
    <p>
      <button type = "button" name = "validate" onclick = "check_guess()">
        Check Guess
      </button>
    </p>

</form>
```

The first two statements display a heading and a paragraph that explains the rules for playing the game. Next, a form named guess_form is created. The data collected by this form will remain local and will not be passed on to a web server for further processing. As a result, the form elements required action attribute has been set to NumberGuess.html and the optional method attribute has been omitted.

The form itself is made up of a series of radio buttons, created using 10 pairs of input and label elements. Each input element is assigned a numeric value from 1 to 10, representing the range of guesses allowed by the game. The label element that follows each input element displays the radio control's assigned value for the player to see.

The last element that makes up the form is created using a button element. This creates a button control labeled Check Guess. When clicked, a JavaScript function named check_guess(), located in a script in the document's head section, is executed.

When called, the check_guess() function will process the contents of the form and determine whether the player has won the game or has entered a guess that is too high or too low. You will learn all about JavaScript functions and their execution in Chapter 9.

Step 3: Developing the Document's Script

The Number Guessing Game includes a JavaScript that needs to be located in the document's head section. The statements that make up this script, shown below, should be embedded in the head section, immediately following the document's title element.

```
<script type = "text/javascript">
<!-- Start hiding JavaScript statements

  var randomNo = 0;
  var player_choice;
```

```
  randomNo = 1 + Math.random() * 9; //Create random number from 1-10
  randomNo = Math.round(randomNo);  //Convert number to an integer

  function check_guess() {

    var radioButtons = document.getElementsByName('radio');
    for (i = 0; i < 10; i++) {
      if (radioButtons[i].checked == true) {
        player_choice = radioButtons[i].value

        //Analyze the player's guess
        if (player_choice == randomNo) {  //See if the guess is correct

          window.alert("Correct! Reload the web page to play again.");
        } else {
          if (player_choice > randomNo) { //See if the guess is high
            window.alert("Incorrect. Your guess was too high.");
          } else {                  //See if the player's guess is low
            window.alert("Incorrect. Your guess was too low.");
          }
        }

      }
    }

  }

// End hiding JavaScript statements -->
</script>
```

At a high level, what this script does is declare a pair of variables that will be used to store both the game's randomly generated number as well as the player's guesses. Next, a random number between 1 and 10 is generated and assigned to the `randomNo` variable. The rest of the JavaScript consists of a custom function that is executed each time the player clicks on the game's Check Guess button. When executed, this function retrieves the player's choice and compares it to the game's random number. If the two values match, the player wins and the game ends. Otherwise, a message is displayed in a popup dialog window that lets the player know whether the guess was too low or too high.

The Finished HTML Document

At this point, your copy of the GuessNumber.html document should be complete. To make sure that you have everything in order, look at the following example, which shows what the finished document should look like.

```
<!DOCTYPE html PUBLIC "-//W3C//DTD XHTML 1.0 Strict//EN"
  "http://www.w3.org/TR/xhtml1/DTD/xhtml1-strict.dtd">

<html xmlns="http://www.w3.org/1999/xhtml" lang="en" xml:lang="en">

  <head>
    <meta http-equiv="Content-type" content="text/xhtml; charset=UTF-8" />
    <title>Number Guessing Game</title>

    <script type = "text/javascript">
    <!-- Start hiding JavaScript statements

      var randomNo = 0;
      var player_choice;

      randomNo = 1 + Math.random() * 9; //Create random number from 1-10
      randomNo = Math.round(randomNo);  //Convert number to an integer

      function check_guess() {

        for (i = 0; i < document.guess_form.radio.length; i++) {
          if (document.guess_form.radio[i].checked == true) {
            player_choice = document.guess_form.radio[i].value;

            //Analyze the player's guess
            if (player_choice == randomNo) {  //See if the guess is correct

              window.alert("Correct! Reload the web page to play again.");
            } else {
              if (player_choice > randomNo) { //See if the guess is high
                window.alert("Incorrect. Your guess was too high.");
              } else {                 //See if the player's guess is low
                window.alert("Incorrect. Your guess was too low.");
```

```
            }
          }

        }
      }

      if (document.guess_form.radio.value == "5") {
        window.alert("Yup!");
      }

    }

  // End hiding JavaScript statements -->
  </script>

</head>

<body>

  <h1>The Number Guessing Game</h1>
  <p>Try to guess the secret number in as few guesses as possible</p>

  <form name = "guess_form" action = "NumberGuess">

    <p>Select Number:</p>

      <input type = "radio" id = "radio1" name = "radio"
      value = "1" />
      <label for = "radio1">1</label><br />

       <input type = "radio" id = "radio2" name = "radio"
      value = "2" />
      <label for = "radio2">2</label><br />

      <input type = "radio" id = "radio3" name = "radio"
      value = "3"/>
      <label for = "radio3">3<label><br />
```

```
    <input type = "radio" id = "radio4" name = "radio"
    value = "4" />
    <label for = "radio4">4</label><br />

    <input type = "radio" id = "radio5" name = "radio"
    value = "5" />
    <label for = "radio5">5</label><br />

    <input type = "radio" id = "radio6" name = "radio"
    value = "6" />
    <label for = "radio6">6</label><br />

    <input type = "radio" id = "radio7" name = "radio"
    value = "7" />
    <label for = "radio7">7</label><br />

    <input type = "radio" id = "radio8" name = "radio"
    value = "8" />
    <label for = "radio8">8</label><br />

    <input type = "radio" id = "radio9" name = "radio"
    value = "9" />
    <label for = "radio9">9</label><br />

    <input type = "radio" id = "radio10" name = "radio"
    value = "10" />
    <label for = "radio10">10</label>
  </p>

  <p>
    <button type = "button" name = "validate" onclick = "check_guess()">
      Check Guess
    </button>
  </p>

</form>
```

```
  </body>

</html>
```

Step 4: Loading and Testing the Number Guessing Game

Once you are ready, load your new game into your web browser and see how things have turned out. To do so, open your browser and execute the following procedure.

1. Click on File > Open File. A standard file open dialog will appear.
2. Navigate to the folder where you stored the web page and select it.
3. Click on the Open button. The browser will load and render our XHTML document, allowing game play to begin.

Assuming that everything works as expected, load your XHTML document using one or two other browsers in order to ensure that its content displays consistently.

Summary

This chapter showed you how to create and work with tables and forms. Using the information and examples provided, you should be able to display any type of tabular data and collect visitor input using all kinds of form controls, including text, password, multiline text, drop-down list, radio, checkbox, and different types of buttons controls. In addition, this chapter showed you how to add borders, row, and column headers to your tables and even to merge multiple cells together in order to create larger cells. You also learned how to use fieldsets to group form controls together into logical collections in order to make your forms easier to use. On top of all this, you learned how to create the Number Guessing Game.

Challenges

1. **As currently designed, the Number Guessing Game provides the player with a base minimum of instructions. Consider modifying the game to provide the player with additional information on how to play.**
2. **Consider making the game more challenging by expanding the range of numbers from 1 to 10 to 1 to 20 or even higher.**

Part III

Cascading Style Sheets

An Introduction to Cascading Style Sheets

Up to this point in the book, you have relied on the browser to determine how to present the content that makes up your (X)HTML documents. In this chapter you will learn how to exercise greater control over how browsers render document content through the application of Cascading Style Sheets (CSS). CSS allows you to separate presentation from content, making both stronger as a result. You can use it to do things like change foreground and background colors and specify font type and color. You can use it to make content visible and invisible, control content placement, and to move things around the browser window. In short, CSS allows detailed control over the way your content in displayed within your visitor's browsers.

Specifically, you will learn:

- The basics of CSS syntax
- The different ways that CSS can be integrated into your web documents
- About CSS specificity and how CSS's cascading rules are applied
- How to use CSS to modify the presentation of text
- How to use CSS to modify color and backgrounds

Project Preview: The Rock, Paper, Scissors Game

In this chapter's web project, you will learn how to create a new web game named Rock, Paper, Scissors. This game pits the player against the computer as both attempt to outguess one another. As Figure 7.1 shows, the player enters moves by clicking on one of two graphic buttons.

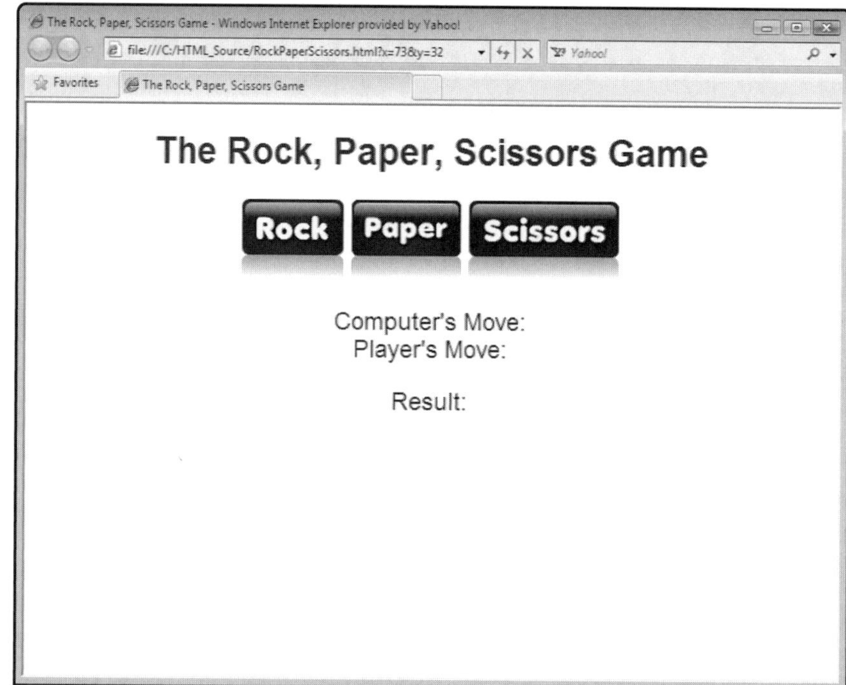

Figure 7.1
The Rock, Paper, Scissors game when first loaded into the browser.

As soon as the player selects a move, the game generates a random move on behalf of the computer. The game analyzes the player and computer's guesses to determine the results of the game. The winner is determined based on the following rules.

- Rock crushes scissors
- Paper covers rock
- Scissors cut paper
- Matching moves result in a tie

Figure 7.2 shows the result of a typical round of play. As you can see, in this example the player's move of Rock has beaten the computer's move of Scissors.

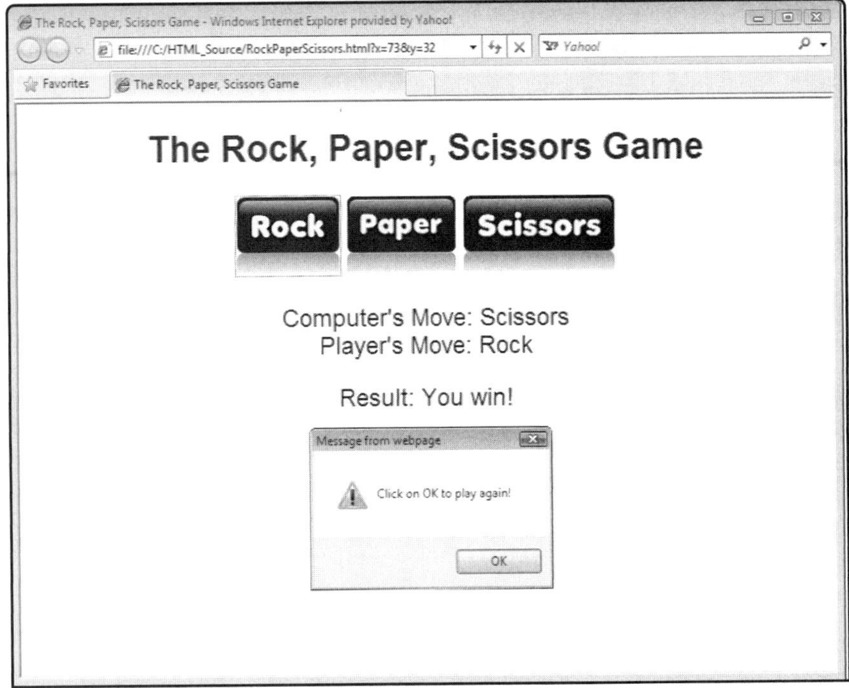

FIGURE 7.2

A popup dialog window is displayed at the end of each round of play.

A popup dialog window is displayed along with the game's results. To play again, the player must click on this OK button. Rather than rely on the browser to determine how to best render the game's content, this application makes use of an external style sheet that specifies font size and color of its heading and paragraph elements and manages the placement of the game's graphics.

INTRODUCING CSS

Cascading Style Sheets or *CSS* is a stylesheet programming language used to describe the way that content written in a markup language is presented. Web developers use CSS to control and influence the presentation of HTML and (X)HTML documents. However, CSS can be used in conjunction with any kind of XML document. CSS provides numerous advantages, including:

- The separation of content and presentation
- The ability to apply style consistently across your web pages
- Reduction of network bandwidth, resulting in pages that load and render more quickly

Prior to the introduction of CSS, (X)HTML presentation could only be influenced using attributes that were added to (X)HTML elements. Unfortunately, this meant intermixing content and presentation, making web documents longer, more complex, and more difficult to maintain. The arrival of CSS provided web developers with the ability to separate content from presentation, simplifying the development and maintenance of both, which of course, resulted in both aspects getting stronger. Instead of having to repeatedly embed presentation attributes in elements strewn repeatedly through web pages, CSS allowed web developers to develop style sheets and to apply the style rules in those sheets to one or more web pages. Thanks to CSS, you could specify and control the presentation of all of the web pages for an entire website using a single style sheet if you wanted. You could later give the entire website a face-lift by modifying only its style sheet. Needless to say, CSS rocks!

As you will learn in this chapter, CSS includes a prioritization scheme that determines how style rules are applied in the event one or more of them matches the same element. As a result of these prioritization rules, CSS rules *cascade* downward to document elements in a predictable manner. CSS rules can be created to control presentation aspects like font type, size, and color as well as background styles, borders, and the content alignment. You can use it to change the way your tables and forms look and to control the presentation of graphics.

The CSS 1.0 specification was published in December 1996. It got off to a somewhat slow start before finally working its way into mainstream web development. CSS 2.0 was published in May 1998 but has yet to be fully supported by modern web browsers. CSS 3.0 is currently under development. As is the case with HTML and XHTML, the W3C is responsible for the ongoing development of CSS.

Due to lack of universal browser support for CSS 2.0, this book's focus in on CSS 1.0 and it is strongly recommended that you do so as well.

CSS is an integral part of web development. As such, both this chapter and the next are dedicated to explaining and demonstrating how to work with it. However, CSS is its own language, with its own unique syntax and worthy of coverage in its own book. Complete coverage of every CSS property and their range of values exceed the space available in this book. Instead, this book's focus is on providing you with a good foundation with sufficient examples to get you well on your way to mastering CSS. To view the full range of CSS properties, visit http://www.w3schools.com/CSS/css_reference.asp, as shown in Figure 7.3.

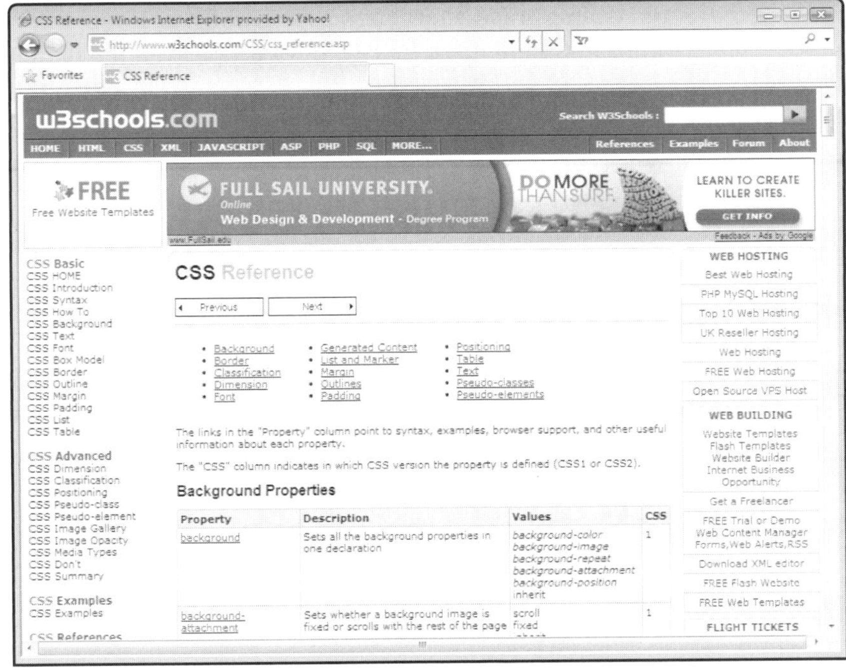

FIGURE 7.3

A complete CSS reference is available online.

Understanding the Basics of CSS Syntax

CSS has a simple syntax. It uses English keywords to specify the styles and their values. There are several ways that CSS can be used, including inline styles, internal style sheets, and external style sheets. This chapter will show you how to work with all three options. CSS style sheets consist of lists of *rules*. CSS rules are roughly analogous to (X)HTML elements. As demonstrated in Figure 7.4, CSS rules are made up of selectors and a declaration block.

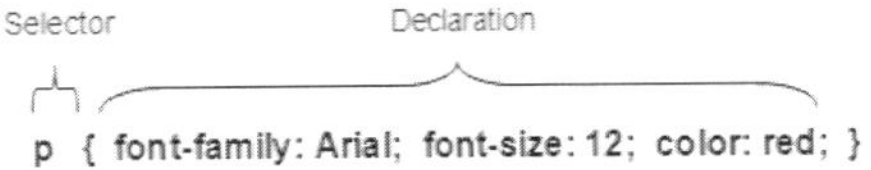

FIGURE 7.4

A CSS rule can have one or more selectors and a declaration block.

Style rules can be written in order to affect the presentation of a specific (X)HTML element or multiple elements. Rules specify the elements they affect through the selector. *Selectors* are used to identify the (X)HTML elements to which style rules are applied. You can specify more than one selector in a rule as long as you separate each one by a comma. The *declaration block* is made up of one or more declarations, allowing you to manipulate more than one aspect of an element's presentation at a time. *Declarations* are embedded inside an opening

{ character and a closing } character. These brace characters are roughly analogous to (X) HTML's ≤ and ≥ characters. Declarations are made up of one or more property/value pairs, as outlined in Figure 7.5.

FIGURE 7.5

Declarations are made up of one or more property/value pairs.

Property Value

```
p { font-family: Arial; font-size: 12; color: red; }
```

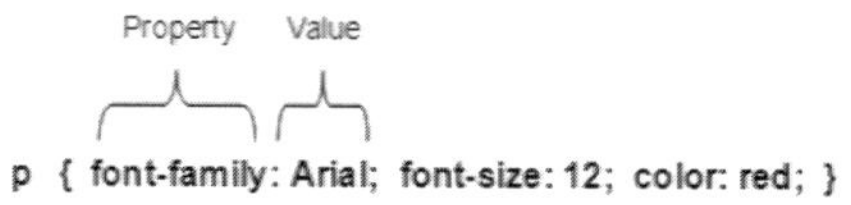

Properties identify the presentation aspect of an element that a rule is modifying. Each declaration property is separated from its corresponding value by a colon. A *value* is a setting that is applied to the specified element(s). In addition, each property/value pair is separated from other property/value pairs by a semicolon. If a declaration has only one property/value pair, you have the option of omitting the semicolon. In addition, you can also leave off the semicolon from the last property/value pair that makes up a declaration. Some properties accept multiple values separated from each other by blank spaces.

Crafting Rule Selectors

In order to effectively use CSS to control the presentation of content on your web pages, you have to understand the concept of specificity. Specificity is a term used to identify the scope that a CSS style rule has within a document (e.g., how many elements the rule affects). When you define a CSS style rule, its selector defines its specificity. CSS supports a wide range of selectors, each with different levels of specificity.

Universal

A universal selector is a selector that matches every element found in a web document. To define a universal selector, you must use the * (wild card) character, as demonstrated here:

```
* {color: red;}
```

When executed, this rule will display all text on the web document in red. Rules defined using a universal selector have the least amount of specificity.

Element

An element selector is one that matches all instances of a given element within a web document, as demonstrated here:

```
p { color: blue;}
```

This rule will display the text of all paragraphs on the web document in blue. Although element selectors have greater specificity than universal selectors, they are still not very specific.

Class

A class selector is one that matches any elements assigned a specified class name attribute. As discussed in Chapter 2, any number of elements on a web document can be assigned to the same class. Though only moderately specific, the class selector is more specific than the element class.

```
.total {color: green;}
```

Note that to specify a class as a selector, you must precede the class name with a . character.

Pseudo Class

A pseudo class selector is used to match elements that exist in a specific state. In terms of specificity, pseudo class selectors are roughly equivalent to class selectors. Only five types of pseudo classes are supported. These classes are:

- :link
- :visited
- :active
- :hover
- :focus

As you can see, all pseudo classes begin with the : character followed by one of five keywords that represent the status of document links. The following rule demonstrates how to work with pseudo class selectors.

```
:hover {color: purple;}
```

This CSS style rule instructs the browser to display in purple any link on the web page when the mouse pointer is hovered over it.

ID

An ID selector is one that matches a unique element based on its assigned attribute ID. Since each element's ID, when assigned, must be unique within a web document, an ID selector is very specific. To reference an ID in a selector, you must precede the ID with the # character, as demonstrated here:

```
#score {color: blue;}
```

When processed, this CSS style rule will display in blue text the element that has been assigned an ID attribute of `score`.

Specifying More Complex Selectors

In addition to specifying individual selectors, CSS lets you create a number of more granular selectors by combining, grouping, and supporting descendant selectors. As demonstrated here, two or more selectors can be combined to create a more complex selector.

```
h1.main {color: blue;}
```

Here, a selector has been defined that matches all level 1 headers that are assigned to the `.main` class.

You can also create more complex selectors by adding together two or more comma-separated selectors, as demonstrated here:

```
h1, h2, h3 {color: green;}
```

Here, all level 1, 2, and 3 headings will be displayed as green text.

Another type of complex selector, referred to as a descendant selector, can be defined by using two or more selectors separated by blank spaces. This type of selector matches up against elements that have a specified contextual relationship to one another, as demonstrated here:

```
.score strong {color: red;}
```

Here, any strong elements located within an element assigned to the `score` class are displayed in red.

Integrating CSS into Your HTML Pages

To use CSS, you need a means of integrating CSS into your web documents. (X)HTML provides several different ways of doing so, as outlined here:

- **Inline Styles.** Styles embedded within (X)HTML element tags.
- **Embedded Style Sheets.** Style rules embedded within the `head` section of your (X)HTML pages.
- **External Style Sheets.** Style rules stored in external files and linked back to your (X) HTML pages.

Using Inline Styles

To use inline styles, you embed CSS styles inside your (X)HTML element tags. To do so, add an optional `style` attribute to each element whose presentation you want to modify. Inline styles are not constructed as CSS rules. They do not make use of selectors. Instead, only declaration blocks are included in inline styles. For example, the following statements add an inline style to a paragraph tag, instructing the browser to display the color of the element's text in `green`.

```
<p style = "color: green";>Hello World!<p>
```

If needed, you can include as many property/value pairs in your declaration as you want. Just remember to keep each one separated by a semicolon, as demonstrated here:

```
<p style = "font-size: 9; color: red; text-align: center;">Hello World!</p>
```

As a general rule, you will want to avoid using inline styles and to defer to using external style sheets or perhaps embedded style sheets. Inline styles require that you intermix presentation with your (X)HTML markup. This eliminates one of CSS's primary advantages: the ability to separate presentation from content and structure. Another challenge in working with inline styles is that since they are applied only to individual elements, you must repeatedly use them on similar types of elements to ensure that your web page has a consistent presentation. This eliminates another advantage of CSS, the ability to present from a single location. Worse still, what if you later change your mind about how things work and want to give your (X)HTML documents a face-lift? You'd have to revisit every element in every page to make those changes. Smart web developers avoid this mistake, only using inline elements in very specific situations when it is necessary to ensure that a particular element's presentation is fine-tuned.

Managing Individual Documents with Embedded Style Sheets

While working with inline styles may be okay for a small (X)HTML document, it is not a good idea to use it with documents whose presentation requires a lot of detailed customization. For this type of situation, a much better option is the use of embedded style sheets. Embedded style sheets help to make it easier to apply a consistent look and feel to your web document by enabling you to globally apply style rules to all matching elements.

To add an embedded style sheet to a web page, you must work with the `style` element. The `style` element is a block-level element that must be placed in a document's `head` section, which helps to keep presentation separate from document structure. Any CSS rules placed within the `style` element are then globally applied to any matching elements found throughout the document.

As an example of the effects of adding an embedded style sheet to an (X)HTML document, look at the following example.

```
<!DOCTYPE html PUBLIC "-//W3C//DTD XHTML 1.0 Strict//EN"
  "http://www.w3.org/TR/xhtml1/DTD/xhtml1-strict.dtd">

<html xmlns="http://www.w3.org/1999/xhtml" lang="en" xml:lang="en">

  <head>
    <meta http-equiv="Content-type" content="text/xhtml; charset=UTF-8" />
    <title>Chapter 7 - Sample Web Page</title>
  </head>

  <body>
    <h1>This heading should be purple, underlined, and centered</h1>
    <p>This paragraph should be bold, italic, and blue.</p>
    <h2>This heading should be orange on a black background and centered</h2>
    <p id="p1">This paragraph should be red, bold, and italic.</p>

  </body>

</html>
```

As you can see, this document consists only of markup and a little content and relies on the browser to handle the document's presentation. Every web browser has its own built-in default browser style sheet. Figure 7.6 shows the resulting web page that is rendered when this document is loaded into the browser.

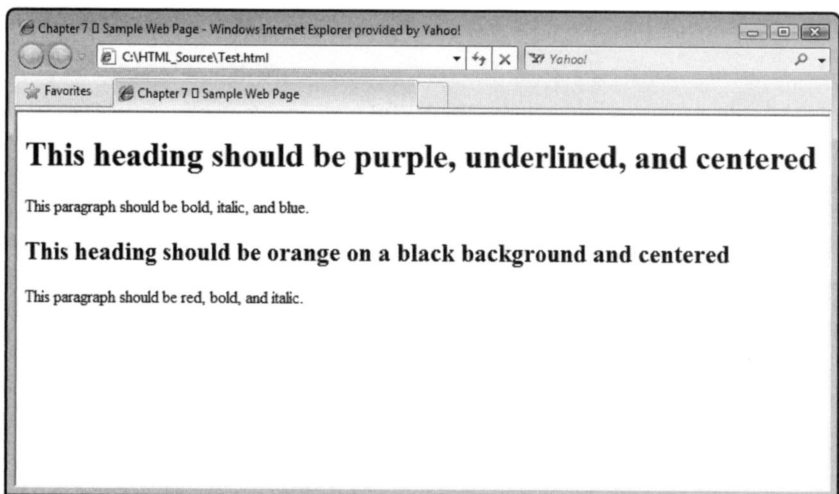

FIGURE 7.6

An example of a small web document.

To spruce things up a bit, let's modify the document by adding an embedded style sheet, as demonstrated in the following example.

```
<!DOCTYPE html PUBLIC "-//W3C//DTD XHTML 1.0 Strict//EN"
  "http://www.w3.org/TR/xhtml1/DTD/xhtml1-strict.dtd">


<html xmlns="http://www.w3.org/1999/xhtml" lang="en" xml:lang="en">

  <head>
    <meta http-equiv="Content-type" content="text/xhtml; charset=UTF-8" />
    <title>Chapter 7 - Working with an Embedded Style Sheet</title>

    <style type = "text/css">

      /*This rule formats all level 1 headings*/
      h1 {
        color: purple;
        text-decoration: underline;
        text-align: center;
      }

      /*This rule formats all level 2 headings*/
      h2 {
        color: orange;
        background-color: black;
        text-align: center;
      }

      /*This rule formats all paragraphs*/
      p {
        font-weight: bold;
        font-style: italic;
        color: blue;
      }

      /*This rule formats a paragraph whose id = p1*/
      #p1 {
```

```
        color: red;
      }

    </style>

  </head>

  <body>
    <h1>This heading should be purple, underlined, and centered</h1>
    <p>This paragraph should be bold, italic, and blue.</p>
    <h2>This heading should be orange on a black background and centered</h2>
    <p id="p1">This paragraph should be red, bold, and italic.</p>

  </body>

</html>
```

As you can see, an embedded style sheet has been added to the document that is made up of four separate CSS style rules. The first rule modifies the appearance of all `h1` elements, displaying the color of their text in purple, making it underlined and centered. The second rule modifies the appearance of all `h2` elements and displays their text in orange on a black background that is centered. The third rule governs the presentation of paragraphs, displaying them in bold, italic, and blue text. The fourth rule affects a specific paragraph on the page. This paragraph is identified by an assigned ID attribute of `p1` (CSS denotes IDs by pre-appending a # character to them).

The fourth rule demonstrates CSS's ability to cascade overlapping rules, by modifying the presentation of one specific paragraph tag. The color property assignment in the fourth rule conflicts with the color property assignment of the third rule. CSS resolves this situation by allowing the most specific selector's color property assignment to override the change made by the third rule. In CSS, rules with greater specificity take precedent.

Note the inclusion of a comment located just before each style rule in the previous example. As you can see, CSS comments begin with the /* characters and end with the */ characters.

Figure 7.7 demonstrates the effect that the addition of the embedded style sheet has had on the web document's appearance once rendered by the web browser.

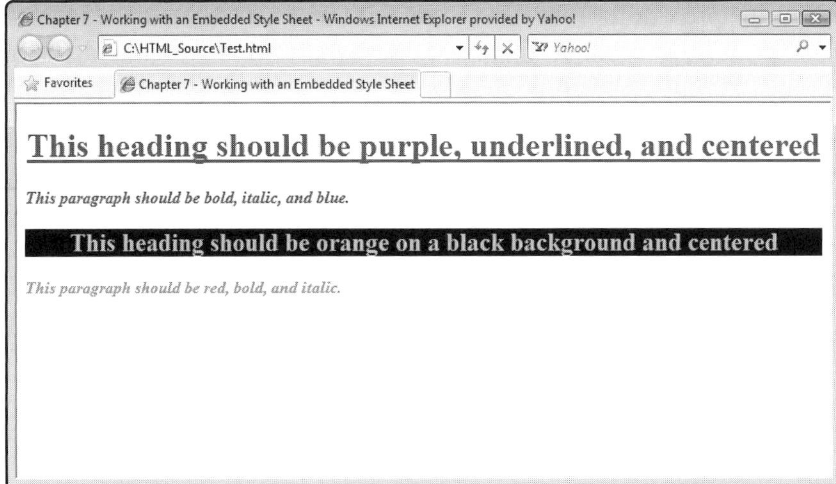

FIGURE 7.7

Examples of how an embedded style sheet can be used to control the presentation of text.

When formulating style sheets you can format your CSS rules any way you want as long as you follow CSS basic syntax. This means you are free to add blank space and carriage returns to help improve readability. For example, you can format your CSS rules in a compact manner, as demonstrated here:

```
h1{color:purple;text-decoration:underline;text-align:center;}
```

Alternatively, you can open things up a bit and make your rules easier to understand by being generous with white space, as demonstrated here:

```
h1 {color: purple; text-decoration: underline; text-align: center;}
```

If your style rules are rather long, you may find it easier to write them in an extended format, as demonstrated here:

```
h1 {
   color: purple;
   text-decoration: underline;
   text-align: center;
}
```

All three of the preceding examples, though laid out differently, are functionally identical. Which format you choose to work with is up to you.

Leveraging the Power of External Style Sheets

The obvious limitation of an embedded style sheet is that you are limited to using it in a single document. To apply the same set of style rules to multiple documents using embedded style sheets, you must copy and paste the embedded style sheets into each document. If you later want to make a change to the presentation of your pages, you will have to revisit each document and make the same update over and over again. The answer to this problem is external style sheets.

An external style sheet is a plain text file made up of CSS style rules. It is arguably your best option for applying CSS to your (X)HTML documents because it provides all of CSS's primary advantages: the separation of content and presentation, the ability to apply style across multiple web pages, and reduced use of network bandwidth. By using external style sheets you can significantly reduce the overall size and complexity of web documents.

Another way of using external style sheets in your web document is to add an `@import` statement inside a style element, as demonstrated here:

```
<style type = "text/css">
  @import "text.css"
  .
  .
  .
</style>
```

In this example, an external style sheet named text.css has been imported into an embedded style sheet. When imported in this manner, the rules in the external style sheet are processed before any of the rules in the embedded style sheet.

Using the previous example as a starting point, you can easily convert an embedded style sheet into an external style sheet. All you have to do is cut and paste the style rules from the `<style>` element into an external text file (don't forget to also remove the opening `<style>` and closing `</style>` tags from the `head` section of the (X)HTML document).

You can name your external style sheets anything you want as long as you assign them a .css file extension. For example, the following CSS file was created by extracting rules from the previous (X)HTML document. It has been named style.css.

```
h1 {
   color: purple;
   text-decoration: underline;
   text-align: center;
}
h2 {
   color: orange;
   background-color: black;
   text-align: center;
```

```
}
p {
  font-weight: bold;
  font-style: italic;
  color: blue;
}
#p1 {
  color: red;
}
```

Once the style element has been removed from the (X)HTML document, the document has become substantially smaller as shown below. As a result, the document is easier to read, understand, and modify.

```
<!DOCTYPE html PUBLIC "-//W3C//DTD XHTML 1.0 Strict//EN"
  "http://www.w3.org/TR/xhtml1/DTD/xhtml1-strict.dtd">

<html xmlns="http://www.w3.org/1999/xhtml" lang="en" xml:lang="en">

  <head>
    <meta http-equiv="Content-type" content="text/xhtml; charset=UTF-8" />
    <title>Chapter 7 - Working with an External Style Sheet</title>
    <link href = "style.css" type = "text/css" rel = "stylesheet" />
  </head>

  <body>
    <h1>This heading should be purple, underlined, and centered</h1>
    <p>This paragraph should be bold, italic, and blue.</p>
    <h2>This heading should be orange on a black background and centered</h2>
    <p id="p1">This paragraph should be red, bold, and italic.</p>
  </body>

</html>
```

To connect the new external style sheet to the (X)HTML document, a link element has been added to the head section. This element contains three elements, explained next.

- **href.** Specifies the URL of the external style sheet.
- **type.** Identifies the MIME type of the document that is being linked.
- **rel.** Specifies the relationship of the linked file to the (X)HTML document.

When the web browser loads this web document, it automatically downloads and applies all of the CSS style rules found in the external style sheet to the document. Even better, the browser automatically caches the style sheet in memory. As a result, if the user loads another one of your web pages that uses the same external style sheet, the style sheet won't have to be downloaded again. As a result, things will occur more quickly, making for happier users. No wonder external style sheets are preferred by most web developers.

You are not limited to working with a single style sheet in your web document. If you want to use more than one external style sheet, place a link to each one in the `head` section. You might, for example, have a style sheet that you link to all of the documents that make up your website and then apply a second more specific style sheet to a given set of pages in order to further customize the presentation of any unique content they might have.

You can also include more than one embedded style sheet in your documents, placing each within its own `style` elements. In fact, while I would not recommend it, you can use inline styles, embedded style sheets, and external style sheets all within a single document.

Understanding How CSS Rules Are Applied

CSS style rules can often conflict with and overlap one another. To ensure that these conflicts are resolved in a predictable and orderly manner, CSS makes use of two resolution techniques, specificity and cascading. Specificity dictates that more specific selectors override less specific selectors. Cascading means that when two selectors of equal specificity conflict, the style rules occurring later override those that occur earlier.

Specificity

Because selectors can be both specific and general, it does not take much for them to come into conflict with one another. When that happens, you must look at the specificity of each selector in order to determine which one will take precedence. While specificity conflicts may be easy to avoid on small web documents, they tend to occur with greater frequency on larger and more complicated documents. Specificity is one of the most difficult concepts to understand when it comes to CSS. In CSS, different weights are assigned to selectors based on their specificity. When you have a web page with elements whose presentation is not being rendered as expected, it is usually because of problems with specificity. A good understanding of CSS specificity rules is therefore critical to web developers.

In CSS, more specific selectors override less specific selectors. In order for you to be able to predict and understand how conflicting style rules will be applied, you need to understand the relative amount of specificity that is assigned to different types of selectors, as outlined in the following list.

- Universal selectors are not specific.
- Element selectors are more specific than universal selectors.
- Class selectors are more specific than element selectors.
- Pseudo class selectors have the same level of specificity as call selectors.
- ID selectors are more specific than class and pseudo selectors.
- Inline styles have a higher specificity than ID selectors.

In addition to understanding how specificity applies to different types of selectors, you also need to understand the following basic rules, which further govern how conflicts are resolved.

Selectors with more specificity override selectors with less specificity. If selectors have equal specificity, the last one wins. The number of selectors in a rule is also cumulative. So a rule with more selectors has a greater specificity than a rule with few selectors of the same type. However, a rule with more selectors of lesser type cannot outweigh a rule with a selector of a higher type (e.g., 5 element selectors do not provide more weight than a single class selector, and a group of class selectors cannot outweigh a single ID selector).

As an example of how all this works, look at a couple of examples, starting with the following rules.

```
p div {color: green;}
p {color : blue;}
```

While you might instinctively think that after processing these rules the browser would display all paragraph text in blue, it does not. Instead, paragraph text is displayed in green because the first selector is regarded as being more specific since it specifies more elements than the second rule. Next, consider the following example.

```
h1 {color: green;}
.firstheading {color: red;}
```

In addition to these rules, let's assume that you have the following element in the web document.

```
<h1 class = ".firstheading">Welcome!<h1>
```

What do you think happens here? Well, the color of all headings in the document would be green except for the heading assigned to the `.firstheading` class. Why? Because class selectors have a greater specificity than element selectors.

Cascading

Okay, so what happens when two rules with equal specificity come into conflict, as demonstrated in the following example?

```
p {color : blue;}
p {color : green;}
```

Since the level of specificity is the same, the browser turns to cascading to determine the result. As a result, the last specified rule cascades over top of the previous rule and is the rule that is applied.

CSS also uses cascading to help determine how style rules should be applied when multiple style sheets are used. For example, a document may have links to two external style sheets. When this occurs, CSS applies rules in each style sheet in the order their associated `link` elements are listed. So in the case of a tie, the style rules on the second external style sheet will override those of the first external style sheet.

If multiple embedded style sheets are present, they are processed in the order in which they are defined, with later embedded style sheets overriding previous ones. Embedded style sheets take precedence over external style sheets and both of these style sheets take precedence over the browser's built-in style sheet. Modern browsers also allow users to configure their own user style sheet. If present, user style sheets take precedence over the browser style sheet. However, embedded and external style sheets take precedence over both user and browser style sheets. If this is not confusing enough, if your web documents make use of any inline styles, they take precedence over all style sheets.

What to Do When All Else Fails

Sometimes trying to figure out why a given piece of content is not being presented the way you want it to be can be very difficult, especially with big web documents with large or multiple style sheets. If you run into a situation where you are unable to work out precisely what is going on, you can exercise a little extra muscle by adding the `!important` keyword to the CSS style rule you want given extra preference.

Note that use of the `!important` keyword is generally discouraged and should only be used in exceptional situations where you have run out of ideas for remedying the situation any other way. The following example demonstrates the use of this keyword.

```
p {color : green !important;}
```

Note that only two things override a CSS rule that uses the `!important` keyword. First is the use of the keyword in a conflicting rule that has greater specificity over which occurs later in the cascade order. The second is the use of the `!important` keyword in a user style sheet, which always takes precedence.

Styling Fonts and Color

You have seen numerous examples of number style rules in this chapter. Most have focused on the presentation of text color or fonts. Let's spend a little time digging deeper into CSS font, text color, and background properties so that you will better understand what you have seen.

Influencing Font Presentation

CSS provides you with control over the selection and appearance of fonts. Using different CSS properties, you can specify font type, size, and a number of other attributes. Table 7.1 provides a list of CSS properties that you can use to control the selection of fonts and to configure their size, width, style, and weight.

Table 7.1 CSS Font Properties

Property	Description
font-family	A prioritized list of font types, such as Arial and Verdana, that specify the font to be used. The list of fonts must be separated by commas. The first available font on the user's computer is automatically used.
font-size	Specifies the size of the font.
font-stretch	Expands or condenses a font's width. Available options include: `normal`, `wider`, and `narrower`.
font-style	Specifies how the font should be displayed. Available options include: `normal`, `italic`, and `oblique`.
font-weight	Specifies font boldness. Available options include: `normal`, `bold`, `bolder`, and `lighter`.

The following example demonstrates how to specify font selection, font style, and font size for various document elements.

```
<!DOCTYPE html PUBLIC "-//W3C//DTD XHTML 1.0 Strict//EN"
  "http://www.w3.org/TR/xhtml1/DTD/xhtml1-strict.dtd">

<html xmlns="http://www.w3.org/1999/xhtml" lang="en" xml:lang="en">
```

```
  <head>
    <meta http-equiv="Content-type" content="text/xhtml; charset=UTF-8" />
    <title>Chapter 7 - Working with an External Style Sheet</title>
    <link href = "style.css" type = "text/css" rel = "stylesheet" />
  </head>

  <body>

    <h1>This heading is displayed in the Arial font using italics</h1>
    <p>This paragraph is displayed in the Garamond font at 150% default
size.</p>

  </body>

</html>
```

As you can see, this XHTML page's content includes a heading and a paragraph element. A link located in the `head` section configures the document's presentation using an external style sheet named style.css. The contents of this style sheet are shown here:

```
h1 {
  font-family: Arial;
  font-style: italic;
}

p {
  font-family: Garamond;
  font-size: 150%;
}
```

As you can see, the first style rule selects the Arial font (`font-family: Arial;`) for any level 1 headings. This font family is universally available on virtually every type of computer. The second declaration in the first rule assigns a value of `italic` to the `font-style` property, so that the browser will display any level 1 headings in italic. The second rule shown above affects the presentation of any paragraphs, setting the `font-family` property to `Garamond` and the `font-size` property to `150%`.

Figure 7.8 shows how this example looks once it has been loaded into the web browser.

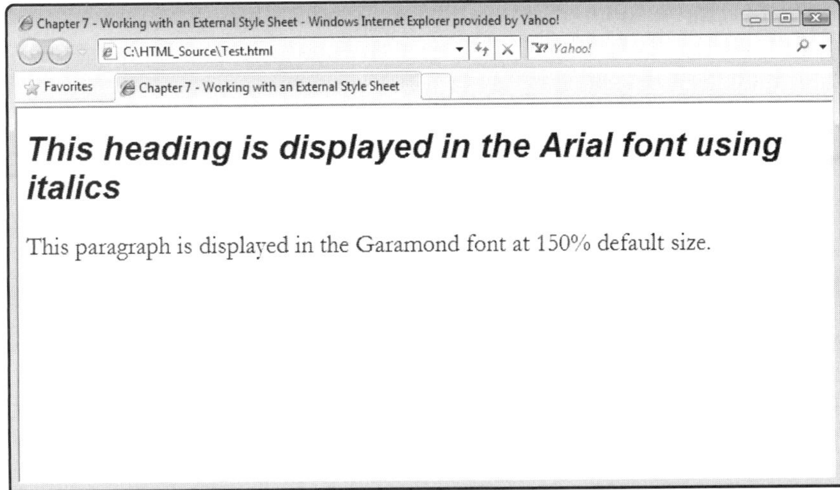

FIGURE 7.8

Examples of how to use CSS to modify different properties.

Take note of both the `font-family` and `font-size` properties used in this example style sheet. Both merit additional discussion. The `font-family` property lets you specify a list of one or more font families as part of a CSS style rule. A *font family* control consists of a collection of font definitions for a given font type. These definitions include different-sized fonts. For example, the Arial font family typically consists of font sizes that range from 8 to 72 points.

When you specify a lot of font families using the `font-family` property, you are really outlining your preferred font type. If the first font family in the list is found on the user's computer, it will be used. If it is not found, the browser will look for the next font in the list. If none of the fonts in the family is found, the browser will default back to its default font type.

CSS supports five generic font families. If you want, you can specify these font families as part of the list in your style rules. These generic font families provide you with a fallback mechanism in the event none of the other font families you specify in your style rules are found on your visitors' computers. When used, the browser will locate a font type on the user's computer that fits the characteristics of the font family, allowing you at least minimal influence of the presentation of text.

- **Cursive.** Fonts in this font family typically have joined strokes and other presentation characteristics that resemble cursive writing. Examples of compatible fonts include Sanvito, Caflisch Script, Corsiva, and Ex Ponto.
- **Fantasy.** Fonts in this family are highly decorative and ornamental. Examples of compatible fonts include Cottonwood, Critter, and Studz.
- **Monospace.** Fonts in this family are proportionately spaced, much like the font used by typewriters. Examples of compatible fonts include Courier, Prostige, and Everson Mona.

- **San Serif.** Fonts in this family have decorative finishes like flaring and cross strike. Examples of compatible fonts include MS Tohoma, MS Arial, Helvetica, and MS Verdana.
- **Serif.** Fonts in this family are among the most decorative and ornamental. They have distinguished finishing strikes and/or tapered endings. Examples of fonts in this family include Times New Roman, MS Georgia, Garamond, and Bodoni.

You can use the `font-family` property in any style rule that works with fonts (e.g., headings, paragraphs, etc.). CSS allows for the downward inheritance of font property assignment. In most cases, property assignments will be inherited by any elements embedded within the element where the property assignment is made. Therefore, it is often desirable to specify a rule that sets font properties for the `body` element, and to allow these property assignment values to be inherited by the rest of the elements in the `body` section, as demonstrated here.

```
body {font-family: "Times New Roman", Georgia, Serif;}
```

Note that the Times New Roman entry in the previous example was enclosed in quotation marks. This is required for any multi-word font names that include spaces.

When it comes to the use of the `font-size` property, CSS supports a number of different ways of specifying measurements, which you can use when specifying CSS properties. The full range of measurement options available are listed in Table 7.2.

Table 7.2 CSS Measurement Units

Unit	Description
%	Percentage
cm	Centimeter
em	One em is equal to the current font size. Two em is two times the size of the current font, etc.
ex	One ex is equivalent to the x-height of a font (which is approximately half the current font size)
in	Inch
mm	Millimeter
pc	Pica (one pc is equivalent to 12 points)
pt	Point (one pt is equivalent to 1/72 inch)
px	Pixels (the smallest addressable area on a computer screen)

Controlling the Presentation of Text

In addition to providing you with the ability to specify different font properties, CSS also allows you to modify properties that affect the presentation of text content. Table 7.3 lists style properties that provide control over presentation features like height, letter spacing, and indentation.

Table 7.3 CSS Text Formatting Properties

Property	Description
text-align	Sets text alignment. Available options include `left`, `right`, `center`, and `justify`.
text-indent	Indents the first line of text.
text-decoration	Applies a decoration to text. Available options include `none`, `underline`, `overline`, `blink`, and `line-through`.
line-height	Specifies the distance between lines.
letter-spacing	Specifies the amount of space between characters.
word-spacing	Specifies the amount of space between words.

As an example of how to work with various CSS text-formatting properties, look at the following example.

```
<!DOCTYPE html PUBLIC "-//W3C//DTD XHTML 1.0 Strict//EN"
  "http://www.w3.org/TR/xhtml1/DTD/xhtml1-strict.dtd">

<html xmlns="http://www.w3.org/1999/xhtml" lang="en" xml:lang="en">

  <head>
    <meta http-equiv="Content-type" content="text/xhtml; charset=UTF-8" />
    <title>Chapter 7 - Working with an External Style Sheet</title>
    <link href = "style.css" type = "text/css" rel = "stylesheet" />
  </head>

  <body>

    <h1>Centered Heading</h1>
    <p id = "p1">Right justified paragraph (underlined)</p>
    <p id = "p2">Left justified paragraph</p>
```

```
  </body>

</html>
```

Here, a document has been created that displays a heading and two paragraphs. The first paragraph has been assigned an ID of `p1` and the second paragraph has been assigned an ID of p2. Note that an external style sheet named style.css has been referenced using a `link` statement located in the document's `head` section. The contents of that style sheet are shown here:

```
h1 {
  text-align: center;
}

#p1 {
  text-decoration: underline;
  text-align: right;
}

#p2 {
  text-align: left;
}
```

When displayed, this example produces the results shown in Figure 7.9.

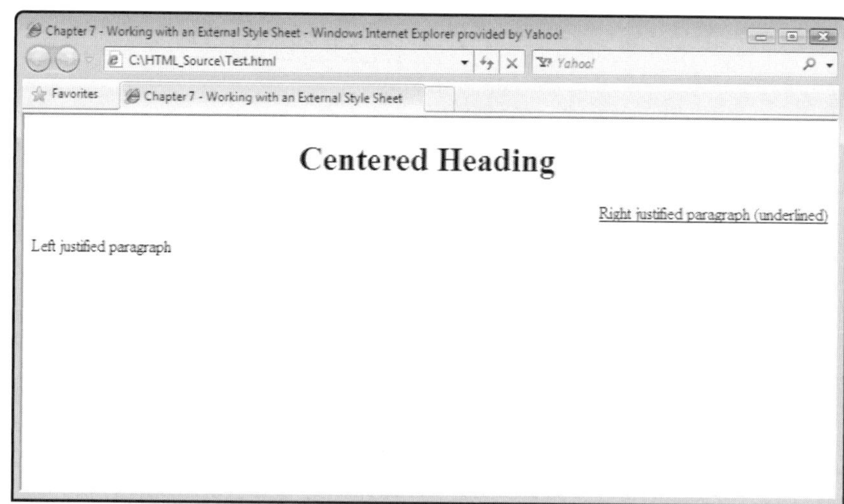

FIGURE 7.9

Examples of how to use CSS to control text alignment.

Specifying Foreground and Background Properties

CSS also allows you to specify the colors and backgrounds that are displayed on your web pages. Table 7.4 lists CSS style properties you can use to control presentation features like text color and window background color.

Table 7.4 CSS Color and Background Properties

Property	Description
color	Specifies the color to be used as the foreground color.
background-image	Specifies the URL of an image file to be used as the background.
background-color	Specifies the color to be used as the background color.
background-repeat	Specifies whether the background image should be tiled. Available options include `no-repeat`, `repeat-x`, and `repeat-y`.
background-position	Specifies the starting position for the background. Available options include `center`, `top`, `bottom`, `right`, and `left`.

CSS provides a number of different ways of specifying color values. You can specify a color using its color name (blue, green, purple, etc). If you prefer, you can specify a color using its hexadecimal value (example: #FFFFFF equals white, #000000 equals black, #FF0000 equals red). Alternatively, you can determine color using the JavaScript `rgb()`, in which you just specify three numbers in the range of 1 to 255, representing different red, green, and blue values (example: `rgb(255, 255, 255)` equals white, `rgb(0, 0, 0)` equals black, and `rgb(255, 0, 0)` equals red). Lastly, you can specify color using the `rgb()` function along with percentages of red, green, and blue `rgb(r%, g%, b%)`.

The following example demonstrates how to work with a number of the properties listed in Table 7.4.

```
<!DOCTYPE html PUBLIC "-//W3C//DTD XHTML 1.0 Strict//EN"
  "http://www.w3.org/TR/xhtml1/DTD/xhtml1-strict.dtd">

<html xmlns="http://www.w3.org/1999/xhtml" lang="en" xml:lang="en">

  <head>
    <meta http-equiv="Content-type" content="text/xhtml; charset=UTF-8" />
    <title>Chapter 7 - Working with an External Style Sheet</title>
    <link href = "style.css" type = "text/css" rel = "stylesheet" />
```

```
  </head>

  <body>
    <h1>All text on this page should appear in green</h1>
    <p>The background color for this page is yellow.</p>
  </body>

</html>
```

As you can see, this document links to a style sheet named style.css, which contains the following CSS style rule.

```
body {
  color: green;
  background-color: yellow;
}
```

This style rule configures all text displayed in the web pages as green on a yellow background. Note that the `color` property assignment here has been made to the `body` section. However, through a process referred to as inheritance, this property assignment flows down to elements declared within the document's body. Figure 7.10 shows an example of what you will see when you load this example into the web browser.

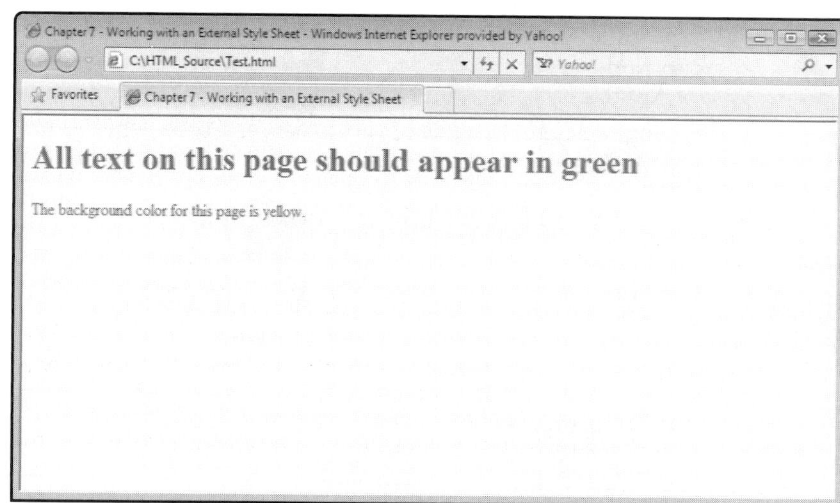

FIGURE 7.10

Examples of how to use CSS to modify a web page's text and background colors.

Validating CSS Syntax

Just as is the case with (X)HTML, the W3C provides free access to a CSS validation service located at http://jigsaw.w3.org/css-validator/, as shown in Figure 7.11. Use this site to ensure that your style sheets are well formed and syntactically valid. Failure to create a valid style sheet can render one or more of its rules completely ineffective and may even result in the entire style sheet failing, leaving your (X)HTML page's presentation to the mercy of your visitor's browser.

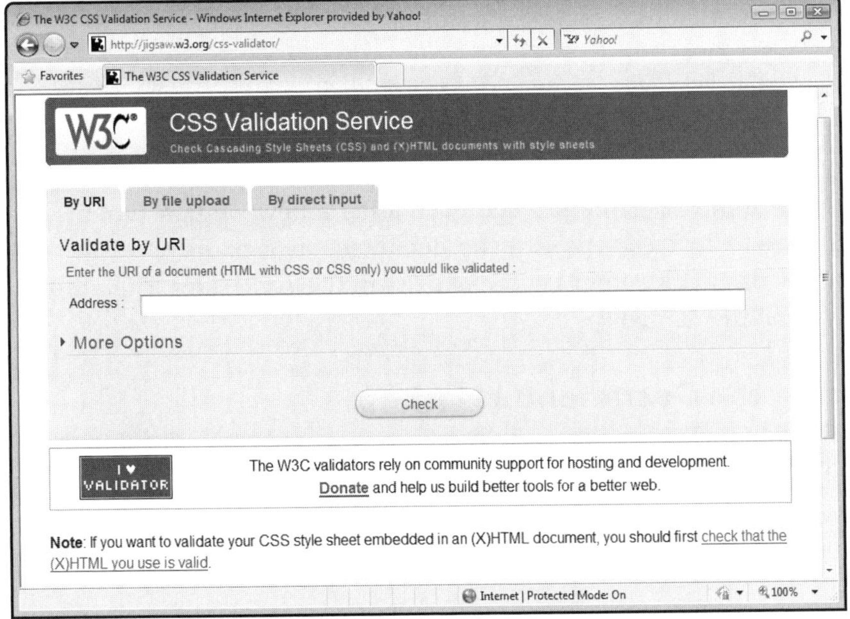

Figure 7.11

Use the free CSS style sheet analyzer provided by W3C to ensure all your style sheets are valid and well formed.

Back to the Rock, Paper, Scissors Game

All right, now it is time to return your attention to this chapter's project, the Rock, Paper, Scissors game. This game will be created using a combination of XHTML, JavaScript, CSS, and the DOM. Together these four technologies can be used to create interactive web pages that dynamically update the display of web content. Collectively, these four technologies are sometimes referred to as *DHTML*, which stands for *Dynamic HTML*. As you'll learn by following along with this project, DHTML helps to take web development to the next level by turning static web pages into an interactive experience.

Designing the Application

This web project is more complicated than any of the previous projects you have worked on so far. To help make things easier to digest, the development of this web application will be broken down into a series of seven steps, as outlined here:

1. Create a new XHTML document.
2. Develop the document's markup.
3. Add `meta` and `title` elements.
4. Create the document's script.
5. Specify document content.
6. Create an external style sheet.
7. Load and test Rock, Paper, Scissors.

Step 1: Creating a New XHTML Document

Let's begin the development of this game project by creating a new web document. Do so using your preferred code or text editor. Save the document as a plain text file named RockPaperScissors.html. This web document will make use of CSS style rules. Therefore, you will need to create a second file named rps.css.

Step 2: Developing the Document's Markup

The next step in the development of the Rock, Paper, Scissors game is to assemble the web document's markup. To do so, add the following elements to the RockPaperScissors.html file.

```
<!DOCTYPE html PUBLIC "-//W3C//DTD XHTML 1.0 Strict//EN"
  "http://www.w3.org/TR/xhtml1/DTD/xhtml1-strict.dtd">

<html xmlns="http://www.w3.org/1999/xhtml" lang="en" xml:lang="en">

  <head>

  </head>

  <body>

  </body>

</html>
```

Step 3: Adding meta and title Elements

Next, let's ensure that the head section is well formed by adding the following elements to it.

```
<meta http-equiv="Content-type" content="text/xhtml; charset=UTF-8" />
<title>The Rock, Paper, Scissors Game</title>
```

This web application is made up of both a web document and an external style sheet named rps.css. As we are working on the document's head section, let's go ahead and set up the link to the external style sheet by adding the following statement to the end of the head section.

```
<link href = "rps.css" type = "text/css" rel = "stylesheet" />
```

Step 4: Specifying Document Content

Now it is time to define a form that the user will use to interact with the game. This form will display three graphic controls labeled Rock, Paper, and Scissors. The player will click on these buttons when making moves during game play. To add the form to the document, add the following statements to the body section.

```
<h1>The Rock, Paper, Scissors Game</h1>

<form action = "RockPaperScissors.html">

  <div>
   <input type = "image" src = "rock.png" onClick = play("Rock") />
   <input type = "image" src = "paper.png" onClick = play("Paper") />
   <input type = "image" src = "scissors.png" onClick = play("Scissors") />
  </div>

</form>
```

Note that the form consists of three input elements embedded within a div element and that the form element's action attribute has been set to the web page itself and not to a server-side form handler. Also, note that the form has no Submit button (and thus no need for a form handler).

Each of the <input> tags displays a different graphic, representing the game's graphic button controls. Each input element also ends with a javascript statement that uses the onClick() event handler to execute a JavaScript function, which you will create in a minute, passing a text string representing the player's move.

The game will dynamically display text that shows the player and computer's moves as well as a message showing who won each time a new round is played. To facilitate the display of this information, add the following elements to the end of the document's body section.

```
<p>
  Computer's Move: <span id="computer"> </span> <br />
  Player's Move: <span id="player"> </span>
</p>

<p>
  Result: <span id="result"> </span>
</p>
```

As you can see, two paragraphs containing three span elements have been used to develop a template through which text can be dynamically displayed. Each span element has been assigned a unique ID, allowing the application's JavaScript statements to dynamically update content using the DOM.

Step 5: Creating the Document's Script

Now that you have added all of the document's markup, it is time to create the JavaScript responsible for controlling the operation of the game. Let's begin by adding the following statements to the document's head section.

```
<script type = "text/javascript">
<!-- Start hiding JavaScript statements

// End hiding JavaScript statements -->
</script>
```

These statements provide the markup needed to support the definition of the script. The JavaScript itself is just one large function named playerMove(). It will be called to execute whenever the player clicks on one of the game's graphic button controls. To create this function, embed the following statements inside the script element's opening <script> tag and closing </script> tags:

```
function play(playerMove) {

  randomNo = 1 + Math.random() * 2; //Generate a random number
                                    //from 1 - 3
```

```
randomNo = Math.round(randomNo);  //Change number to an integer

//Assign the computer's move based on the random number
if (randomNo == 1) computerMove = "Rock"
if (randomNo == 2) computerMove = "Paper"
if (randomNo == 3) computerMove = "Scissors"

//Compare the computer's and the player's move
switch (computerMove) {
  case "Rock":
    if (playerMove == "Rock") {
      document.getElementById('result').innerHTML = "You tie!"
    }
    if (playerMove == "Paper") {
      document.getElementById('result').innerHTML = "You win!"
    }
    if (playerMove == "Scissors") {
      document.getElementById('result').innerHTML = "You lose!"
    }
    break;
  case "Paper":
    if (playerMove == "Rock") {
      document.getElementById('result').innerHTML = "You lose!"
    }
    if (playerMove == "Paper") {
      document.getElementById('result').innerHTML = "You tie!"
    }
    if (playerMove == "Scissors") {
      document.getElementById('result').innerHTML = "You win!"
    }
    break;
  case "Scissors":
    if (playerMove == "Rock") {
      document.getElementById('result').innerHTML = "You win!"
    }
    if (playerMove == "Paper") {
      document.getElementById('result').innerHTML = "You lose!"
    }
```

```
      if (playerMove == "Scissors") {
        document.getElementById('result').innerHTML = "You tie!"
      }
    break;
  }

  document.getElementById('computer').innerHTML = computerMove
  document.getElementById('player').innerHTML = playerMove

  window.alert("Click on OK to play again!");

}
```

This script is executed when the player clicks on one of the game's graphic controls, causing the control's `onClick` event to trigger and pass a text string representing the selected button control. The function definition includes a parameter named `playerMove`. The text string argument passed as input to the script is mapped to this parameter, assigning the text string as the value of the parameter, which acts as a variable. The function compares the player's move to the computer's move, automatically generated by the script on behalf of the computer, to determine the result.

The first two statements in the script generate a random number from 1 to 3, representing the computer's move. The random number is assigned to a variable named `randomNo`. The next three statements assign a text string to a variable named `computerMove`. The value assigned depends on the value of the random number. A value of `1` results in an assignment of `Rock`. A value of `2` results in the assignment of `Paper`, and a value of `3` results in the assignment of `Scissors` as the text string representing the computer's move.

Now that both the player and the computer's moves are known, the script needs to compare their values in order to determine a result. This is accomplished using a `switch` code block that contains a number of embedded `if` statement code blocks.

The first `case` statement executes if the computer's assigned move is `Rock`. It is followed by three `if` statement code blocks. Only one `if` statement code block executes, depending on the value of the player's move. Lastly, a `break` statement is executed, terminating the execution of the rest of the `switch` code block. In similar fashion, the second and third `case` statements execute when the computer's assigned move is `paper` or `scissors`.

At this point, the script has determined whether the player has won, lost, or tied. What happens next is a little complicated and is what causes the script to dynamically update the web page, without requiring the page to be refreshed or reloaded. In simple terms, depending on the result of the script's analysis of the player and computer's moves, a statement like the one shown here is executed.

```
document.getElementById('result').innerHTML = "You tie!"
```

This script statement merits some explanation. It requires some understanding of the DOM, as was covered in Chapter 1. It begins by referring to the document object, which is always the top-most document in the DOM tree. Next, the `getElementById()` method is executed. This method retrieves a reference to a document element based on its assigned ID, which is passed to the method as a string argument. Lastly, the `innerHTML` property is used to assist a text string as the document element's new value, dynamically updating it on the fly. Note that the dot (`.`) character is used to glue together the different parts of this statement, referred to as dot notation. The last three statements use similar logic to dynamically update the `span` elements responsible for displaying the player and computer's moves and then display a popup dialog window that instructs the player to reload the web page in order to play again.

Step 6: Creating an External Style Sheet

The RockPaperScissors.html document uses an external style sheet to configure the presentation of its content. This style sheet is saved in a file named rps.css. The rules stored in this style sheet are shown here:

```
h1 {
      color: MidnightBlue;
      text-align: center;
      font-family: Arial;
      font-size: 36px;
   }

div {
      text-align: center;
    }

p { text-align: center;
    font-family: Arial;
    font-size: 24px;
  }
```

The first rule in the style sheet applies to all of the `h1` headings in RockPaperScissors.html. It will display them using a color of `MidnightBlue`, centering the text using the `Arial` font using a font size that is 36 pixels high. The second rule applies to the document's `div` element, which contains the three graphic button controls. The third and final style rule specifies the presentation of the document's paragraphs, centering them and displaying them using an `Arial` font that is 24 pixels high.

Step 7: Loading and Testing the Rock, Paper, Scissors Game

At this point, your copy of the RockPaperScissors.html document should be complete. To help ensure you've assembled it correctly, take a look at the following example, which shows a complete copy of the finished document.

```
<!DOCTYPE html PUBLIC "-//W3C//DTD XHTML 1.0 Strict//EN"
  "http://www.w3.org/TR/xhtml1/DTD/xhtml1-strict.dtd">

<html xmlns="http://www.w3.org/1999/xhtml" lang="en" xml:lang="en">

  <head>
    <meta http-equiv="Content-type" content="text/xhtml; charset=UTF-8" />
    <title>The Rock, Paper, Scissors Game</title>
    <link href = "rps.css" type = "text/css" rel = "stylesheet" />

    <script type = "text/javascript">
    <!-- Start hiding JavaScript statements

      function play(playerMove) {

        randomNo = 1 + Math.random() * 2; //Generate a random number
                                          //from 1 - 3

        randomNo = Math.round(randomNo);  //Change number to an integer

        //Assign the computer's move based on the random number
        if (randomNo == 1) computerMove = "Rock"
        if (randomNo == 2) computerMove = "Paper"
        if (randomNo == 3) computerMove = "Scissors"

        //Compare the computer's and the player's move
        switch (computerMove) {
          case "Rock":
            if (playerMove == "Rock") {
```

```
      document.getElementById('result').innerHTML = "You tie!"
    }
    if (playerMove == "Paper") {
      document.getElementById('result').innerHTML = "You win!"
    }
    if (playerMove == "Scissors") {
      document.getElementById('result').innerHTML = "You lose!"
    }
    break;
  case "Paper":
    if (playerMove == "Rock") {
      document.getElementById('result').innerHTML = "You lose!"
    }
    if (playerMove == "Paper") {
      document.getElementById('result').innerHTML = "You tie!"
    }
    if (playerMove == "Scissors") {
      document.getElementById('result').innerHTML = "You win!"
    }
    break;
  case "Scissors":
    if (playerMove == "Rock") {
      document.getElementById('result').innerHTML = "You win!"
    }
    if (playerMove == "Paper") {
      document.getElementById('result').innerHTML = "You lose!"
    }
    if (playerMove == "Scissors") {
      document.getElementById('result').innerHTML = "You tie!"
    }
    break;
}

document.getElementById('computer').innerHTML = computerMove
document.getElementById('player').innerHTML = playerMove

window.alert("Click on OK to play again!");
```

```
      }

    // End hiding JavaScript statements -->
    </script>

  </head>

  <body>

    <h1>The Rock, Paper, Scissors Game</h1>

    <form action = "RockPaperScissors.html">

      <div>
        <input type = "image" src = "rock.png" onClick = play("Rock") />
        <input type = "image" src = "paper.png" onClick = play("Paper") />
        <input type = "image" src = "scissors.png"
          onClick = play("Scissors") />
      </div>

    </form>

    <p>
      Computer's Move: <span id="computer"> </span> <br />
      Player's Move: <span id="player"> </span>
    </p>

    <p>
      Result: <span id="result"> </span>
    </p>

  </body>

</html>
```

Okay, if you have not done so already, now is the time to load your new web page and to see how your new game works.

A complete copy of the source code for this project, including its style sheet, and the graphics needed to create its graphic controls is available on the book's companion web page, located at www.courseptr.com/downloads.

Summary

This chapter provided an introduction to CSS and explained its role in helping to influence the presentation of content on web pages. You learned the basic syntax required to formulate CSS style rules. This included how to work with inline styles, embedded style sheets, and external style sheets. You also learned how to use CSS to style fonts, text, and foreground and background colors. On top of all this, you learned how to create the Rock, Paper, Scissors game.

Challenges

1. The Rock, Paper, Scissors game currently makes the assumption that the player knows the rules for playing the game. Rather than rely on this assumption, consider creating another document with detailed instructions for playing the game and add a link to that document on the RockPaperScissors.html document.
2. Let's spruce things up a bit by modifying the color of the document's paragraph to something more attractive than the default color of black.
3. Lastly, using the `em` element, enclose the `span` element, so that the `player`, `computer`, and `result` values are given additional emphasis when displayed.

Digging Deeper into CSS

In the previous chapter, you learned different ways of integrating CSS into your web documents and the basic syntax rules used to formulate style rules. In this chapter, you will expand your understanding of CSS by learning how to use it to take control of the placement of content, customize the display of lists, and to style both text and graphic links and buttons. You will also learn how to use CSS to style the flow of graphics and text, to display background images, to style your tables in numerous ways, and to influence the presentation of text in (X)HTML forms.

Specifically, you will learn:

- How to work with and configure containers
- Different options for specifying the presentation of content
- How to modify the display of markers used to identify ordered and unordered list items
- Create rollover links, controls, and buttons
- A number of ways that you can improve the presentation of graphics, tables, and forms

Project Preview: The Fortune Teller Game

This chapter's web project is the development of the Fortune Teller game. When first started, this game displays the screen shown in Figure 8.1.

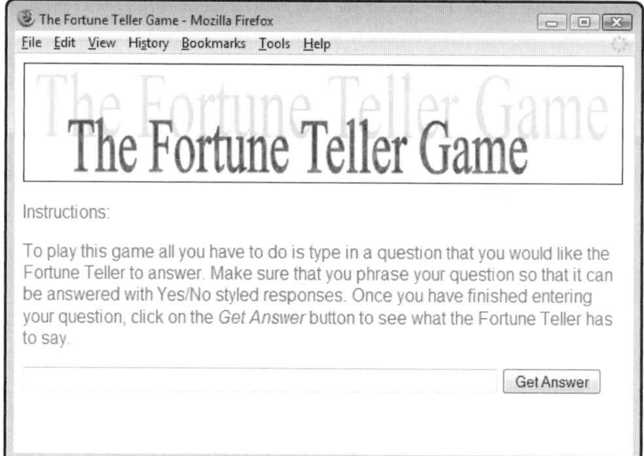

Figure 8.1 The game's presentation is controlled using an external style sheet.

To play, type in a question in the text control located in a form at the bottom of the browser window and then click on the Get Answer button. For the game to work properly, the player must submit all questions in a form that allows for Yes/No responses. Once the Get Answer button is clicked, the game will display one of ten randomly selected responses, as demonstrated in Figure 8.2.

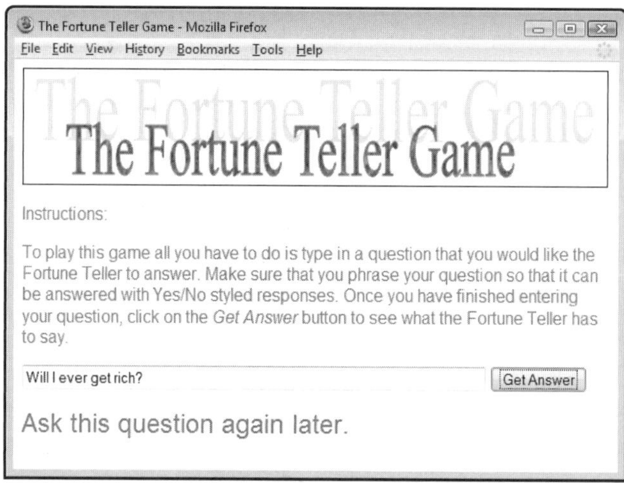

Figure 8.2 The game's answer to the player's question is displayed at the bottom of the browser window.

After a short three-second pause, the game will automatically clear out both the player's question and the game's answer, readying the game to accept a new question while also providing the player with plenty of time to view and consider the game's answer. In the event that the player clicks on the Get Answer button without entering a question, the game will display the following popup dialog window, notifying the player of his error.

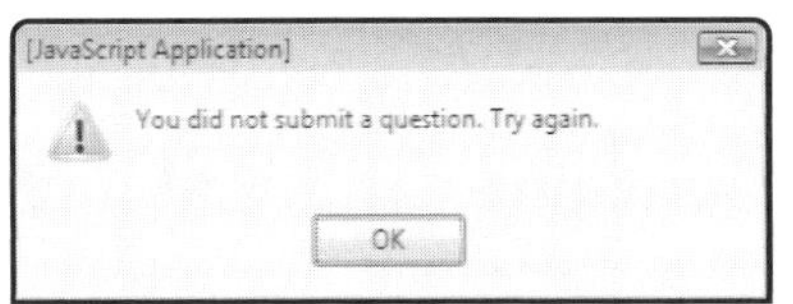

FIGURE 8.3

Game play resumes as soon as the player clicks on the OK button.

WORKING WITH CONTAINERS

One of the most useful features of CSS is its ability to control the position at which elements are displayed on web pages. Key to understanding how this works is the concept of a container. A *container* is an entity to which you can apply CSS. In addition, many elements can serve as containers for other elements. To help illustrate this point, look at the following example.

```
<body>
  <p>
    Who did <em>Roger Rabbit</em> marry?
  </p>
</body>
```

Here, the paragraph is used to display a little text. In addition, an `em` element is embedded within the paragraph. Both the paragraph and the `em` elements are containers. Therefore, both can be styled.

In most cases, any style you apply to an element is automatically inherited by any embedded elements. So, if you add a style rule that displays all text within the paragraph in red, the embedded `em` element inherits that color styling as well.

A container has three common presentation attributes that affect how its content is blended in with other content. These container attributes are margins, padding, and borders.

Setting Container Margins

A margin is the space that encloses the container. By changing container margins, you can make things feel less cluttered by adding a little extra white space. Setting a container's margin is easy. All you have to do is use the `margin` property, as demonstrated here:

```
p {margin: 10cm 10cm 5cm 5cm;}
```

Here, the left and right margins have been set to 10 centimeters and the top and bottom margins have been set to 5 centimeters.

If you prefer to be more explicit, you can specify each margin separately, as demonstrated here:

```
p {margin-left: 10cm; margin-right: 10cm; margin-top: 5cm;
    margin-bottom: 5cm;}
```

Padding Space Between the Container and Its Border

All containers have a border, whether it is visible or not. The border represents the outside edge of the container. If you want, you can add additional padding between a container and its border using the `padding` attribute. The `padding` attribute works just like the `margin` element, as demonstrated here.

```
p {padding: 10cm 10cm 5cm 5cm;}
```

Configuring a Container's Border

By default, container borders are invisible. However, you can display and configure them using the `border-width` and `border-style` properties. The `border-style` property lets you enable and disable the display of the container's border (disabled by default). Take, for example, the following rule.

```
p {border-style: solid;}
```

This rule will display a solid border around every paragraph in the document. The following list outlines the possible range of values supported by the `border-style` property. The last value (`none`) is the default.

- hidden
- dashed
- dotted
- double
- groove
- inset
- outset
- ridge
- solid
- none

Once you have used the `border-style` property to select and display a container's border, you can use the `border-width` property to specify the thickness of that border. You have four choices, as outlined here:

- **thin.** Displays the container using a thin border.
- **medium.** Displays the container using a medium border.
- **thick.** Displays the container using a thick border.
- *value.* Displays the container with a border whose thickness depends on what value you assign (example: 2 cm).

The following example demonstrates how to display a border around all paragraphs in a document using an inset border that is medium thick.

```
<!DOCTYPE html PUBLIC "-//W3C//DTD XHTML 1.0 Strict//EN"
  "http://www.w3.org/TR/xhtml1/DTD/xhtml1-strict.dtd">

<html xmlns="http://www.w3.org/1999/xhtml" lang="en" xml:lang="en">

  <head>
    <meta http-equiv="Content-type" content="text/xhtml; charset=UTF-8" />
    <title>Chapter 8 - Working with Borders</title>
    <style type = "text/css">
      p {border-style: double; border-width: medium;}
    </style>
  </head>

  <body>
    <p>
      Who did <em>Roger Rabbit</em> marry?
    </p>
  </body>

</html>
```

Figure 8.4 shows how the paragraph element's border looks when rendered by the browser.

Note that in this example and in the rest of the examples that you will see in this chapter, embedded style sheets are used to simplify examples and make things easier to present. However, use of external style sheets is still recommended for most real-life web documents.

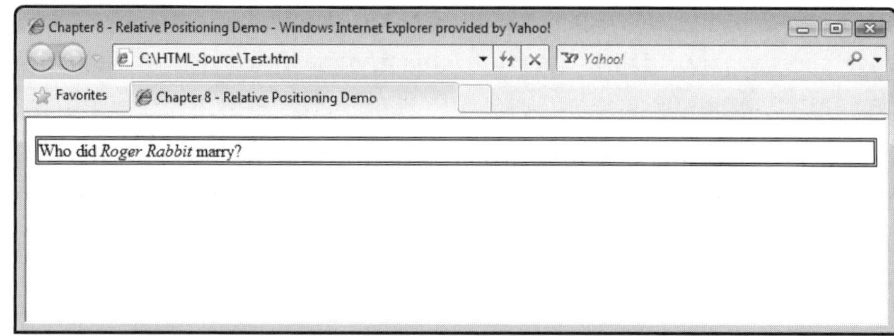

FIGURE 8.4

An example of how to display and configure an element's content in a container.

TAKING CONTROL OF ELEMENT PLACEMENT

CSS provides you a number of different properties that you can use to take control over the placement of document content within the browser window. CSS supports a coordinate system along with properties that you can use to interact with that system. Figure 8.5 provides a visual depiction of CSS's coordinate system. As you can see, coordinate 0,0 is located in the upper-left corner of the browser window. 0,0 represents vertical and horizontal values. As the display of an element is moved down the browser window, the value of its y (vertical) coordinate increases. Likewise, as an element moves from left to right, the value of its x (horizontal) coordinate increases.

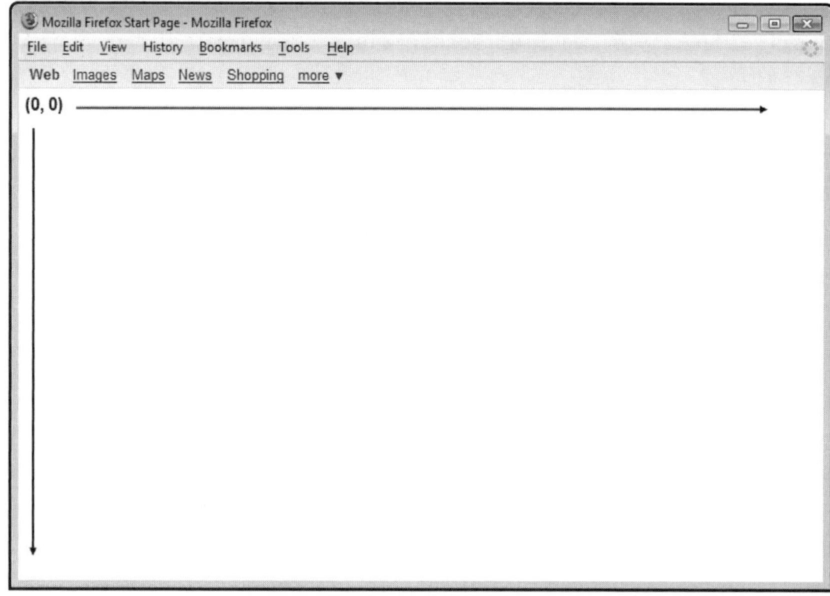

FIGURE 8.5

A depiction of CSS's coordinate system.

Table 8.1 provides a list of CSS properties that you can use to affect element positioning.

Table 8.1 CSS Properties that Affect Element Positioning

Property	Property	Description
top	pixel value	Offset from the top of the browser's display area (absolute) or from its default location as determined by the browser.
bottom	pixel value	Offset from the bottom of the browser's display area (absolute) or from its default location as determined by the browser.
left	pixel value	Offset from the top-left side of the browser's display area (absolute) or from its default location as determined by the browser.
right	pixel value	Offset from the top-right side of the browser's display area (absolute) or from its default location as determined by the browser.
position	static, absolute, relative, fixed, float	Determines how to position an element.
z-order	numeric value	A value that determines the order in which elements appear when they overlap one another.

Static Positioning

Static is the default positioning option, and it is the option you have been using throughout this book. With static positioning, elements are displayed in the order they are laid out in your documents, one after another, as demonstrated in the following example.

```
<!DOCTYPE html PUBLIC "-//W3C//DTD XHTML 1.0 Strict//EN"
  "http://www.w3.org/TR/xhtml1/DTD/xhtml1-strict.dtd">

<html xmlns="http://www.w3.org/1999/xhtml" lang="en" xml:lang="en">

  <head>
    <meta http-equiv="Content-type" content="text/xhtml; charset=UTF-8" />
    <title>Chapter 8 - Static Positioning Demo</title>
    <style type = "text/css">
      p {border-width: thin; border-style: groove; height: 200px;
```

```
        width: 200px;}
      #yellowbox {background-color: yellow;}
      #bluebox {background-color: blue;}
    </style>
  </head>

  <body>
    <p id = "yellowbox">
      Yellow Box
    </p>
    <p id = "bluebox">
      Blue Box
    </p>
  </body>

</html>
```

Figure 8.6 shows how the resulting web page is laid out when this example is rendered by the browser.

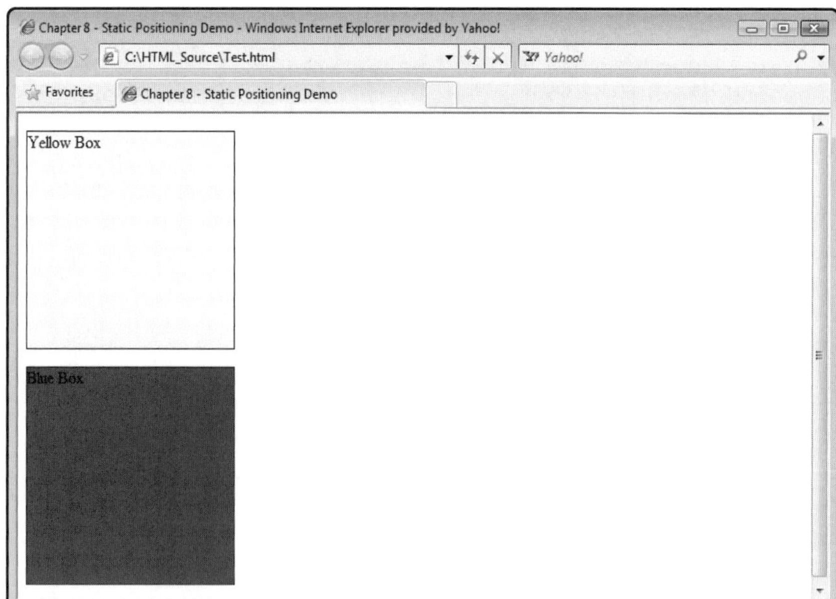

FIGURE 8.6

An example of how to control container placement using static positioning.

Absolute Positioning

Absolute positioning provides precise control over the placement of your content. You simply specify the location where you want an element's content to appear using the `top`, `bottom`, `left`, and `right` properties, as demonstrated by the following example.

```
<!DOCTYPE html PUBLIC "-//W3C//DTD XHTML 1.0 Strict//EN"
  "http://www.w3.org/TR/xhtml1/DTD/xhtml1-strict.dtd">

<html xmlns="http://www.w3.org/1999/xhtml" lang="en" xml:lang="en">

  <head>
    <meta http-equiv="Content-type" content="text/xhtml; charset=UTF-8" />
    <title>Chapter 8 - Static Positioning Demo</title>
  </head>

  <body>

    <p style = "position: absolute; left: 50px; top: 25px; z-index: 20;" >
      <img src = "cats.jpg" width = "270" height = "200"
        alt = "Picture of two cats" />
    </p>

    <p style = "position: absolute; left: 200px; top: 150px; z-index: 10;">
      <img src = "river.jpg" width = "270" height = "200"
        alt = "Picture of a river" />
    </p>

  </body>

</html>
```

As you can see, in this example two images are displayed on the browser window. The assigned coordinates cause the images to overlap. As a result, the image with the highest specified `z-index` value is displayed on top of the other figure. Figure 8.7 shows how this example's context looks when rendered by the browser.

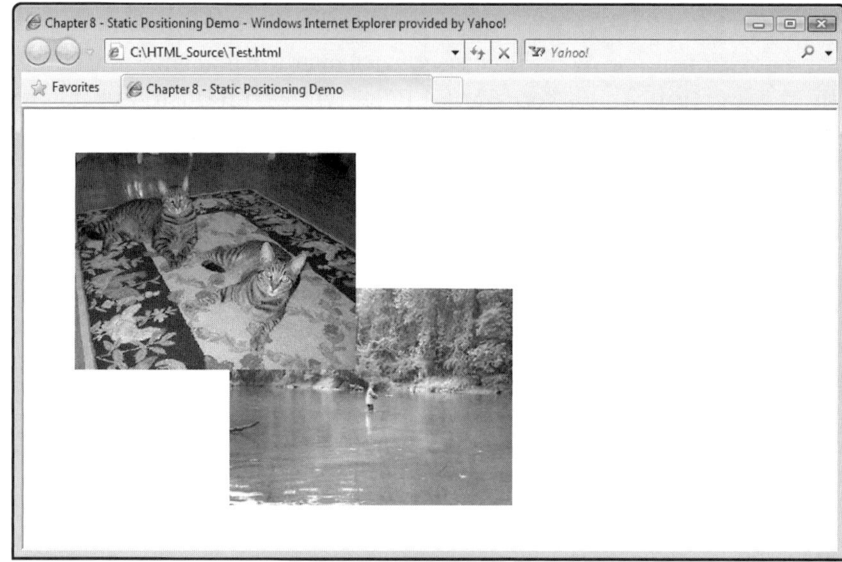

FIGURE 8.7

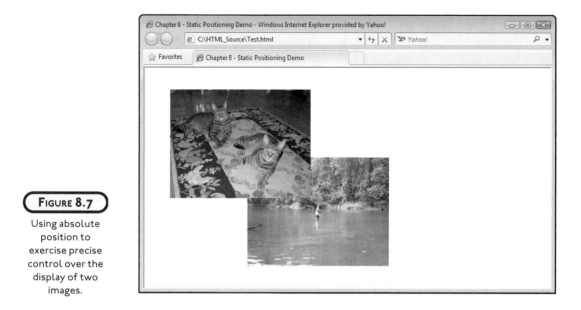

Using absolute position to exercise precise control over the display of two images.

Relative Positioning

A problem with absolute positioning is that not all computers are set up with the same screen resolution. Therefore, the coordinates system changes from user to user. As a result, it can be difficult to ensure web pages look the way you want them to at different resolutions. Relative positioning sets an element's position relative to other elements.

Using relative positioning, you can create an application that automatically repositions its elements based on window resolution. This helps keep things from overlapping or from being pushed out of view. As an example of how relative positioning works, look at the following example.

```
<!DOCTYPE html PUBLIC "-//W3C//DTD XHTML 1.0 Strict//EN"
  "http://www.w3.org/TR/xhtml1/DTD/xhtml1-strict.dtd">

<html xmlns="http://www.w3.org/1999/xhtml" lang="en" xml:lang="en">

  <head>
    <meta http-equiv="Content-type" content="text/xhtml; charset=UTF-8" />
    <title>Chapter 8 - Relative Positioning Demo</title>
  </head>

  <body>
```

```
    <p>
      Man
      <span style = "position: relative; top: 5px;">went</span>
      <span style = "position: relative; top: 10px;">to</span>
      <span style = "position: relative; top: 20px;">the</span>
      <span style = "position: relative; top: 30px;">moon</span>
      <span style = "position: relative; top: 40px;">and</span>
      <span style = "position: relative; top: 50px;">came</span>
      <span style = "position: relative; top: 60px;">back</span>
      <span style = "position: relative; top: 50px;">again</span>
      <span style = "position: relative; top: 40px;">only</span>
      <span style = "position: relative; top: 30px;">to</span>
      <span style = "position: relative; top: 20px;">find</span>
      <span style = "position: relative; top: 10px;">the</span>
      <span style = "position: relative; top: 5px;">urge</span>
      <span style = "position: relative; top: 0px;">to</span>
      <span style = "position: relative; top: 5px;">return</span>
      <span style = "position: relative; top: 10px;">so</span>
      <span style = "position: relative; top: 20px;">compelling</span>
      <span style = "position: relative; top: 30px;">that</span>
      <span style = "position: relative; top: 40px;">he</span>
      <span style = "position: relative; top: 50px;">wished</span>
      <span style = "position: relative; top: 60px;">he</span>
      <span style = "position: relative; top: 50px;">had</span>
      <span style = "position: relative; top: 40px;">never</span>
      <span style = "position: relative; top: 30px;">left</span>
      <span style = "position: relative; top: 20px;">in</span>
      <span style = "position: relative; top: 10px;">the</span>
      <span style = "position: relative; top: 5px;">first</span>
      <span style = "position: relative; top: 0px;">place.</span>
    </p>
  </body>

</html>
```

Figure 8.8 demonstrates how this page will look when loaded into the browser.

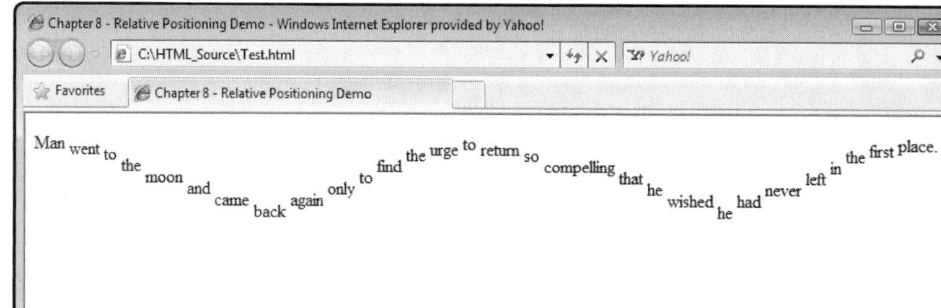

FIGURE 8.8

Using relative positioning to control text presentation.

Fixed Positioning

Elements that are positioned using fixed positioning do not scroll or change position when the user scrolls up and down the web page. Instead, the elements remain visible at the same location while the rest of the page's content scrolls behind them. Fixed positioning is often used to keep report headings visible at the top of a web page at all times. The following example demonstrates how to work with fixed positioning.

```
<!DOCTYPE html PUBLIC "-//W3C//DTD XHTML 1.0 Strict//EN"
  "http://www.w3.org/TR/xhtml1/DTD/xhtml1-strict.dtd">

<html xmlns="http://www.w3.org/1999/xhtml" lang="en" xml:lang="en">

  <head>
    <meta http-equiv="Content-type" content="text/xhtml; charset=UTF-8" />
    <title>Chapter 8 - Fixed Positioning Demo</title>
    <style type = "text/css">
      p {border-width: thick; border-style: solid; height: 55px;
         width: 189px; position: fixed; top: -16px; left: 0px;}
    </style>
  </head>

  <body>
    <p>
      <img src = "nba.png" alt = "A graphic NBA header" />
    </p>
    <pre>
```

```
      Celtics
      Nets
      Knicks
      76ers
      Raptors
      Mavericks
      Rockets
      Grizzlies
      Hornets
      Spurs
      Bulls
      Cavaliers
      Pistons
      Pacers
      Bucks
      Nuggets
      Timberwolves
      Trail Blazers
      City Thunder
      Jazz
      Hawks
      Bobcats
      Heat
      Magic
      Wizards
      Warriors
      Clippers
      Lakers
      Suns
      Kings
    </pre>
  </body>

</html>
```

Note that the four blank lines in the previous document are no accident.

FIGURE 8.9

Using fixed positioning to set up a non-scrolling graphic heading.

Figure 8.10 demonstrates how this page will look when first loaded into the browser.

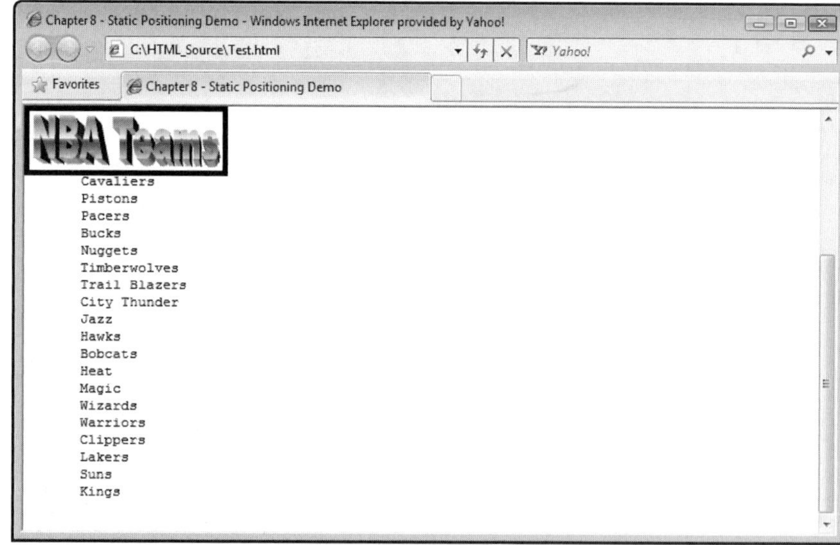

FIGURE 8.10

The graphic heading remains in place as the page's content is scrolled.

Float Positioning

The position option supported by CSS is float. When an element is set up to float, it can be assigned to shift or float right or left on its current vertical line. The `float` property can be assigned any of the following values; `left`, `right`, `none`. A floated element will shift position in the specified direction until it makes contact with the edge of the container in which it is defined or until it makes contact with another float. Any text displayed on the page will follow down and around the floated element.

```
<!DOCTYPE html PUBLIC "-//W3C//DTD XHTML 1.0 Strict//EN"
  "http://www.w3.org/TR/xhtml1/DTD/xhtml1-strict.dtd">

<html xmlns="http://www.w3.org/1999/xhtml" lang="en" xml:lang="en">

  <head>
    <meta http-equiv="Content-type" content="text/xhtml; charset=UTF-8" />
    <title>Chapter 8 - Float Positioning Demo</title>
    <style type = "text/css">
      p {float: right;}
    </style>

  </head>

  <body>
    <p>
      <img src = "cats.jpg" alt = "Picture of two little kittens." />
    </p>
  </body>

</html>
```

Figure 8.11 demonstrates how this page will look when first loaded into the browser.

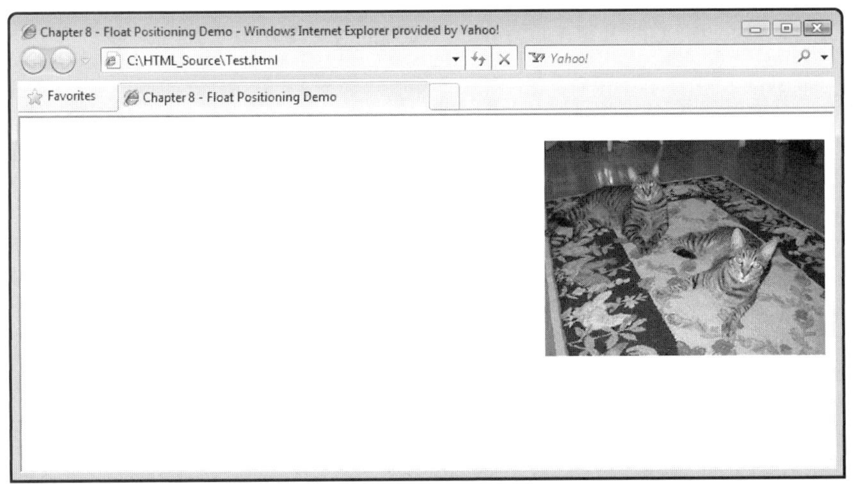

FIGURE 8.11

Using float positioning to control the horizontal positioning of an element.

Using CSS to Style Your Lists

You can use CSS to style just about any content you embed in your web pages. This includes styling ordered and unordered lists. By default, ordered lists are displayed using Arabic numerals (1,2,3...) and ordered lists are displayed using a round disk shaped bullet. Using CSS, you can modify these defaults, displaying your lists using a variety of different markers.

Customizing Markers for Ordered Lists

If you prefer to use something other than the standard Arabic numerals when defining ordered lists, you can use the `list-style-type` property to select any of the alternative numeric styles listed in Table 8.2.

Table 8.2 Values Supported by the list-style Property

Numeric Style	Description	Example
Decimal	Displays Arabic numeral characters (default)	1, 2, 3, 4, 5, ...
lower-alpha	Displays lowercase alphabetic characters	a, b, c, d, e, ...
lower-roman	Displays lowercase Roman numeral characters	i, ii, iii, iv, v, ...
upper-alpha	Displays uppercase alphabetic characters	A, B, C, D, E, ...
upper-roman	Displays uppercase Roman numeral characters	I, II, III, IV, V, ...
none	Suppresses the display of characters	N/A

Actually, CSS supports a number of other numeric styles, including: armenian, decimal-leading-zero, georgian, inherit, lower-greek, lower-latin, and upper-latin. However, Internet Explorer does not currently support any of these numeric style types, so it is recommended that you avoid their usage.

As an example of how to work with the `list-style-type` property to change the presentation of your ordered lists, look at the following:

```
<!DOCTYPE html PUBLIC "-//W3C//DTD XHTML 1.0 Strict//EN"
  "http://www.w3.org/TR/xhtml1/DTD/xhtml1-strict.dtd">

<html xmlns="http://www.w3.org/1999/xhtml" lang="en" xml:lang="en">

  <head>
    <meta http-equiv="Content-type" content="text/xhtml; charset=UTF-8" />
    <title>Chapter 8 - Ordered List</title>
```

```
  </head>

  <body>
    <h1>Directions</h1>
    <ol>
      <li>Start off on Maple Street.</li>
      <li>Go two lights and turn right on Puff Puff Lane.</li>
      <li>Go half a mile and veer right on Santa Claus Parkway.</li>
      <li>Go another 3.5 miles and turn right onto Puff'n Stuff Avenue.</li>
      <li>Go 1.2 miles and turn left into the main entrance of the fun
          park.</li>
    </ol>
  </body>

</html>
```

Here, a list of five ordered items has been defined. Figure 8.12 shows how this list looks when rendered by the browser.

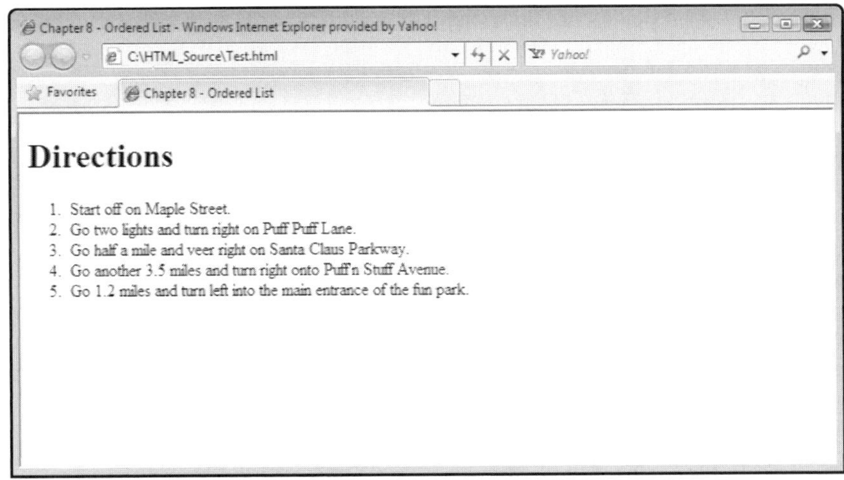

FIGURE 8.12

An example of an ordered list displayed using the default marker.

Now, let's rework the example as shown below.

```
<!DOCTYPE html PUBLIC "-//W3C//DTD XHTML 1.0 Strict//EN"
  "http://www.w3.org/TR/xhtml1/DTD/xhtml1-strict.dtd">

<html xmlns="http://www.w3.org/1999/xhtml" lang="en" xml:lang="en">
```

```
  <head>
    <meta http-equiv="Content-type" content="text/xhtml; charset=UTF-8" />
    <title>Chapter 8 - Styled Ordered List</title>
    <style type = "text/css">
      ol {list-style-type: upper-roman;}
    </style>
  </head>

  <body>
    <h1>Directions</h1>
    <ol>
      <li>Start off on Maple Street.</li>
      <li>Go two lights and turn right on Puff Puff Lane.</li>
      <li>Go half a mile and veer right on Santa Claus Parkway.</li>
      <li>Go another 3.5 miles and turn right onto Puff'n Stuff Avenue.</li>
      <li>Go 1.2 miles and turn left into the main entrance of the fun
          park.</li>
    </ol>
  </body>

</html>
```

As you can see, this example includes a style rule that uses the `list-style-type` property to alter the display of the marker to upper-roman, as shown in Figure 8.13.

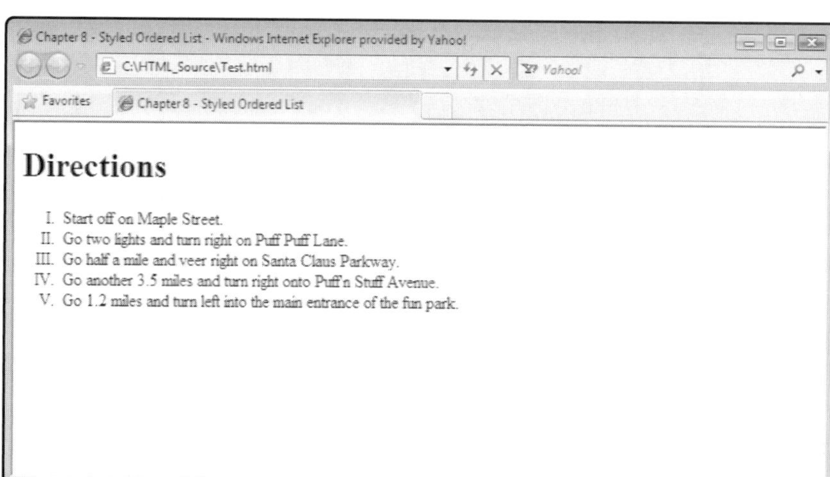

FIGURE 8.13

An example of an unordered list that has been configured to use the upper-roman marker.

Changing Markers for Unordered Lists

By taking advantage of the `list-style-type` property, you can modify the appearance of the markers used to style your unordered lists. You can even hide the markers altogether. The following lists outlines various markers that can be assigned to this property.

- **disc.** A darkened round marker (default).
- **circle.** A hollow or empty circle marker.
- **square.** A darkened square marker.
- **none.** A blank or hidden marker.

As an example of how to work with the `list-style-type` property to change the presentation of your unordered lists, look at the following.

```
<!DOCTYPE html PUBLIC "-//W3C//DTD XHTML 1.0 Strict//EN"
  "http://www.w3.org/TR/xhtml1/DTD/xhtml1-strict.dtd">

<html xmlns="http://www.w3.org/1999/xhtml" lang="en" xml:lang="en">

  <head>
    <meta http-equiv="Content-type" content="text/xhtml; charset=UTF-8" />
    <title>Chapter 8 - Unordered List</title>
  </head>

  <body>
    <h1>School Supplies</h1>
    <ul>
      <li>Two No. 2 pencils</li>
      <li>Ruler</li>
      <li>Three spiral notebooks</li>
      <li>Two 3-ring binders</li>
      <li>500 sheets of college lined notebook paper</li>
    </ul>
  </body>

</html>
```

Here, a list of five unordered items has been defined. Figure 8.14 shows how this list looks when rendered by the browser.

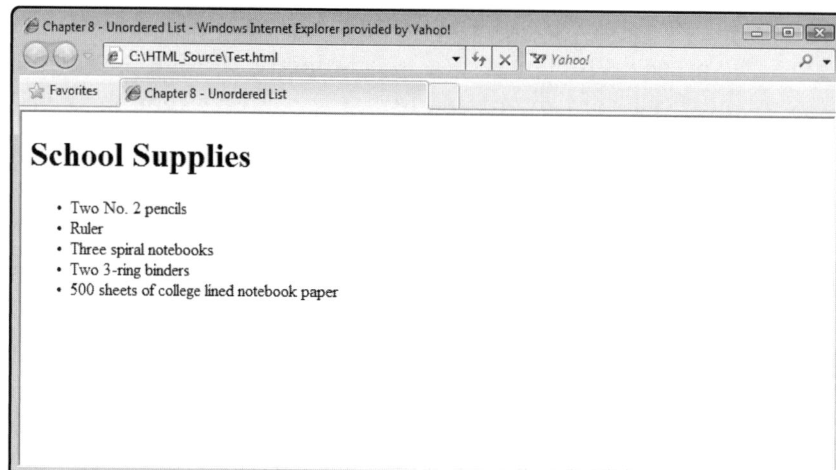

FIGURE 8.14

An example of an unordered list displayed using the default marker.

Now, let's rework the example as shown below.

```
<!DOCTYPE html PUBLIC "-//W3C//DTD XHTML 1.0 Strict//EN"
  "http://www.w3.org/TR/xhtml1/DTD/xhtml1-strict.dtd">

<html xmlns="http://www.w3.org/1999/xhtml" lang="en" xml:lang="en">

  <head>
    <meta http-equiv="Content-type" content="text/xhtml; charset=UTF-8" />
    <title>Chapter 8 - Styled Unordered List</title>
    <style type = "text/css">
      ul {list-style-type: circle;}
    </style>
  </head>

  <body>
    <h1>School Supplies</h1>
    <ul>
      <li>Two No. 2 pencils</li>
      <li>Ruler</li>
      <li>Three spiral notebooks</li>
      <li>Two 3-ring binders</li>
      <li>500 sheets of college lined notebook paper</li>
    </ul>
```

```
  </body>

</html>
```

As you can see, this example includes a style rule that uses the `list-style-type` property to alter the display of the maker to a circle, as shown in Figure 8.15.

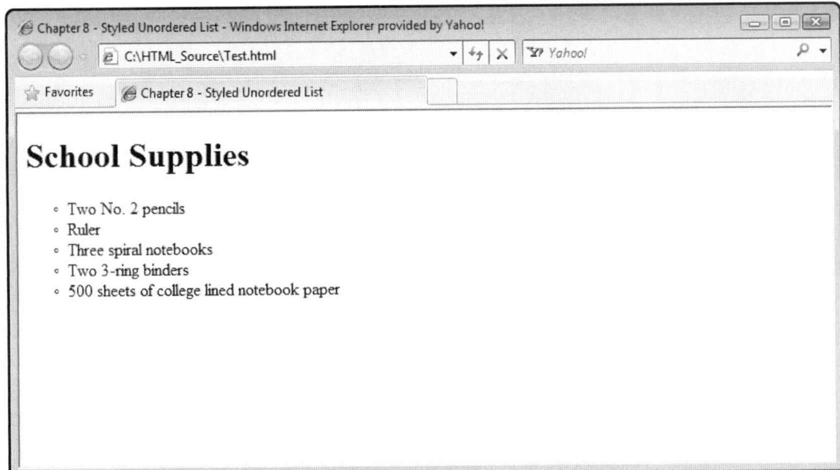

FIGURE 8.15
An example of an unordered list that has been configured to use the circle marker.

As demonstrated in both of the previous examples, take note that regardless of which marker type you elect to use, CSS automatically sizes the marker to ensure that it is kept proportional with its associated text.

Creating Custom List Markers

If you are not satisfied with the set of graphic markers made available by CSS, you can create and use your own marker using the `list-style-image` property. To use this property to supply your own custom marker, you must specify the URL of the graphic file where the marker resides. In addition, you must ensure that the marker is proportionally sized to match up with its associated text. CSS will not automatically scale your custom marker.

As an example of how to use the `list-style-image` property, look at the following document.

```
<!DOCTYPE html PUBLIC "-//W3C//DTD XHTML 1.0 Strict//EN"
  "http://www.w3.org/TR/xhtml1/DTD/xhtml1-strict.dtd">

<html xmlns="http://www.w3.org/1999/xhtml" lang="en" xml:lang="en">
```

```
  <head>
    <meta http-equiv="Content-type" content="text/xhtml; charset=UTF-8" />
    <title>Chapter 8 - Customized List Markers</title>
    <style type = "text/css">
      body {font-size: 1.6pc;}
      ul {list-style-image: url("ball.jpg");}
    </style>
  </head>

  <body>
    <h1>Popular NBA Teams</h1>
    <ul>
      <li>Boston Celtics</li>
      <li>Orlando Magic</li>
      <li>Cleveland Cavaliers</li>
      <li>Dallas Mavericks</li>
    </ul>
  </body>

</html>
```

As you can see, this example uses a custom graphic named ball.jpg as the basis for creating a customized marker. Figure 8.16 shows how this example looks when rendered by the browser.

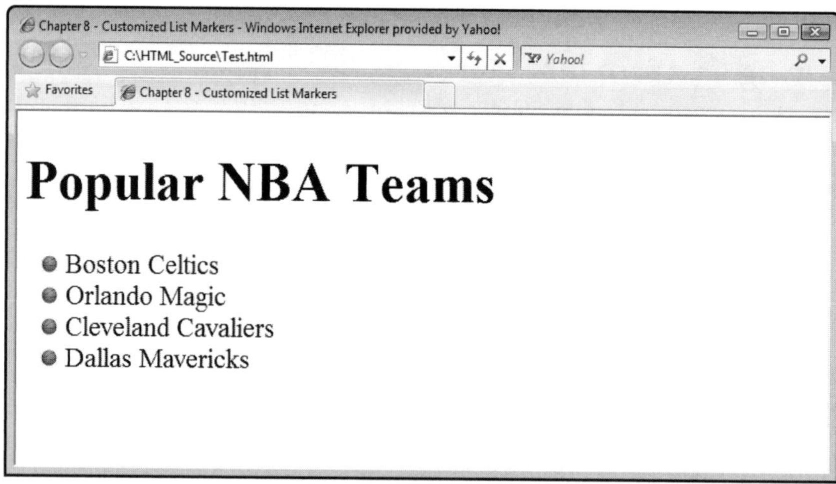

FIGURE 8.16

An example of an unordered list that uses a customized marker.

Styling Links

Another useful application of CSS is in style links. This includes both text and graphic links. For example, by default, browsers generally underline links and change the color in which they are displayed based on their status. Blue may be used to identify a link that has not been touched, while links that have been visited may be displayed in purple. If this color scheme is not consistent with the color scheme of your website you may want to modify the style of those links. This is accomplished by applying style rules to the anchor element while using pseudo classes.

Modifying the Presentation of Text Links

You were introduced to pseudo classes in Chapter 7. CSS supports five pseudo classes, all of which are designed to work with the anchor element. The following document demonstrates how you can use them in conjunction with CSS to take control over the appearance of all your links.

```
<!DOCTYPE html PUBLIC "-//W3C//DTD XHTML 1.0 Strict//EN"
  "http://www.w3.org/TR/xhtml1/DTD/xhtml1-strict.dtd">

<html xmlns="http://www.w3.org/1999/xhtml" lang="en" xml:lang="en">

  <head>
    <meta http-equiv="Content-type" content="text/xhtml; charset=UTF-8" />
    <title>Chapter 8 - Customized Links</title>
    <style type = "text/css">
      body {font-size: 1.4pc;}
      a:link {color: blue;}
      a:visited {color: green;}
      a:hover {color: red; font-weight: bolder; text-decoration: none;}
      a:active {color: green;}
      a:focus {color: red; font-weight: bolder; text-decoration: none;}
    </style>
  </head>

  <body>
    <p><a href = "index.html">Home</a></p>
    <p><a href = "products.html">Products</a></p>
    <p><a href = "services.html">Services</a></p>
    <p><a href = "downloads.html">Downloads</a></p>
```

```
    <p><a href = "custserv.html">Customer Service</a></p>
  </body>

</html>
```

Figure 8.17 demonstrates how things look when this document has been loaded into the browser and the mouse-pointer has been moved over the Products link.

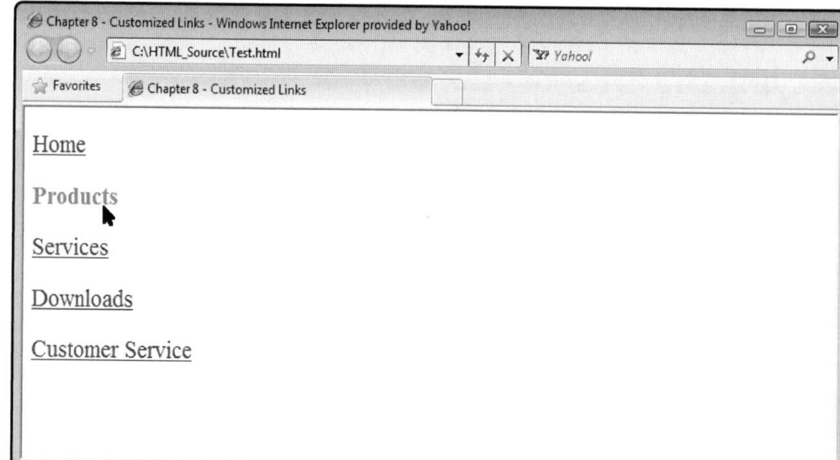

FIGURE 8.17 An example of how to use CSS to alter the presentation of document text links.

Creating Graphical Links

Another common use of CSS is to convert text links into graphic links. To accomplish this, you need to use CSS to add a border to the link, and give it a background color, as demonstrated in the following example:

```
<!DOCTYPE html PUBLIC "-//W3C//DTD XHTML 1.0 Strict//EN"
  "http://www.w3.org/TR/xhtml1/DTD/xhtml1-strict.dtd">

<html xmlns="http://www.w3.org/1999/xhtml" lang="en" xml:lang="en">

  <head>
    <meta http-equiv="Content-type" content="text/xhtml; charset=UTF-8" />
    <title>Chapter 8 - Graphic Links</title>
    <style type = "text/css">
      a {border: 3px solid black;
         display: block;
```

```
        font: 14px Arial;
        text-decoration: none;
        text-align: center;
        width: 200px;
        height: 20px;
        background: yellow;
        color: blue;
      }
    a:focus, a:hover, a:active {
        background: red;
      }

    </style>
  </head>

  <body>
    <p><a href = "index.html">Home</a></p>
    <p><a href = "products.html">Products</a></p>
    <p><a href = "services.html">Services</a></p>
    <p><a href = "downloads.html">Downloads</a></p>
    <p><a href = "custserv.html">Customer Service</a></p>
  </body>

</html>
```

When this document is loaded into the browser, the first CSS style rule configures all of the links so that they are displayed with a solid black border that is 150 pixels wide and 30 pixels high. Their containers have been given a yellow background. The second rule uses two pseudo classes to modify the background color of each link's container whenever the mouse pointer is moved over it or when it becomes active. The result is a simple but impressive set of graphic menu controls that when clicked control navigation to other web pages.

Figure 8.18 demonstrates how things look when this document has been loaded into the browser and the mouse-pointer has been moved over the container for the Services link.

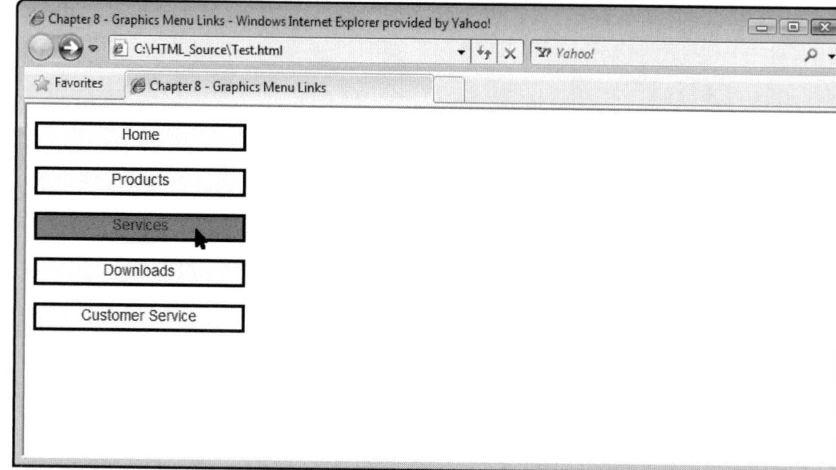

FIGURE 8.18

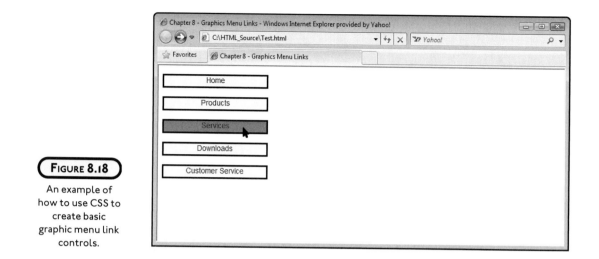

An example of how to use CSS to create basic graphic menu link controls.

If you want to get even fancier, you can use background images in place of background colors, as demonstrated in the following example.

```
<!DOCTYPE html PUBLIC "-//W3C//DTD XHTML 1.0 Strict//EN"
  "http://www.w3.org/TR/xhtml1/DTD/xhtml1-strict.dtd">

<html xmlns="http://www.w3.org/1999/xhtml" lang="en" xml:lang="en">

  <head>
    <meta http-equiv="Content-type" content="text/xhtml; charset=UTF-8" />
    <title>Chapter 8 - Graphic Button Links</title>
    <style type = "text/css">
      a {display: block;
         font: 14px Arial;
         text-decoration: none;
         text-align: center;
         width: 200px;
         height: 20px;
         /*background: yellow;*/
         background-image: url("yellow.png");
         color: blue;
      }
    a:focus, a:hover, a:active {
         /*background: red;*/
```

```
        background-image: url("red.png");
      }
    </style>
  </head>

  <body>
    <p><a href = "index.html">Home</a></p>
    <p><a href = "products.html">Products</a></p>
    <p><a href = "services.html">Services</a></p>
    <p><a href = "downloads.html">Downloads</a></p>
    <p><a href = "custserv.html">Customer Service</a></p>
  </body>

</html>
```

The differences between this example and the one before it are highlighted in bold. As you can see, instead of using the `background` property, this new version of the document uses the `background-image` property to display graphic files. This example makes use of two graphic image files. These two images contain a copy of an almost identical graphic button, the only difference being the color of the buttons. When loaded into the browser, CSS automatically centers and displays link text on the graphic button. Figure 8.19 demonstrates how this example looks when loaded into the browser.

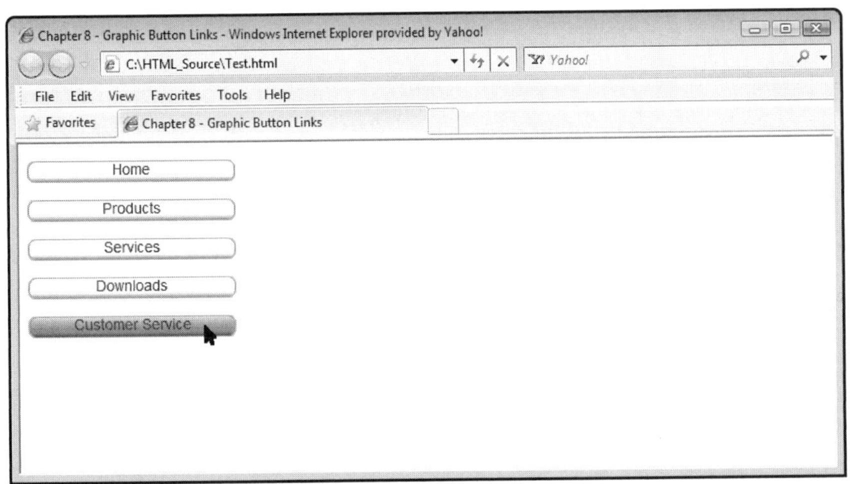

FIGURE 8.19

An example of how to use CSS to create fancy graphic menu link controls.

Using CSS to Better Integrate Text and Images

Another good use of CSS is to help better integrate and style the presentation of the flow of text and graphics on your web pages. Using CSS, you can, for example, wrap text around graphics in much the same way as is done in magazines and newspapers. CSS also makes easy work of adding graphics as backgrounds for your web pages.

Wrapping Text Around Graphics

The trick to wrapping text around graphics lies in the application of the `float` property. An element that is floated, in this case a graphic, is shifted to the right or left, allowing text to flow around it. The `float` property supports the following values: `left`, `right`, and `none`. The following example demonstrates how to use the `float` property to flow text around the right side of a figure (as opposed to displaying it over or under the figure).

```
<!DOCTYPE html PUBLIC "-//W3C//DTD XHTML 1.0 Strict//EN"
  "http://www.w3.org/TR/xhtml1/DTD/xhtml1-strict.dtd">

<html xmlns="http://www.w3.org/1999/xhtml" lang="en" xml:lang="en">

  <head>
    <meta http-equiv="Content-type" content="text/xhtml; charset=UTF-8" />
    <title>Chapter 8 - Styled Graphic Demo</title>
    <style type = "text/css">
      p {
        border-width: thin;
        border-style: solid;
        width: 500px;
        height: 210px;
      }
      #logo {
        float: left;
      }
    </style>
  </head>

  <body>
    <p>
      <img id = "logo" src = "TwoCats.jpg" width = "149" height = "149"
        alt = "Two Cats Logo" />
```

```
      Welcome to <em>Two Cats Consignment Shop</em>. We buy and sell
      anything and everything. Stop by and see what we have got in
      store for you! We specialize in antique furniture and rare
      artwork. However, we have a little something for everyone. This week
      we are featuring hand-crafted tableware from mid-18th century Europe.
      We are open from 8am to 5pm Monday - Friday and from noon to 4pm on
      Saturdays. If you have something you would like to put on
      consignment, please call for an appointment. Our phone number is
      (999) 888 - 1234. We look forward to seeing or hearing from you soon!

    </p>
  </body>

</html>
```

If you look closely, you will see that the document's image `img` element has been assigned an ID of `Logo` and that a style rule has been used to apply the `float` property to the element. Note that the value of `float` has been set to `left` and that a paragraph rule has also been added that wraps up the paragraph and all its contents, including the `img` element, in a solid border.

Figure 8.20 shows how this example output is rendered by the browser.

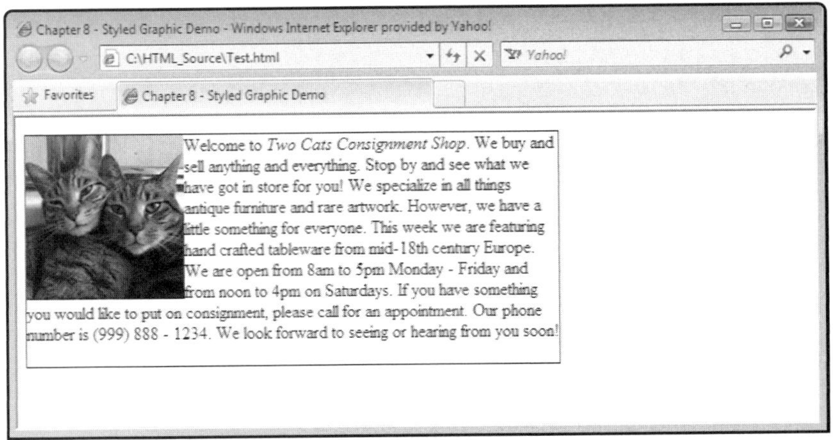

FIGURE 8.20 Using the `float` property to allow text to flow around the side of an image.

Note that while the text now wraps around the right side of the graphic, things look a little crowded because the text is so tightly placed up against the side of the graphic. However, this can easily be remedied by modifying the style rule and configuring the margin for the `img` element as demonstrated here.

```
<style type = "text/css">
  p {
    border-width: thin;
    border-style: solid;
    width: 500px;
    height: 210px;
  }
  #logo {
    float: left;
    margin-right: 10px;
    margin-bottom: 2px;
  }
</style>
```

As you can see, rather than use the `margin` property to set the margin for all four sides of the `img` element, the `margin-right` and `margin-bottom` properties were used to modify both the element's right and lower margins. Figure 8.21 shows how these changes to the style rule have affected the resulting web page.

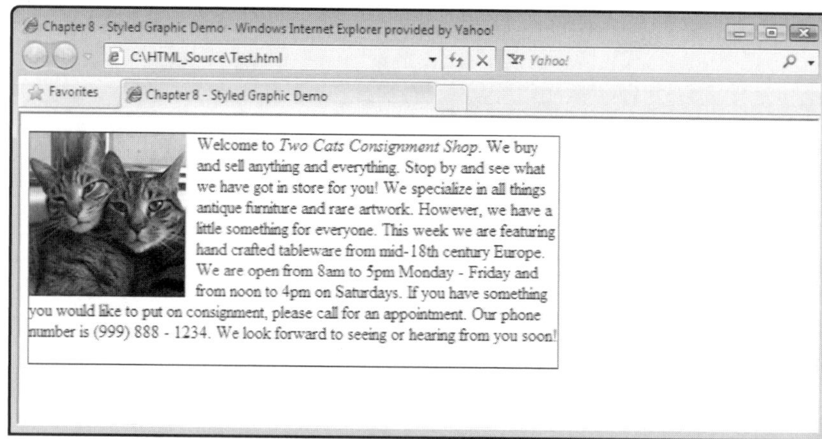

FIGURE 8.21

You can improve presentation by setting the image's right and bottom margins.

Adding a Background Image to Your Web Page

You have no doubt visited different websites that display graphic images as background on web pages. You can do the same thing using the `background-image` property. Of course, to be effective, the image you display must not overpower the content that you want to display. To use the `background-image` property, all you have to do is specify the URL of the graphic file you want to use, as demonstrated in the following example.

```
<!DOCTYPE html PUBLIC "-//W3C//DTD XHTML 1.0 Strict//EN"
  "http://www.w3.org/TR/xhtml1/DTD/xhtml1-strict.dtd">

<html xmlns="http://www.w3.org/1999/xhtml" lang="en" xml:lang="en">

  <head>
    <meta http-equiv="Content-type" content="text/xhtml; charset=UTF-8" />
    <title>Chapter 8 - Background Demo</title>
    <style type = "text/css">
      body {
        background-image: url(background.png);
      }
      h1 {
        font-size: 3pc;
      }
      p {
        font-size: 2pc;
      }
    </style>
  </head>

  <body>

    <h1>Welcome to "Who is asking?"</h1>

    <p>
      Our guest tonight is funny man Tim Soboring. Tim is currently hosting
      the hit TV comedy
      "What's on my Mind."
    </p>

    <p>
      Tomorrow's guest will be movie star and civic activist Carolyn
      Crywithme.
    </p>

  </body>

</html>
```

Here, an image file named background.png is used as the document's background, accomplished using the `background-image` property with a rule that styles the document's `body` element. Figure 8.22 shows an example of how this document looks when rendered by the browser.

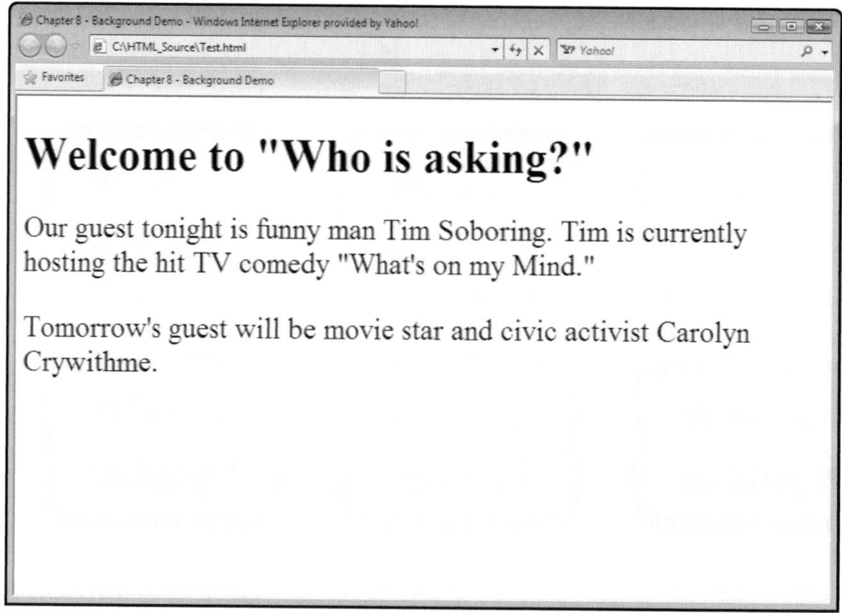

FIGURE 8.22

An example of how to use CSS to add a background to your web pages.

Note that by default, the image is tiled, both horizontally and vertically, in the event the image is too small to fill the entire browser window. You can modify this behavior by adding the `background-repeat` property to the `body` element's style rule. This property supports the following values.

- **repeat-x.** Tiles the image horizontally.
- **repeat-y.** Tiles the image vertically.
- **no-repeat**. Disables image tiling.

STYLING YOUR TABLES

CSS provides extensive control over the presentation of tables. You can create CSS rules that add table borders, pad table cells, collapse individual cell borders, add background color, set border color, and control text alignment.

In Chapter 6, you learned how to add borders to your tables using the `table` element's `border` attribute. Though effective, it is better to use CSS's `border-style` property to add borders to your tables. Not only is using the `border-style` property considered better form, but it also provides the ability to specify any of the following values:

- dashed
- dotted
- double
- groove
- hidden
- inset
- none
- outset
- solid

The following document provides an example of how to set a table's border using the `border-style` property.

```
<!DOCTYPE html PUBLIC "-//W3C//DTD XHTML 1.0 Strict//EN"
  "http://www.w3.org/TR/xhtml1/DTD/xhtml1-strict.dtd">

<html xmlns="http://www.w3.org/1999/xhtml" lang="en" xml:lang="en">

  <head>
    <meta http-equiv="Content-type" content="text/xhtml; charset=UTF-8" />
    <title>Chapter 8 - Background Demo</title>
    <style type = "text/css">
      table {
        border-style: solid;
      }
      th, td {
        border-style: solid;
      }
    </style>
  </head>

  <body>
```

```
    <table>
      <tr>
        <th scope = "col">Team</th>
        <th scope = "col">City</th>
        <th scope = "col">Conference</th>
      </tr>
      <tr>
        <td>Lakers</td>
        <td>Los Angeles</td>
        <td>West</td>
      </tr>
      <tr>
        <td>Celtics</td>
        <td>Boston</td>
        <td>East</td>
      </tr>
      <tr>
        <td>Magic</td>
        <td>Orlando</td>
        <td>East</td>
      </tr>
      <tr>
        <td>Cavaliers</td>
        <td>Cleveland</td>
        <td>East</td>
      </tr>
    </table>

  </body>

</html>
```

Figure 8.23 shows how the table produced by this example looks when rendered by the browser.

By default, the browser allocated only enough space to a row or column to accommodate its largest cell entry. You can often make a table look better by using the padding property to add a little extra white space to its cells. To demonstrate how this works, let's modify the embedded style sheet from the previous example as shown here:

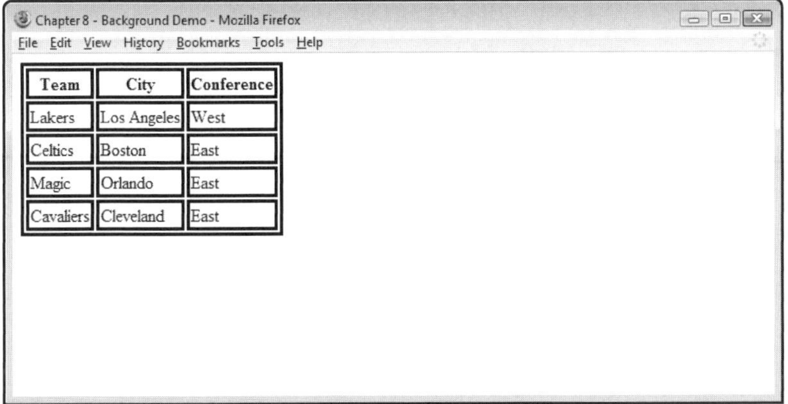

FIGURE 8.23

Using CSS to add a border to your table.

```
<style type = "text/css">
  table {
    border-style: solid;
  }
  th, td {
    border-style: solid;
    padding: 10px
  }
</style>
```

Figure 8.24 shows how the table looks once it has been rendered using the updated style rule.

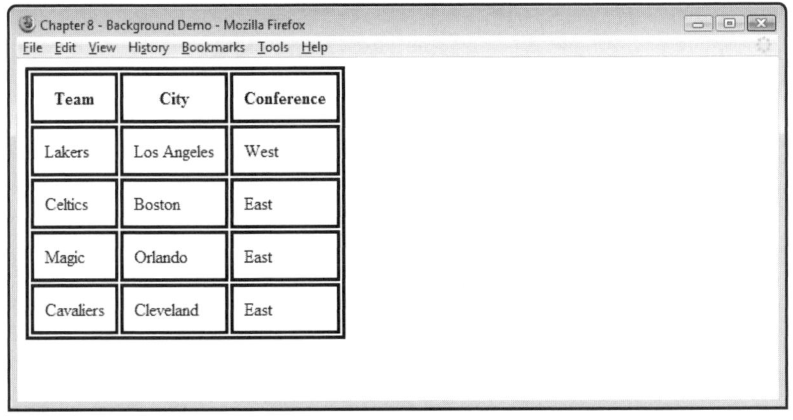

FIGURE 8.24

Using CSS to add a little padding to table cells.

If you look closely at Figure 8.24, you will notice that every cell in the table has its own individual border. If you want, you can modify the `table` element's style rule by adding the `border-collapse` property to it (with a value of `collapse`) to disable this presentation effect, as demonstrated here:

```
<style type = "text/css">
  table {
    border-style: solid;
    border-collapse: collapse;
  }
  th, td {
    border-style: solid;
    padding: 10px
  }
</style>
```

Figure 8.25 shows the effect that this rule change has on the table.

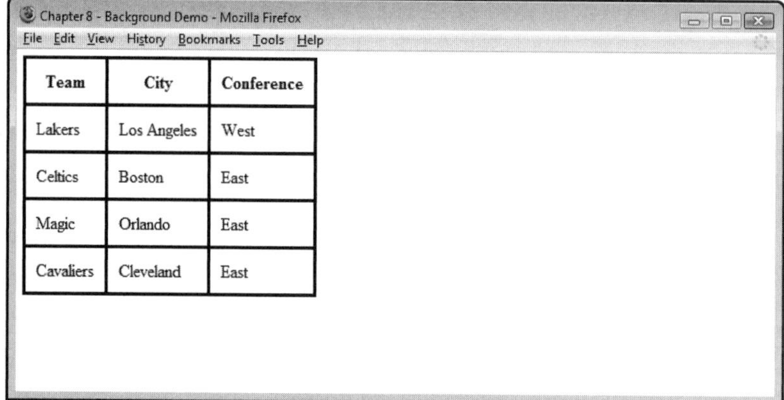

FIGURE 8.25

Using CSS to collapse individual cell borders.

Often table headings are highlighted by assigning a background color to them. This makes them stand out and helps make table data easier to scan. To add background color to cells in your tables, all you have to do is add the `background-color` property to the style rule for the appropriate table elements, as demonstrated here:

```
<style type = "text/css">
  table {
    border-style: solid;
    border-collapse: collapse;
```

```
  }
  th, td {
    border-style: solid;
    padding: 10px
  }
  th {
    background-color: gray;
  }
</style>
```

Figure 8.26 shows the effect that this rule change has on the table.

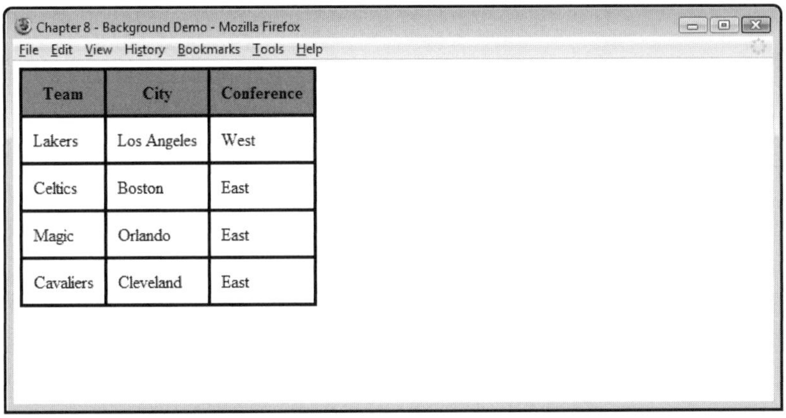

Team	City	Conference
Lakers	Los Angeles	West
Celtics	Boston	East
Magic	Orlando	East
Cavaliers	Cleveland	East

FIGURE 8.26
Using CSS to add background color to your tables.

If you want, you can even specify the color of your tables by assigning a color to them, as demonstrated here:

```
<style type = "text/css">
  table {
    border-style: solid;
    border-collapse: collapse;
  }
  th, td {
    border-style: solid;
    padding: 10px;
    border-color: blue;
  }
  th {
```

```
    background-color: gray;
  }
</style>
```

You can even use CSS to control the alignment of text within labels using the `text-align` property, assigning it a value of `left`, `right`, `center`, or `justify`. To demonstrate how to work with this property, let's modify the previous style sheet as shown here:

```
<style type = "text/css">
  table {
    border-style: solid;
    border-collapse: collapse;
  }
  th, td {
    border-style: solid;
    padding: 10px;
    border-color: blue;
  }
  th {
    background-color: gray;
    text-align: left
  }
</style>
```

Figure 8.27 shows the effect that this style modification has on the table.

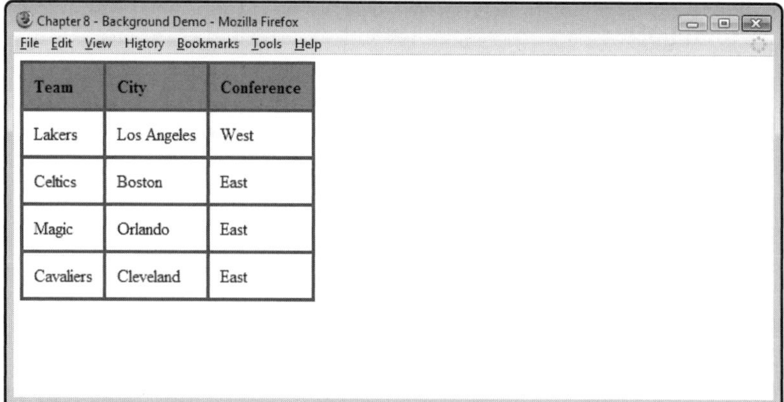

FIGURE 8.27

Using CSS to control cell alignment.

Styling Your Forms

One final area where we will look at applying CSS is in the modification of form presentation. Forms are challenging to style because every browser displays them differently. Form elements are closely tied to the operating system. To try to provide users with a consistent environment in which to work, browsers rely on the operating system to render form controls. As such, form appearance is heavily affected by the operating system's native presentation scheme. This scheme not only varies from operating system to operating system, but it also often varies between different versions of the same operating system. For example, Windows Vista's controls have a distinct look and feel from those provided by Windows XP.

Given the above restrictions, it is all but impossible to create forms that look exactly the same on every computer that loads your web documents. As such, it's often best to allow the browser to render forms using its default style. This brings with it the benefit that your visitors will see your form presented in a manner consistent with their experience and expectations. So, while you should avoid tinkering around with your form's controls, there is often plenty of value in modifying the presentation of the other elements on your forms, including headings, paragraphs, labels, and fieldsets.

As an example of how you might go about modifying a form's appearance, look at the following, which you might recognize from Chapter 6.

```
<!DOCTYPE html PUBLIC "-//W3C//DTD XHTML 1.0 Strict//EN"
  "http://www.w3.org/TR/xhtml1/DTD/xhtml1-strict.dtd">

<html xmlns="http://www.w3.org/1999/xhtml" lang="en" xml:lang="en">

  <head>
    <meta http-equiv="Content-type" content="text/xhtml; charset=UTF-8" />
    <title>Chapter 6 - Building Forms</title>
    <style type = "text/css">
      body {
        color: blue;
      }
      fieldset {
        padding: 10px;
        max-width: 300px;
        border: double;
      }
      .textbox {
```

```
      float: left;
      width: 220px;
    }
  </style>
</head>

<body>

  <h1>Joe's Custom T-Shirts</h1>

  <form action = "/cgi-bin/processdata.cgi" method = "post">

    <p>
      <label class = "textbox" for = "name">Last name: (8 character
        max.)</label>
      <input type = "text" id = "name" name = "name" size = "8"
        maxlength = "8" />
    </p>

    <p>
      <label class = "textbox" for = "number">Jersey number: (2
        character max.)</label>
      <input type = "text" id = "number" name = "number" size = "2"
        maxlength = "2" />
    </p>

    <fieldset>
      <legend>Pick your size:</legend>
      <input type = "checkbox" id = "checkbox1" name = "checkbox1"
        value = "Small" checked = "checked" />
      <label for = "checkbox1">Small</label><br />
      <input type = "checkbox" id = "checkbox2" name = "checkbox2"
        value = "Medium" />
      <label for = "checkbox2">Medium</label><br />
      <input type = "checkbox" id = "checkbox3" name = "checkbox3"
        value = "Large"/>
      <label for = "checkbox3">Large</label><br />
      <input type = "checkbox" id = "checkbox4" name = "checkbox4"
```

```
        value = "Extra Large" />
      <label for = "checkbox4">Extra Large</label>
    </fieldset>

    <fieldset>
      <legend>Choose a color:</legend>
      <input type = "radio" id = "radio1" name = "radio"
        value = "Red" />
      <label for = "radio1">Red</label><br />
      <input type = "radio" id = "radio2" name = "radio"
        value = "Blue" checked = "checked" />
      <label for = "radio2">Blue</label><br />
      <input type = "radio" id = "radio3" name = "radio"
        value = "Green" />
      <label for = "radio3">Green</label><br />
    </fieldset>

    <p>
      <input type = "submit" id = "submit_button" name = "submit_button"
        value = "Submit Order Information" />
      <input type = "reset" id = "reset_button" name = "reset_button"
        value = "Reset Form" />
    </p>

  </form>

 </body>

</html>
```

If you look at this example's style rules, you will see that the first rule configures the display of the form's text in blue. In addition, a rule has been set up that modifies the appearance of the form's `fieldset` element in several ways. For starters, a little extra padding has been added to keep things from being too bunched up. Second, the width of the `fieldset` element is set to 300 pixels, overriding the default behavior of making the `fieldset` span the width of the entire browser window. Last, the `fieldset` element's border has been set to `double` just to spice things up a bit. The final style rule affects the presentation of the two labels assigned to the `textbox` class. The rule makes the labels float to the left and sets their width to 220 pixels.

As a result, the text control associated with the label becomes vertically aligned, as shown in Figure 8.28.

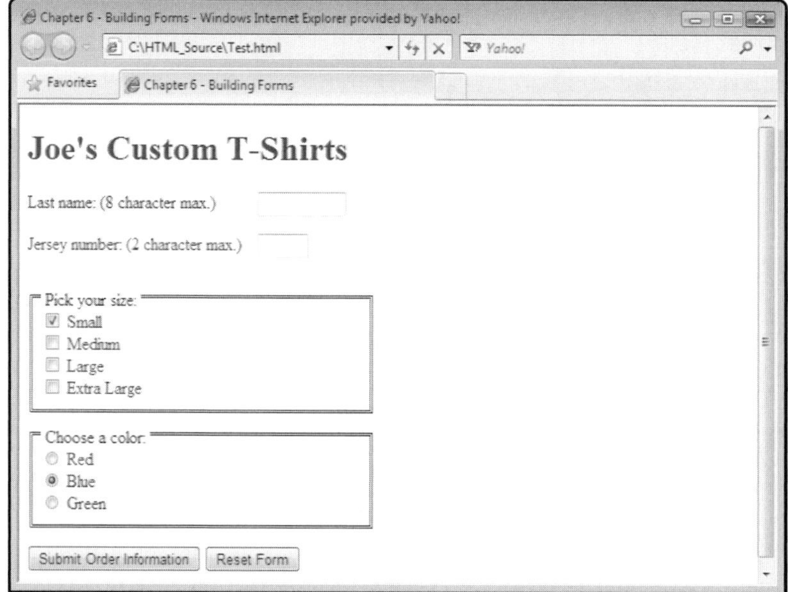

FIGURE 8.28

Using CSS to customize form presentation.

Styling Based on Output Device

Depending on your target audience, you may find that you need to configure CSS to present your content differently. For example, if your web content is targeted at an audience that is visually disabled, you might want to make sure your style is directed towards braille output devices. To define the type of media you want to target, you need to include the `style` element's optional `media` attribute. This attribute specifies the type of media your content should be styled for. The following list of values can be assigned to the `media` attribute.

- all
- aural
- braille
- handheld
- print
- projection
- screen

- tty
- tv

If you want, you can use the @media rule, which will allow you to specify more than one media type, as demonstrated in the following example.

```
<style type = "text/css">
  @media print {
    body { font-size: 12pt; }
  }
  @media screen {
    body { font-size: 14px; }
  }
  @media screen, print {
    body { color: blue; }
  }
</style>
```

Here, a font size of 12 points was specified for the text when printed. However, a font size of 14 points was specified for text when displayed in the browser window. In addition, the third rule has configured the use of blue when printing and displaying text.

Back to the Fortune Teller Game

All right, now it is time to return your attention to this chapter's project, the Fortune Teller game. This game simulates a session with a Fortune Teller, allowing the player to enter any number of questions. Answers to the player's questions are randomly generated and dynamically displayed in the browser window. To make the applications more appealing, an external style sheet will be used to improve various aspects of its presentation.

Designing the Application

To help make things easier to digest, this web project will be completed in a series of steps, as outlined here:

1. Create a new XHTML document.
2. Develop the document's markup.
3. Add meta and title elements.
4. Specify document content.
5. Create the document's script.
6. Create an external style sheet.
7. Load and test the Fortune Teller game.

Step 1: Creating a New XHTML Document

The first step in the development of the Fortune Teller game is to create a new web document. Do so using your preferred code or text editor. Save the document as a plain text file named FortuneTeller.html. This web document will make use of CSS style rules. Therefore, you will need to create a second file named ft.css.

Step 2: Developing the Document's Markup

The next step in the development of this project is to assemble the document's markup. To do so, add the following elements to the FortuneTeller.html file.

```
<!DOCTYPE html PUBLIC "-//W3C//DTD XHTML 1.0 Strict//EN"
  "http://www.w3.org/TR/xhtml1/DTD/xhtml1-strict.dtd">

<html xmlns="http://www.w3.org/1999/xhtml" lang="en" xml:lang="en">

  <head>

  </head>

  <body>

  </body>

</html>
```

Step 3: Adding meta and title Elements

Next, add the following elements to the document's `head` section.

```
<meta http-equiv="Content-type" content="text/xhtml; charset=UTF-8" />
<title>The Fortune Teller Game</title>
```

As previously stated, this web application will make use of an external style sheet named ft.css. To set this up, add the following link to the external style sheet to the end of the `head` section.

```
<link href = "ft.css" type = "text/css" rel = "stylesheet" />
```

Step 4: Specifying Document Content

Now it is time to work on laying out this document's markup. Begin by adding the following elements to the document's `body` section.

```
<div>
  <img src = "title.png" width = "550px" height = "104px" alt = "Game Logo" />
</div>
```

As you can see, these elements place an image inside a div element. The img element is used to display a graphic showing the game's logo, which is displayed at the top of the browser window. The rest of the document's markup is made up of a form and its elements.

Note that the form element's action attribute has been set to the web page itself and not to a server-side form handler. Also, note that the form has no Submit button (and thus no need for a form handler). The form has two input elements, one with a text control and one for a button control. Both elements are assigned a unique ID. In addition, the button element ends with a JavaScript statement that uses the onClick() event handler to execute a JavaScript function named AnswerQuestion().

The game will dynamically display text that shows the Fortune Teller answers each time a new question is asked. To facilitate the display of this information a span element has been added to the end of the form and assigned an ID of answer.

```
<form action = "FortuneTeller.html">


  <p>
    Instructions:
  </p>
  <p>
    To play this game all you have to do is type in a question that
    you would like the Fortune Teller to answer. Make sure that you
    phrase your question so that it can be answered with Yes/No styled
    responses. Once you have finished entering your question, click on
    the <em>Get Answer</em> button to see what the Fortune Teller has
    to say.
  </p>

  <p>
    <input type = "text" size = "68px" id = "inputField" />

    <input type = "button" value = "Get Answer" id = "checkBtn"
      Onclick = "AnswerQuestion()" />
  </p>
```

```
  <p><span id = "answer"> </span></p>

</form>
```

By assigning the span element a unique ID, you enable the application's JavaScript statements to dynamically update its content using the DOM.

Step 5: Creating the Document's Script

Now that the document's markup is complete, it is time to lay out its JavaScript code. Begin by adding the following statements to the document's head section.

```
<script type = "text/javascript">
<!-- Start hiding JavaScript statements

// End hiding JavaScript statements -->
</script>
```

These statements provide the markup needed to support the definition of the script. The JavaScript itself consists of two functions named AnswerQuestion() and ResetScreen(). The AnswerQuestion() function is executed whenever the player clicks on the game's button control. To create this function, embed the following statements inside the script element's opening <script> and closing </script> tags:

```
function AnswerQuestion() {
  var checkButton = document.getElementById("checkBtn");

  if (document.getElementById('inputField').value == "") {
    window.alert("You did not submit a question. Try again.");
  } else {

    randomNo = 1 + Math.random() * 9;
    randomNo = Math.round(randomNo);

    switch (randomNo) {
    case 1:
      document.getElementById('answer').innerHTML = "Yes!";
      break;
    case 2:
      document.getElementById('answer').innerHTML = "No.";
      break;
```

```
    case 3:
      document.getElementById('answer').innerHTML = "Maybe.";
      break;
    case 4:
      document.getElementById('answer').innerHTML = "Doubtful.";
      break;
    case 5:
      document.getElementById('answer').innerHTML =
        "Not in this lifetime.";
      break;
    case 6:
      document.getElementById('answer').innerHTML =
        "The answer is unclear.";
      break;
    case 7:
      document.getElementById('answer').innerHTML =
        "Ask this question again later.";
      break;
    case 8:
      document.getElementById('answer').innerHTML =
        "Today is your lucky day... Yes!";
      break;
    case 9:
      document.getElementById('answer').innerHTML =
        "Sorry but the answer is no.";
      break;
    case 10:
      document.getElementById('answer').innerHTML = "No way!";
      break;
    }
    setTimeout("ResetScreen()", 3000)

  }
}
```

The `AnswerQuestion()` function begins by declaring a variable named `checkButton`, which is used to set up a reference to the document's button control. Next, a check is made to ensure that the user actually typed a question before clicking on the button control. If not, an error message is displayed in a popup dialog window. If a question was submitted, a random number from 1 to 10 is generated and stored in a variable named `randomNo`. A `switch` statement code block is then used to compare the value stored in `randomNo` against ten `case` statements, each of which is assigned a value from 1 to 10. When a match is found, that `case` statement is executed. The first of these statements used dot notation and the DOM to assign (display) a text string inside the document's `span` element. This element assigned an ID of `answer`. The assignment is made using the `document` object's `getElementById()` method along with the `innerHTML` property. As soon as the assignment is made, a `break` statement is executed, terminating the execution of the rest of the `switch` statement code block.

The JavaScript `SetTimeout()` function is then executed. This function accepts two arguments, the name of a JavaScript to execute and a numeric value specifying how many milliseconds to pause before the specified function is executed (300 milliseconds equals 3 seconds).

So, after a three-second pause, the `ResetScreen()` function, shown below, is executed. This function uses dot notation and the DOM to clear out the player's questions and the game's answer in order to ready the game for a another question.

```
function ResetScreen() {
  document.getElementById('inputField').value = "";
  document.getElementById('answer').innerHTML = "";
}
```

Step 6: Creating an External Style Sheet

The FortuneTeller.html document is styled using an external style sheet named ft.css. The rules stored in this style sheet are shown here:

```
body {
  background-color: white;
  }

div {
  border-width: thin;
  border-style: solid;
  width: 550px;
  height: 104px;
  }

p {font-family: Arial;
  color: green;
```

```
  font-size: 1pc; }

span {
  font-size: 1.5pc }
  font-weight: bold;
  color: green;
  }
```

The first rule explicitly assigns white as the web page's background color. The second rule formats the document's `div` element, assigning it a thin, solid border that is 550 pixels wide and 104 pixels high (e.g., the exact dimension of the `img` element embedded inside the `div` element). The third rule assigns the font type, color, and size for all text stored in the document's paragraph elements. The last rule assigns the font size, height, and color of the text displayed inside the document's `span` element, making it a little larger than that of its paragraph text.

Step 7: Loading and Testing the Fortune Teller Game

Assuming you have followed along carefully, your copy of the FortuneTeller.html document should be complete. To make sure you have assembled it correctly, look at the following example, which shows a complete copy of the finished document.

```
<!DOCTYPE html PUBLIC "-//W3C//DTD XHTML 1.0 Strict//EN"
  "http://www.w3.org/TR/xhtml1/DTD/xhtml1-strict.dtd">

<html xmlns="http://www.w3.org/1999/xhtml" lang="en" xml:lang="en">

  <head>
    <meta http-equiv="Content-type" content="text/xhtml; charset=UTF-8" />
    <title>The Fortune Teller Game</title>
    <link href = "ft.css" type = "text/css" rel = "stylesheet" />

    <script type = "text/javascript">
    <!-- Start hiding JavaScript statements

      function AnswerQuestion() {
        var checkButton = document.getElementById("checkBtn");

        if (document.getElementById('inputField').value == "") {
          window.alert("You did not submit a question. Try again.");
```

```
} else {

  randomNo = 1 + Math.random() * 9;
  randomNo = Math.round(randomNo);

  switch (randomNo) {
  case 1:
    document.getElementById('answer').innerHTML = "Yes!";
    break;
  case 2:
    document.getElementById('answer').innerHTML = "No.";
    break;
  case 3:
    document.getElementById('answer').innerHTML = "Maybe.";
    break;
  case 4:
    document.getElementById('answer').innerHTML = "Doubtful.";
    break;
  case 5:
    document.getElementById('answer').innerHTML =
      "Not in this lifetime.";
    break;
  case 6:
    document.getElementById('answer').innerHTML =
      "The answer is unclear.";
    break;
  case 7:
    document.getElementById('answer').innerHTML =
      "Ask this question again later.";
    break;
  case 8:
    document.getElementById('answer').innerHTML =
      "Today is your lucky day... Yes!";
    break;
  case 9:
    document.getElementById('answer').innerHTML =
      "Sorry but the answer is no.";
    break;
```

```
        case 10:
          document.getElementById('answer').innerHTML = "No way!";
          break;
        }
        setTimeout("ResetScreen()", 3000)

      }
    }

    function ResetScreen() {
      document.getElementById('inputField').value = "";
      document.getElementById('answer').innerHTML = "";
    }

  // End hiding JavaScript statements -->
  </script>

</head>

<body>

  <div>
    <img src = "title.png" width = "550 height = "104"
     alt = "Game Logo" />
  </div>

  <form action = "FortuneTeller.html">

    <p>
      Instructions:
    </p>
    <p>
      To play this game all you have to do is type in a question that
      you would like the Fortune Teller to answer. Make sure that you
      phrase your question so that it can be answered with Yes/No styled
      responses. Once you have finished entering your question, click on
      the <em>Get Answer</em> button to see what the Fortune Teller has
      to say.
```

```
      </p>

      <p>
        <input type = "textfield" size = "68" id = "inputField">

        <INPUT type = "button" value = "Get Answer" id = "checkBtn"
          onclick= AnswerQuestion()>
      </p>

      <p><span id = "answer"> </span></p>

    </form>

  </body>

</html>
```

If you have not already done so, save your document and load it into your web browser to see how things have turned out.

A complete copy of the source code for this project, including its style sheet and the graphics needed to create its graphic controls is available on the book's companion web page, located at www.courseptr.com/downloads.

Summary

This chapter rounded out your understanding of cascading style sheets by demonstrating its use in a variety of circumstances. This included learning how to use CSS to control the configuration of containers and including their placement, border, margins, and padding. You learned how to create CSS rules that modify the display of list markers and to create rollover links, controls, and buttons. This chapter also showed you how to use CSS to better integrate the presentation of text and images. On top of all this, you learned how to influence the presentation of forms and tables. This chapter wrapped things up by walking you through the creation of the Fortune Teller game.

Now, before you move on to Chapter 10, take a few minutes and enhance the Fortune Teller game by implementing the following challenges.

Challenges

1. As currently designed, the Fortune Teller Game displays one of ten randomly selected answers to player questions. However, it does not take long for the player to realize the limited range of answers. Make things more interesting by increasing the number of available answers.
2. As written, the Fortune Teller Game left justifies its graphic, text, and form. As a result, things look a little out of place if a user fully expands the browser window. To fix this, use CSS to center the display of all content.

Part IV

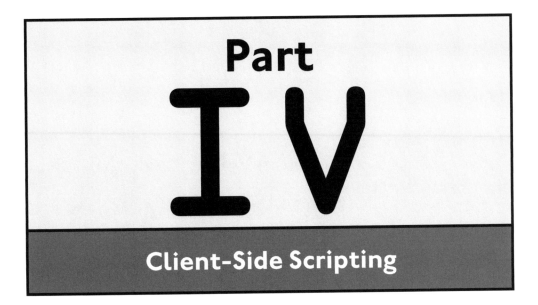

Client-Side Scripting

Client-Side Scripting

You have seen JavaScript used in most of the web projects presented in this book. That's because without JavaScript or some other equivalent type of programming language, it is impossible to create truly interactive web pages and applications. Of all browser-based programming languages currently available, JavaScript is by far the most popular and universally supported. JavaScript helps bind together (X)HTML, CSS, and the DOM. A good understanding of JavaScript is essential to any serious web developer.

Specifically, you will learn how to:

- Create and embed JavaScript in web pages
- Collect, store, and modify data using variables and to apply conditional and iterative programming logic
- Organize JavaScript statements into functions that process and return data
- Use arrays to store and process collections of data
- Trigger function execution when browser events occur

Project Preview: The Word Decoder Challenge

In this chapter's web project, you will learn how to create a new game called the Word Decoder Challenge. This game will present the player with a series of scrambled words and challenge him to attempt to unscramble them. When first started, the screen shown in Figure 9.1 is displayed. Game play occurs within a white rectangle area that is centered horizontally on the browser window.

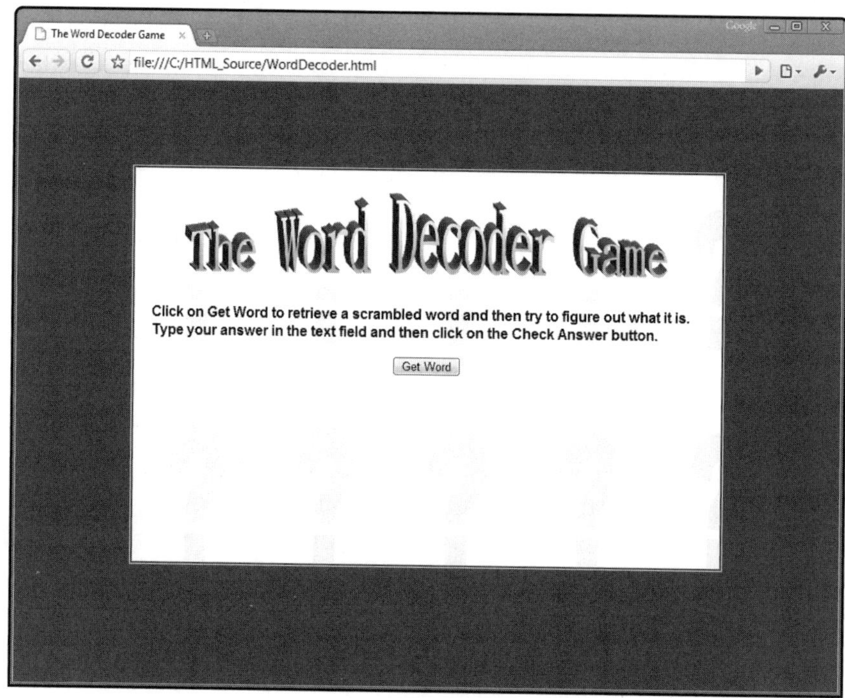

FIGURE 9.1

To begin game play the player clicks on the Get Word button.

Each time a new word is displayed, a browser window dynamically refreshes its content and displays a scrambled word in red, as demonstrated in Figure 9.2.

Once the player thinks the word has been properly decoded, he clicks on the Check Answer button to see the results of his effort. If the player's answer is correct, the player is notified via a message displayed in a popup dialog window. Similarly, if the answer supplied is not correct or if the player failed to key in anything, other messages are displayed.

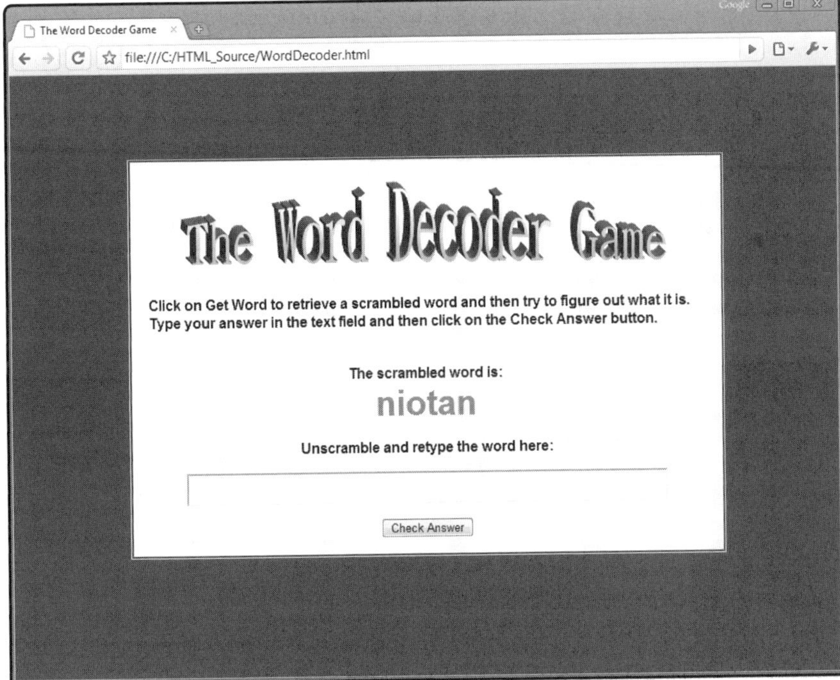

Figure 9.2

The player's job is to correctly retype the word in unscrambled form in the text field.

Introducing JavaScript

JavaScript is a computer programming language used in the development of scripts. Scripts are small programs embedded inside HTML pages. Scripts allow you to add interactive content to web pages. JavaScript is an interpreted programming language. This means that scripts are not converted to an executable form until the HTML page they reside in is processed. The drawback to interpreted scripts is that they execute slower than programs written in compiled programming languages, which are converted into executable code at development time.

JavaScript is an object-based programming language, seeing everything within web documents and the browser as *objects*. To JavaScript, image files, text controls, and button controls are all just different types of objects. All objects have properties. *Properties* describe attributes about an object. For example, buttons display text specified using the `value` property. `img` elements also have properties. For example, there are properties that you can set to control a graphic's height and width and that you can use to specify its URL.

Objects also have *methods*, which are collections of statements that can be called upon to perform specified actions and tasks. For example, you can define methods within your JavaScripts that when called will validate form content. Object properties and methods enable JavaScripts to dynamically alter both content and its presentation on web pages.

JavaScript is also capable of interacting with the user and responding to changes that occur within the browser. This is facilitated by JavaScript's ability to initiate code execution based on the occurrence of different events. An *event* is an action initiated as a result of user interaction with your web page in the browser. Events occur when the user clicks on or interacts with form elements. Events occur when web pages are opened and closed. Events also occur when the user moves the mouse pointer or enters keystrokes.

Working with JavaScript

As you have already seen, JavaScripts are inserted into HTML pages using the script element. Figure 9.3 outlines the syntax that you must follow when working with this element.

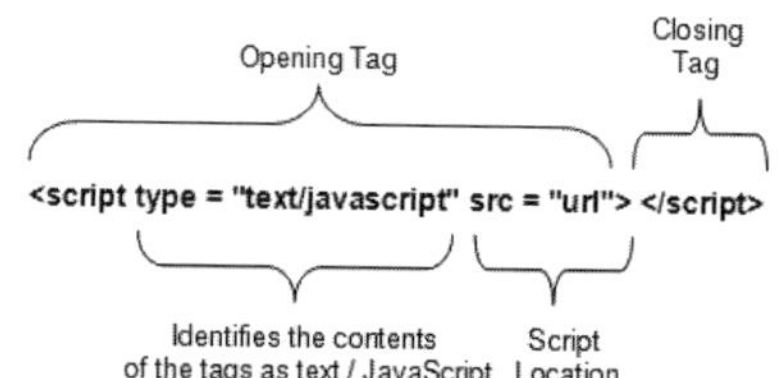

Figure 9.3
An examination of the syntax required to integrate (X)HTML and JavaScript in your documents.

The syntax outlined in Figure 9.3 includes the use of two key attributes, both of which are located in the opening `<script>` tag. The keyword `type` attribute is always set equal to `text/javascript` and the optional `scr` tells the browser where to locate an external JavaScript file (used in situations where you want to keep your markup and JavaScript code separate).

JavaScript is a case-sensitive programming language. In order to prevent errors from occurring, you must use correct capitalization when writing JavaScript code. For example, JavaScript requires that whenever you use the `document` object on any of its methods and properties that you use all lowercase.

Case-sensitivity aside, JavaScript is regarded as a very flexible programming language. It imposes a minimal set of rules regarding statement syntax. Statements begin and end on the same line. However, you can continue a statement onto another line using concatenation (explained later in this chapter). If desired, you can place multiple statements on a single line if you separate them with semicolons (;). In JavaScript, semicolons are used to identify the end of statements. Technically, the use of semicolons to mark the end of statements is optional; however, it is considered good form to use them anyway.

Like (X)HTML and CSS, JavaScript allows you to make liberal use of white space. You may insert blank lines in between statements or indent statements to make your scripts more readable.

What about Browsers That Do Not Support JavaScript?

Today, there are still many people surfing the Internet with web browsers that do not support JavaScript or that have been configured not to support it. This makes things challenging for web developers. To address this challenge, most web developers use (X)HTML comments to hide JavaScript statements from non-supporting browsers. As you know, (X)HTML comments are created using the `<!--` and `-->` characters. Anything placed in a comment is ignored by the browser.

All browsers, even those that do not support JavaScript, know not to display the `<script>` tags. However, browsers without support for JavaScript do not know how to process statements embedded within the `<script>` tags. As a result, these browsers will display the script statements as part of the web page. The result is not pretty. To keep this from occurring, enclose any JavaScript statements located inside the `script` elements within (X)HTML comments. Doing this prevents browsers that do not support JavaScript from displaying any statements on your web pages (intermixed with real content). The following example demonstrates how to do this.

```
<!DOCTYPE html PUBLIC "-//W3C//DTD XHTML 1.0 Strict//EN"
  "http://www.w3.org/TR/xhtml1/DTD/xhtml1-strict.dtd">

<html xmlns="http://www.w3.org/1999/xhtml" lang="en" xml:lang="en">

  <head>
    <meta http-equiv="Content-type" content="text/xhtml; charset=UTF-8" />
    <title>Ch. 9 - Hiding JavaScript from non-supporting browsers</title>
    <script type = "text/javascript">
    <!-- Start hiding JavaScript statements
      document.write("If you see this your browser supports JavaScript!");
    // End hiding JavaScript statements -->
    </script>
  </head>

  <body>
  </body>

</html>
```

Creating a Simple JavaScript

Now that you know the syntax required to work with the script element, let's put this knowledge to use by creating a simple JavaScript and adding it to an XHTML document. The markup and JavaScript statements that make up this example are shown here:

```
<!DOCTYPE html PUBLIC "-//W3C//DTD XHTML 1.0 Strict//EN"
  "http://www.w3.org/TR/xhtml1/DTD/xhtml1-strict.dtd">

<html xmlns="http://www.w3.org/1999/xhtml" lang="en" xml:lang="en">

  <head>
    <meta http-equiv="Content-type" content="text/xhtml; charset=UTF-8" />
    <title>Chapter 9 - A simple JavaScript</title>
  </head>

  <body>
    <script type = "text/javascript">
    <!-- Start hiding JavaScript statements
      document.write("Here I am!");
    // End hiding JavaScript statements -->
    </script>
  </body>

</html>
```

In this example, a simple JavaScript has been embedded directly into the body section of the web document. The first and last JavaScript statements are the script's opening and closing tags. The statement in the middle instructs the browser to write a text string of "Here I am " to the current document (e.g., on the web page).

Running Your JavaScripts

To test the execution of your new JavaScript, simply open the web document that contains it using your web browser. In response, the browser will render the document's markup and then execute the scripts. Figure 9.4 shows the result that you will see in your web browser.

Assuming you did not mistype the document's JavaScript when keying it in, you should see the sentence Here I Am! on the browser window.

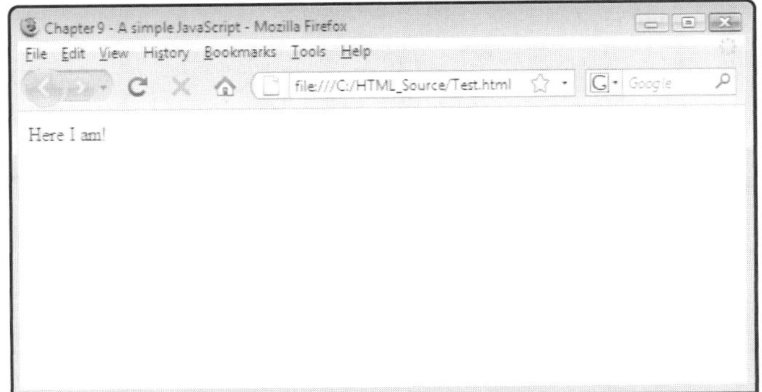

FIGURE 9.4

Testing the execution of a JavaScript embedded within an XHTML document.

DIFFERENT WAYS OF INTEGRATING JAVASCRIPT INTO YOUR DOCUMENTS

You can integrate JavaScript into your web documents in a variety of ways, including embedding scripts into either the `head` or `body` sections. You can also execute external JavaScript files, separating JavaScript code from your markup. You can even embed JavaScript statements directly into (X)HTML markup.

Embedding JavaScripts in the head Section

Most Ajax developers embed their JavaScripts in the `head` sections of their (X)HTML pages. JavaScripts placed in the `head` section can be automatically or conditionally executed when your (X)HTML pages load. By placing your JavaScript functions and variable declarations in the `head` section, you ensure they are defined when the web page loads, making them ready and available when called upon for execution.

A *variable* is a pointer or reference to a location in memory where data is stored. A *function* is a named collection of code statements that can be called on to execute and perform a specific task.

The following XHTML document provides an example of how to embed a JavaScript in a document's `head` section. In this example, the script is automatically executed when the web browser loads the document.

```
<!DOCTYPE html PUBLIC "-//W3C//DTD XHTML 1.0 Strict//EN"
  "http://www.w3.org/TR/xhtml1/DTD/xhtml1-strict.dtd">

<html xmlns="http://www.w3.org/1999/xhtml" lang="en" xml:lang="en">
```

```
  <head>
    <meta http-equiv="Content-type" content="text/xhtml; charset=UTF-8" />
    <title>Chapter 9 - Embedding a JavaScript in the head section</title>
    <script type = "text/javascript">
    <!-- Start hiding JavaScript statements
      document.write("Up, up, and away!");
    // End hiding JavaScript statements -->
    </script>
  </head>

  <body>
  </body>

</html>
```

In the previous example the `window` object's `alert` method (`window.alert`) is used to display a text string in a popup dialog window. This method is often used to display a simple message that does not require user interaction. The `alert` method has the following syntax.

```
window.alert("message");
```

message represents a text string that is to be displayed. The popup dialog window that is used to display the message includes an OK button that when clicked closes the window. More about how to work with objects and methods is provided later in this chapter.

Figure 9.5 shows the output that is generated when this example is loaded into the browser.

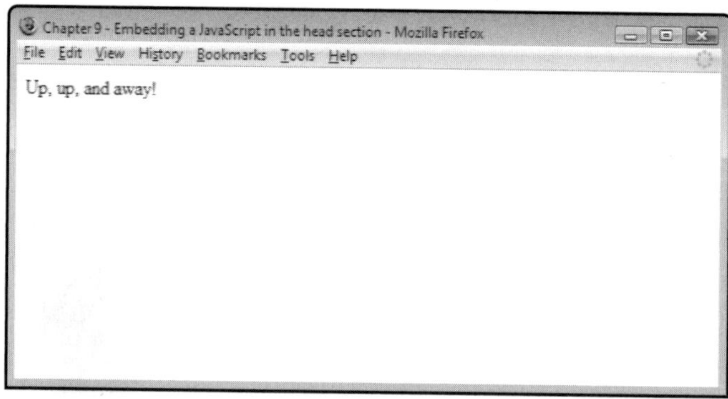

FIGURE 9.5

By default, any JavaScript embedded in an (X)HTML document's `head` section is automatically executed when loaded by the browser.

By default, any JavaScript embedded inside a document's head section is automatically executed when the page loads. However, any JavaScript statements organized into functions are only executed when explicitly called to run. The following document shows just such an example. Here, an XHTML page contains an embedded JavaScript that is made up of a function named Fly(). When the document that contains it is loaded, the function is not automatically executed.

```
<!DOCTYPE html PUBLIC "-//W3C//DTD XHTML 1.0 Strict//EN"
  "http://www.w3.org/TR/xhtml1/DTD/xhtml1-strict.dtd">

<html xmlns="http://www.w3.org/1999/xhtml" lang="en" xml:lang="en">

  <head>
    <meta http-equiv="Content-type" content="text/xhtml; charset=UTF-8" />
    <title>Chapter 9 - Creating a JavaScript function</title>
    <script type = "text/javascript">
    <!-- Start hiding JavaScript statements
      function Fly() {
        window.alert("Up, up, and away!");
      }
    // End hiding JavaScript statements -->
    </script>
  </head>

  <body>
  </body>

</html>
```

You will learn all about functions and how to control their execution later in this chapter.

Embedding JavaScripts in the body Section

As you have seen, JavaScripts can also be placed in the body section of your (X)HTML document. These scripts are automatically executed when the document loads.

```
<body>
  <script type = "text/javascript">
  <!-- Start hiding JavaScript statements
      window.alert("Up, up, and away!");
```

```
  // End hiding JavaScript statements -->
  </script>
</body>
```

Storing Your JavaScripts Externally

Large (X)HTML documents can be made of many different scripts with various levels of complexity. As with CSS, it is often a good idea to keep your markup and JavaScript separate. This is easily accomplished using external JavaScript files. To create an external JavaScript file, all you have to do is create a plain text file, add your JavaScript code to it, and save it with a .js file extension. Once created, you can refer to it using the `script` element's `scr` attribute as demonstrated here:

```
<script src = "Test.js" type = text/javascript"> </script>
```

The external JavaScript file can be used to store any number of JavaScript statements. It cannot, however, contain any (X)HTML markup. If any markup is found, an error will occur.

There are many benefits to using external JavaScripts. External JavaScripts mean smaller (X) HTML documents, which makes your (X)HTML documents easier to manage. External JavaScripts can be used by more than one document, allowing for code reuse. If you ever need to modify an external JavaScript, you can do so without having to edit every (X)HTML document that references it.

Embedding JavaScript Statements inside HTML Tags

One last option for integrating JavaScript into your (X)HTML document is to embed individual JavaScript statements within individual (X)HTML tags, as demonstrated here:

```
<body onLoad = document.write("Hello!")> <body>
```

In this example, a JavaScript statement `(onLoad = document.write("Hello!")` has been embedded within the document's opening `<body>` tag. This statement executes when the document is loaded into the browser. It instructs the browser to display a text string directly in the browser window. Embedding JavaScript statements within (X)HTML elements in this manner provides an easy way to execute small JavaScript statements.

Documenting Your Scripts

In order to make your JavaScripts self-documenting and easier to maintain, you should include embedded comments in your code that document what is going on in your web documents. Comments do not affect script performance, so use them liberally. JavaScript supports two types of comments. You can add a single line comment to a script by typing // followed by the comment, as demonstrated here:

```
//The following statement displays a greeting
document.write("Hello!");
```

If you want, you can append comments to the end of statements as shown here.

```
document.write("Hello!");  //The following statement displays a greeting
```

You can also create multi-line comments by enclosing text inside the /* and */ characters, as shown here:

```
/* The following statement displays a text message in the browser windows
that greet the user */
document.write("Hello!");
```

Dealing with Different Types of Values

Most JavaScripts store and process some type of data when they execute. JavaScript automatically does its best to make a determination about the type of data it is presented with. This determination has a direct impact on how the data is handled. Table 9.1 outlines different types of values supported by JavaScript.

Table 9.1 Values Supported by JavaScript

Value	Description
Boolean	A value indicating a condition of either `true` or `false`
Null	An empty value
Numbers	A numeric value
Strings	A string of text enclosed in matching quotation marks

Once specified or collected, you can store data in your scripts using variables. A *variable* is a pointer or reference to a location in memory where a piece of data is stored.

Storing and Retrieving Data

JavaScript allows you to store and retrieve individual pieces of data as well as collections of data. Individual pieces of data are managed using variables. Collections of data are managed using arrays. You will learn how to work with both variables and arrays in the sections that follow.

Defining JavaScript Variables

In order to use a variable in a JavaScript, it must be declared (or defined). You can declare a variable explicitly or implicitly. An explicitly declared variable is defined before it is referenced using the `var` keyword. The following example demonstrates how to explicitly declare a variable.

```
var playerScore = 1000;
```

Note that in the preceding example a numeric value of `1000` was assigned to the variable. If you assign a text string to a variable, you must enclose the string inside quotation marks, as demonstrated here:

```
var playerCharacter = "Wizard";
```

Here, a variable named `playerScore` has been declared. It has also been assigned an initial value of `1000`. To implicitly declare a variable, you simply reference it for the first time without first declaring it, as demonstrated here:

```
playerScore = 1000;
```

Explicit variable declaration is considered to be good form and is highly recommended.

It is not necessary to assign a variable a value at declaration time. However, doing so can make your script code easier to understand and also helps JavaScript determine the type of data the variable will be used to store.

Naming Your Variable

When assigning names to your variables, you should take care to assign names that are descriptive of the variable's purpose. For example, `totalScore` is a much more descriptive variable name than `x`. In addition, you must follow the rules outlined below when assigning variable names.

- Variable names must start with a letter or the underscore character.
- Variable names cannot contain blank spaces.
- Variable names can only be made of letters, numbers, and the underscore character.
- You cannot use reserved words as variable names.

JavaScript variables are case-sensitive. If you assign a variable a name of `totalScore`, you must use the exact same case when referring to it in other parts of your JavaScript. If you accidently make a typo of `totalscore` or use a different case like `TOTALSCORE` or `totalscore`, JavaScript will regard each of these as being different variables.

Understanding Variable Scope

Variable scope refers to the location within a script where a variable is accessible. JavaScript supports both global and location scope. Global variables can be accessed by any script embedded within an (X)HTML document. Local variables exist within functions and can only be accessed by statements located in the functions where the variables are defined.

Global variables are accessible by any script located within a web document. There are two ways of defining global variables. These include:

- Making an initial reference to a new variable from inside a function (without using the `var` keyword).
- Declaring a variable outside of a function (with or without the `var` keyword).

A *local variable* is declared inside a function by preceding its initial reference with the `var` keyword. A *function* is a named collection of code statements. Functions can be called from different locations within a document. The following example demonstrates how to create a local variable.

```
function DisplayMsg() {
  var message = "Well, hello there!";
  document.write(message);
}
```

In this example, a function named `DisplayMsg()` has been defined. When executed statements in the function declare a local variable named `message`, assign it a text string, and then display the string (in the browser window). Because it is a local variable, the value assigned to `message` is not accessible from outside the function.

Working with Collections of Data

Depending on how much data you need to collect and process on your web pages, there may be times when working with individual variables becomes impractical. In these situations, you can use arrays to store large collections of data. An *array* is an indexed list of values. Arrays can store any type of value. For example, the following statements declare an array and then use it to store three text strings.

```
powers = new Array(2);
powers[0] = "Flight";
powers[1] = "Super Strength";
powers[2] = "Heat Vision";
```

The first statement declares an array named `powers` using the required `new` keyword. The array has been set up to store five values. The remaining statements populate the array with data. In JavaScript, array's indices begin with an index position of 0. So, in the previous example, the `powers` array can store three values, in index positions 0 through 2.

Accessing Array Elements

To access a value stored in an array, you must specify the array's name followed by the value's index position enclosed in square brackets. As an example, look at the following document.

```
<!DOCTYPE html PUBLIC "-//W3C//DTD XHTML 1.0 Strict//EN"
  "http://www.w3.org/TR/xhtml1/DTD/xhtml1-strict.dtd">

<html xmlns="http://www.w3.org/1999/xhtml" lang="en" xml:lang="en">

  <head>
    <meta http-equiv="Content-type" content="text/xhtml; charset=UTF-8" />
    <title>Ch. 9 - Working with arrays</title>
    <script type = "text/javascript">
    <!-- Start hiding JavaScript statements
      powers = new Array(2);
      powers[0] = "Flight";
      powers[1] = "Super Strength";
      powers[2] = "Heat Vision";
      document.write("The first super power is " + powers[0]);
    // End hiding JavaScript statements -->
    </script>
  </head>

  <body>
  </body>

</html>
```

Remember, JavaScript arrays begin at index position 0. The first item in the array is located at index position 0 (e.g., `Flight`).

Processing Arrays with Loops

Processing the array elements an element at a time is impractical for large arrays containing dozens, hundreds, or thousands of elements. Instead, web developers use loops to process array contents as demonstrated here:

```
<!DOCTYPE html PUBLIC "-//W3C//DTD XHTML 1.0 Strict//EN"
  "http://www.w3.org/TR/xhtml1/DTD/xhtml1-strict.dtd">

<html xmlns="http://www.w3.org/1999/xhtml" lang="en" xml:lang="en">

  <head>
    <meta http-equiv="Content-type" content="text/xhtml; charset=UTF-8" />
    <title>Ch. 9 - Working with functions</title>

    <script type = "text/javascript">
    <!-- Start hiding JavaScript statements
      powers = new Array(2);
      powers[0] = "Flight";
      powers[1] = "Super Strength";
      powers[2] = "Heat Vision";
      document.write("List of Super Powers <br />");
      for (var i = 0; i < powers.length; i++) {
        document.write("* " + powers[i] + "<br />");
      }
    // End hiding JavaScript statements -->
    </script>

  </head>

  <body>
  </body>

</html>
```

In this example, an array named `powers` has been defined and populated with three values. A `for` loop is used to process the array, starting at `powers[0]`. Each time the loop iterates, the value of `i` is incremented by 1, causing the loop to process the next element stored in the array. Take note of the use of the array object's `length` property. This property stores a numeric value representing the array's length. It is used to control loop execution, halting the loop when the end of the array is reached. Figure 9.6 shows the output produced when this example is executed.

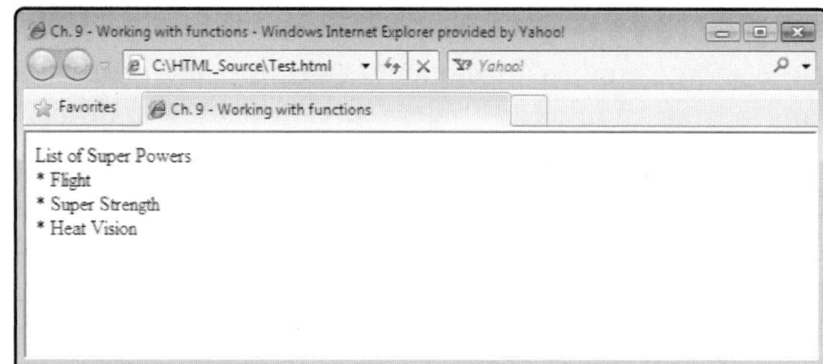

FIGURE 9.6

Processing the contents of an array using a loop.

Manipulating and Comparing Data

There is a lot more to working with data than collecting, storing, retrieving, and displaying it. Most scripts analyze data in some manner. To do this, you need to learn how to work with a number of operators that facilitate mathematic operations, data assignment, and value comparison.

Performing Mathematic Calculations

JavaScript supports a range of arithmetic operations that facilitate the development of arithmetic calculations when working with numeric data. Table 9.2 outlines and demonstrates the use of these operations. With this collection of operators at your disposal, you can develop programming logic that performs virtually any type of calculation you might want to process.

While use of the first four operators shown in Table 9.2 is self-explanatory, the remaining operators require explanation. The `x++` and `++x` operators are used to increment a value of a numeric variable by 1. The difference between these two operators lies in when the update occurs. Suppose you had two variables, `totalScore` and `points`. If `points` was equal to `100` when the following statement executed, the value of `points` would first be incremented by 1 and then its value (101) would be assigned to `totalScore`.

```
totalScore = ++points;
```

As demonstrated next, use the `x++` operator in place of the `++x` operators to generate a different result.

```
totalScore = points++;
```

Table 9.2 JavaScript Operators

Operator	Description	Example
+	Adds two values together	`totalScore = 5 + 10`
-	Subtracts one value from another	`totalScore = 10 - 5`
*	Multiplies two values together	`totalScore = 5 * 10`
/	Divides one value by another	`totalScore = 10 / 5`
-x	Reverses a variable's sign	`count = -count`
x++	Post-increment (returns x, then increments x by one)	`x = y++`
++x	Pre-increment (increments x by one, then returns x)	`x = ++y`
x--	Post-decrement (returns x, then decrements x by one)	`x = y--`
--x	Pre-decrement (decrements x by one, then returns x)	`x = --y`

Here, the value of `points` (e.g., 100) is first assigned to `totalScore` (setting it equal to 100). Then the value of `points` is incremented by 1 to 101. The `--x` and `x--` operators work just like the `++x` and `x++` operators—the difference being that they decrement a variable's value instead of incrementing it.

Assigning Values to Variables

To assign a value to a variable, you use the = (equals) operator. To change a variable's value, all you have to do is assign it a different value, as demonstrated here.

```
totalScore = 0;
.
.
.
total = 100;
```

In addition to the = operator, JavaScript supports all of the operators listed in Table 9.3.

Table 9.3 JavaScript Assignment Operators

Operator	Description	Examples
=	Sets a variable value equal to some value	x l y + l
+=	Shorthand for x l x + y (addition)	x +l y
-=	Shorthand for x l x – y (subtraction)	x -l y
*=	Shorthand for x l x * y (multiplication)	x *l y
/=	Shorthand for x l x / y (division)	x /l y
%=	Shorthand for x l x % y (remainder)	x %l y

Let's look at an example of how to work with each of the operators shown in Table 9.3.

```
<!DOCTYPE html PUBLIC "-//W3C//DTD XHTML 1.0 Strict//EN"
  "http://www.w3.org/TR/xhtml1/DTD/xhtml1-strict.dtd">

<html xmlns="http://www.w3.org/1999/xhtml" lang="en" xml:lang="en">

  <head>
    <meta http-equiv="Content-type" content="text/xhtml; charset=UTF-8" />
    <title>Ch. 9 - Working with JavaScript assignment operators</title>
    <script type = "text/javascript">
    <!-- Start hiding JavaScript statements
      var a = 3;
      var b = 10;
      var c = 0;
      c = a + b;
      document.write("a = " + a + ", b = " + b + ", c = " + c + "<br />");
      document.write("<br />a + b = " + c + "<br />");
      c += 2
      document.write("<br />c += 2 = " + c + "<br />");
      c -= 5
      document.write("<br />c -= 5 = " + c + "<br />");
      c *= 3
      document.write("<br />c *= 3 = " + c + "<br />");
      c /= 2
      document.write("<br />c /= 2 = " + c + "<br />");
      c %= 7
```

```
      document.write("<br />c %= 7 = " + c + "<br />");
    // End hiding JavaScript statements -->
    </script>
  </head>

  <body>
  </body>

</html>
```

Notice that the <br /> tag has been embedded within various statements as a means of controlling line breaks. Also note the use of the + operator. When used with strings, the + operator joins or concatenates two strings together to create a new larger string.

Figure 9.7 shows the output generated when this example is loaded into the browser.

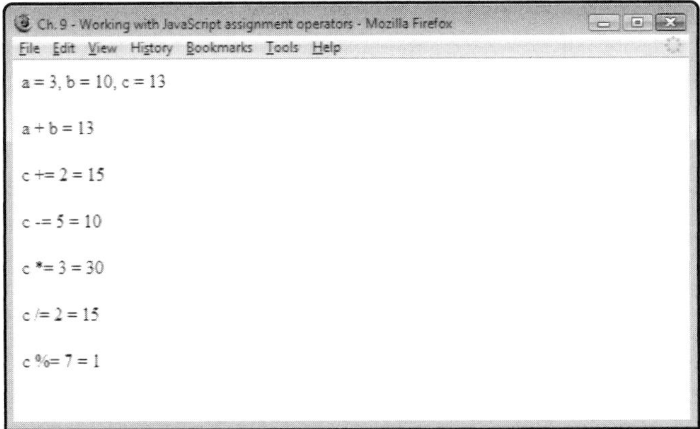

FIGURE 9.7

A demonstration of how to work with JavaScript's operators.

Comparing Values

To be useful, data generally needs to be analyzed. With numeric data this typically means performing different types of comparison operations. Based on the results of this analysis, a JavaScript can alter its execution. A JavaScript might, for example, take one action if the value of a variable is greater than 1000 and another action if it is not. Table 9.4 provides a listing of the different types of comparison operators supported by JavaScript.

Table 9.4 JavaScript Comparison Operators

Operator	Description	Example
==	Equal to	x == y
!==	Not equal to	x !== y
>	Greater than	x > y
>=	Greater than or equal to	x >= y
<	Less than	x < y
<=	Less than or equal to	x <= y

To determine if two values are equal, you must use the == comparison operator (not the = assignment operator). If you get these two operators mixed up an error will occur. As an example of how to work with these operators, look at the following example.

```
if (x == y) {
document.write("x equals y");
}
```

Here, a comparison is made between two values stored in the x and y variables. If the values are equal a text string is displayed. If you modify this example, as demonstrated here, you can determine if the value of x is greater than or equal to the value of y.

```
if (x >= y) {
document.write("x is greater than or equal to y");
}
```

Making Decisions

Conditional programming logic gives you the ability to make decisions and to alter the logical execution flow of code statements in your JavaScripts based on the result of comparison operations. Conditional logic allows you to execute a set of statements based on whether a tested condition evaluates as true.

Working with the if Statement

The `if` statement gives you the ability to compare two values and to conditionally execute one or more statements based on the result of that analysis. In its most basic form, the `if` statement uses the following syntax.

```
if (condition) statement
```

Here, ***condition*** is an expression that when evaluated generates a value of `true` or `false`. Note that the expression that is analyzed must be enclosed in parentheses. Take a look at the following example which shows you how to apply this version of the `if` statement.

```
<!DOCTYPE html PUBLIC "-//W3C//DTD XHTML 1.0 Strict//EN"
  "http://www.w3.org/TR/xhtml1/DTD/xhtml1-strict.dtd">

<html xmlns="http://www.w3.org/1999/xhtml" lang="en" xml:lang="en">

  <head>
    <meta http-equiv="Content-type" content="text/xhtml; charset=UTF-8" />
    <title>Ch. 9 - An example of how to work with the if statement</title>
    <script type = "text/javascript">
    <!-- Start hiding JavaScript statements
      var totalScore = 1000;
      if (totalScore > 1001) document.write("You win!");
    // End hiding JavaScript statements -->
    </script>
  </head>

  <body>
  </body>

</html>
```

In this example, a variable named `totalScore` is declared and assigned a value of `1000`. Next, an `if` statement is used to determine if the value of `totalScore` is greater than 1001 (which it is not). Had it been greater than 1001, a message would have been displayed. However, since `totalScore` is equal to `1000`, nothing happens.

Generating Multiline if Statements

If you include { and } characters, as demonstrated in the following example, you can use the `if` statement to create a code block, which can include any number of statements. Every statement in the code block will execute if the tested condition evaluates as `true`.

```
<!DOCTYPE html PUBLIC "-//W3C//DTD XHTML 1.0 Strict//EN"
  "http://www.w3.org/TR/xhtml1/DTD/xhtml1-strict.dtd">

<html xmlns="http://www.w3.org/1999/xhtml" lang="en" xml:lang="en">
```

```
  <head>
    <meta http-equiv="Content-type" content="text/xhtml; charset=UTF-8" />
    <title>Ch. 9 - An example of how to work with the if statement</title>
    <script type = "text/javascript">
    <!-- Start hiding JavaScript statements
      var totalScore = 20000;
      if (totalScore > 10000) {
        document.write("Game over. You win!");
      }
    // End hiding JavaScript statements -->
    </script>
  </head>

  <body>
  </body>

</html>
```

In this example, two statements are executed if the value assigned to `totalScore` is greater than or equal to `10000`.

Handling Alternative Conditions

The `if` statement supports an optional `else` keyword that when used lets you modify an `if` statement code block so that it can execute an alternative set of statements if the tested condition proves `false`. An example of how this works is provided here:

```
<!DOCTYPE html PUBLIC "-//W3C//DTD XHTML 1.0 Strict//EN"
  "http://www.w3.org/TR/xhtml1/DTD/xhtml1-strict.dtd">

<html xmlns="http://www.w3.org/1999/xhtml" lang="en" xml:lang="en">

  <head>
    <meta http-equiv="Content-type" content="text/xhtml; charset=UTF-8" />
    <title>Ch. 9 - An example of how to work with the if statement</title>
    <script type = "text/javascript">
    <!-- Start hiding JavaScript statements
      var totalScore = 9999;
      if (totalScore <= 10000) {
        document.write("Game over. You lose.");
```

```
      }
      else {
        document.write("Game over. You win.");
      }
    // End hiding JavaScript statements -->
    </script>
  </head>

  <body>
  </body>

</html>
```

In this example, the message `Game over. You lose.` is displayed if `totalScore` is less than or equal to `10000` and a string of `Game over. You win!` is displayed if `totalScore` is not less than or equal to `10000`. Note that in this example two separate code blocks have been defined, each of which has its own set of opening `{` and closing `}` characters.

Nesting if Statements

If you need to perform complex conditional logic that involves comparing multiple values, where one decision is based on the outcome of another decision, you can nest `if` statements to outline the required logic. The following example demonstrates how to nest `if` statements.

```
<!DOCTYPE html PUBLIC "-//W3C//DTD XHTML 1.0 Strict//EN"
  "http://www.w3.org/TR/xhtml1/DTD/xhtml1-strict.dtd">

<html xmlns="http://www.w3.org/1999/xhtml" lang="en" xml:lang="en">

  <head>
    <meta http-equiv="Content-type" content="text/xhtml; charset=UTF-8" />
    <title>Ch. 9 - An example of how to work with the if statement</title>
    <script type = "text/javascript">
    <!-- Start hiding JavaScript statements
      var gameOver = false;
      var totalScore = 9999;
      if (gameOver == true) {
       if (totalScore <= 10000) {
          document.write("Game over. You lose.");
        }
```

```
        else {
          document.write("Game over. You win.");
        }
      }
      else {
        document.write("Please try again.");
      }
    // End hiding JavaScript statements -->
    </script>
  </head>

  <body>
  </body>

</html>
```

Here, the value assigned to `gameOver` is analyzed to determine if it is equal to `true`. If it does not equal `true`, the statement embedded in the `else` code block is executed.

Evaluating Conditions with the switch Statement

If you need to evaluate a series of possible values to determine a match, you can do so using a series of `if` statements. However, an easier and more efficient option is to use the `switch` statement. The `switch` statement specifies an expression which is then compared to a series of `case` statements to see if a match can be found. If a match is found, statements belonging to the matching `case` statement are executed. The `switch` statement's syntax is outlined here:

```
switch (expression) {
  case label:
    statements;
  break;
    .
    .
    .
  case label:
    statements;
  break;
  default:
   statements;
}
```

The value of ***expression*** is compared to the expression outlined in each `case` statement's ***label***. The statements of the first `case` statement that result in a match are executed. If no match is found, the statements that belong to the optional `default` statement, if specified, are executed.

The `break` statement at the end of each set of statements belonging to the `case` statement is optional. When specified, the `break` statement instructs JavaScript to exit the `switch` statement. If you do not specify a `break` statement at the end of each `case` statement code block, the script will execute the statements of any `case` statement that matches (instead of just the statements belonging to the first `case` statement that matches).

To better understand how to work with the `switch` statement, let's look at an example.

```
<!DOCTYPE html PUBLIC "-//W3C//DTD XHTML 1.0 Strict//EN"
  "http://www.w3.org/TR/xhtml1/DTD/xhtml1-strict.dtd">

<html xmlns="http://www.w3.org/1999/xhtml" lang="en" xml:lang="en">

  <head>
    <meta http-equiv="Content-type" content="text/xhtml; charset=UTF-8" />
    <title>Ch. 9 - An example of how to work with the switch statement</title>
    <script type = "text/javascript">
    <!-- Start hiding JavaScript statements
      var color = window.prompt("Pick a color: red, green, or blue.");
      switch (color) {
        case "red":
          document.write("Rose petals are red.");
          break;
        case "green":
          document.write("Stems are green.");
          break;
        case "blue":
          document.write("Violets are blue.");
          break;
        default:
          document.write("Error: Invalid input.");
      }
    // End hiding JavaScript statements -->
    </script>
  </head>
```

```
  <body>
  </body>

</html>
```

In this example, the user is prompted to enter a color. Once the user's input is collected, it is assigned to a variable named `color`. The value of `color` is then analyzed. The message displayed depends on the result of that analysis.

Note the manner in which the `color` variable's value is assigned in the previous example. The `window` object's `prompt` method is used to display the message in a popup dialog window that prompts the user to input. The `prompt` method's syntax is outlined here:

```
window.prompt("message" [, "default"]);
```

message represents the string displayed in the popup dialog window. ***default*** is an optional parameter. If specified, it displays default input in the popup dialog window's text field. The `window` object's `prompt` method is great for situations where you need to collect a small piece of data from the user.

Using Loops to Work Efficiently

A *loop* is a collection of statements that are executed repeatedly. Programmers use loops to process large amounts of data and to execute repetitive tasks. The power of loops lie in the fact that with just a few lines of code you can process an unlimited amount of data or perform a given task an infinite number of times.

Creating a Loop Using the for Statement

The `for` statement allows you to set up a loop that executes for as long as a specified condition remains `true`. A variable is used to manage loop execution. The `for` loop consists of three parts: a starting expression, a tested condition, and an increment statement. The loop's syntax is outlined here:

```
for (expression; condition; increment) {
  statements;
}
```

You may place as many JavaScript statements as you want in between the loop's opening and closing bracket. These statements are executed every time the loop iterates (repeats). As an example of how to work with the `for` statement, look at the following example.

```
<!DOCTYPE html PUBLIC "-//W3C//DTD XHTML 1.0 Strict//EN"
  "http://www.w3.org/TR/xhtml1/DTD/xhtml1-strict.dtd">

<html xmlns="http://www.w3.org/1999/xhtml" lang="en" xml:lang="en">

  <head>
    <meta http-equiv="Content-type" content="text/xhtml; charset=UTF-8" />
    <title>Ch. 9 - Executing a for loop</title>
    <script type = "text/javascript">
    <!-- Start hiding JavaScript statements
      for (i = 1; i <= 10; i++) {
        document.write(i,"<br />");
      }
    // End hiding JavaScript statements -->
    </script>
  </head>

  <body>
  </body>

</html>
```

In this example, a loop has been set up to repeat 10 times. In its first iteration, the value of `i` is set to 1. The loop repeats 10 times, terminating when the value exceeds 10. Figure 9.8 shows the output generated when this example executes.

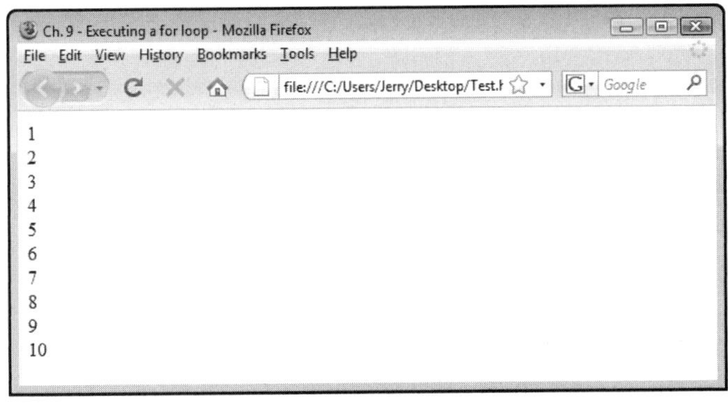

FIGURE 9.8

Using a `for` loop to count from 1 to 10.

Creating a Loop Using the while Statement

JavaScript also supports the `while` statement, which you can use to set up a loop that executes for as long as a specified condition is `true`. The `while` loop's syntax is outlined here:

```
while (condition) {
  statements;
}
```

The following example demonstrates how to work with the `while` statements.

```
<!DOCTYPE html PUBLIC "-//W3C//DTD XHTML 1.0 Strict//EN"
  "http://www.w3.org/TR/xhtml1/DTD/xhtml1-strict.dtd">

<html xmlns="http://www.w3.org/1999/xhtml" lang="en" xml:lang="en">

  <head>
    <meta http-equiv="Content-type" content="text/xhtml; charset=UTF-8" />
    <title>Ch. 9 - Executing a while loop</title>
    <script type = "text/javascript">
    <!-- Start hiding JavaScript statements
      var counter = 10;
      document.write("<p>Begin countdown.</p>");
      while (counter > 0) {
        document.write(counter + "<br />");
        counter = counter - 1;
      }
      document.write("<br />Blastoff!");
    // End hiding JavaScript statements -->
    </script>
  </head>

  <body>
  </body>

</html>
```

In this example, a `while` loop is configured to iterate for as long as the value of `counter` is greater than 0. Every time the loop repeats, the value of `counter` is displayed and decremented by 1. Figure 9.9 shows the output that is displayed when this example is executed.

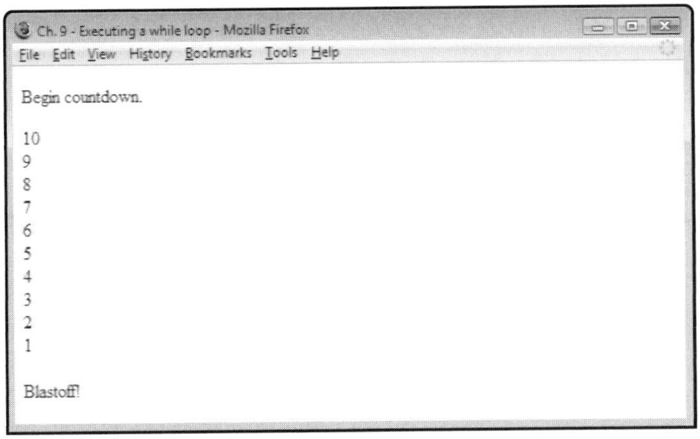

FIGURE 9.9

An example of how to use a `while` loop to iterate 10 times.

Creating a Loop Using the do. . .while Statement

Another type of loop supported by JavaScript is the `do. . .while` loop. This loop repeats until a tested condition becomes `false`. The `do...while` loop's syntax is outlined here:

```
do {
  statements;
} while (condition)
```

The `do. . .while` loop distinguishes itself from the `while` loop in that it always executes at least once. This is because the loop's *condition* is not evaluated until the end of the loop. The following example demonstrates how use the `do...while` loop.

```
<!DOCTYPE html PUBLIC "-//W3C//DTD XHTML 1.0 Strict//EN"
  "http://www.w3.org/TR/xhtml1/DTD/xhtml1-strict.dtd">

<html xmlns="http://www.w3.org/1999/xhtml" lang="en" xml:lang="en">

  <head>
    <meta http-equiv="Content-type" content="text/xhtml; charset=UTF-8" />
    <title>Ch. 9 - Executing a do...while loop</title>

    <script type = "text/javascript">
    <!-- Start hiding JavaScript statements
      var counter = 11;
      document.write("<p>Begin countdown.</p>");
      do {
        counter = counter - 1;
```

```
        document.write(counter, "<br />");
      } while (counter > 1)
      document.write("<br />Blastoff!");
    // End hiding JavaScript statements -->
    </script>
  </head>

  <body>
  </body>

</html>
```

The output generated by this example is the same as that produced by the `while` loop example.

Breaking out of Loops

Loops automatically execute over and over again from beginning to end. While this is usually what you want, there may be times you will want to halt loop execution or skip an iteration of the loop. The following example shows you can use the `break` statement to halt a loop's execution.

```
for (i = 1; i <= 5; i++) {
  document.write(i,"<br />");
  if (i == 3) break;
}
```

When executed, this example displays the following output on the browser window.

```
1
2
3
```

In this example, the `break` statement has been used to halt the loop when the value of i becomes 5. In similar fashion, you can use the `continue` statement to prematurely terminate the current execution of a `while` loop. This allows the loop to continue running. The following example demonstrates how this works.

```
for (i = 1; i <= 5; i++) {
  if (i == 3) continue;
  document.write(i,"<br />");
}
```

When executed, this example displays the following output on the browser window.

```
1
2
4
5
```

Note that the number 3 is missing from this output as a result of the premature termination of the fifth iteration of the loop.

Organizing Your JavaScripts into Functions

A *function* is a collection of code statements that can be called by name to execute and perform a specific task. Web developers that use JavaScript usually store functions in the `head` section of (X)HTML documents ensuring they are available as soon as the web document is loaded by the browser. Placing all your functions in one place also makes them easier to find and maintain.

Defining Functions

A function must be defined before it can be executed. If an attempt is made to create a function that has not been defined, an error will occur. The syntax that you must follow when defining functions is outlined here:

```
function FunctionName(p1, p2,....pn) {
  statements;
return
}
```

`FunctionName` represents the function's name. The function's name must be immediately followed by parentheses. The parentheses are used to define an optional list of comma-separated arguments for the function to process. You must provide the parentheses even if a function does not define any arguments. A function can hold as many statements as you want. These statements must be embedded within the function's opening and closing curly braces. Functions can include an optional `return` statement that, when present, halts the function's execution. The result statement can also return an optional value back to the statement that executed the function.

In the following example a function named `Verify()` is defined. It accepts one argument as input. The function automatically assigns the incoming argument to a local variable named `age`. It then analyzes the value assigned to `age` to determine if the user is old enough to play and then displays either of two messages:

```
function Verify(age) {
  if (age < 21) {
    window.alert("Sorry, you are not old enough to play this game.");
    return "true"
   } else {
    window.alert("Let's get ready to rumble...");
    return "false"
  }
}
```

JavaScript functions are not automatically executed. They must be explicitly called upon in order to execute. Functions facilitate code reuse by allowing you to call upon a function from any location within a document. This eliminates the need to duplicate script statements and results in smaller scripts.

Executing Functions

You can execute a JavaScript function in two different ways. First, you can call on a function by typing its name, as shown here:

```
DisplayMsg();
```

Here, a function named `DisplayMsg()` is executed. No arguments are passed to the function but the parentheses are required anyway. When called, the function executes. When finished, processing flow is returned to the next statement in the script.

Functions designed to process arguments can be passed data when called, as demonstrated here:

```
UpdateScore(1000);
```

In this example, a function named `UpdateScore()` is executed and passed a value of `1000`. You can pass any number of arguments to a function as demonstrated below (provided the function has been set up to handle them).

```
UpdateAllScores(1000, 850, 75);
```

A second way of executing a function is to call on the function as part of an expression. This option requires that the function be set up to return a value. As an example, the following statement executes the `UpdateScore()` function and stores the result that is returned in a variable named `totalScore`.

```
totalScore = UpdateScore();
```

To make sure that you have a good understanding of how to execute functions and return a result from them, look at the following example.

```
<!DOCTYPE html PUBLIC "-//W3C//DTD XHTML 1.0 Strict//EN"
  "http://www.w3.org/TR/xhtml1/DTD/xhtml1-strict.dtd">

<html xmlns="http://www.w3.org/1999/xhtml" lang="en" xml:lang="en">

  <head>
    <meta http-equiv="Content-type" content="text/xhtml; charset=UTF-8" />
    <title>Ch. 9 - Working with functions</title>
    <script type = "text/javascript">
    <!-- Start hiding JavaScript statements
      function Verify() {
        var result;
        result = window.prompt("How old are you?","");
        return result;
      }
    // End hiding JavaScript statements -->
    </script>
  </head>

  <body>
    <script type = "text/javascript">
    <!-- Start hiding JavaScript statements
      playerAge = Verify();
      if (playerAge > 17) {
        window.alert("Let's get ready to rumble...");
      } else {
        window.alert("Sorry. Come back and play when you are 18.");
      }
    // End hiding JavaScript statements -->
    </script>
  </body>

</html>
```

In this example, a function named `Verify()` is defined. When executed, the function displays a popup dialog window that asks the user to enter his age. The user's input is then assigned to a variable named `result`, which is then returned to the calling statement. The function is executed by a statement located in the `body` section. The script in the `body` section takes the value that is returned by the function and assigns it to a local variable named `playerAge`, which it then analyzes.

Creating Interactive Web Pages Using Event-Driven Scripts

Events are things that occur within the browser. Events execute when the mouse clicks on something. Events occur when the mouse moves, when keys are pressed, and the browser window is moved, opened, or closed. Web browsers know how to recognize events and respond to them. For example, if you click on a link, the `onClick` event occurs and the browser's default response is to load the link's URL.

Using JavaScript you can create functions and associate them with specific events. To do this you need to know how to work with event handlers. An *event handler* detects events and reacts to them. Event handlers can be used to execute individual JavaScript statements or to call on JavaScript functions. Events are associated with objects. The following example demonstrates how to set up an event handler.

```
<body onload = "window.alert('Ta Da!')">
```

This event handler executes when the `load` event occurs, triggering the display of an alert message. As this example demonstrates, you can execute any JavaScript statement using an event handler. However, the real benefit of event handlers is their ability to execute functions.

Different Types of Javascript Events

JavaScript can react to a host of events. Table 9.5 provides a list of commonly used events along with their associated event handlers.

Each event has an accompanying event handler. Examples of how to work with these event handlers are provided in the sections that follow.

Table 9.5 JavaScript Events and Event Handlers

Event	Handler	This event occurs when:
abort	onabort	An action is aborted
blur	onblur	An item loses focus
change	onchange	A control's data is changed
click	onclick	When an element is clicked
dblclick	ondblclick	When an element is double clicked
dragdrop	ondragdrop	An element is dragged and dropped
error	onerror	A JavaScript error occurs
focus	onfocus	An element receives focus
keydown	onkeydown	A keyboard key is held down
keypress	onkeypress	A keyboard key is pressed
keyup	onkeyup	A keyboard key is released
load	onload	A web page is loaded
mousedown	onmousedown	One of the mouse buttons is pressed
mousemove	onmousemove	The mouse is moved
mouseout	onmouseout	The mouse is moved off an element
mouseover	onmouseover	The mouse is moved over an element
mouseup	onmouseup	The mouse's button is released
reset	onreset	A form's Reset button is clicked
resize	onresize	An element is resized
submit	onsubmit	A form's Submit button is clicked
unload	onunload	The browser unloads a web page

Managing Window Events

JavaScript can react to a number of different events that involve the browser window. These events include the `load`, `unload`, and `resize` events. To create web pages that can respond to these events all you need do is place the appropriate event handlers in your (X)HTML document's opening `<bodytag`, as demonstrated here:

```
<!DOCTYPE html PUBLIC "-//W3C//DTD XHTML 1.0 Strict//EN"
  "http://www.w3.org/TR/xhtml1/DTD/xhtml1-strict.dtd">

<html xmlns="http://www.w3.org/1999/xhtml" lang="en" xml:lang="en">

  <head>
    <meta http-equiv="Content-type" content="text/xhtml; charset=UTF-8" />
    <title>Ch. 9 - Working with window events</title>
```

```
  </head>

  <body onload = "window.alert('Page loaded!')"
    onresize = "window.alert('Ouch, that hurts!')"
    onunload = "window.alert('Goodbye cruel world...')">
  </body>

</html>
```

Figures 9.10 through 9.12 show the output displayed when this document is loaded by the browser, when its web page is resized, and when it is unloaded.

FIGURE 9.10

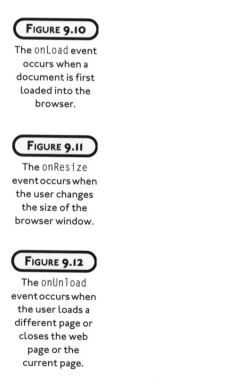

The `onLoad` event occurs when a document is first loaded into the browser.

FIGURE 9.11

The `onResize` event occurs when the user changes the size of the browser window.

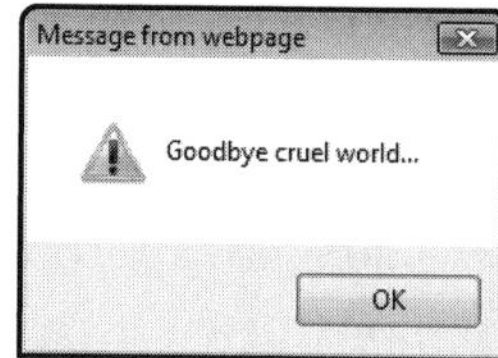

FIGURE 9.12

The `onUnload` event occurs when the user loads a different page or closes the web page or the current page.

Handling Mouse Events

Events are also triggered when the user moves or clicks the mouse within the confines of the browser window. Examples of mouse-related events include the `onMouseOver` and `onMouseOut` events. As an example of how to develop a script that reacts to these two events, look at the following document.

```
<!DOCTYPE html PUBLIC "-//W3C//DTD XHTML 1.0 Strict//EN"
  "http://www.w3.org/TR/xhtml1/DTD/xhtml1-strict.dtd">

<html xmlns="http://www.w3.org/1999/xhtml" lang="en" xml:lang="en">

  <head>
    <meta http-equiv="Content-type" content="text/xhtml; charset=UTF-8" />
    <title>Ch. 9 - Working with mouse events</title>
    <script type = "text/javascript">
    <!-- Start hiding JavaScript statements
      function ShowMsg(input) {
        document.getElementById('placeholder').innerHTML = input;
      }
    // End hiding JavaScript statements -->
    </script>
  </head>

  <body>
    <p>
      <a href="http://www.courseptr.com"
        onmouseover = 'ShowMsg("Visit www.courseptr.com")'
        onmouseout = 'ShowMsg(" ")'>
        Go to www.courseptr.com</a>
   </p>
   <div id = "placeholder"> </div>
  </body>

</html>
```

In this example, a link is displayed on the browser window. `onMouseOver` and `onMouseOut` event handlers are displayed and clear the display of text on the browser window whenever the mouse pointer is moved over and away from the link. Each time the mouse pointer moves over the link, the `DisplayMessage()` function is executed. The function establishes a reference to the document's `div` element and modifies its content. It does this using the `getElementByID()` method in conjunction with the object's `innerHTML` property. This allows it to display text string that was passed to it as an argument.

Back to the Word Decoder Challenge Project

It is time to turn your attention back to this chapter's project, the Word Decoder Challenge game. This game presents the player with a scrambled word and challenges the player to decode it. To complete this game you will have to develop a JavaScript that makes use of variables, arrays, conditional logic, and events. The JavaScript will have to make use of methods and properties that interact with the DOM. To help give the game a little extra pizzazz, CSS will be used to enhance presentation.

Designing the Application

As with every game project covered in this book, this game will be developed in a series of steps, as outlined here:

1. Create a new XHTML document.
2. Develop the document's markup.
3. Add `meta` and `title` elements.
4. Specify document content.
5. Create the document's script.
6. Create an external style sheet.
7. Load and Test the Word Decoder Challenge Project.

Step 1: Creating a New XHTML Document

The first step in the development of the Word Decoder Challenge game is to create a new web document. Do so using your preferred code or text editor. Save the document as a plain text file named WordDecoder.html. This web document will make use of CSS style rules. Therefore, you will need to create a second file named wd.css.

Step 2: Developing the Document's Markup

The next step in the development of this project is to assemble the document's markup. To do so, add the following elements to the WordDecoder.html file.

```
<!DOCTYPE html PUBLIC "-//W3C//DTD XHTML 1.0 Strict//EN"
  "http://www.w3.org/TR/xhtml1/DTD/xhtml1-strict.dtd">

<html xmlns="http://www.w3.org/1999/xhtml" lang="en" xml:lang="en">

  <head>

  </head>
```

```
  <body>

  </body>

</html>
```

Step 3: Adding meta and title Elements

Now it is time to complete the document head section by adding the elements responsible for defining its meta and title elements. To do so, add the following elements to the document's head section.

```
<meta http-equiv="Content-type" content="text/xhtml; charset=UTF-8" />
<title>The Word Decoder Game</title>
```

This web page will use an external style sheet named wd.css to enhance its presentation. Therefore, you will need to add the following tag to the end of the head section to make the connection to the external style sheet.

```
<link href = "wd.css" type = "text/css" rel = "stylesheet" />
```

Step 4: Specifying Document Content

The markup for this document, shown below, is very straightforward. It uses div and p elements to group content and insert blank spaces. It displays a graphic image at the top of the web page using an img element. It also makes use of a form that contains two button controls and a text field. Note that this game also makes use of inline styles that set the initial visibility state of these controls (to either visible or hidden). Later in the document's JavaScript you will add programming logic that takes control over the visible state of form control during game play, making the control dynamically appear and disappear during game play.

```
<div id = "mainDiv">

 <img src="logo.png" alt = "A graphic logo that displays the game's name" />

 <p id = "instructions">
   Click on Get Word to retrieve a scrambled word and then try to
   figure out what it is. Type your answer in the text field and then click
   on the Check Answer button.
 </p>

 <form action = "WordDecorder.html">
```

```
    <div>

      <input type = "button" id = "GetWordBtn" value = "Get Word"
        onclick = "StartGame()"/>

      <div id = "ScrambledHeading" style="visibility: hidden">The scrambled
        word is:
      </div>

      <div id = "ScrambledDiv" > </div>

      <div id = "UnscrambledHeading" style = "visibility:hidden">
        <p>Unscramble and retype the word here:</p>
      </div>

      <input type = "text" size = "45" style = "visibility: hidden"
        id = "inputField"/>

      <p>
        <input type = "button" id = "checkAnswerBtn" value = "Check Answer"
          style="visibility:hidden" onclick = "CheckAnswer()"/>
      </p>

    </div>

  </form>

</div>
```

Note the including of the ID attribute in various elements throughout the markup. This provides hooks into each element, allowing the document's JavaScript to interact with and control these elements.

Step 5: Creating the Document's Script

The document's markup is now complete. The next step in the development of this game is to lay out its JavaScript code. Begin by adding the following statements to the document's head section.

```
<script type = "text/javascript">
<!-- Start hiding JavaScript statements

// End hiding JavaScript statements -->
</script>
```

Now that the script's opening and closing tags are in place, add the following statements to the script.

```
//Define global variables and an array
var Request = false;
var wordArray = new Array(10);
var scrambledWord = "";
var unscrambledWord = "";

//Populate the array in a string made up of copies of the same word (one
//unscrambled and the other scrambled
wordArray[0] = "dog gdo";
wordArray[1] = "cat tac";
wordArray[2] = "lion niol";
wordArray[3] = "elephant tnaphele";
wordArray[4] = "car rac";
wordArray[5] = "desk ksed";
wordArray[6] = "pen epn";
wordArray[7] = "envelope evneelop";
wordArray[8] = "nation niotan";
wordArray[9] = "imperial liaimper";
```

The first three statements above define three global variables and an array named `wordArray`. The next ten statements populate the array with ten strings containing two versions of the same word, separated by a blank space. The first version of the word is the word in its unscrambled format. The second version of the word is the word in a scrambled format.

The rest of the script is made up of three functions. The `StartGame()` function, shown here, is called for execution when the player clicks on the `Get Word` button (e.g., `GetWordBtn`). It passes the `getElementById()` method `ID` of five form elements in order to establish a reference to those elements. The statements then use the element's `style` property's `visibility` property to control whether each element is visible. The next two statements clear out any text displayed in the form's text control and in the `div` element named `ScrambledDiv`. The last thing the function does is call on the `GetWord()` function to execute.

```
//This function is executed when the game's Get Word button is clicked.
function StartGame() {

  //These statements control form element visibility
  document.getElementById("checkAnswerBtn").style.visibility = "visible";
  document.getElementById("GetWordBtn").style.visibility = "hidden";
  document.getElementById("inputField").style.visibility = "visible";
  document.getElementById("ScrambledHeading").style.visibility = "visible";
  document.getElementById("UnscrambledHeading").style.visibility =
    "visible";

  //These statements clear out any text displayed by these elements
  document.getElementById("inputField").value="";
  document.getElementById('ScrambledDiv').innerHTML = "";

  //This statement executes the getWord() function
  getWord();

}
```

The code statements that make up the `getWord()` function are shown below and should be added to the end of the document's JavaScript. The function begins by declaring a number of variables used within the function. It then generates a random number between 0 and 9 and uses that number to select an element from the `wordArray` array, which is then assigned to a variable named `selectedWord`. Next, the `indexOf()` method is used to locate the character position of the blank space within the string stored in `selectedWord`. The `substr()` method is used to assign the unscrambled portion of the string, starting at character position 0 out to the character position of the blank space, to the `unscrambled` variable. Similarly, the `substr()` function is used a second time to assign the scrambled portion of the string to the `scrambledWord` variable, starting at one character position past the blank space out to the end of the string. Lastly, the scrambled word is displayed on the browser window for the player to see.

```
//This function retrieves a random word string for the player to guess
function getWord() {

  //Declare variables used within the function
  var randomNo = 0;
  var selectedWord = "";
```

```
  var loc = 0;

  //Generate a random number from 0 to 9 and use it to select an element
  //from the array
  randomNo = Math.random() * 9;
  randomNo = Math.round(randomNo);
  selectedWord = wordArray[randomNo]

  loc = selectedWord.indexOf(" ");                 //Locate the blank space
  unscrambledWord = selectedWord.substr(0, loc); //Assign the unscrambled
                                                   //word
  scrambledWord = selectedWord.substr(loc + 1); //Assign the scrambled word

  //Display the scrambled version of the word in the browser window
  document.getElementById('ScrambledDiv').innerHTML = scrambledWord;

}
```

The `indexOf()` method is a built-in JavaScript method that is used to locate the starting character position of one string within another string. The `substr()` method is used to extract a portion of a string. To learn more about these and other built-in methods that come with JavaScript, visit http://www.w3schools.com/jsref/jsref_obj_string.asp.

The last function in the document's JavaScript is the `CheckAnswer()` function, which is executed when the player clicks on the button control labeled Check Answer (e.g., `checkAnswerBtn`). It retrieves the player's input and determines whether the player successfully decoded the scrambled word. It ends by resetting the form's elements back to their starting state, readying the game for another round of play.

```
//This function analyzes the player's input and resets the form to its
//starting state
function CheckAnswer() {

  //Analyze the player's input
  switch (document.getElementById("inputField").value) {
    case unscrambledWord:
      window.alert("Correct. You successfully decoded the secret word!");
      break;
```

```
    case "":
      window.alert("You did not type anything!");
      break;
    default:
      window.alert("Incorrect. The secret word was " +
        unscrambledWord + ".");
  }

  //Reset the form back to its starting state
  document.getElementById("checkAnswerBtn").style.visibility = "hidden";
  document.getElementById("GetWordBtn").style.visibility = "visible";
  document.getElementById("inputField").style.visibility = "hidden";
  document.getElementById("ScrambledHeading").style.visibility = "hidden";
  document.getElementById("UnscrambledHeading").style.visibility = "hidden"
  document.getElementById('ScrambledDiv').innerHTML = "";
  document.getElementById("inputField").value = "";

}
```

Step 6: Creating an External Style Sheet

The WordDecoder.html document is styled using an external style sheet named wd.css. The rules stored in this style sheet are shown here:

```
body {
  background-color: blue;
  font-family: Arial, sans-serif;
  font-weight: bold;
  text-align: center;
  }

#mainDiv {
  border-width: thick;
  border-style: double;
  border-color: blue;
  background-image: url("questionmark.png");
  width: 640px;
  height: 400px;
  padding: 20px;
  margin-top: 10%;
```

```
  margin-left: auto;
  margin-right: auto;
  }

#ScrambledDiv {
  color: red;
  font-size: 2.5pc;
  }

#inputField {
  color: midnightblue;
  background-color: honeydew;
  font-size: 1.5pc;
  font-weight: bold;
  }

#instructions {
  text-align: left;
  }
```

The first style rule affects the document's `body` section, setting the background color of the browser window to blue, setting Arial as the font type, and assigning a bold font weight. In addition, the alignment of text is set to center.

The second rule applies to the `div` element named `mainDiv` (e.g., a `div` element wrapped around all of the elements located in the `body` section). The `div` element's border is set to thick and displayed using double blue lines. A background image is assigned to the `div` element that will repeatedly display a light blue character as the element's background. Next, the height and width of the `div` element is set and a padding of 20 pixels is applied. Lastly, a margin is applied to the top, left, and right side. Note the assignment of `auto` as the value of the `margin-left` and `margin-right` properties. Together these properties instruct the browser to horizontally center the `div` element and all its contents in the browser window.

The third rule styles a `div` element named `ScrambledDiv`, setting its color to red and its font size to 2.5 times its default size. This rule controls the presentation of the scrambled word on the browser window.

The fourth rule modifies the presentation of text in the form's text control, setting its color to midnight blue, its background to honeydew, its font size to 1.5 times its default size, and its weight to bold. The last rule overrides the centered text alignment setting, inherited from the first rule, left aligning the text for the `p` element whose `ID` is `instructions`.

Step 7: Loading and Testing the Word Decoder Challenge Game

As long as you have followed along carefully with all of the instructions that have been provided, your copy of the WordDecoder.html document should now be ready for testing. If you have not already saved your new game, do so now and then load it into your web browser to see how it works. Once you are confident that everything is working just right, post a copy of it online at your website so that the world can play.

A complete copy of the source code for this project, including its style sheet and the graphics needed to create its graphic controls, is available on the book's companion web page, located at www.courseptr.com/downloads.

Summary

In this chapter you learned how to program using JavaScript. You learned different ways of embedding JavaScripts in your web pages. You learned how to collect, store, and process data using variables and to apply conditional and iterative programming logic. You also learned how to use arrays to store and process collections of data. This chapter explained the importance and benefits of using functions to improve script organization. You learned how to create functions that process arguments and return data. You also learned how to trigger function execution back on the occurrence of events. On top of all this, you learned how to create the Word Decoder Challenge Game.

Before you move on to Chapter 10, consider setting aside a few minutes to enhance the Word Decoder Challenge game by implementing the following challenges.

Challenges

1. **As currently written, the Word Decoder Challenge game only has 10 words from which to choose. These words are stored in an array named `wordArray`. Consider doubling or tripling the size of this array and its contents.**
2. **Consider modifying the game by replacing its words with more complex words and also adding the display of a sentence that provides the player with an extra hint about what the word means. One way of accomplishing this is to add a blank space to the end of each array element followed by a string describing the word. Another option is to display a third button on the browser window that the player can click on if he wants a hint.**

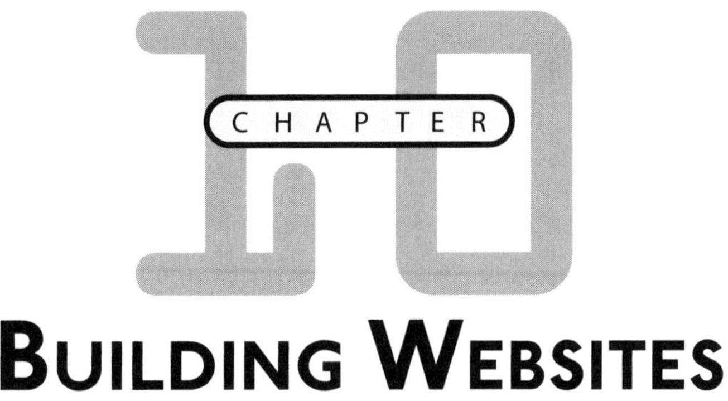

Building Websites

Throughout this book, you have learned the fundamentals of web development using HTML, XHTML, and CSS. These technologies provide a robust development environment designed to support the creation of web sites. This final chapter is designed to tie together everything you have learned by guiding you through the development of a new website. Along the way, you will learn the basic design steps involved in the development of new sites. By the time you are done, you will be ready to start creating websites of your own.

Specifically, you will learn:

- Fundamental steps and principles involved in website development
- The importance of proper planning and content organization prior to web development
- How to develop an effective navigation system to facilitate movement between the site's web pages
- How to apply a consistent look and feel to all your web pages

Project Preview: www.tech-publishing.com

In the previous chapters, you learned how to work with both HTML and XHTML and to use CSS to develop style rules that influence how the resulting markup is rendered. As this book's final project, you will learn how to develop an entire website. The premise behind the development of this website is that its owner, an author of a number of computer books, wants to create a new website designed to provide additional value and support to his readers.

The website you'll develop in this chapter can be found online at www.tech-publishing.com. There is one difference from the website presented here and the one you will find online: The online version of this website's library and downloads have been modified to use Ajax to supply some of their content, dynamically using data supplied by a web server. Ajax, which stands for Asynchronous JavaScript and XML, is a collection of web development technologies that uses (X)HTML, CSS, JavaScript, the DOM, the XMLHttpRequest object, and XML to create web applications that provide dynamic content provided by a web server.

If you really want to be a great web developer, learning Ajax is a must and is a logical next step to this book. To learn more, check out *Ajax Programming for the Absolute Beginner*(ISBN: 1598635646).

This website will consist of four document styles using a single CSS style sheet. The main landing page for this website is its welcome page, shown in Figure 10.1.

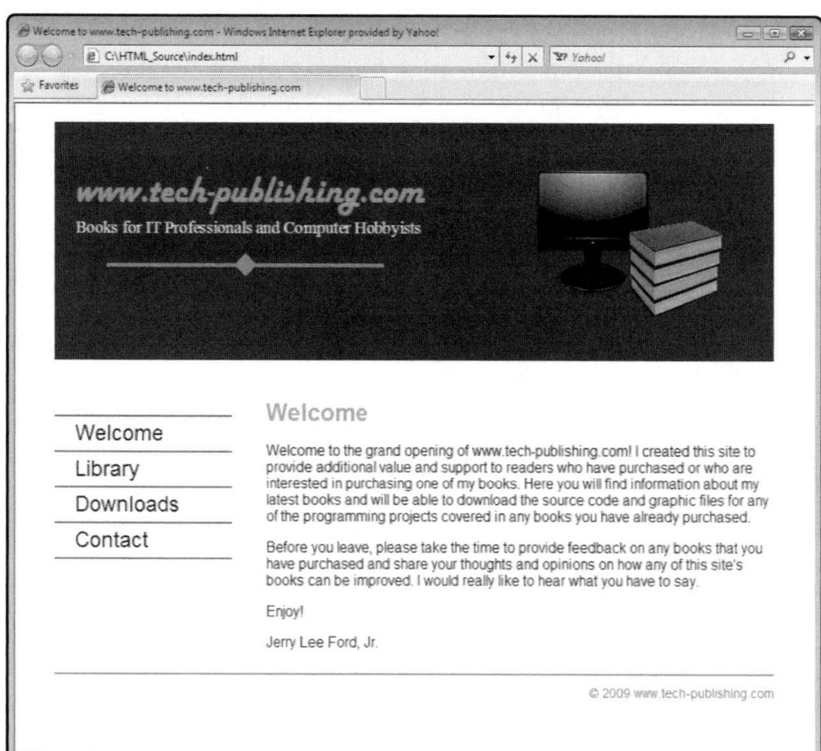

FIGURE 10.1

The other pages that make up this website are accessed via a series of links that make up the site menu system.

The website's library page, shown in Figure 10.2, provides information on the author's latest books and displays a link to amazon.com where the books can be purchased.

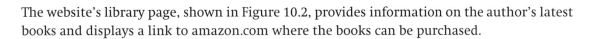

FIGURE 10.2

Every page on the website features the same banner, menu, and font/ color scheme.

The Downloads page, shown in Figure 10.3, provides easy access to the source code and graphic files belonging to the author's books. Access to these files is provided by a series of links stored as an unordered list.

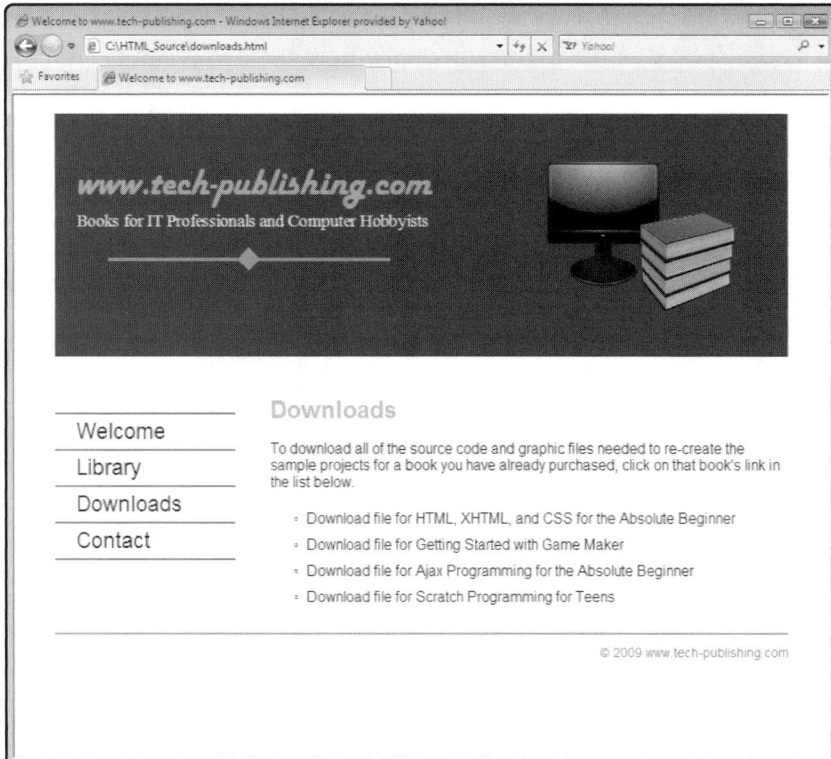

FIGURE 10.3

An unordered list provides single-click access to files containing each book's source code and graphics.

A copyright statement is provided at the bottom of every page in the lower-right corner, immediately after an orange-colored graphic separator bar. The website's final document generates its Contact page, shown in Figure 10.4. This page displays a form that visitors can fill in to provide feedback to the author.

Figure 10.4

A form provides a mechanism for readers to interact with the author.

Designing a Website from the Ground Up

It is important to realize from the very start that there is no specific procedure that must be followed when designing and developing new websites. However, in general it is a good idea to spend a little time thinking about what you hope to accomplish and then figuring out how you want to go about it before you start working. Failure to do so can lead to frustration and a lot of wasted time.

Document Project Objectives

When starting any new development project, a good first step is to begin by documenting your objectives for the project. What information are you trying to share or what products or services are you attempting to sell? Take a look at any competitive websites that might already serve the same population you are targeting. Once you have documented this information, you will be able to use it to help guide any development decisions as you work on your project.

Organization Content

Once you have a good understanding of your objectives, you can begin thinking about how you should lay out the website's overall organization and structure. A good way of doing this is to create a graphic structure chart like the one shown in Figure 10.5.

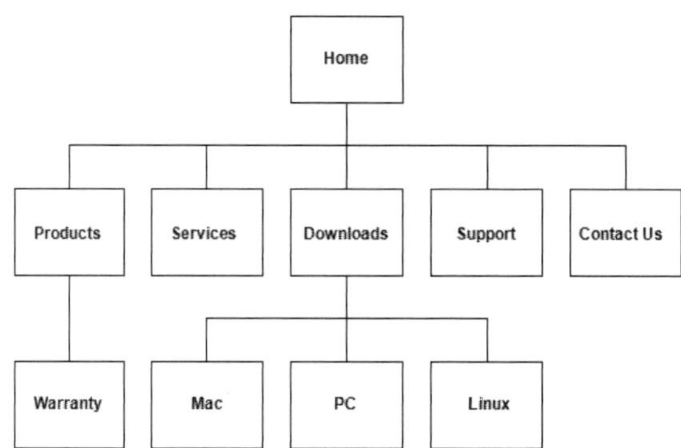

FIGURE 10.5

An example of a website's layout documented using a structure chart.

As Figure 10.5 shows, it is important at this stage to determine the different types of content you plan to provide and to group that content into sections (web documents). By laying out the website's content using a structure chart, you can accomplish multiple objectives. For starters, you will end up with a structure that can be used to layout the design of all of the web documents you will need to create as part of the website. In addition, the structure chart helps define how these documents relate to one another, showing their interconnections and providing a basis for formulating navigation links or menus for your website.

For example, using the structure chart shown in Figure 10.5, you can see that the website has a landing page where all visitors are expected to enter, though thanks to bookmarks and search engine results, this may not always be the case. The landing page provides direct access to five other pages. Your website's navigation links should most likely be based on these five pages. Pages that are connected to one of the individual pages can be accessed by links on those individual pages. However, regardless of where visitors are, it is almost always a good idea to make sure that the website's navigation links or menu is made available on every page, making it easy for visitors to get back to the website's primary pages.

All websites have an initial landing page, intended to be used as the entry point for the people who visit. When you sign up with a web service provider, be sure to find out the name you must assign to your web page's landing page. Usually this file is named index.html. However, in some cases your web service provider may require you to name it default.html, home.html, or something similar.

Outlining a Common Page Structure

In order to ensure that all of the web documents that make up a website share a common look and feel, many web developers begin web development by outlining all of the features that you see as being common to each web document. Once outlined, this list can be used as the basis for creating a template document that outlines the overall layout of the site's web pages. For example, many web pages display a heading at the top with a series of menu links following under it or along the left-hand side of the browser window. In addition, a large area of space is usually reserved for displaying content. Many websites also display a copyright message at the bottom of the window.

Creating a Rough Mockup of the Web Page Template

A good next step at this point is to spend a little time sketching out your idea as to how the website should look. If you have more than one idea, then sketch them all out and then choose whichever one looks best. Assuming that you have created a common page structure layout as previously suggested, you can use it as the basis for ensuring that your page sketch addresses all of the basic requirements.

If you are being paid to build this web page as a part of your job then you can share your sketch with your boss or customer and ask them to review and approve it. This way you will not end up wasting any time and energy developing a website that nobody wants. Your visual outline can be as simple as a hand-drawn sketch or you may instead want to use your favorite graphics program to render a more detailed and realistic example.

Creating a Common Document Template

Assuming that your sketch meets the needs of boss or customer, or you own personal requirements, then you can proceed with the process of constructing a template document. The markup for this document should define all of the content previously outlined. As you lay out the markup for this document, make sure that you keep your focus on defining content based on the order of its importance and not based on the order in which you want it to appear in the browser window. Right now, what you want to do is give your markup a good well-reasoned structure. You can use CSS, as explained in the next step, to reposition content.

Developing a Common CSS Style Sheet for the Website

Once your website's common template has been constructed, you should start working on the website's style rules, preferably using an external style sheet. Make sure that you style all of the content located in the template document so that it is rendered the way you want it to be. If necessary, you can always come back and tweak the CSS style sheet as needed as you work through the development of the entire website. For example, you may find that you need to come back and add additional CSS rules to fine-tune the presentation of content of some of the individual documents that you will ultimately be creating.

Build-out the Documents That Make Up the Website

Once your common template has the look you want, you can use copies of it as the starting point for each page you plan to add to the website. Assuming that you have carefully worked through the entire development process as just described, then you should find that the development of individual web documents goes pretty smoothly and that when you are done, each resulting web page is rendered with a presentation and style that makes it feel like it's part of a greater whole.

Back to the www.tech-publishing.com Website

It is time to turn your attention back to this book's final project, the creation of the www.tech-publishing.com website. The development of this website will follow the development process previously outlined in this chapter, demonstrating the effectiveness of this common development approach. However, there is more than one way to skin a cat, and you are of course free to follow any development approach you want.

Designing the Website

To keep things as simple and straightforward as possible, this website will be developed by following a specific series of steps, as outlined here:

1. Outline site objectives.
2. Sketch the site's overall structure.
3. Outline template content.
4. Sketch web page design.
5. Create the template markup.
6. Develop the site's CSS file.
7. Assemble document files.
8. Test your new website.

Step 1: Outlining Objectives for the Website

In keeping with the overall methodology outlined earlier in this chapter, let's begin this development effort by outlining the objective for this website. First, it has been stated that its overall purpose is to assist the author in providing additional value and support to his readers. To this end, the website needs to provide the author with a place to talk about his books. Second, since many of the author's books include sample code and graphics, the website needs to make it easy for the reader to locate and download these files. Lastly, the website should facilitate communication with visitors and provide them with the ability to send messages to the author.

Step 2: Sketching Out the Site's Structure

With these objectives now outlined, it is time to sit down and sketch out an overall outline for the website. For starters, like most websites, this site's general expectation is that visitors will arrive at the website most of the time through its main landing page (although some visitors may arrive at other pages thanks to previously set bookmarks or through search results).

Given the three objectives outlined in the previous step, it makes good sense to organize the rest of the website into three web documents, one to provide information about books, one to allow for source file downloads, and one to provide the reader a means of contacting the author. Figure 10.6 provides a high-level sketch of the website that follows the outline just provided.

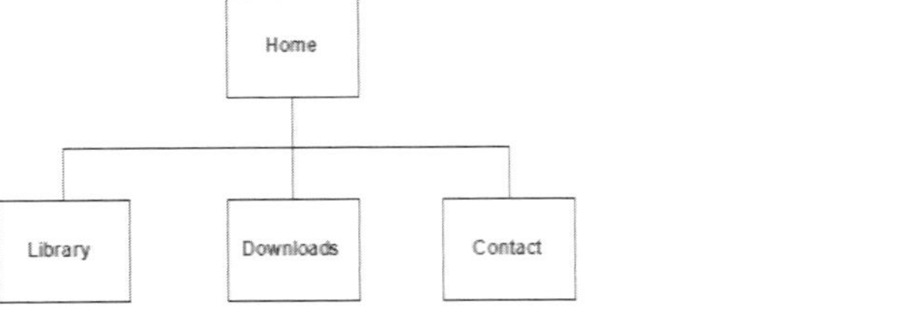

Figure 10.6

This www.tech-publishing.com website consists of four documents.

Step 3: Outlining Template Content

Now that we know the objectives and have laid out a sketch of the overall organization of the website, it is time to outline the content that should be provided on each of the site's web pages. For starters, let's brand the website by giving it a distinctive banner that is displayed across the top of each web page. Using graphics supplied by the author, display the www.tech-publishing.com logo as well as a graphic showing a computer and a stack of books on the banner.

Some type of navigation controls are required in order to control navigation between the pages that make up the website. To this end, let's develop a simple, text-based navigation menu with links to each of the site's four pages. Of course, each page has specific content that needs to be provided. To facilitate this, a specific portion of the browser window needs to be set aside. To help provide a consistent look and feel, this content area should always be set up to display a heading followed by a paragraph, after which additional content can be displayed.

Lastly, like most websites, a copyright notice needs to be displayed somewhere on the browser window, protecting the author's intellectual property rights. To make all of this information easier to digest, let's rework it as a bulleted list as shown here.

- Solid gray banner along the top of the browser window
  - www.tech-publishing.com graphic logo
  - Graphic image of a computer and books
- A text-based navigation menu
  - Links to each of the site's web documents
- A content area
  - A heading that identifies page content
  - A paragraph for displaying content
- A copyright notice

Now that we have this list of contents, let's use it as the basis for sketching out the overall design of all of the site's web documents and for developing the web page's markup.

Step 4: Sketching Out a Web Page Design

Rather than simply beginning the development of all of the website's documents, it's a good idea to pause and sketch out your vision as to how you plan to lay out the presentation of the web pages. In the case of the www.tech-publishing.com website, the sketch depicted in Figure 10.7 provides a vision of how the final result will look.

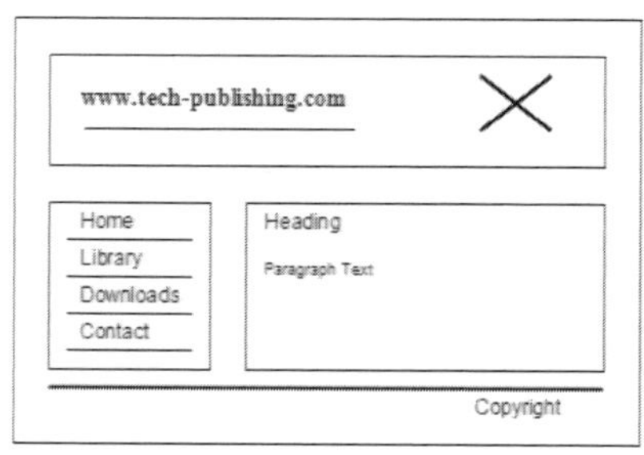

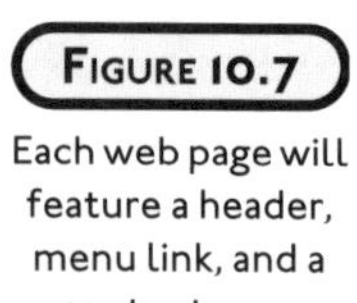

FIGURE 10.7

Each web page will feature a header, menu link, and a content area.

As you can see, the vision here is to display a heading that spans across the top of the browser window. The header will display the www.tech-publishing.com logo on the left-hand side as well as a graphic showing a computer and stack of books, represented by a bold X on the right-hand side of the header. A text-based collection of links will be displayed on the left-hand side of the browser window to provide navigation controls for every page that makes up the website. To the right of the menu links is the main display area for the web page, where the real content for each page will be displayed.

Beneath all of this, at the bottom of the web page is a graphic separator followed by a copyright notice located at the lower-right corner. The color scheme used to develop the website is orange on dark gray. The www.tech-publishing.com logo, menu headings, and the separate bar will be displayed in orange. The graphic header background color is dark gray. All text displaying in the menu and content area is displayed in black. However, when the mouse pointer is moved over or clicks on a text menu, its color changes to orange.

With this sketch now complete, you can approach the author and show him your idea for how the website will look and feel. Assuming he approves, you can begin working on the website's markup, confident that you are moving in the right direction. If, on the other hand, the author disapproves, you can make changes to your plans without losing a lot of time and effort.

Consider creating a number of different sketches outlining different presentation options for the website and giving all of them to your customer to consider. For example, you might create a sketch to show the page's links listed horizontally across the top of the web page, just under its header. Or you might sketch out a page that uses different types of graphic navigation buttons. The idea here is get the customer to agree to the content being provided and then to a number of different presentation options. Once the customer has made a selection, you can use it as the basis for developing the web page's external CSS file.

Step 5: Creating Template Markup

Once the author has given his approval to your plans, it is time to get to work. Begin by creating a template page that contains all of the content elements outlined in step 3. Don't worry about presentation at this point. All that matters is that you lay out the template document content in a logical and well-structured manner. Name your template document template.html, add the following content to it, and save it.

```
<!DOCTYPE html PUBLIC "-//W3C//DTD XHTML 1.0 Strict//EN"
  "http://www.w3.org/TR/xhtml1/DTD/xhtml1-strict.dtd">

<html xmlns="http://www.w3.org/1999/xhtml" xml:lang="en" lang="en">

  <head>
    <meta http-equiv = "Content-Type" content = "text/html; charset = utf-8" />
    <title>Welcome to www.tech-publishing.com</title>
    <link rel = "stylesheet" type = "text/css" href = "tech-pub.css" />
  </head>

  <body>
```

```
    <div id = "logo">
      <img src = "banner.png" width = "426" height = "192"
        alt = "Books for Professional and Computer Hobbyists" />
    </div>

    <div id = "concept">
      <img src = "pcandbooks.png" width = "210" height = "160"
        alt = "Picture of a computer and books" />
    </div>

    <ul id = "menu">
      <li><a href="index.html">Welcome</a></li>
      <li><a href="library.html">Library</a></li>
      <li><a href="downloads.html">Downloads</a></li>
      <li><a href="contact.html">Contact</a></li>
    </ul>

    <div id = "content">
      <h1>Page Title</h1>
      <p>Page content.</p>
    </div>

    <div id = "copyright">
      &copy; 2009 www.tech-publishing.com
    </div>

  </body>

</html>
```

As you can see, the head section already contains a link element that references a CSS file named tech-pub.css. Even though you have not created this file yet, it is a good idea to link to it now. This will not cause any errors and will ensure that the element is already in place when you later use this template as the basis of creating the site's documents.

The page's body section uses a series of div elements, each of which is assigned a unique ID attribute. The first two div elements each enclose an img element. The first image element references an image file named banner.png, which contains a graphic showing the website's graphic logo. The second div element references a graphic file named pcandbooks.png, which contains a graphic image of a computer and a stack of books.

The next `div` element contains an unordered list, made up of four links that when clicked, load each of the website's pages. Another `div` element, assigned an `ID` of content, has been added to define the area on the document where its content can be assigned. Lastly, a final `div` element is used to display a text string representing the website's copyright message.

Note the inclusion of `©` at the beginning of the copyright message. `©` is an example of a common character reference. It is necessary to use common character references to generate the display of certain types of characters like the copyright (©) character. For a complete list of common character references, check out http://www.w3schools.com/tags/ref_entities.asp.

Right now, the focus of this step is on laying out the markup for template.html in a manner that is well structured. Presentation of content is not important at the moment. Presentation will be addressed in the next step when you develop the document's external style sheet. Figure 10.8 shows how the browser renders the content of this document when loaded.

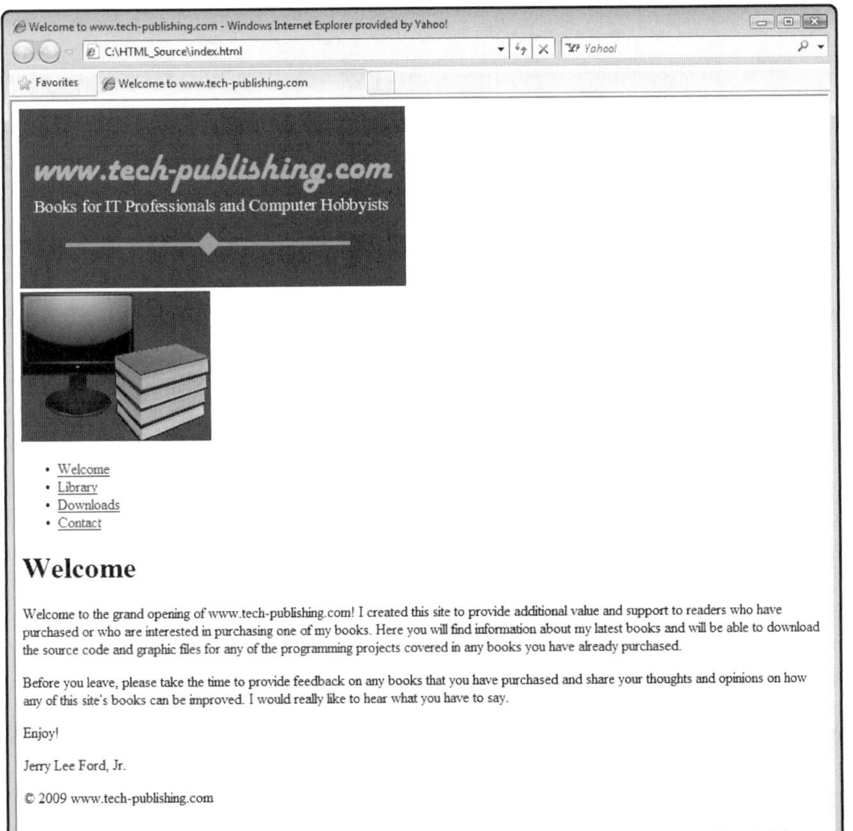

FIGURE 10.8

An example of how the resulting web page looks when the document is rendered by the browser using default style rules.

Step 6: Developing the Site's External CSS File

Now that the markup for the template.html page has been developed, it is time to create the style rules needed to modify the presentation of the resulting web page so that it looks like the sketch that was approved by the author. Begin by creating a CSS file named tech-pub.css and then add the following rule to it.

```
/*Configure minimum page width, available width, margins and default*/
/*font family for the document*/
body {
  min-width: 800px;
  width: 90%;
  margin: 0 auto;
  padding: 0;
  font-family: Arial, sans-serif;
}
```

This rule sets a minimum width of 800 pixels for the web page. It then sets the available area within this space to 90%. Browsers have a tendency to add a little extra padding to elements that make precise control over the presentation of content challenging. To overcome this problem, you simply need to remove any extra margin or padding that may be automatically added by the browser, which you can do by setting the `margin` and `padding` properties to 0. Lastly, `Arial` is set up as the default font for the entire web page.

Next, let's configure the colors used to display the document's links. To do so, add the following style rules to the end of the CSS file.

```
/*Configure the colors when displaying links*/
a:link, a:visited {
  color: black;
}
a:hover, a:focus, a:active  {
  color: orange;
}
```

The first rule configures the display of all links as black. The second rule turns the links to orange when the user moves the mouse pointer over a link or uses the Tab key to select a link. The content area on the web page consists of an `h1` heading. Let's change its color to orange, display its text content at 160 percent of the document's default size, and remove any top margin the browser may add to the heading by adding the following rule to the end of the style sheet.

```
/*Configure the size and color of level 1 headings*/
h1 {
  color: orange;
  font-size: 160%;
  margin-top: 0;
}
```

Next, let's begin configuring the display of the page's banner by adding the following rule to the end of the style sheet. The banner is made up of a dark gray heading with the website logo on it. In addition, a second graphic showing a computer and a stack of books will be displayed on it as well. You can use the `div` element whose `ID` is `logo` to reference the banner. Because this `div` element includes an embedded `img` element, that element will automatically be displayed on the resulting banner. Note that its position is set to relative. This will allow any content you place within it to be absolutely positioned.

Next, the height of the banner is specified and a small margin added to put a little extra space at the top of the banner and the top of the browser window. A little padding and a margin are then added to the `div` element, and a graphic file named background.png is used to repeatedly draw a graphic, which is 260 pixels tall by 10 pixels wide, repeatedly across the top of the browser window. Lastly, the `color` property is used to set the display of any character text to white.

Note that the background.png file used to draw the banner is only 260 pixels tall and 10 pixels wide. This is a relatively small file that can be downloaded quickly and repeatedly drawn over and over horizontally across the screen. This helps speed up the rendering of the page since small graphic files take less time to download.

```
/*Configure the location, height, and width of the document's logo*/
/*located at the left-hand side of the banner*/
#logo {
  position: relative;
  height: 260px;
  margin-top: 20px;
  padding: 10px;
  margin-bottom: 20px;
  background: url(background.png) repeat-x;
  color: white;
}
```

There are no plans to display on the banner. However, in the event that either of the graphic files that will be displayed on the banner becomes unavailable, each `img` element alternative text is displayed (in white instead of black).

With the presentation of the banner and the website's logo now configured, let's configure the display of the graphic image showing a computer and books on the banner by adding the following rule to the end of the style sheet. As you can see, the margin has been set to 0, positioning has been set to absolute, and the graphic's placement is specified using absolute positioning.

```
/*Specify the placement of the computer/book graphic at the top*/
/*of the screen*/
#concept {
  margin: 0;
  position: absolute;
  top: 50px;
  right: 40px;
  width: 30%;
  color: white;
  text-align: center;
}
```

Next, let's reserve space for the presentation of the page's content by adding the following rule to the end of the style sheet. Since the display of content is handled within a `div` element whose `ID` is `content`, this rule uses the `content ID` as its hook, allocating 70 percent of all available horizontal space to the display of content. This section of the web page is floated right.

```
/*Set the size of the area where content is displayed and float it*/
/*to the right*/
#content {
  width: 70%;
  float: right;
  padding-bottom: 20px;
  margin-left: 10px;
  padding: 2px;
}
```

The presentation of the web page's menu links is handled next by adding the following three rules to the end of the style sheet.

```
/*Set width of menu and float it to the left, disabling list style*/
/* and displaying a border on top of the first menu item*/
#menu {

  width: 25%;
  float: left;
  margin-top: 20px;
  margin-bottom: 20px;
  padding: 0;
  list-style: none;
  border-top: 2px solid gray;
}

/*Display a border below each menu item and increase menu font size*/
#menu li {
  border-bottom: 2px solid gray;
  font: 150% Arial, sans-serif;
  padding: 5px 0 5px 25px;
}

/*Disable the underlining of links*/
#menu a {
  text-decoration: none;
}
```

The first style rule allocates 25 percent of the available horizontal space to the `div` element that contains the menu's text links. This `div` element is floated to the left. Also, take note of the use of the `list-style` property, which is set to `none`. This hides the display of the menu list's bullets, which would otherwise be displayed. Also take note of the use of the `border-top` property, which has been configured to display a two-pixel thick solid gray line just above the first link.

By allocating 70 percent of available horizontal space to the content area and 25 percent for the display of the menu links, a total of 5 percent is left unaccounted for. Given that the menu links are floated to the left and the content is floated to the right, the leftover five percent represents unused white space in between these two entities.

The second rule shown above is responsible for displaying two-pixel thick solid gray lines under each link and for enlarging the display of link text. Lastly, a little extra padding is added to improve link presentation. The last rule shown above sets the `text-decoration` property to `none`. This eliminates the automatic underlining of links by the browser.

Last but not least, add the following style rule to the end of the style sheet. This rule begins by setting the `clear` property to `both`. This is needed because of the use of floated elements in the web document. Floated elements defy the normal flow of content presentation. When elements are floated, the browser is unable to determine the element's lower boundary. As a result, any content that follows can end up being displayed over the top of previously floated content. The use of the `clear` property prevents this from occurring by instructing the browser to set an arbitrary invisible line above which new content is not to be displayed.

```
/*Configure the display of the copyright statement*/
#copyright {
  clear: both;
  text-align: right;
  font-size: 90%;
  color: gray;
  padding-top: 20px;
  margin-bottom: 20px;
  background: url(separator.png) repeat-x;
}
```

After setting the value of the `clear` property, the rest of the rule sets the location, font size, and color of the copyright element and then uses the `background` property to display an orange graphic separator bar graphic along the bottom of the web page.

Okay, at this point the external style sheet for the website is complete. Figure 10.9 shows how the application of this style sheet has affected the presentation of the web page.

The presentation of content using the steps outlined above results in a fluid display that automatically adjusts its presentation based on the width of the browser window as demonstrated in Figure 10.10.

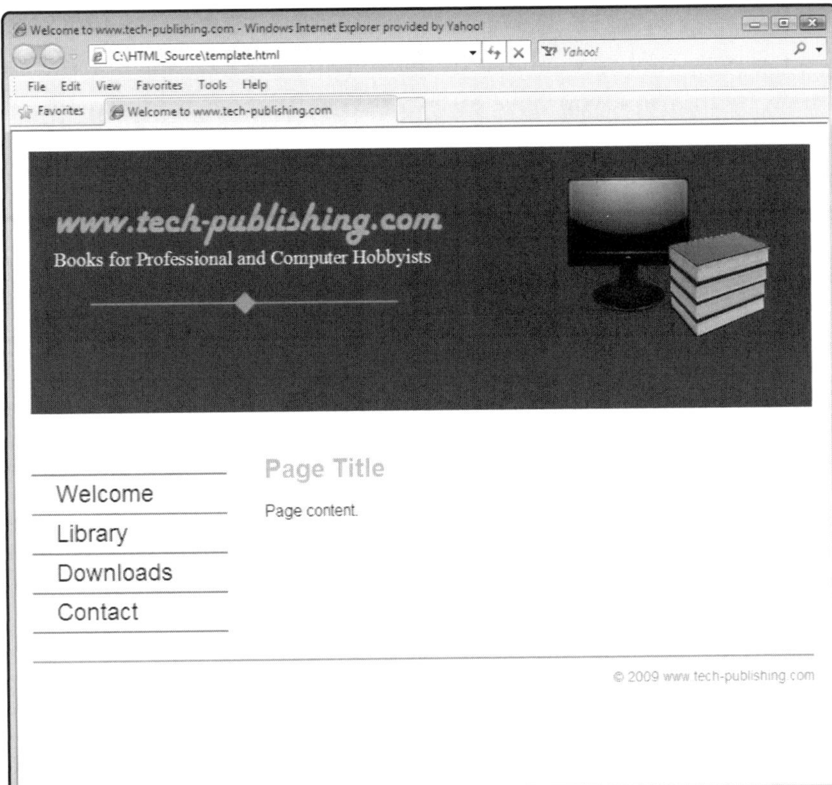

FIGURE 10.9 An example of how the website looks when viewed using a small browser window.

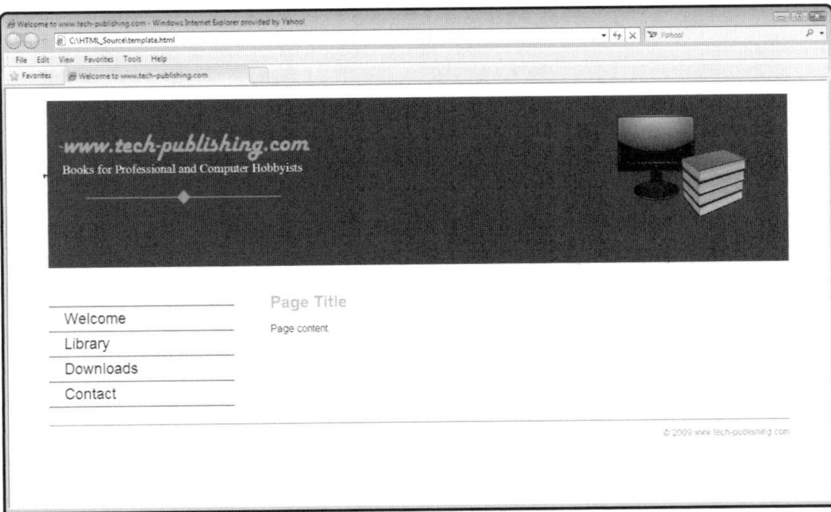

FIGURE 10.10 An example of how the website looks when viewed using a larger browser window.

Step 7: Assembling Document Files

At this point you have a template that you will use as the starting point for each of the website's four document files. In addition, you have an external style sheet that manages the presentation of any content defined in these pages. As you build out these web documents, you will find it necessary to return and add style rules to the external style sheet, specifically designed to handle the presentation of the new content that you are going to add. This is a normal and expected part of the development process.

Creating the index.html Document

The first web document to be created is the index.html document, which will be used to create the website's primary landing page. To create it, make a copy of the template.html page, renaming it index.html and then modify its markup by adding the elements and content highlighted below in bold exactly as shown.

```
<!DOCTYPE html PUBLIC "-//W3C//DTD XHTML 1.0 Strict//EN"
  "http://www.w3.org/TR/xhtml1/DTD/xhtml1-strict.dtd">

<html xmlns="http://www.w3.org/1999/xhtml" xml:lang="en" lang="en">

  <head>
    <meta http-equiv = "Content-Type" content = "text/html; charset = utf-8" />
    <title>Welcome to www.tech-publishing.com</title>
    <link rel = "stylesheet" type = "text/css" href = "tech-pub.css" />
  </head>

  <body>

    <div id = "logo">
      <img src = "banner.png" width = "426" height = "192"
        alt = "Books for Professional and Computer Hobbyists" />
    </div>

    <div id = "concept">
      <img src = "pcandbooks.png" width = "210" height = "160"
        alt = "Picture of a computer and books" />
    </div>
```

```
    <ul id = "menu">
      <li><a href="index.html">Welcome</a></li>
      <li><a href="library.html">Library</a></li>
      <li><a href="downloads.html">Downloads</a></li>
      <li><a href="contact.html">Contact</a></li>
    </ul>

    <div id = "content">
      <h1>Welcome</h1>
      <p>Welcome to the grand opening of www.tech-publishing.com! I created
         this site to provide additional value and support to readers who
         have purchased or who are interested in purchasing one of my books.
         Here you will find information about my latest books and will
         be able to download the source code and graphic files for any of the
         programming projects covered in any books you have already
         purchased.
      </p>
      <p>
         Before you leave, please take the time to provide feedback on any
         books that you have purchased and share your thoughts and opinions on
         how any of this site's books can be improved. I would really
         like to hear what you have to say.
      </p>
      <p>Enjoy!</p>
      <p>Jerry Lee Ford, Jr.</p>
    </div>

    <div id = "copyright">
      &copy; 2009 www.tech-publishing.com
    </div>

  </body>

</html>
```

As you can see, all that has happened here is the modification of the document's `h1` element along with addition of a little content, embedded within paragraph elements.

Creating the library.html Document

Now let's move on to the creation of the library.html document. To create this document, make a copy of the template.html file and rename it library.html. Modify the document's markup by adding the elements and content highlighted below in bold print exactly as shown.

```
<!DOCTYPE html PUBLIC "-//W3C//DTD XHTML 1.0 Strict//EN"
  "http://www.w3.org/TR/xhtml1/DTD/xhtml1-strict.dtd">

<html xmlns="http://www.w3.org/1999/xhtml" xml:lang="en" lang="en">

  <head>
    <meta http-equiv = "Content-Type" content = "text/html; charset = utf-8" />
    <title>Welcome to www.tech-publishing.com</title>
    <link rel = "stylesheet" type = "text/css" href = "tech-pub.css" />
  </head>

  <body>

    <div id = "logo">
      <img src = "banner.png" width = "426" height = "192"
        alt = "Books for Professional and Computer Hobbyists" />
    </div>

    <div id = "concept">
      <img src = "pcandbooks.png" width = "210" height = "160"
        alt = "Picture of a computer and books" />
    </div>

    <ul id = "menu">
      <li><a href="index.html">Welcome</a></li>
      <li><a href="library.html">Library</a></li>
      <li><a href="downloads.html">Downloads</a></li>
      <li><a href="contact.html">Contact</a></li>
    </ul>

    <div id = "content">
      <h1>Library</h1>
      <p>Scroll down to learn more about my latest books. If you find one
```

```
    you like, you can purchase it online by clicking on the link to
    amazon.com located at the bottom of this page.</p><br />
<p><img src = "xhtml-css.jpg" width = "93" height = "115"
    alt = "HTML, XHTML, and CSS for the Absolute Beginner" /></p>
<p><em>HTML, XHTML, &amp; CSS For the Absolute Beginner</em> provides
    Beginner-level programmers with an entry-level introduction
    to HTML, XHTML, and CSS. This book serves as a primer for
    client-side web development. To make learning fun, the book
    uses a games-based instructional approach that provides working
    examples that demonstrate how HTML, XHTML, and CSS can be applied
    to the development of web pages and sites.</p><br />
<p><img src = "gamemaker.jpg" width = "93" height = "115"
    alt = "Getting Started with Game Maker" /></p>
<p><em>Getting Started with Game Maker</em> shows aspiring game
    developers how to create their very own, professional-quality computer
    games, no programming knowledge required. Using Game Maker and
    its drag-and-drop environment and following along with the
    step-by-step instructions, you will learn how to create
    arcade-style 2D and 3D games complete with graphics, sound
    effects, and music. Game Maker provides everything you need to
    create, test, debug, and run your games in a Windows
    environment.</p><br />
<p><img src = "ajax.jpg" width = "93" height = "115"
    alt = "Ajax Programming for the Absolute Beginner" /></p>
<p><em>Ajax Programming for the Absolute Beginner</em> teaches the
    principles of programming through simple game creation. You will
    acquire the skills that you need for more practical programming
    applications and learn how these skills can be put to use
    in real-world scenarios.</p><br />
<p><img src = "scratch.jpg" width = "93" height = "115"
    alt = "Scratch Programming for Teens" /></p>
<p><em>Scratch Programming for Teens</em> teaches you everything
    you need to know to get up and running quickly with Scratch.
    Scratch is a programming language intended to make programming
    easier to learn for novice programmers. It can be used to create
    computer games, interactive stories, graphic artwork, and
    computer animation, and all sorts of other multimedia projects.
    Scratch can also be used to play digital music and sound
```

```
        effects. If you aspire to one day become a professional
        programmer, Scratch provides everything you need to build a
        foundation.</p><br />
      <p><a href="http://www.amazon.com">Visit amazon.com to purchase a
        book</a></p>

    </div>

    <div id = "copyright">
      &copy; 2009 www.tech-publishing.com
    </div>

  </body>

</html>
```

As you can see, the content that has been added to the document consists primarily of paragraph and link elements as well as an `img` element for each of the four books that are displayed. The additional markup ends with the link to www.amazon.com at the bottom of the `div` element to which all of the new content has been added.

Creating the downloads.html Document

Next, let's create the downloads.html document. To create this document, make a copy of the template.html file and rename it downloads.html. Modify the document's markup by adding the elements and content highlighted below in bold print to it exactly as shown.

```
<!DOCTYPE html PUBLIC "-//W3C//DTD XHTML 1.0 Strict//EN"
  "http://www.w3.org/TR/xhtml1/DTD/xhtml1-strict.dtd">

<html xmlns="http://www.w3.org/1999/xhtml" xml:lang="en" lang="en">

  <head>
    <meta http-equiv = "Content-Type" content = "text/html; charset = utf-8" />
    <title>Welcome to www.tech-publishing.com</title>
    <link rel = "stylesheet" type = "text/css" href = "tech-pub.css" />
  </head>

  <body>
```

```
<div id = "logo">
  <img src = "banner.png" width = "426" height = "192"
    alt = "Books for Professional and Computer Hobbyists" />
</div>

<div id = "concept">
  <img src = "pcandbooks.png" width = "210" height = "160"
    alt = "Picture of a computer and books" />
</div>

<ul id = "menu">
  <li><a href="index.html">Welcome</a></li>
  <li><a href="library.html">Library</a></li>
  <li><a href="downloads.html">Downloads</a></li>
  <li><a href="contact.html">Contact</a></li>
</ul>

<div id = "content">
  <h1>Downloads</h1>
  <p>To download all of the source code and graphic files needed to
     re-create the sample projects for a book you have already purchased,
     click on that book's link in the list below.</p>

  <ul id = "downloads">
    <li><a href="xhtml-css.zip">Download files for HTML, XHTML, and CSS for
         the Absolute Beginner</a></li>
    <li><a href="gamemaker.zip">Download file for Getting Started with
         Game Maker</a></li>
    <li><a href="ajax.zip">Download file for Ajax Programming for the
         Absolute Beginner</a></li>
    <li><a href="scratch.zip">Download file for Scratch Programming for
         Teens</a></li>
  </ul>

</div>

<div id = "copyright">
  &copy; 2009 www.tech-publishing.com
```

```
    </div>

  </body>

</html>
```

The additional markup that has been added to this document primarily consists of an unordered list containing a series of four links, each of which references a different zip file stored alongside the website's other content on the web server. When clicked, these links allow visitors to download and save a copy of the source code and graphic files for the author's books.

The addition of the new content in the downloads.html document requires that you go back and modify the tech-pub.css document by adding the style rules shown below to the end of the website's external style sheet.

```
/*Additional style rules for downloads.html*/

/*Set font size, type, add extra padding and set list style*/
#downloads li {
  font: 100% Arial, sans-serif;
  padding: 5px 0px 5px 0px;
  list-style: circle;
}

/*Disable the underlining of links*/
#downloads a {
  text-decoration: none;
}
```

As you can see, the first of these two new rules set and configure the size of the font used to display the download links, add a little padding around each list item (link), and then configure each link to display a circle bullet. The second rule removes the underlining of links.

Creating the contact.html Document

Now it is time to create the website's final document, contact.html. To create this document, make a copy of the template.html file and rename it contact.html. Modify the document's markup by adding the elements and content highlighted below in bold.

```
<!DOCTYPE html PUBLIC "-//W3C//DTD XHTML 1.0 Strict//EN"
  "http://www.w3.org/TR/xhtml1/DTD/xhtml1-strict.dtd">

<html xmlns="http://www.w3.org/1999/xhtml" xml:lang="en" lang="en">

  <head>
    <meta http-equiv = "Content-Type" content = "text/html; charset = utf-8" />
    <title>Welcome to www.tech-publishing.com</title>
    <link rel = "stylesheet" type = "text/css" href = "tech-pub.css" />

    <script type = "text/javascript">
    <!-- Start hiding JavaScript statements
      function ProcessMsg() {
        if (document.getElementById("name").value != "") {
          if (document.getElementById("email").value != "") {
            if (document.getElementById("message").value != "") {
              document.getElementById("msgForm").submit();
            }
            else {
              window.alert("Error: You must enter a message.");
            }
          }
          else {
            window.alert("Error: You must enter your email address.");
          }
        }
        else {
          window.alert("Error: You must enter your name.");
        }
      }
    // End hiding JavaScript statements -->
    </script>

  </head>

  <body>

    <div id = "logo">
```

```
  <img src = "banner.png" width = "426" height = "192"
    alt = "Books for Professional and Computer Hobbyists" />
</div>

<div id = "concept">
  <img src = "pcandbooks.png" width = "210" height = "160"
    alt = "Picture of a computer and books" />
</div>

<ul id = "menu">
  <li><a href="index.html">Welcome</a></li>
  <li><a href="library.html">Library</a></li>
  <li><a href="downloads.html">Downloads</a></li>
  <li><a href="contact.html">Contact</a></li>
</ul>

<div id = "content">
  <h1>Contact</h1>
  <p>Have any thoughts on how this site or one of my books might be
     improved? I would like to hear them. Simply fill out the form
     below and click on Send.</p><br />
  <form id = "msgForm" method = "post" action = "process_form.php">
    <fieldset id = "submitmsg">
      <ol>
        <li><label for = "name">Name:</label>
            <input type = "text" id = "name" name = "name" />
        </li>
        <li><label for = "email">E-mail:</label>
            <input type = "text" id = "email" name = "email" />
        </li>
        <li><label for = "message">Message:</label>
            <textarea id = "message" name = "message" cols = "50"
              rows = "12"></textarea>
        </li>
        <li><label for = "submit"> Submit:</label>
          <input type = "submit" id = "submit" name = "submit"
            value = "Send" onclick = "ProcessMsg()"/>
        </li>
```

```
        </ol>
      </fieldset>
    </form>
  </div>

  <div id = "copyright">
    &copy; 2009 www.tech-publishing.com
  </div>

</body>

</html>
```

As you can see, the additional markup added to this page is used to create a form that collects visitor feedback. Note that the opening `<form>` tag's `action` attribute points to a PHP file located on the web server (in the same folder as the html page). In addition, note that the `input` element configured as a Submit button includes an `onclick` event handler that executes a JavaScript function named `ProcessMsg()` when clicked.

The `ProcessMsg()` function uses the `getElementById()` method to retrieve any text typed into the form's `text` and `textarea` controls. If any of these controls are found to be empty, an error message is displayed, instructing the user what information has been omitted. If all required information has been provided, the `getElementById()` method is used to establish and reference the document's form and then to execute its `submit()` method.

The addition of the form and its various form elements requires that you go back and modify the tech-pub.css document one last time, adding the style rules shown below to the end of the website's external style sheet.

```
/*Additional style rules for contact.html*/

/*Hide the fieldset element's border*/
#submitmsg {
  border: none;
}

/*Disable the display of list numbering*/
#submitmsg ol {
  list-style: none;
  margin: 0;
  padding: 0;
```

```
}

/*Add some space between form fields*/
#submitmsg li {
  margin-bottom: 10px;
}

/*Set width of labels to 15 percent and configure them*/
#submitmsg label {
  width: 15%;
  float: left;
  text-align: right;
  margin-right: 5%;
}

/*Set the width of the form button*/
#submit {
  min-width: 80px;
}
```

The first of these five style rules removes the display of the default border that is normally displayed by the `fieldset` element. The form's elements are organized and displayed as an ordered list. The second rule disables the display of the list's numbers and eliminates any margin or padding that the browser may add to the list. The third rule adds a little space between form controls by adding a padding of 10 pixels to the end of each list element. The fourth rule modifies the presentation of form labels, configuring them so that label text is left aligned. By assigning each label the same width, the controls also end up aligned when displayed. Finally, the fifth and final rule sets the minimum width assigned to the form's Submit button.

In order for the contact.html document to work as previously explained, you must have a program named process_form.php located in the same folder on your web server as your web documents. The process_form.php program is a PHP script. PHP is a server-side scripting language used in the creation of web applications. A discussion of PHP is well outside the scope of this book.

PHP is one of the most universally supported server-side scripting languages. Chances are that your web host supports it. Assuming this is the case, all you have to do to enable the proper operation of the Contact form is to create a text file named process_form.php and then add the following statement to it.

While I will not go into any detail describing what this PHP script does, I will point out that it consists of two parts. The first part is written in PHP and its purpose is to process data submitted to it by the contact.html page's form. The second part of the script contains a copy of the template.html page. Its content has been modified to display a message that lets visitors know that their messages have been submitted. This XHTML content is returned by the PHP program to the browser, where it is displayed in the browser window.

```
<?
if (($_POST[name] == "") ||
    ($_POST[email] == "") ||
    ($_POST[message] == "")) {
    header("Location: contact.html");
    exit;
}

$msg = "Email sent  from www.tech-publishing.com\n";
$msg .= "Sender Name:\t$_POST[name]\n";
$msg .= "Sender Email:\t$_POST[email]\n";
$msg .= "Message:\t$_POST[message]\n";

$to = "jlf04@yahoo.com";
$subject = "Reader Feedback";
$mailheaders = "From: www.tech-publishing.com\n";
$mailheaders .= "Reply-To: $_POST[sender_email]\n";
mail($to, $subject, $msg, $mailheaders);
?>

<!DOCTYPE html PUBLIC "-//W3C//DTD XHTML 1.0 Strict//EN"
  "http://www.w3.org/TR/xhtml1/DTD/xhtml1-strict.dtd">

<html xmlns="http://www.w3.org/1999/xhtml" xml:lang="en" lang="en">

  <head>
    <meta http-equiv = "Content-Type" content = "text/html; charset = utf-8" />
    <title>Welcome to www.tech-publishing.com</title>
    <link rel = "stylesheet" type = "text/css" href = "tech-pub.css" />
  </head>
```

```
  <body>

    <div id = "logo">
      <img src = "banner.png" width = "426" height = "192"
        alt = "Books for Professional and Computer Hobbyists" />
    </div>

    <div id = "concept">
      <img src = "pcandbooks.png" width = "210" height = "160"
        alt = "Picture of a computer and books" />
    </div>

    <ul id = "menu">
      <li><a href="index.html">Welcome</a></li>
      <li><a href="library.html">Library</a></li>
      <li><a href="downloads.html">Downloads</a></li>
      <li><a href="contact.html">Contact</a></li>
    </ul>

    <div id = "content">
      <h1>Contact</h1>
      <p>Your message has been sent. Thanks!</p><br />
    </div>

    <div id = "copyright">
      &copy; 2009 www.tech-publishing.com
    </div>

  </body>

</html>
```

Step 8: Testing the New Website

Well, that's it! As long as you followed along carefully with the instructions that have been provided, your copy of the www.tech-publishing.com website should be ready for testing. Start by loading the index.html document into your web browser and then explore the site and make sure that everything works as advertised.

A complete copy of the source code for this project, including its style sheet, and the graphics needed to create its graphic controls is available on the book's companion web page, located at www.courseptr.com/downloads.

Summary

Congratulations on making it through to the end of this book! By making it this far, you have learned the fundamentals of web development using HTML, XHTML, and CSS. Not only that but you have a basic understanding of the document object model (DOM) and a good understanding of JavaScript programming. By mastering the basics of all of these web development technologies, you have positioned yourself to make the leap from web surfer to web developer. As a result, you are ready to begin developing your own websites and to begin making a name for yourself by carving out your own little piece of space on the World Wide Web.

Before you put this book down and move on to other things, why don't you take a few minutes to implement the following challenges?

Challenges

1. **Using the www.tech-publishing.com website as a starting point, create a new website of your own.**
2. **Replace the graphics and modify the color scheme and layout to suit your own preferences.**
3. **If you don't already have one, find a website host and upload your new website for the world to see.**

Part V

Appendixes

What's on the Companion Website?

Now that you have made your way through all the chapters in this book, you have a strong foundation on which you can continue to build and learn. Do not think of this book as the end of your HTML, XHTML, and CSS education; think of it as the beginning. There is a lot left to learn and experience—a lot more than can be covered in any single book.

As you continue working with all of the different web development languages and technologies that you learned in this book, you will find that it helps to have a collection of reliable examples and source code upon which you can draw for inspiration and use as examples as how to perform certain types of tasks. If you have been faithfully following along and re-creating all of the sample projects, then you already have access to such a collection of code and examples. As you continue experimenting, learning, and tackling more and more challenging projects, you should continue to add to this collection.

By continuing to refer to and study these examples, you will learn to be a better web developer. Further, by copying and pasting portions of source code from these examples into new applications, you can modify and adapt them to perform different types of tasks. This will allow you to work smarter and faster and will save you from having to reinvent the wheel every time you start a new web development project.

Downloading the Book's Source Code

The best way to use this book is to set aside the time required to re-create every project that has been presented. However, in the event that you do not have the time to re-create all of this book's projects, you can download all of the (X)HTML code, CSS style sheets, and JavaScripts that were presented. This way you can still work with and learn from them. You will find copies of all these resources available for download on the book's companion website, located at http://www.courseptr.com/downloads.

Table A.1 provides an overview of all the project code presented in this book, which you will find ready for download on this book's companion website. This includes all of the (X)HTML code, CSS style sheets, and JavaScripts that were used in the creation of these projects.

Table A.1 Project Source Code Available on the Companion Website

Chapter	Overview
Chapter 1	**The HTML Joke Page**—Displays a joke and its punch line.
Chapter 2	**The Linked Jokes Application**—Tells two jokes, displaying the punch lines on different web pages.
Chapter 3	**The Math Quiz**—A 15-question math quiz.
Chapter 4	**A Knight's Tale**—Tells a story that incorporates user input.
Chapter 5	**The (X)HTML Typing Quiz**—A game that evaluates the player's typing skills.
Chapter 6	**The Number Guessing Game**—Challenges the player to guess a randomly generated number in as few guesses as possible.
Chapter 7	**The Rock, Paper, Scissors Game**—Pits the player against the computer as both attempt to outguess one another.
Chapter 8	**The Fortune Teller Game**—Simulates a session with a fortune teller, answering the player's every question.
Chapter 9	**The Word Decoder Challenge**—Challenges the player to decode a series of scrambled words.
Chapter 10	**The www.tech-publishing.com Website**—A complete sample website.

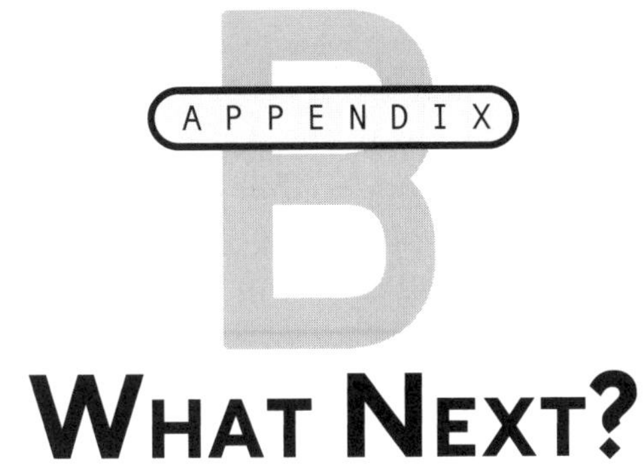

What Next?

To truly become an effective web developer, you must put in the time and effort required to learn and master your craft. This means developing all kinds of websites and projects, experimenting as you learn more about how and why things work. By reading this book cover to cover and taking the time to re-create all of the projects that have been presented, you are off to an excellent start as a web developer. To keep the momentum going and further your understanding of all of the technologies and programming languages involved, this appendix provides a list of online resources that you can visit to learn more about (X)HTML, CSS, XML, and JavaScript. This appendix also provides you with a list of tools you may find will make valuable additions to your development toolset. These tools include web page editors, graphics editors, FTP clients, and link checkers.

HTML Resources

This book has taught you a lot about HTML and XHTML. While you should now be familiar with all the basics, there is a lot more to be learned. The following set of websites provide you with names and URLs where you can go to learn more about both of these markup languages.

Wikipedia's HTML and XHTML Pages

If you want to stay abreast of the latest happenings about HTML and XHTML then two of the best places to visit are Wikipedia's HTML and XHTML pages. As shown in Figure B.1, Wikipedia's HTML page is located at http://en.wikipedia.org/wiki/HTML. You will find a lot of good information about HTML, its origins, and major elements. You will also find lots of links, including links to numerous online tutorials.

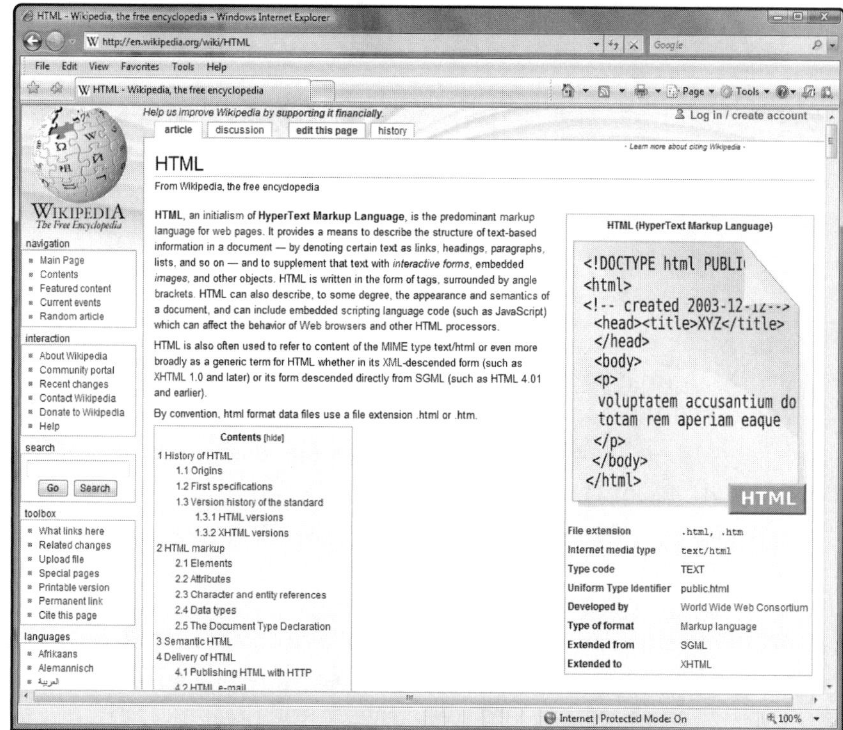

FIGURE B.1

You can frequent Wikipedia's HTML page to keep up with the current and future status of HTML.

Similarly, an easy way to stay on top of what is going on with XHTML is to visit Wikipedia's XHTML page, located at http://en.wikipedia.org/wiki/XHTML.

WC3's HTML 4.01 Specification Page

Another essential source of HTML information that every serious web developer should be aware of is the W3C HTML 4.01 Specification page located at http://www.w3.org/TR/html401, as shown in Figure B.2. Here you will find everything there is to know about HTML 4.01.

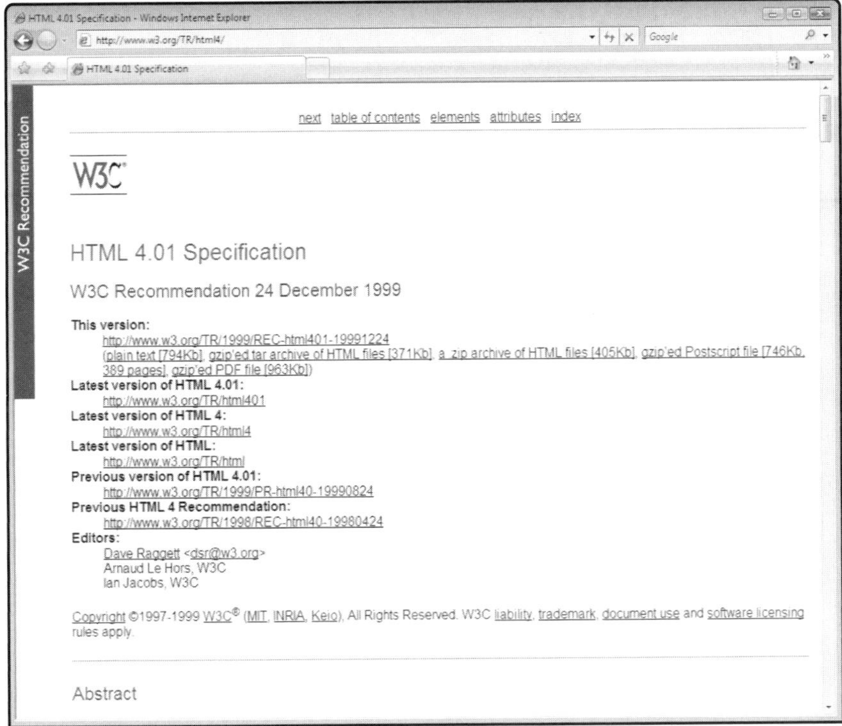

Figure B.2

WC3's HTML 4.01 Specification page is the Holy Grail of information on HTML.

WC3's XHTML Specifications

As with HTML, W3C is also responsible for managing the specification of XHTML. So far, there have been two drafts of XHTML: XHTML 1.0 and XHTML 1.1. In addition, a new XHTML 2.0 standard is currently under development. To review these specifications, visit the following URLs.

- **XHTML 1.0**—www.w3.org/MarkUp/
- **XHTML 1.1**—www.w3.org/TR/xhtnl11/
- **XHTML 2.0**—www.w3.org/TR/xhtml1/

Resources for Cascading Style Sheets

Cascading Style Sheets (or CSS) is a style sheet language whose purpose is to facilitate the presentation of documents written using a markup language like HTML and XHTML. CSS allows you to create style templates that specify the layout of web page items. CSS lets web developers define font attributes, spacing, borders, and many other types of visual and organizational characteristics that govern the display on web pages.

Wikipedia's Cascading Style Sheets Page

An understanding of the proper use of cascading style sheets in controlling content presentation on web pages is essential to web developers. One of the easiest and fastest ways of staying abreast of the latest developments of CSS is to keep an eye on the Wikipedia Cascading Style Sheets page located at http://en.wikipedia.org/wiki/Cascading_style_sheets as shown in Figure B.3.

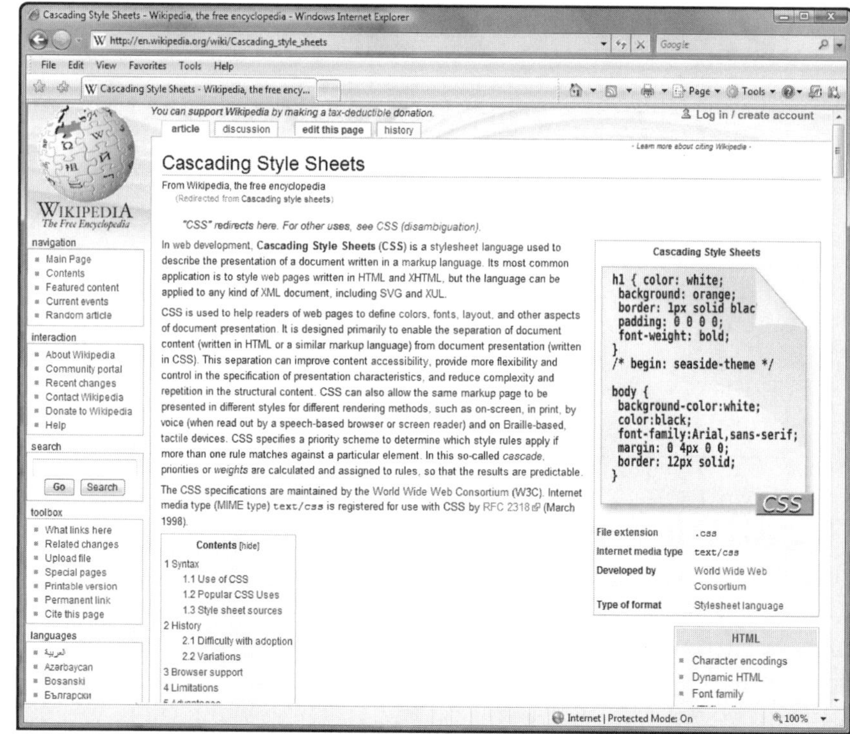

FIGURE B.3

Wikipedia's Cascading Style Sheets page provides up-to-date information on the latest happenings with CSS.

Wikipedia's Cascading Style Sheets page provides background information about CSS and provides an overview of its many uses and limitations. Just as important, this web page is an excellent source of links to other websites dedicated to CSS.

WC3's Cascading Style Sheets Page

Like HTML and XHTML, CSS specifications are managed by W3C. So far, there have been two major versions. To review these specifications, visit the following URLs.

- **CSS Level 1**—www.w3.org/TR/CSS1
- **CSS Level 2**—www.w3.org/TR/CSS21

In addition to these two versions, there is a third version currently in the process of being defined. To learn more about the future of CSS development, visit http://www.w3.org/Style/CSS/current-work, as shown in Figure B.4.

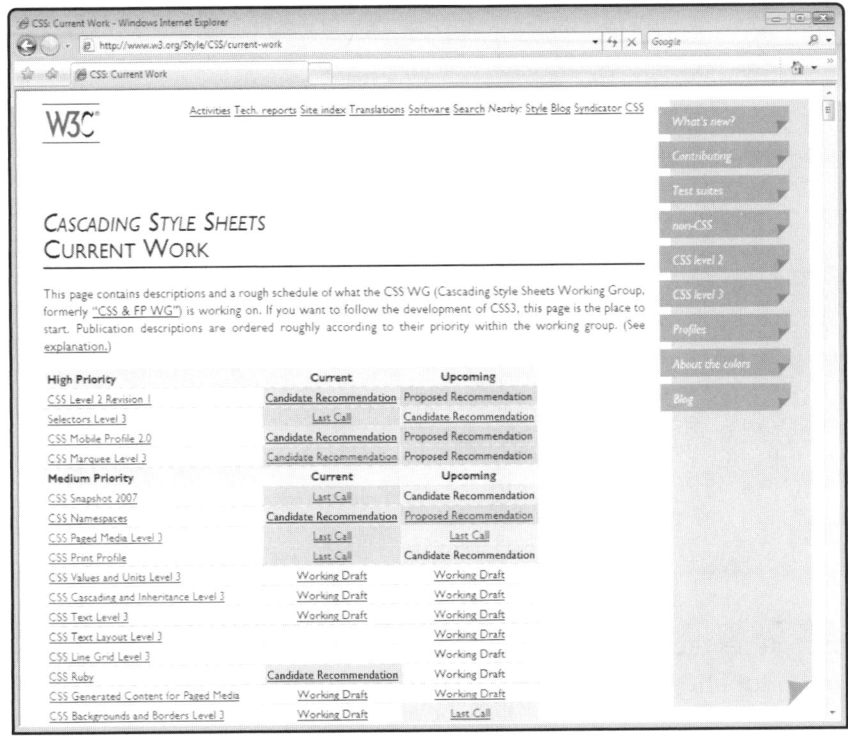

FIGURE B.4

WC3's Cascading Style Sheets Current Work page provides information on the future development direction of CSS.

XML RESOURCES

XML is a document processing standard that describes the structure of data. XML is an integral part of XHTML. XML allows web developers to create custom tags and define a structure for describing data. A good understanding is therefore important to any web developer.

Wikipedia's XML Page

This book has provided you with a basic overview of XML. However, there is a lot more to XML than could be fit into this book. To learn more, visit http://en.wikipedia.org/wiki/Xml, as shown in Figure B.5.

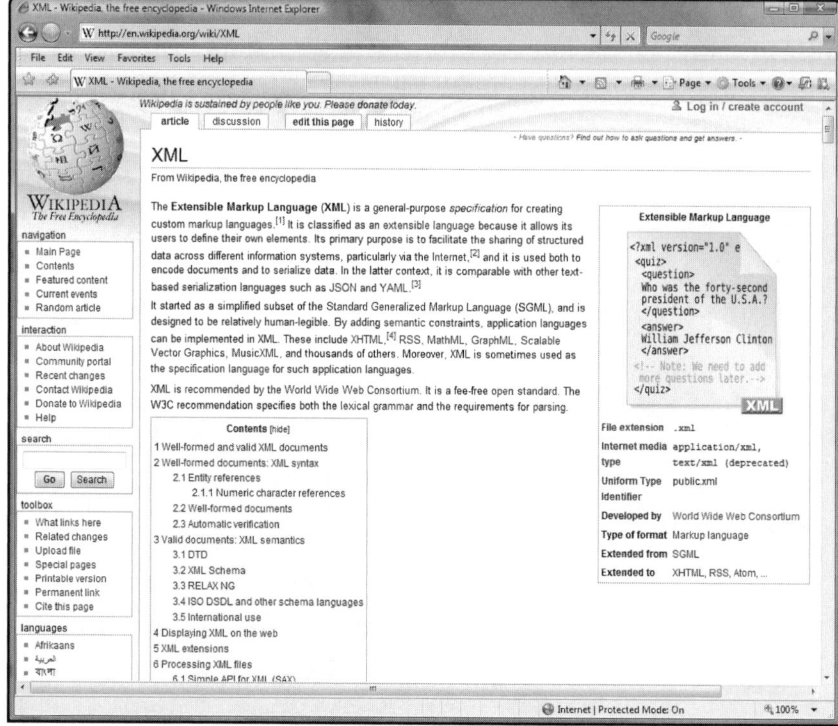

FIGURE B.5

Wikipedia's XML page provides an excellent overview of XML.

Wikipedia's XML page explores the history behind XML and outlines its advantages and disadvantages. In addition, it supplies an abundance of links to other websites.

W3C's Extensible Markup Language (XML) Page

The ultimate authority on XML is the W3C's XML page located at http://www.w3.org/XML/, as shown in Figure B.6. You will not only find a good overview of XML but will find plenty of information and links to different groups dedicated to the development of XML.

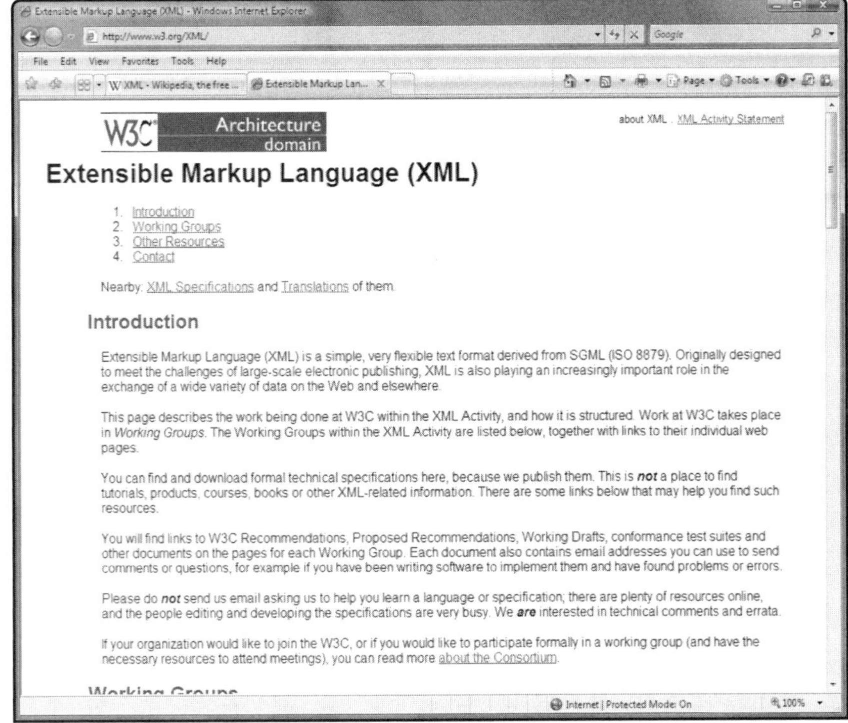

FIGURE B.6

The W3C's Extensible Markup Language (XML) page is the ultimate resource for XML.

JavaScript Resources

JavaScript is the most broadly supported web page scripting language. Web developers use JavaScript to create scripts that make web pages more dynamic and interactive. Originally developed by Netscape, JavaScript's development is now overseen by the European Computer Manufactures Association (ECMA), which now refers to it as ECMAScript.

Wikipedia's JavaScript Page

JavaScript appeared in 1995 and has been the dominant web scripting language ever since. A good working knowledge of JavaScript is important to your success as a web developer. To further your understanding of JavaScript, visit http://en.wikipedia.org/wiki/Javascript, as shown in Figure B.7.

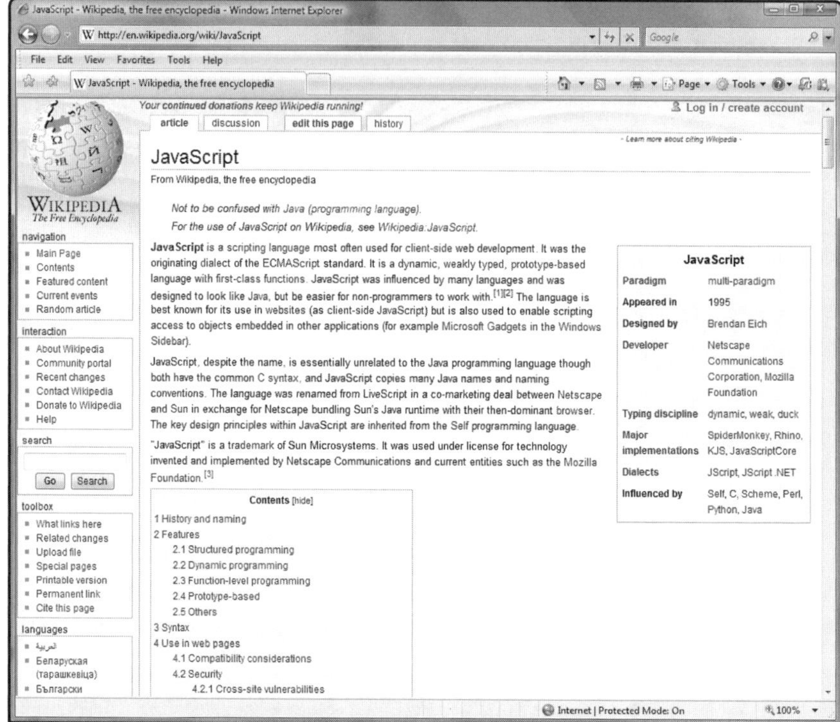

FIGURE B.7

Wikipedia's JavaScriptpPage provides a good overview of JavaScript and its roots.

JavaScript Tutorial

To learn more about how to develop scripts using JavaScript, you may benefit from completing a JavaScript tutorial located at http://www.w3schools.com/JS/default.asp, as shown in Figure B.8. This website will also provide access to all kinds of examples and sample code from which you can learn.

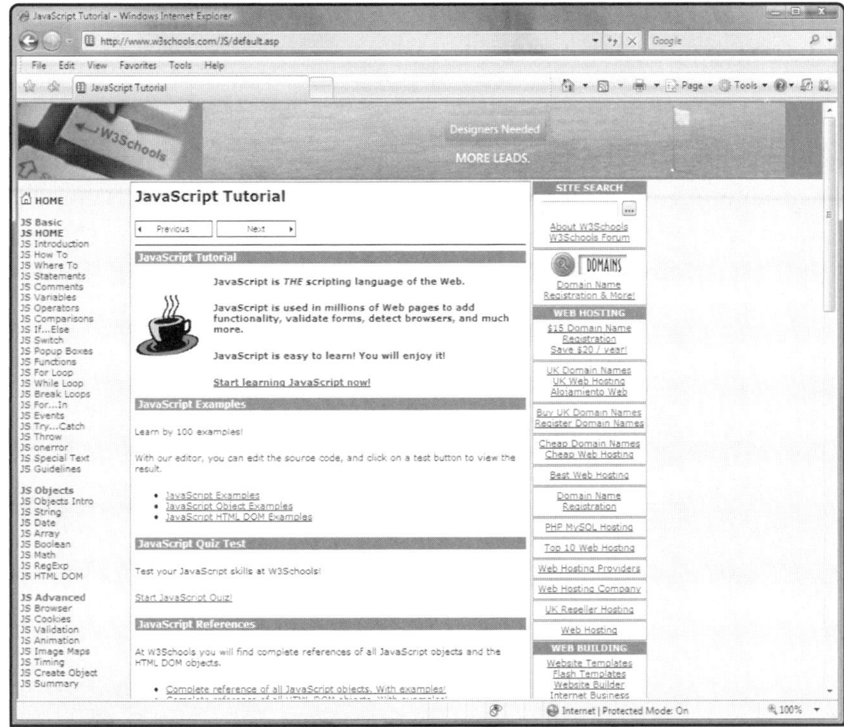

FIGURE B.8

The tutorial provides a step-by-step walk through of JavaScript programming.

Essential Development Tools

Web developers need to know how to work with many different types of technologies and languages. Web development involves different disciplines, like programming and graphics development. As such, web developers assemble a collection of software tools designed to assist them in working with all of the different aspects of web page development. These tools include things like:

- Web page editors
- Graphic editors
- FTP clients
- Link checkers

Web Page Editors

Although you can create a web page using a simple text editor like Windows Notepad or the Mac Text Edit application, there are a number of very good web page editors that you can use when developing your web pages. These web page editors provide web page editing features like tag color coding and spell checking. These web editors also may include a WYSIWYG editor that automatically generates markup for you using features similar to those provided by word processors and desktop publishing software.

CoffeeCup

CoffeeCup HTML Editor 2008 provides a robust code editor as well as a WYSIWYG editor. It even provides CSS code completion assistance and works well with JavaScript. It also provides a web library that includes plenty of graphics from which to choose. At the time this book was being published, you could purchase CoffeeCup HTML Editor 2007 for $49 from the CoffeeCup website located at www.coffeecup.com, as shown in Figure B.9.

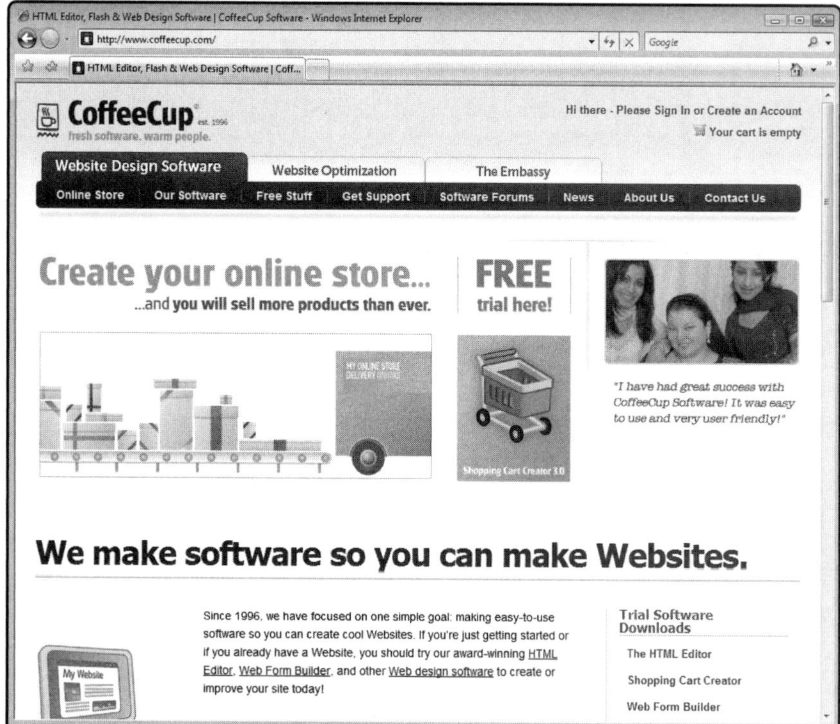

FIGURE B.9

CoffeeCup provides powerful web page editor features at a reasonable price.

HotDog

HotDog Pro provides both code editing and WYSIWYG editing. It provides native support for HTML and JavaScript and simplifies working with CSS through the use of wizards. It includes tools for editing images and managing your websites. You can download and try HotDog Pro from various shareware sites on the Internet. It costs around $100 to purchase. To learn more about HotDog Pro, visit http://www.sausagetools.com/, as shown in Figure B.10.

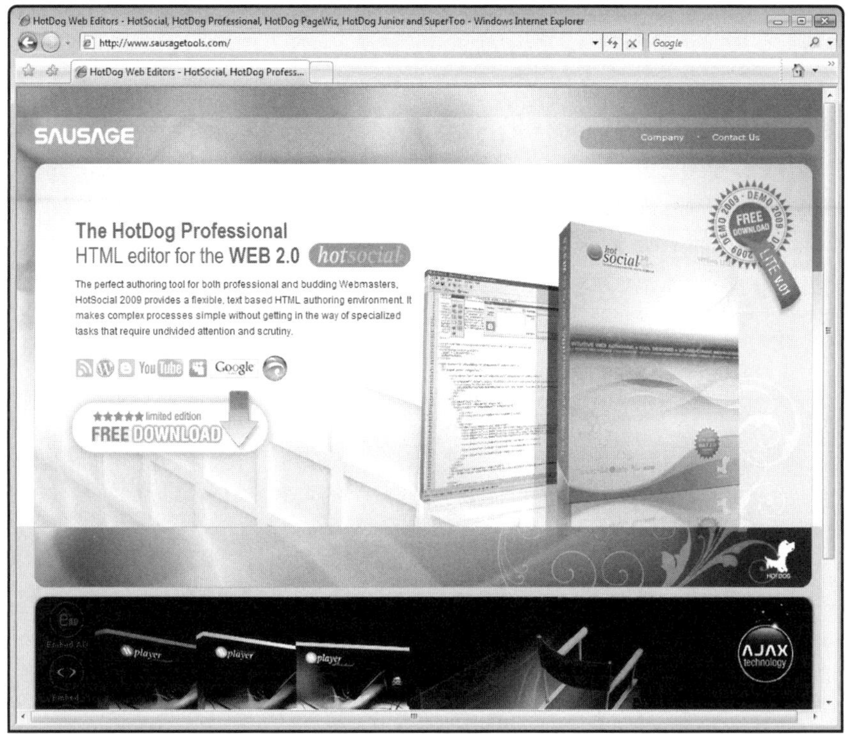

FIGURE B.10
HotDog Pro provides an advanced (X) HTML authoring environment.

Graphics Editors

One of the most challenging components of website development is figuring out how to come up with all the graphics and images needed to create exiting eye-catching web pages. One way of meeting this challenge is to learn how to create graphics from scratch using graphic editors. Another option is to purchase a graphic tool that specializes in creating web graphics. Of course, you can always partner with a graphic artist or try finding content on the Internet.

Paint Shop Pro Photo X2

There are many different graphic editors available today. Once of the easiest and most affordable to work with is Paint Shop Pro Photo X2. Paint Shop Pro Photo X2 runs on Microsoft Windows and costs $79. You can download and purchase it by visiting www.corel.com, as shown in Figure B.11.

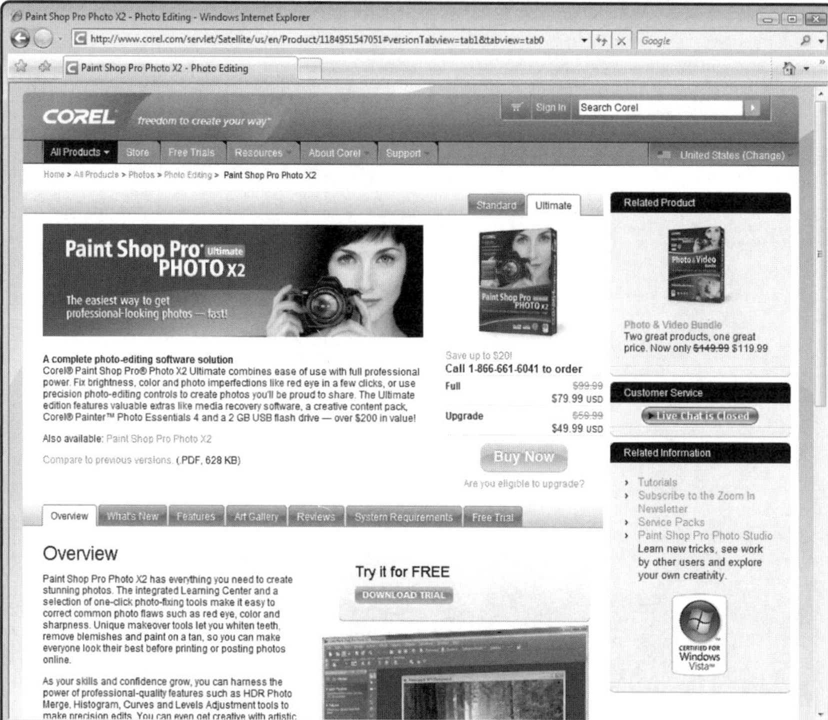

FIGURE B.11

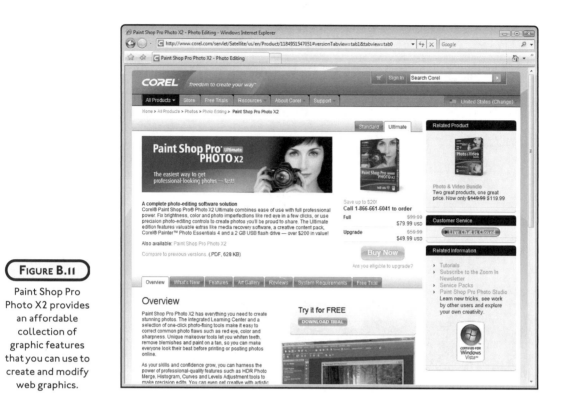

Paint Shop Pro Photo X2 provides an affordable collection of graphic features that you can use to create and modify web graphics.

Paint Shop Pro Photo X2 has everything you need to create web graphics. You can use it to import pictures from your digital camera and then edit them. In addition, you can use it to edit any graphic images and apply a host of special effects to them.

Adobe Photoshop Elements

Adobe Photoshop Elements is another low-cost graphics editor you can download and purchase from www.adobe.com, as shown in Figure B.12. Adobe Photoshop Elements cost $139.99 and can be run on either Windows or the Mac.

FIGURE B.12

Adobe Photoshop Elements provides everything you need to create graphic content for your web pages.

Using Adobe Photoshop Elements, you can create and edit graphic files. You can use it to download photos from your digital camera and apply any of a large number of special effects.

NetStudio

Rather than creating graphics from scratch, you might want to consider buying an application like NetStudio, which is specifically designed to support the development of web graphics. Using wizards, NetStudio quickly guides you through the process of creating things like buttons, web page banners, and custom navigation bars.

NetStudio runs on Windows and sells for $199. To learn more about it or to download and purchase it, visit www.netstudio.com, as shown in Figure B.13.

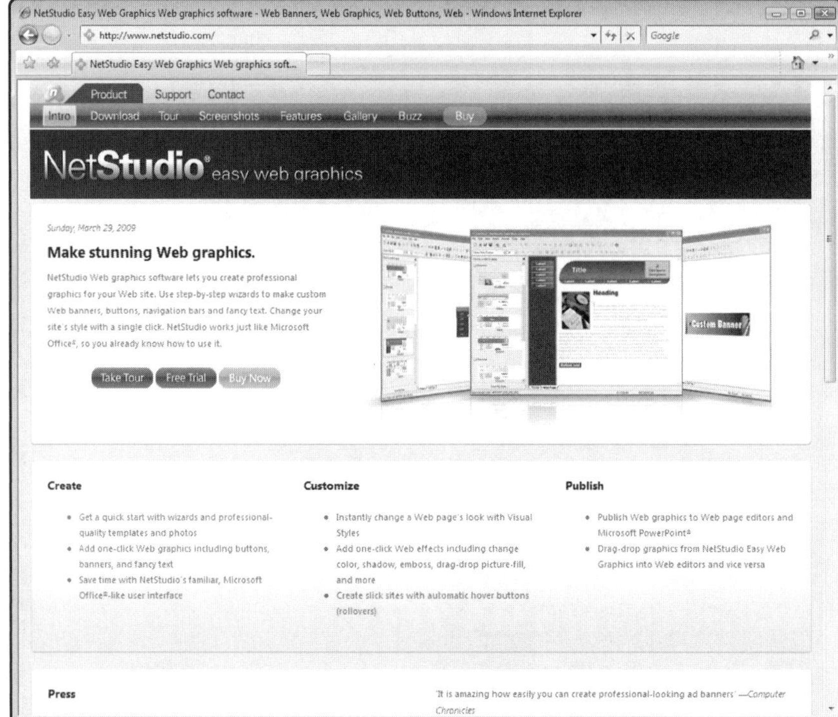

FIGURE B.13

NetStudio looks and works a lot like Microsoft Office.

FTP Clients

Many web server hosts allow you to to upload web pages via a graphical administrator interface. This works well in situations where you have a limited number of files to upload. Another option provided by most web server hosts is the ability to use the file transfer protocol or FTP. The easiest way of using FTP is to download and install a good FTP client application.

One such FTP client is FileZilla. FileZilla is a free open source FTP client that runs on either Windows or the Mac. It sports an intuitive graphical user interface that is easy to learn and allows you to upload files to your website using drag and drop. FileZilla supports many advanced features that allow you to configure things like transfer speed and logging. You can download FileZilla by visiting www.filezilla-project.org, as shown in Figure B.14.

FIGURE B.14

FileZilla is an FTP client that can be used on Windows, Mac, and Linux.

Another FTP client that is popular with Mac users is Fetch. Fetch costs just $25 and runs on Mac OS X 10.3.9 or higher. To learn more about Fetch, or to download and try it, visit www.fetchsoftworks.com.

If you are a Windows user, you might want to try SmartFTP, which at the time this book was published cost $36.95 and could be downloaded from www.smartftp.com. SmartFTP has a very handy thumbnail preview feature that allows you to easily preview the files you are transferring, without having to actually open them. Like FileZilla and Fetch, SmartFTP supports drag and drop. It also provides a command-line FTP interface.

Link Checkers

One of the worst things that can happen on any website is the occurrence of broken links, resulting in the display of a 404 Object Not Found message. Maintaining links to web pages within your own website is easy but when you start linking to web pages on websites that you do not manage, you run the risk that somewhere along the way the developers in charge of these other sites may make changes that break your links. It is therefore important that you keep a close eye on all of your links so that you can identify when they break and fix them before your visitors find them. The easiest way of doing this is to use a link validation program or service.

An easy way of checking on your site's links is to use the free online W3C Link Checker services located at http://validator.w3.org/checklink, as shown in Figure B.15.

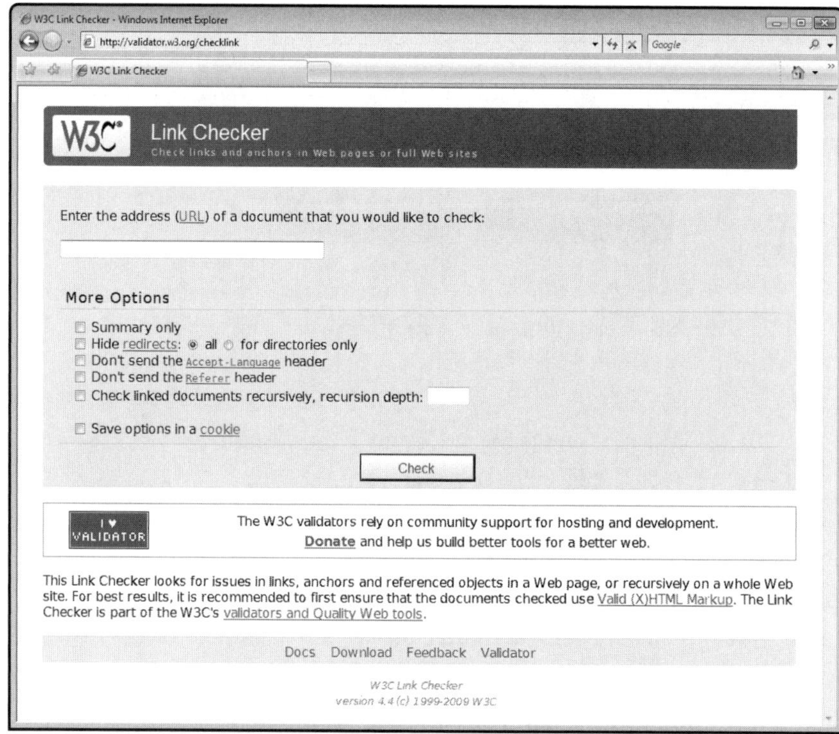

FIGURE B.15

W3C Link Checker is a free online link checker service.

Alternatively, you can download and install a link checker program on your computer. Several examples of such programs are listed here:

- Link Checker Pro—http://www.link-checker-pro.com ($75)
- HTML Link Validator—http://lithopssoft.com/hlv/ ($35)
- Inspyder InSite—https://secure.inspyder.com ($59.95)

THE AUTHOR'S WEBSITE

If you enjoyed this book and are interested in learning about other web development technologies like Ajax or other programming languages, visit my website located at http://www.tech-publishing.com, as shown in Figure B.16. While you are there drop me a message to let me know what you think of the book or how you think it might be improved.

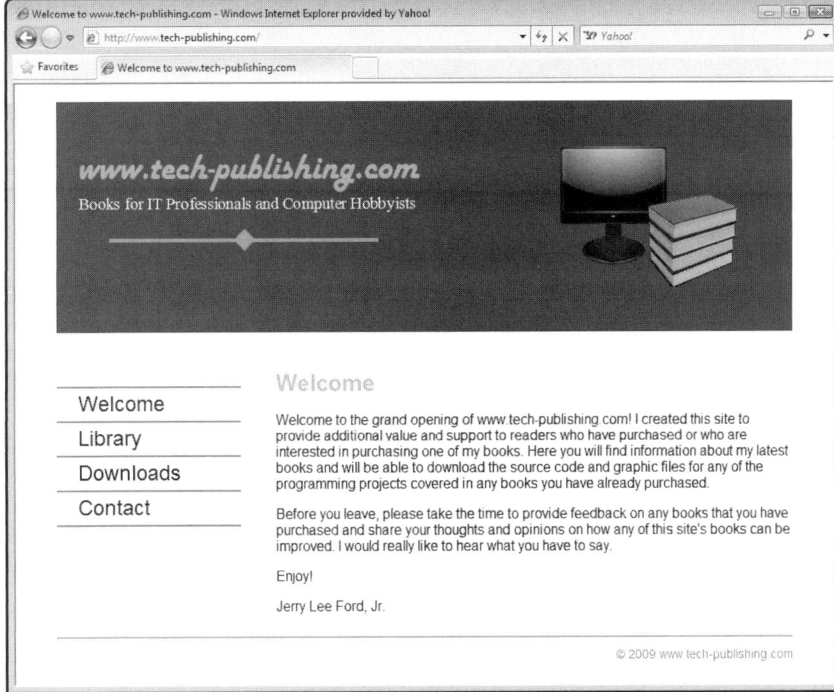

Figure B.16

Visit www.tech-publishing.com and provide your feedback on this book.

Glossary

Absolute URL. A URL that specifies a fully qualified path identifying the exact location of a resource on the Internet.

Argument. A piece of data passed to a function or script as input.

Array. A collection of data that is indexed and can be programmatically manipulated.

Boolean. A value that is either a `true` or `false` value.

Browser. A software application that displays web pages.

Camino. A Mac OX S browser (caminobrowser.org).

Cascade. A CSS prioritization scheme in which CSS rules flow downward to document elements in a predictable manner.

Comments. Statements added to markup, style rules, and scripts that are ignored by the browser but which provide valuable information to anyone editing these resources.

Compiling. The process of converting a program to machine code before it can be executed.

Concatenation. The process of combining two or more strings into a single string.

Conditional Logic. A programming construct that enables scripts and programs to make decisions and to alter the logical execution flow of code statements based on the result of comparison operations.

Container. An entity to which CSS style rules can be applied.

Content. A term that loosely refers to everything that people see and hear when they load web pages into their web browser. Content includes text, graphics, audio, and video.

CSS (Cascading Style Sheet). A stylesheet language that web developers use to specify the presentation of web page content.

Deepnet Explorer. A Windows browser (www.deepnetexplorer.com).

Divitis. A term that describes the excessive use of `div` elements within web documents.

Doctype (Document Type Declaration). Instructs web browsers as to what version of (X)HTML is being used so that the browsers know what set of rules to follow when rendering and displaying the document content.

DOM (Document Object Model). A browser object model that provides CSS and JavaScript with access to all the elements on a web document.

Domain Name. The primary address (or URL) of a particular Web site where a web page or resource resides.

Element. The building block of markup, made up of special tags that outline the structure of content stored in web documents.

Embedded Style Sheets. Style rules embedded within the `head` section of your (X)HTML pages.

External Style Sheets. Style rules stored in external files and linked back to your (X)HTML pages.

Event. An action initiated as a result of user interaction with your web page in the browser.

Event handler. A JavaScript construct that automatically executes when a given event occurs such as when the `Click` event initiates the execution of the `onclick` event handler.

Expression. A statement that evaluates the value of variables and constants.

Form. A location on a web page where visitors can provide input. Forms are made up of controls like text, checkbox, radio, drop-down, and button controls.

Form handler. A program or script, usually executed on a web server, that processes the data entered into the form.

Firefox. A Windows, Mac OS X, and Linux browser (www.firefox.com).

Frameset. A mechanism for laying out a web page into separate frames or panes, each of which displays its own web page. Frames are a deprecated feature in both Strict and Transitional (X)HTML.

FTP (File Transfer Protocol). A communication protocol that facilitates the movement of files between computers over a network.

Function. A collection of JavaScript statements that can be called by name to execute and perform a specific task.

GIF (Graphics Interchange Format). A graphic file format best used for images with less than 256 colors but which require great detail.

Global Variable. Accessible by any script located within a web document.

Google Chrome. A Windows browser (www.google.com/chrome).

HTML (Hypertext Markup Language). A markup language that was created based on SGML or Standard Generalized Markup Language.

HTML 4.01 Frameset. A version of HTML identical to HTML 4.01 Transitional but with additional support for dealing with frames.

HTML 4.01 Strict. A version of HTML that excludes support for older presentation-based HTML elements, deferring to CSS to provide for web page presentation.

HTML 4.01 Transitional. A version of HTML designed to help web developers make the transition from earlier versions of HTML to HTML 4.01.

HTTP (HyperText Transfer Protocol). A protocol that governs the transmission of hypertext-encoded data between computers on a network.

Inline Styles. Styles embedded within (X)HTML element tags.

Internet Explorer. A Windows browser (www.microsoft.com/windows/Internet-explorer/).

Interpreted language. A programming language used to develop programs or scripts that are not compiled in advance of their execution.

JavaScript. A programming language that supports the development of client-side scripts that execute inside web browsers.

JPEG (Joint Photographic Experts Group). A graphic file format best used for photos and other types of graphics that contain a larger range of colors.

Konqueror. A Linux browser (www.konqueror.org).

Links. Also known as hyperlinks, are used to connect things together on the Internet.

Local variable. A variable whose scope is limited to the function in which it is declared.

Loop. A collection of statements that are executed repeatedly. Programmers use loops to process large amounts of data and to execute repetitive tasks.

Lynx. A text-based, non-graphical Internet browser noted for its speed and exceptional performance.

Margin. The space that encloses a container.

Metadata. A term used to describe data about data. The use of metadata is an important component in the marketing of web pages.

Method. A function associated with an object, containing a collection of statements that can be called upon to perform specified actions and tasks.

Object. A programming construct that contains its own properties and methods.

Opera. A Windows, Mac OS X, and Linux browser (www.opera.com).

Parameter. An argument passed to a script or function at run time as input.

Path. A hierarchical list of folders in which a web page or file resides.

PNG (Portable Network Graphics). A graphic file format best used for photos and other graphics files that contain a large range of colors.

Program. A collection of stored programming statements that constitute a script or application.

Property. A variable associated with an object that controls or describes a particular object feature.

Protocol. A set of rules that governs communication and the exchange of data between computers over a network.

Quirks mode. A browser mode to which browsers fall back to when rendering non-compliant (X)HTML markup.

Relative URL. A URL that specifies the location of a file relative to the location of the current web page.

Reserved words. A collection of language-specific words that cannot be used as variables and function names within a script.

Rollover. A graphical effect that swaps between two images or text colors as the pointer selects or passes over a graphic image.

Safari. A Mac OS X browser (www.apple.com/safari/).

Script. A group of program statements that are interpreted and executed by a web browser.

Selector. The portion of a CSS style rule that identifies the (X)HTML elements to which the style rule is applied.

Specificity. A CSS process that assigns different weights to selectors based on how specific they are. More specific selectors override less specific selectors.

Statement. A line of code in a JavaScript.

String. A group of text characters enclosed within quotation marks.

Style rule. Collections of CSS properties that together modify the presentation of (X)HTML elements.

Table. An HTML construct that allows page content to be organized and presented within predefined tables, providing a convenient way of displaying collections of related data in tabular format.

URL (Universal Resource Locator). An address used to identify a site, page, or file on the World Wide Web.

Validation. The process of verifying that the data typed into a form conforms to required specifications.

Variable. A pointer or reference to a location in memory where data is stored.

Variable scope. Refers to the location within a script where a variable can be accessed.

W3C(*World Wide Web Consortium*). A non-profit organization dedicated to the development of open standards, ensuring that things on the Internet work smoothly by providing everyone with a consistent and agreed upon set of rules.

Web document. A term referring to a text file containing markup code.

Web page. A term referring to the result that is displayed and made visible when a web document is loaded and rendered by a web browser or similar device.

Web server. A specially configured server that is connected to the Internet and whose purpose is to accept requests from web browsers and return specified web pages and other types of content.

Well formed. (X)HTML markup that meets the syntactical requirements of the HTML and XHTML specifications.

(X)HTML. A term that generically refers to both HTML and XHTML.

XHTML (Extensible Hypertext Markup Language). A markup language that is very similar to HTML, except that it is based on XML rather then SGML.

XHTML 1.0 Frameset. A version of XHTML designed to support web pages that still rely on the use of framesets.

XHTML 1.0 Strict. A version of XHTML where presentation and other deprecated features are not allowed and syntax rules must be rigidly adhered to in order for an XHTML document to be regarded as being well formed.

XHTML 1.0 Transitional. A version of XHTML designed to support web developers who are in the process of converting from HTML to XHTML.

XML (Extensible Markup Language). A restrictive subset of SGML that results in tighter syntax that yields more consistent results.

INDEX

!– tag, 82, 289
– tag, 82, 289

A

a tags, 82
  with links, 121
abbr tag, 82
abort event, 319
absolute positioning, 237–238
absolute URLs, 15–16
accept attribute for file controls, 159
acronym tag, 82
action attribute, 155
addition operator in JavaScript, 301–302
address element, 93–94
address tag, 82
Adobe Photoshop Elements, 380–381
Ajax Programming for the Absolute Beginner, 332
alert() function in Knights Tale project, 108
alert method, 292
align attribute, 87
alignment, 87
  CSS formatting property, 213–214
  of graphics and text, 119
  tables, alignment of text in labels for, 266
alt attribute
  empty string with, 118
  with graphics, 116
anchor (a) element, 121–124
and characters, 34
Apple Safari 3, 13
  file controls for, 159
  headings, example of, 88–89
  HTML Joke Page on, 5
applet tag, 82
area / tag, 82
Arial font, selecting, 210–211
arithmetic calculations, JavaScript support for, 300–304
armenian numeric style, 244
arrays. *See* JavaScript
attributes. *See also* specific types
  configuring, 38–39
  standard element attributes, 39–40
  syntax rules for, 38–39
audio playback, integrating, 131–132
aural output, styling for, 270
author's website, 384–385

B

b tag, 82
background-color property, 264–265
background colors
  CSS specifying, 215
  links, creating for, 252–255
  tables, adding to, 264–265
background-image property, 255
  web page, adding background image to, 258–260
background images
  links, adding to, 254–255
  web page, adding to, 258–260
background-repeat property, 260

banner for www.tech-publishing.com, 345–346
base tag, 61–62
bdo tag, 82
big element, 96–97
big tag, 82
blank space. *See* white space
block-level elements, 40
  form element as, 155
  text and graphics, separating, 230
  textarea element as, 166
blockquote element, 92–93
blockquote tag, 82
blur event, 319
Bodoni font, 212
body section
  developing, 81–82
  for HTML Joke Page, 20–21
  JavaScripts, embedding, 293–294
  tags available in, 82–84
  for www.tech-publishing.com markup, 342
body tag, 81
boldfacing headings, example of, 88–89
Boolean values, JavaScript support for, 295
border attribute, 147–148
border-style property, 232–234
  tables, adding borders to, 261–262
border-width property, 232–234
borders. *See also* tables
  container borders, configuring, 232–234
  with fieldset element, 174
bottom element positioning, 235
br / tag, 82
  in JavaScript statements, 303
br element, 100–102
  with preformatted text, 90–91
brackets for tags, 32
braille output, styling for, 270
break statement. *See* JavaScript
broken links, 123, 383–384
browsers, 13
  JavaScript support, 289
  quirks mode, 30
button element, adding buttons with, 165
button tag, 82
buttons
  button element, adding buttons with, 165
  general controls, creating, 161–162
  image controls for buttons, creating, 162–163
  reset button controls, creating, 163–165
  submit button controls, creating, 163–165

C

Caflisch Script font, 211
Camino, 13
caption element for table headings, 150–151
caption tag, 83
Cascading Style Sheets. *See* CSS
case-sensitivity of JavaScript, 288
case statement
  in JavaScript, 309
  for Rock, Paper, Scissors Game, 222
cells. *See* tables
center tag, 83
centering text, CSS property for, 214
change event, 319
charset attribute for meta tags, 59
checkbox controls. *See* forms
circle markers, 247
cite tag, 83
class attribute, 40
class selectors. *See* CSS
click event, 319
client-side programming language, 9
code tag, 83
CofeeCup HTML Editor 2008, 278

col span attribute, 153–154
col tag, 83
colgroup tag, 83
colors. *See also* background colors
  CSS properties for, 215–216
  internal style sheet for, 64
  for links, 252–255
  tables, specifying colors for, 265–266
columns and rows. *See* tables
comma-separated selectors, 198
comments
  CSS comments, 202
  embedding, 42
  with JavaScripts, 294–295
companion website, information on, 367–368
comparison operators in JavaScript, 303–304
concatenation, 104
contact information
  adding, 93–94
  contact.html document for www.tech-publishing.com, creating, 356–362
  links, setting up, 127–129
contact.html document for www.tech-publishing.com, creating, 356–362
containers, 231–234
  borders, configuring, 232–234
  margins, setting, 231–232
  padding space in, 232
  widths of borders, 233
content. *See also* body section
  defined, 81
  grouping content, 84–86
  proper management of, 82–84
content attribute for meta tags, 59
controls. *See* forms
coordinate system, CSS supporting, 234
copyright notice for website, 339
Corsiva font, 211
Cottonwood font, 211
Courier font, 211
Critter font, 211
CSS, 6, 8–9, 191. *See also* containers; embedded style sheets; external style sheets; fonts
  absolute positioning with, 237–238
  advantages of, 193–194
  background properties, specifying, 215–216
  blank space, rules for, 203
  browser style sheets, precedence of, 208
  cascading, use of, 208
  class selectors, 197
    specificity of, 207
  color properties, specifying, 215–216
  comma-separated selectors, 198
  comments, 202
  complex selectors, specifying, 198
  for control presentation, 94
  coordinate system, 234
  declaration blocks, 195
    with inline styles, 199
  declarations, 195–196
  descendant selectors, 198
  element placement with, 234–243
  element selectors, 196–197
    specificity of, 207
  fixed positioning with, 240–242
  float positioning with, 242–243
  foreground properties, specifying, 215–216
  forms, styling, 267–270
  granular selectors, creating, 198
  horizontal rules, managing, 102
  ID selectors, 197–198
    specificity of, 207
  !important keyword, 208–209
  inline styles, 198–199

specificity of, 207
integrating CSS into HTML pages, 198–206
introduction to, 193–196
links, styling, 251–255
margin size, managing, 102
measurement units, 212
numeric styles with, 244–246
output device, styling based on, 270–271
overlapping rules, cascading, 202
property/values pairs, 196
font properties, 209–212
with inline styles, 199
text formatting properties, 213–214
pseudo class selectors, 197
specificity of, 207
range of properties, website showing, 194–195
relative positioning with, 238–240
resources for, 371–373
rules, 195–196
selectors, 195
complex selectors, specifying, 198
crafting rule selectors, 196–198
specificity of, 206–207
separating presentation from content with, 27–28
specificity of rules, 206–207
static positioning with, 235–237
syntax, 195–196
validating, 217
tables, styling, 260–266
text formatting properties, 213–214
universal selectors, 196–198
specificity of, 207
validating syntax, 217
web browser interpretations, 30
website, development common style sheet for, 337–338
Wikipedia resources, 372
wrapping text around graphics with, 256–258
W3C page, 372–373
cursive fonts, 211

D

dblclick event, 319
dd tag, 83
decimal-leading-zero numeric style, 244
decimal numeric style, 244
declaration blocks. *See* CSS
declarations in CSS, 195–196
Decoder Challenge Project
content, specifying, 323–324
designing application, 322–330
external style sheets for, 328–329
JavaScript, creating, 324–328
loading and testing, 330
markup, developing, 322–323
meta element for, 323
title element for, 323
Deepnet Explorer, 13
definition lists, creating, 99–100
del tag, 83
descendant selectors, 198
dfn tag, 83
dir tag, 83
disc markers, 247
div element, 85–86
for www.tech-publishing.com markup, 342–343
div tag, 83
division operator in JavaScript, 301–302
dl tag, 83
DOCTYPE declaration, 55
DOCTYPE element, 18, 28
for document template, 56
DOCTYPE switching, 30

document object, 10–12
document object model. *See* DOM
document templates
  building, 55–56
  validation of, 56–57
DOM, 10–12
  basics of, 10
  graphic representation of DOM tree, 11–12
  hierarchy for objects, 10
  navigating DOM tree, 10–12
  for Rock, Paper, Scissors Game, script statement for, 222
domain names, 14
do...while statement, creating loops with, 313–314
downloading
  downloads.html document for www.tech-publishing.com, creating, 354–356
  links for document downloads, setting up, 126–127
  source code in book, 368
downloads.html document for www.tech-publishing.com, creating, 354–356
dragdrop event, 319
drop-down lists
  categories, optgroup element for adding, 169–171
  multiline lists, creating, 171–173
  option element, creating with, 167–169
  preselecting options in, 169
  select element, creating with, 167
  substituting returned values, 169
  width, configuring, 168–169
dt element, 99–100
dt tag, 83
DTD Support column, 84

E

editors
  graphics editors, 115, 379–382
  web page editors, 17, 377–379
  WYSIWYG editors, 377–379
  XHTML editor, 17
element attributes. *See* attributes
element selectors. *See* CSS
elements. *See also* comments; inline elements
  absolute positioning, 237–238
  array elements, accessing, 298
  CSS, element placement with, 234–243
  fixed positioning, 240–242
  float positioning, 242–243
  nesting, 41–42
  relative positioning, 238–240
  static positioning, 235–237
else keyword in JavaScript, 306–307
em element, 94–95
em tag, 83
email. *See also* spam
  links facilitating, 127–129
email element, 41
embedded style sheets, 199–203
  cascading, use of, 208
  with containers, 233
  external style sheets imported to, 204
  multiple sheets, working with, 206
equal to (==) in JavaScript, 304
error event, 319
event handlers. *See* JavaScript
events. *See* JavaScript
Everson Mona font, 211
Ex Ponto font, 211
extensions for URLs, 15

external JavaScripts, 68–69, 294
external style sheets, 203–206
  for Decoder Challenge Project, 328–329
  for Fortune Teller Game, 276–277
  link tag with, 66–67
  links for, 205–206
  multiple sheets, working with, 206
  naming, 204
  plain text with, 67
  for Rock, Paper, Scissors Game, 223–224
  rules for, 67
  for www.tech-publishing.com, 344–349

F

fantasy fonts, 211
Fetch, 383
fieldset element
  grouping form elements with, 174–176
  with www.tech-publishing.com, 360
fieldset tag, 83
file controls for forms, creating, 158–159
filenames for URLs, 15
FileZilla, 44, 382–383
Firefox. *See* Mozilla Firefox 3
fixed positioning, 240–242
float positioning, 242–243
float property, 242–243
  wrapping text around graphics with, 256–258
  in www.tech-publishing.com, 348
focus event, 319
folders, URLs specifying, 16
font-family property, 209–212
font-style property, 209–212
font tag, 83
fonts
  big element for, 96–97
  internal style sheet for, 64
  presentation of, 209–212
  properties in CSS, 209–212
  small element for, 96
for statement, creating loops with, 310–311
foreground properties, CSS specifying, 215
form element, 154–156
form handlers, 154–156
form tag, 83
forms, 154–156. *See also* buttons; drop-down lists
  checkbox controls
    creating, 159–161
    example of, 179
  CSS for styling, 267–270
  defined, 154
  descriptive text, adding, 173
  designing good forms, 179–180
  example of complete form, 176–179
  fieldset element, grouping form elements with, 174–176
  file controls, creating, 158–159
  hidden controls, creating, 163
  input element, defining controls with, 156–165
  label element, adding descriptive text with, 173
  labels for controls, 180
  layout, advice on, 179–180
  legend element with fieldset elements, 175–176
  maxlength attribute for, 180
  password controls, creating, 157–158
  radio controls
    creating, 159–161
    example of, 179
  reset button controls, creating, 163–165
  submit button controls, creating, 163–165
  text
    controls, creating, 157
    label element, adding descriptive text with, 173

with legend element, 175–176
multiline text fields, adding, 165–166
Fortune Teller Game, 230–231
content, specifying, 272–274
designing application, 271–280
external style sheets, creating, 276–277
loading and testing, 277–280
markup, developing, 272
meta element for, 272
new XHTML document, creating, 272
script, creating, 274–276
title element for, 272
frame / tag, 83
frameset tag, 83
FTP
clients, 382–383
working with, 44
functions. *See* JavaScript

G

Garamond font, selecting, 210–212
georgian numeric style, 244
get option for forms, 155
GIF (graphics interchange format), 115
global variables, 297
glossary, 387–392
Google
Chrome, 13
web host service, 44
granular selectors, 198
graphics, 14, 114. *See also* background images; img element; links
alternative content, displaying, 118
buttons, creating image controls for, 162–163
dimensions of file, specifying, 116–118
for Rock, Paper, Scissors Game, 219–220
storing files externally, 115
text and graphics, displaying, 118–121
types of, 114–115
wrapping text around graphics with CSS, 256–258
graphics editors, 115, 379–382
greater than (>) in JavaScript, 304
greater than or equal to (>=) in JavaScript, 304

H

h1 tag, 83
h2 tag, 83
h3 tag, 83
h4 tag, 83
h5 tag, 83
h6 tag, 83
handheld media, styling for, 270
head section
adding elements to, 57–58
JavaScripts, embedding, 104–105, 291–293
for Math Quiz application, 70
for www.tech-publishing.com markup, 342
headings, 86–89. *See also* tables
for fieldset elements, 175–176
for HTML Joke Page, 20–21
height
graphic file dimensions, specifying, 116–118
img element specifying, 116–118
line height, CSS formatting for, 213
Helvetica font, 212
hidden controls, creating, 163
horizontal rules, 102–103
HotDog Pro, 378–379
hr element, 102–103
hr / tag, 83
href attribute
for base tag, 61–62
link tag using, 66
with links, 121
.htm extension, 15

HTML. *See also* tags; XHTML
- HTML 4.01 Frameset, 29
- HTML 4.01 Strict, 29
- HTML 4.01 Transitional, 29
- html element in, 31
- introduction to, 5–7
- Joke Page project, 4–24
- for Linked Jokes project, 26–27, 45
- Math Quiz application, creating HTML document for, 69
- resources, 369–371
- standards, 28–29
- versions of, 7–8, 28–29
- Wikipedia's HTML/XHTML pages, 370

html element, 18, 31–32

HTML Joke Page
- designing, 19–23
- document markup, developing, 20–22
- loading and testing, 22–23
- new HTML document, creating, 20

HTML Link Validator, 384

http-equiv attribute for meta tags, 59–60

HTTP (Hyper-Text Transfer Protocol), 14–16

hyperlinks. *See* links

I

i tag, 83

id attribute, 12, 39

ID selectors. *See* CSS

if statement. *See also* JavaScript
- for Rock, Paper, Scissors Game, 222

iframe tag, 83

images. *See* graphics

img element, 116–118. *See also* alt attribute
- width and height of graphic, specifying, 116–118
- and wrapping text around graphics, 257–258

img / tag, 83

@import statement with external style sheets, 204

!important keyword, 208–209

Increase Your Web Traffic in a Weekend (Ford), 59

indentation
- CSS formatting property, 213
- of elements, 18

index.html document for www.tech-publishing.com, creating, 350–351

inherit numeric style, 244

inline elements, 40
- embedding, 40–41
- working with, 94–97

inline styles. *See* CSS

input element, 156–165

input / tag, 83

ins tag, 83

Inspyder InSite, 384

internal style sheets, 64–66
- for Math Quiz application, 73–74

Internet, introduction to, 13–14

Internet Explorer, 13
- XML declaration statement with, 28

isindex tag, 83

italics
- with address element, 83–84
- with em element, 94–95

J

JavaScript, 6, 9–10. *See also* DOM
- alert method, 292
- arithmetic calculations, performing, 300–304
- arrays, 297–300
  - accessing array elements, 298
  - for Decoder Challenge Project, 325
  - loops, processing arrays with, 299–300

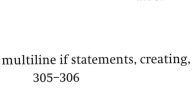

body section, embedding scripts in, 293–294
break statement, 309
loops, halting, 314–315
browser support, 289
case-sensitivity of, 288
case statement, 309
collections of data, working with, 297–304
comments for, 294–295
comparing values in, 303–304
for Decoder Challenge Project, 324–328
documenting, 294–295
do...while statement, creating loops with, 313–314
else keyword with, 306–307
events, 288
creating web pages using, 318
mouse events, managing, 320–321
types of, 318
window events, managing, 319–320
example, 104–105
expression, functions as part of, 316
external JavaScripts, 68–69, 294
for statement, creating loops with, 310–311
Fortune Teller Game, creating script for, 274–276
functions, 291
for Decoder Challenge Project, 325–328
defining, 315–316
executing, 316–318
naming, 315
global variables, 297
for Decoder Challenge Project, 325
head section, embedding scripts in, 104–105, 291–293
HTML tags, embedding JavaScript statements in, 294
if statement, 304–305
else keyword with, 306–307
multiline if statements, creating, 305–306
nesting if statements, 307–308
integrating into web documents, 103–104
introduction to, 287–288
for Knights Tale project, 106–109
local variables, 297
loops
arrays with loops, processing, 299–300
breaking out of, 314–315
do...while statement, creating loops with, 313–314
for statement, creating loops with, 310–311
while statement, creating loops with, 312–313
mathematic calculations, performing, 300–304
methods, 287
prompt method, 310
mouse events, managing, 320–321
multiple statements on single line, 288
naming
functions, 315
variables, 296–297
nesting if statements, 307–308
for Number Guessing Game, 183–184
numeric data in, 300–304
objects, 287
operators in, 300–301
prompt method, 310
properties, 287
resources, 375–377
retrieving data, 295
for Rock, Paper, Scissors Game, 220–223
running scripts, 290–291
scope of variable, understanding, 297
script tags, browsers displaying, 289
semicolons, use of, 104, 288

simple script, creating, 290
storing data, 295
switch statement in, 308–310
syntax in, 288
tutorial, 376–377
values supported by, 295
variables
assigning values to, 301–302
defining, 296–297
naming, 296–297
scope of, 297
while statement, creating loops with, 312–313
white space in, 288
Wikipedia JavaScript page, 375–376
window events, managing, 319–320
working with, 288–291
for XHTML Typing Quiz, 135–137
Joke Page project, 4–24
JPEG (Joint Photographic Experts Group), 115

K

kbd tag, 83
keydown event, 319
keypress event, 319
keyup event, 319
Knights Tale project, 80
designing application, 105–110
finished HTML document, 108–109
loading and testing, 109–110
Konqueror, 13

L

label element
for checkbox controls, 160
forms, adding descriptive text to, 173
label tag, 83
labels for form controls, 180
language attribute
with html element, 31
script tag supporting, 67–68
left element positioning, 235
legend element with fieldset elements, 175–176
legend tag, 83
less than (<) in JavaScript, 304
less than or equal to (<=) in JavaScript, 304
letter-spacing, CSS formatting property for, 213
li tag, 83
library.html document for www.tech-publishing.com, creating, 352–354
line breaks
br element, working with, 100–102
in JavaScript statements, 303
line height, CSS formatting property for, 213
Link Checker Pro, 384
link checkers, 123, 383–384
link element with external style sheets, 205–206
link tag, 66–67
Linked Jokes project, 26–27
designing application, 45–48
loading and testing, 48
links
background colors for, 252–254
background images for, 254–255
borders to links, adding, 252–255
broken links, 123, 383–384
checkers, 123, 383–384
colors for, 252–255
creating, 121–124
CSS for styling, 251–255
document downloads, setting up links for, 126–127
emailing, links facilitating, 127–129
for external style sheets, 205–206
graphics links
CSS for creating, 252–255
setting up, 123–124

new window, links opening, 125–126
text links
CSS for presentation of, 251–252
setting up, 121–123
for www.tech-publishing.com, 347–348
www.tech-publishing.com, developing for, 344–345
Linux Konqueror, 13
list-style-image property, 249–250
list-style-type property
with ordered lists, 244–245
with unordered lists, 247–248
lists. *See also* drop-down lists
CSS for styling, 244–250
definition lists, creating, 99–100
markers
custom list markers, creating, 249–250
ordered lists, customizing markers for, 244–246
unordered lists, customizing markers for, 247–249
ordered lists
creating, 98–99
CSS for customizing markers, 244–246
unordered lists
creating, 97–98
markers, changing, 247–249
load event, 319
local variables, 297
loops. *See* JavaScript
lower-alpha numeric style, 244
lower-greek numeric style, 244
lower-latin numeric style, 244
lower-roman numeric style, 244
Lynx, 13–14

M

Mac Text Edit, 377
mailto: keyword, 155
map tag, 83
margin property for containers, 231–232
margins
container margins, setting, 231–232
CSS for managing, 102
and wrapping text around graphics, 257–258
markers. *See* lists
markup
for Decoder Challenge Project, 322–323
for Fortune Teller Game, 272
for Knights Tale project, 106
languages, 6
for Math Quiz application, 69–72
for Number Guessing Game, 181–183
for Rock, Paper, Scissors Game, 218
validation, 35–38
www.tech-publishing.com template markup, creating, 341–343
for XHTML Typing Quiz, 134–135
Math Quiz application, 54–55
content, specifying, 69–72
designing, 69–77
document markup, developing, 69–72
finished HTML document, 74–76
head section, updating, 70
internal style sheet, embedding, 73–74
loading and testing, 76–77
quick test of document, performing, 72–73
mathematic calculations, JavaScript support for, 300–304
maxlength attribute for forms, 180
measurement units in CSS, 212
@media rule, 271
media types, styling for, 270–271
menu tag, 83
merging table cells, 153–154
meta element
for Decoder Challenge Project, 323
for Fortune Teller Game, 272
for Rock, Paper, Scissors Game, 219

meta tag, 59–61
metadata, 59
method attribute, 155
methods. *See* JavaScript
monospace fonts, 211
mouse events, JavaScript managing, 319–321
mousedown event, 319
mousemove event, 319
mouseout event, 319
mouseover event, 319
mouseup event, 319
movies as content, integrating, 129–130
Mozilla Firefox 3, 13
  HTML Joke Page on, 5
MS Arial font, 212
MS-DOS, 15
MS Georgia font, 212
MS Tohoma font, 212
MS Verdana font, 212
multiline drop-down lists, creating, 171–173
multiline text fields, creating, 165–166
multiple attributes with drop-down lists, 171–173
multiplication operator in JavaScript, 301–302
MySQL, 44

N

name attribute for meta tags, 59–60
naming. *See also* JavaScript
  external style sheets, 204
  initial landing page of website, 336
nesting
  elements, 41–42
  if statements in JavaScript, 307–308
NetStudio, 381–382
noframes tag, 83
noscript tag, 84
not equal to (!==) in JavaScript, 304
null values, JavaScript support for, 295
Number Guessing Game, 144–145
  designing, 181–188
  finished HTML document, 185–188
  loading and testing, 188
  markup, developing, 181–183
  new XHTML document, creating, 181
  script, developing, 183–184
numeric styles with CSS, 244–246
numeric values, JavaScript support for, 295

O

object element
  audio playback, integrating, 131
  PDF files, displaying, 133–134
  video content, adding, 129–130
object tag, 84
objects in JavaScript, 287
ol element, 98–99
ol tag, 84
onClick() event
  in Fortune Teller Game, 273
  in Rock, Paper, Scissors Game, 222
onLoad event, 320
onResize event, 320
onUnload event, 320
OOP (object-oriented programming), 9, 287. *See also* JavaScript
Opera, 13
optgroup element for drop-down lists, 169–171
optgroup tag, 84
option element for drop-down lists, 167–169
option tag, 84
ordered lists. *See* lists

P

p element, 86–88
  text and graphics placed within, 119–120
p tag, 84
  closing p tag, omission of, 86

padding property
for containers, 232
tables, adding white space to, 262–263
Paint Shop Pro Photo X2, 379–380
paragraphs
borders, containers for displaying, 233–234
containers for displaying borders around, 233–234
left-alignment of text, 87
p element for, 86–88
working with, 87–88
param tag, 84
password controls for forms, 157–158
paths for URLs, 15
PDF files
displaying, 133–134
links for document downloads, setting up, 126–127
Perl, 44
Photoshop Elements, Adobe, 380–381
PHP scripts, 44, 360–361
placement of elements with CSS, 234–243
PNG (Portable Network Graphics), 115
position element positioning, 235
post-decrement operator in JavaScript, 301
post-increment operator in JavaScript, 301
post method with form example, 178
post option for forms, 155
pre-decrement operator in JavaScript, 301
pre element with preformatted text, 91
pre-increment operator in JavaScript, 301
pre tag, 84
preformatted text, displaying, 89–91
print output, styling for, 270
projection output, styling for, 270
properties. *See* CSS;
JavaScript
Prostige font, 211
pseudo class selectors. *See* CSS
PunchLine.html documents, creating, 47–48
Python, 44

Q

q element, 92
q tag, 84
quirks mode, 30
quotation marks for multi-word font names with spaces, 212
quotations, displaying, 92–93

R

radio controls. *See* forms
random numbers for Rock, Paper, Scissors Game, 222
rel attribute, link tag using, 66
relative positioning, 238–240
relative URLs, 16
rendering web pages, 6
reset button controls, creating, 163–165
reset event, 319
resize event, 319
resources
CSS resources, 371–373
for graphic buttons, 162
HTML resources, 369–371
JavaScript resources, 375–377
tags, online resources on, 34–35
XHTML resources, 369–371
XML resources, 373–375
right element positioning, 235
Rock, Paper, Scissors Game, 192–193
content, specifying, 219–220
designing application, 218–227
external style sheet, creating, 223–224
loading and testing, 224–226

markup, developing, 218
meta element for, 219
new XHTML document, creating, 218
script, creating, 220–223
title element for, 219
Roman numeral characters, 244
rowspan attribute for merging table cells, 153
Ruby on Rails, 44

S

s tag, 84
Safari. *See* Apple Safari 3
samp tag, 84
san serif fonts, 212
Sanvito font, 211
scope element for defining tables, 148–150
scr attribute
with graphics, 116
script tag supporting, 67–68
screen output, styling for, 270
script element, 67–69, 84. *See also* JavaScript
script tags, browsers displaying, 289
search engines, meta tag for, 59–61
select element for drop-down lists, 167
select tag, 84
selectors. *See* CSS
semicolons in JavaScript, 104, 288
serif fonts, 212
SGML (Standard Generalized Markup Language), 6
sign-reversal operator in JavaScript, 301
simple web page, creating, 17–19
single tags, 33–34
site5.com, 44
small element, 96
small tag, 84
SmartFTP, 383
sound playback, integrating, 131–132
source code in book, downloading, 368
spam
forms and, 155
links and, 129
span element, 86
in Fortune Teller Game, 273–274
span tag, 84
square markers, 247
static positioning, 235–237
strike tag, 84
strings, JavaScript support for, 295
strong element, 41, 95
strong tag, 84
Studz font, 211
style attribute, 40
for inline styles, 198–199
style element with embedded style sheets, 199–203
style sheets. *See* CSS
style tag, 63–66
sub tag, 84
submit button
controls, creating, 163–165
for www.tech-publishing.com, 360
submit event, 319
subtraction operator in JavaScript, 301–302
summary element for defining tables, 148–150
sup tag, 84
switch code block for Rock, Paper, Scissors Game, 222
switch statement in JavaScript, 308–310
syntax. *See also* CSS
in JavaScript, 288

T

table elements, 145–147
table tag, 84
tables, 145–146
alignment of text in labels, 266
background colors, adding, 264–265
border-collapse property, 264

borders
adding, 147–148
border-style property, adding with, 261–262
collapsing, 264
colors, specifying, 265–266
CSS for styling, 260–266
headings
columns and rows headings, defining, 151–152
table heading, assigning, 150–151
labels, aligning text in, 266
merging cells in, 153–154
for non-graphic browsers, 148–150
padding property for adding white space, 262–263
text in labels, aligning, 266
white space, padding property for adding, 262–263
tag pairs, 32–33
tags
body section, tags available in, 82–84
head section supporting, 57
for html element, 31
JavaScript statements, embedding, 294
online resources on, 34–35
pairs, 32–33
single tags, 33–34
target attribute for links, 125–126
tbody tag, 84
td element, 146–147
td tag, 84
tech-publishing.com. *See* www.tech-publishing.com
templates. *See also* document templates
website templates, creating, 337
for www.tech-publishing.com, 339–340
temporary comments, 42
text. *See also* fonts; forms; headings; italics; links; lists
address information, managing, 93–94
big element, working with, 96–97
boldfacing headings, example of, 88–89
button controls displaying, 161–162
CSS formatting properties, 213–214
em element, working with, 94–95
graphics and text, displaying, 118–121
inline elements, working with, 94–97
preformatted text, displaying, 89–91
quotations, displaying, 92–93
small element, working with, 96
strong element, working with, 95
table labels, aligning text in, 266
text fields, creating, 157
wrapping text around graphics with CSS, 256–258
text-based browsing, 13
text-decoration, CSS formatting property for, 213–214
textarea element, 165–166
textarea tag, 84
tfoot tag, 84
th tag, 84
thread tag, 84
tiling background images, 260
Times New Roman font, 212
title attribute, 39
title element
for Decoder Challenge Project, 323
for Fortune Teller Game, 272
for Rock, Paper, Scissors Game, 219
title tag, 58–59
top element positioning, 235
tr element, 146–147
tr tag, 84
tt tag, 84
tty output, styling for, 271
tv mode output, styling for, 271

type attribute
  link tag using, 66
  script tag supporting, 67–68
  for style tag, 63

U

u tag, 84
ul element, 97–98
ul tag, 84
underlining text, CSS property for, 213–214
universal selectors. *See* CSS
unload event, 319
unordered lists. *See* lists
upper-alpha numeric style, 244
upper-latin numeric style, 244
upper-roman numeric style, 244
URLs, 14–16. *See also* href attribute
  absolute URLs, 15–16
  base tag for, 61–62
  protocols for, 14
  relative URLs, 16
  web host providing, 44

V

validation
  of CSS syntax, 217
  of document templates, 56–57
  XHTML markup validation, 35–38
values. *See also* CSS
  JavaScript, values supported by, 295
var tag, 84
variables, 291. *See also* JavaScript
video as content, integrating, 129–130
visually disabled persons, styling for, 270

W

wave files, integrating, 131–132
web browsers. *See* browsers
web document, defined, 6
web hosts, 19
  finding, 44–45
web page editors, 17, 377–379
web pages
  defined, 6
  simple web page, creating, 17–19
web servers, 44
websites. *See also* www.tech-publishing.com
  author's website, 384–385
  building-out documents in, 338
  common page structure, outlining, 337
  companion website, information on, 367–368
  CSS style sheet, creating, 337–338
  initial landing pages, 336
  layout, organizing, 336–338
  mockup of template, creating, 337
  objectives for project, documenting, 335
  organization of content, 336–338
  outlining common page structure, 337
    rough mockup, creating, 337
  statistics, 44
  structure chart for organizing, 336
  templates, creating, 337
while statement, creating loops with, 312–313
white space
  adding, 42–44
  CSS rules for, 102, 203
  in JavaScript, 288
  use of, 18
width
  border-width property, 232–234
  of container borders, 233
  drop-down lists, width element for, 168–169
  graphic file dimensions, specifying, 116–118

Wikipedia
CSS page, 372
HTML/XHTML pages, 370
JavaScript page, 375–376
XML page, 373–374
wild cards (*) for universal selectors, 196–198
windows
JavaScript managing window events, 319–320
new window, links opening, 125–126
Windows Notepad, 377
Word Decoder Challenge, 285–287
word spacing, CSS formatting property for, 213
wrapping text around graphics with CSS, 256–258
W3C, 7–8
CSS page, 372–373
DOM and, 10
HTML 4.01 specifications, 370–371
markup validation service, 36–38
XHTML specifications, 371
XML page, 374–375
W3C Link Checker, 384
www.tech-publishing.com, 331–335
assembling document files, 350
author's website, 384–385
banner, configuring, 345–346
contact.html document, creating, 356–362
copyright notice, 339
designing website, 338–363
downloads.html document, creating, 354–356
external file sheets, developing, 344–349
floated elements in, 348
index.html document, creating, 350–351
library.html document, creating, 352–354
markup for template, creating, 341–343
menu links, presentation of, 346–347
navigation controls, designing, 339–340
objectives, outlining, 338–339
PHP scripts for, 360–361
presentation of web pages, designing, 340–341
sketching out site structure, 339
template content, outlining, 339–340
testing website, 362–363
text links, designing, 347–348
WYSIWYG editors, 377–379

X

XHTML, 6, 7–8. *See also* attributes; document templates; tags
block-level elements, 40
dissecting markup, 32–33
html element in, 31
Knights Tale project, creating document for, 105
for Linked Jokes project, 26–27, 45–46
markup validation, 35–38
resources, 369–371
separating presentation from content, 27–28
with single tags, 33
standards, 29–30
versions of, 7
Wikipedia's HTML/XHTML pages, 370
W3C's XHTML specifications, 371
XHTML 1.0 Frameset, 30
XHTML 1.0 Strict, 30
XHTML 1.0 Transitional, 29–30
XHTML editor, 17
XHTML Typing Quiz, 112–113
designing application, 134–140
finished document, 137–140

loading and testing, 140
markup, developing, 134–135
script, creating, 135–137
XML, 6, 31–32
resources, 373–375
standards, compliance with, 28
Wikipedia's XML page, 373–374
W3C XML page, 374–375
xml: lang attribute with html element, 31
xmlns attribute, 31

Z

z-order element positioning, 235
Zip document downloads, links for setting up, 126–127

the fun way to learn programming

Let's face it. C++, Java, and Perl can be a little intimidating. But now they don't have to be. The *for the absolute beginner*™ series gives you a fun, non-intimidating introduction to the world of programming. Each book in this series teaches a specific programming language using simple game programming as a teaching aid. All titles include source code on the companion CD-ROM or Web site.

C++ Programming for the Absolute Beginner
By Mark Lee
1-59863-875-0 | $29.99 | 464 pages

Microsoft WSH and VBScript Programming for the Absolute Beginner, Third Edition
By Jerry Ford, Jr.
1-59863-803-3 | $34.99 | 480 pages

C Programming for the Absolute Beginner, Second Edition
By Michael Vine
1-59863-480-1 | $29.99 | 336 pages

Microsoft Excel VBA Programming for the Absolute Beginner, Third Edition
By Duane Birnbaum and Michael Vine
1-59863-394-5 | $29.99 | 400 pages

Microsoft Access VBA Programming for the Absolute Beginner, Third Edition
By Michael Vine
1-59863-393-7 | $29.99 | 384 pages

Microsoft Windows Powershell Programming for the Absolute Beginner
By Jerry Lee Ford Jr.
1-59863-354-6 | $29.99 | 376 pages

Microsoft Visual Basic 2008 Express Programming for the Absolute Beginner
By Jerry Lee Ford, Jr.
1-59863-900-5 | $29.99 | 432 pages

Ajax Programming for the Absolute Beginner
By Jerry Ford, Jr.
1-59863-564-6 | $29.99 | 320 pages

Java Programming for the Absolute Beginner, Second Edition
By John Flynt
1-59863-275-2 | $29.99 | 480 pages

COURSE TECHNOLOGY
CENGAGE Learning
Professional • Technical • Reference

Call 1.800.648.7450 to order
Order online at www.courseptr.com

COURSE TECHNOLOGY
CENGAGE Learning
Professional • Technical • Reference

Course Technology PTR...

the ultimate source for all your certification needs.

With step-by-step instructions and extensive end-of-chapter review questions, projects, and exercises, these learning solutions map fully to their certification exams. In-depth and well-organized—there isn't a better way to prepare!

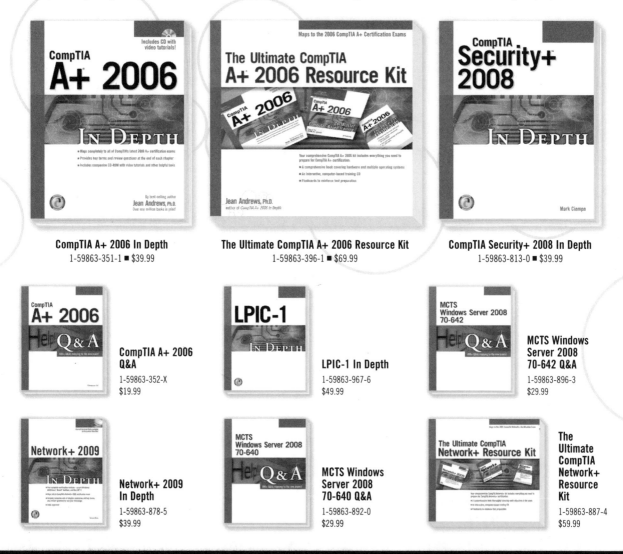

CompTIA A+ 2006 In Depth
1-59863-351-1 ■ $39.99

The Ultimate CompTIA A+ 2006 Resource Kit
1-59863-396-1 ■ $69.99

CompTIA Security+ 2008 In Depth
1-59863-813-0 ■ $39.99

CompTIA A+ 2006 Q&A
1-59863-352-X
$19.99

LPIC-1 In Depth
1-59863-967-6
$49.99

MCTS Windows Server 2008 70-642 Q&A
1-59863-896-3
$29.99

Network+ 2009 In Depth
1-59863-878-5
$39.99

MCTS Windows Server 2008 70-640 Q&A
1-59863-892-0
$29.99

The Ultimate CompTIA Network+ Resource Kit
1-59863-887-4
$59.99

For more information on our offerings and to order, call **1.800.648.7450**, go to your favorite bookstore, or visit us at **www.courseptr.com**.